Border Law

Border Law

The First Seminole War and American Nationhood

Deborah A. Rosen

Harvard University Press
Cambridge, Massachusetts
London, England
2015

Second Printing

Cataloging-in-Publication Data available from the Library of Congress

ISBN: 978-0-674-96761-8 (alk. paper)

For Susan

Contents

List of Maps

Border Law

Introduction

During the Florida campaigns of 1816–1818, U.S. troops led by General Andrew Jackson crossed the southeastern border into Spanish territory, seized forts, destroyed towns, and occupied Pensacola, the main seat of Spanish government in West Florida. They summarily hanged two prominent Creek prisoners, executed two British allies of the Seminoles, and killed or captured numerous Seminoles, Creeks, and African-descended people, carrying some into slavery in the United States.[1]

Americans vigorously debated whether the United States was legally justified in entering territory claimed by a European sovereign, destroying property on foreign soil, and implementing its legal presumptions extraterritorially. They discussed who qualified as a prisoner of war, what rights and protections wartime prisoners legally held, and whether the law of nations applied to non-Europeans and their European allies. This book analyzes those debates and evaluates their implications for American nation-building.[2]

The Florida expeditions, known at the time as the "Seminole War," played an important role in American political development.[3] In the Republic's first few decades, foreign nations questioned the United States' ability to fulfill its international obligations and Americans themselves were unsure whether their newly declared nation could survive. The forcefulness, decisiveness, and assertiveness of the Florida incursions demonstrated American determination to both domestic and foreign audiences. Even more important than military accomplishments on the ground was the United States' aggressive legal, political, and diplomatic defense of its armed hostilities against Spaniards, Creeks and Seminoles, African-heritage people, and Britons. In the wake of the war, the United States boldly asserted its new status in the world.

Crucial to the new American national identity at home and abroad were its borders of law and nationhood. The requirements for "nationhood" were unsettled in this era. Therefore, when making their case to other nations, Americans focused on elements of nationhood that were most important to them: They constituted a people distinct from and independent of—yet equal to—the British. Moreover, their government exercised supreme and exclusive authority over a defined territory and had the right to rule the inhabitants and defend the borders of that territory as it saw fit.[4] In the Seminole War debates, the United States used a legal framework to declare that vision in four ways: first, it expanded the boundaries of the European family of nations to include the United States; second, it demarcated a line of differentiation between the New World and the Old; third, it defined the borders of the American polity and the limits of legal protection along racial and cultural lines; and fourth, it changed the rules for acting across territorial borders in order to secure its interests beyond the nation's spatial boundaries. To advance these goals, supporters of the Florida campaigns articulated a fresh approach to the sources, the applicability, and the substance of law.

First, the United States insisted that it was a full-fledged member of the European diplomatic and legal community. The United States redrew the line defining the "civilized" international community, contending that the community's border did not stop at the edges of Europe but included European-heritage nations as well. The United States claimed that it not only was a fully "sovereign" nation—that is, a politically independent state that governed itself without interference from outside authorities—but was equal to any European country.

The U.S. relationship with European states helped define the United States as a nation. In fact, the realm of foreign affairs was a crucial locus, perhaps even the most important locus, for defining American national identity in the early Republic. Projecting a collective identity in foreign relations was essential, even at a time when, on the domestic front, Americans were still developing a cohesive sense of being a single nation. Diplomats, military officers, and government officials who focused on the United States' relations with other nations played an important role in creating American nationhood. One of the principal purposes of the Constitutional Convention had been to convey to an international audience a more unified American national policy than was evident under the Articles of Confederation and, especially, to reassure skeptical Europeans of American capacity to act as a nation. The framers designed a number of constitutional provisions to assure other nations in the Atlantic world that they could safely and confidently engage in diplomacy and commerce with the United States. In this regard, the Constitution was only partially successful: at the end of the 1780s, Europeans understood that the Constitution created a more cohesive nation, but they still did not regard the United States as equal to European countries.[5]

In the early 1790s, the United States remained weak, and many Americans and foreigners alike remained uncertain about its ability to survive. Britain refused to remove its troops from forts in the Northwest Territory or to open the West Indies to American trade, Spain closed the Mississippi River and the port at New Orleans to American ships, and both countries supplied arms to Indians who were in conflict with Americans. Gradually, though, the United States fortified its position on the continent by negotiating a treaty in which Britain agreed to vacate the western forts (1795), a treaty with Spain that gave Americans access to the Mississippi River and a right of deposit in New Orleans (1795), and an agreement with France that secured the Louisiana Territory (1803).[6] Moreover, during the first decade of the nineteenth century the U.S. government tacitly, secretly, or overtly supported a number of filibuster missions against territories in the Spanish domain, not only in Florida but in South America as well. For example, the participation of prominent Americans in outfitting Francisco de Miranda's 1806 expedition to overthrow Spanish rule in Venezuela, the Jefferson administration's reputed behind-the-scenes support for the venture, the federal court's refusal to punish the filibusters, and the popular support they enjoyed indicate that the United States was moving in the direction of a more assertive national presence, prepared to project its ideals outward. The U.S. declaration of war against Britain in 1812 was another step toward asserting national independence. Though the Treaty of Ghent essentially restored the *status quo ante bellum,* Americans celebrated the war as a second American Revolution, and nationalistic pride surged after Andrew Jackson led U.S. troops to a major victory in the Battle of New Orleans in January 1815.[7]

Close on the heels of the War of 1812, the Seminole War provided an opportunity for the United States to flex its muscle and assert American strength and authority. "It is alone by a just and a bold course of conduct that we can expect to obtain and ensure respect from Europe, and not by a timid, temporizing policy," General Andrew Jackson wrote to the secretary of war in the summer of 1818; "the first commands admiration and esteem, the latter contempt."[8] Most Americans agreed. They were confident that the Florida campaigns reinforced U.S. power by ensuring that the young nation would be viewed from abroad with respect and admiration. Less than a year after the war, Spain ceded Florida to the United States and consented to a boundary line extending to the Pacific Ocean. Britain finally agreed to a treaty that resolved boundary issues, secured American fishing rights, and extended

U.S.-U.K. commercial regulations. Victory in the Seminole War heralded a new world in which the United States took its place as a nation that Europeans had to take seriously.

Just as important, on the domestic front, too, U.S. armed hostilities between 1816 and 1818 strengthened the national image of military prowess. Fostering strong national pride and cohesiveness was particularly important in a relatively new republic, whose citizens had reason to harbor insecurities about their nation's fragility. For Americans, Jackson's campaigns in Florida were just the kind of decisive, forceful action that proved the country was strong. U.S. sovereignty seemed more secure as a result of Jackson's feats.

The United States asserted its sovereignty and equality with European nation-states by vigorously defending the security of its borders and the safety of its citizens, taking a strong position against foreign interference, and participating in the shaping of rules governing international relations. The United States demanded expansion of the boundaries of the civilized family of nations, claiming for itself membership in that family.

Second, the United States differentiated between the Old World and the New World. Although Americans needed the respect, powers, and rights that a recognized sovereign member of the European diplomatic community enjoyed, they also wanted European recognition that, in certain regards, Americans inhabited a separate and distinct cultural, political, legal space. As will be shown, Americans asserted this position during the Seminole War and the subsequent debate in four interconnected ways: They refused, on principle, to allow a European country to mediate the territorial dispute about Florida on the ground that it was American turf. They insisted that the United States was the natural dominant power in the Americas and that European nations and European agents had no right to interfere with U.S. interests or policies there. They claimed that they were entitled to have different rules with regard to slavery and territorial dispossession than Europeans followed within Europe. And, in what seems today like a contradiction, they maintained that the New World was a place of liberty and republicanism, a refuge from Old World oppression and tyranny. Thus, Americans expressed their presumption of American exceptionalism—the notion that the United States had a unique history, a unique destiny, and unique qualities—and reinforced the concept of American continentalism—Americans' vision of a continent-wide domain. Even before the term "manifest destiny" was coined, Americans believed such an extended territory was their political and providential destiny.[9]

Americans' belief that they constituted a unique nation that was fated to hold continental or even hemispheric hegemony provided a rationale for demarcating the Western and Eastern Hemispheres as distinct spheres. In the 1810s, that conception was gaining traction. Just a few years before the Seminole War, Thomas Jefferson had asserted in a private letter that "America has a hemisphere to itself."[10] Yet the idea had never before been exposed to such a full public debate nor been so significantly justified in terms of law. Just a few years after the United States successfully swept the Spanish out of Florida, the Monroe Doctrine would formalize the conviction that the United States had natural primacy in the Americas and could demand that Europeans desist from further colonization there. Yet the idea was inconsistent with the notion of a universal global order because it identified a particular geographic region with its own rules. It also introduced a new element to Europeans' view of their own legal and diplomatic community—that a member of the community could not only enact its own national laws relating to internal matters but also set international rules that would be applicable within a particular extra-European region.

Third, the United States openly rejected the prevailing theory that nations had an obligation to provide the protections of fundamental law universally. The Seminole War took place at a time when universalist natural law language still dominated legal thought. In principle, natural law was eternal, unchanging law that applied universally to all. Medieval theologians attributed natural law to divine will, while ancient Roman and Enlightenment-era jurists were more likely to emphasize secular origins in nature or in human reason. Whatever the source, in the early modern period natural law doctrine presented an ideal that all human beings were entitled to certain fundamental protections.[11]

During the revolutionary era, natural law had been popular in the United States. In fact, it was an essential foundation of the American Revolution. For Americans of the 1760s and 1770s, the natural law argument was particularly compelling because it provided a way of challenging imperial legislation at a time when the British regarded Parliament's decisions as the highest law. Most prominently, the Declaration of Independence relied heavily on natural law as a source of Americans' rights. Addressing the colonies' collective rights, the Declaration proclaimed the necessity of the United States' assuming "the separate and equal station to which the Laws of Nature and of Nature's God entitle them." The Declaration also addressed natural law on an individual level. Perhaps the document's most famous sentence is based squarely on natural or divine law expressed in broad, universalist language: "We hold these truths to be self-evident, that all men are created equal, that they are endowed by their Creator with certain unalienable Rights, that among these are Life, Liberty and the pursuit of Happiness."[12]

On the international front, transcendent natural law principles also dominated the law of nations, which was the law governing relations among nations in peacetime and wartime. In the early nineteenth century, there were no official documents definitively laying out either the broad law of nations or its component part that focused on the laws of war. The United States and other nations had never formally agreed on a set of principles to govern military behavior. Although there were some bilateral international agreements in the eighteenth century, multilateral treaties that codified broadly applicable international legal principles would only appear much later in the nineteenth century. At the time of the Seminole War, the laws of war were based primarily on jurists' treatises and unwritten customary practices. Natural law provided a foundation for the legal thought of most early modern jurists and theologians who wrote about law, including Thomas Aquinas, Francisco de Vitoria, Hugo Grotius, Samuel von Pufendorf, Jean Jacques Burlamaqui, and Emer de Vattel.[13]

Yet, in an apparent contradiction, in the Seminole War the United States distanced itself from universalist natural law doctrine in order to establish itself as a lawful nation among civilized nations. Rather than extending equal rights to everyone, Americans preferred to limit rights to selected categories of people. The line they drew between people with or without rights was inconsistent with idealized theories of natural law but was an important step in creating national identity.

In the wake of the Seminole War, Americans took the lead in openly asserting a selectively applicable international law that bound only European and European-descended nations in their relationships with each other. Though not in conformity with universalistic theories that formally dominated European literature on the law of nations, some aspects of that American version of the laws of war had roots in Renaissance and early modern European discourse and were consistent with actual practice in North America, especially with the style of warfare commonly employed in conflicts with Indians. Although there was considerable precedent in customary usages, however, neither military nor political leaders had previously explained the legal basis for such practices, and jurisprudential writings had not yet fully incorporated them. Moreover, although European legal treatises left open the possibility for exceptions to universalism in special circumstances, Americans went far beyond European jurists when they formalized vast legal distinctions based on race and culture. The American articulation of those principles in the 1810s, which Henry Wheaton later incorporated into the first American treatise on international law, constituted a significant shift that had long-term influence.

The United States' blatant legal line-drawing based on race and culture helped solidify an exclusionary vision that would firmly displace universalism in European thought by the end of the nineteenth century. By 1900, the old concept of universal international law would give way to a growing popular belief in the existence of a sharp racially inflected line between "savage" and "civilized" people, in the superiority of European over non-European civilizations, in the propriety of having different rules to govern relations with "barbarians" than with "civilized" nations, and in the necessity to apply different political standards to indigenous populations in the colonies than were applied to Europeans.[14] In their Seminole War discourse, Americans anticipated—and helped forge—that shift.

In parallel fashion, the United States made manifest its internal lines of law and nationhood during the Florida expeditions. As the nation increasingly emphasized popular sovereignty, it reframed domestic natural law discourse. The United States rejected the notion that law applied equally to all groups within the nation. Derived from the will of the people expressed through their representatives, rather than from God or nature, law was particular, not universal. U.S. law fully protected only European-descended people, not people of other ancestries, yet all inhabitants of the United States were subject to American law. These ideas, which Americans asserted in the Seminole War, presaged doctrines of legal modernism that firmly took hold in the United States in the late nineteenth and early twentieth centuries.[15]

Fourth, the United States proposed a new approach to the application of law across territorial borders. The nation's extraterritorial armed hostilities were a way of both claiming membership in the European family of sovereign nations and making clear the legal ramifications of the distinction between "civilized" and "savage" people. The reverse was also true: the United States used the distinctions between European- and non-European-heritage nations, between sovereign and nonsovereign polities, and between civilized and savage people to justify its extraterritorial activities.

Americans believed that their extraterritorial activity in pursuit of geographic expansion was justified by their right to conquer territory inhabited by "uncivilized" people, because such conquest would make the land more productive and would spread American values of liberty and republican government. Accordingly, a profound influence on the U.S. approach to Florida in the 1810s was the commitment to American exceptionalism and American continentalism. The United States' justifications for its extraterritorial military actions, as well as its rationale for extraterritorial application of U.S. law and racial status designations, were based on a complex understanding of the United States' own mission as a nation. Despite the particularity and distinctiveness of the Americans' exceptionalist notions of continentalism and manifest destiny, some of the fundamental legal ideas underlying those concepts later bolstered American and European overseas expansion. In the mid-to-late nineteenth century, European and European-heritage nations continued their adherence to a law of nations that guaranteed their own territorial sovereignty and right of self-determination while nonetheless finding room in international law for conquest of other lands in the name of a civilizing mission. Thus, the American explanation of circumstances in which the law of nations permitted a nation to act outside of its own borders, as articulated in connection with the Seminole War, proved useful for empire-building ventures around the world later in the century.

Thus, in justifying the Florida campaigns, the United States deployed law to advance several interrelated goals: asserting itself as a formidable sovereign nation, claiming its position as the hegemonic continental power, defining itself as a white/European-heritage nation, and claiming the right to act extraterritorially to further its national interests. Successful achievement of these goals served both domestic and international purposes. The United States craved European respect and acceptance as a member of the civilized community of nations. Americans believed they would earn respect through forceful extraterritorial military action and would gain acceptance by demonstrating that they were a European-heritage community. Their exclusionary legal borders conveyed that neither Native Americans nor African-descended people were equal members of the American civic community, thus establishing the nation's European credentials. Yet the United States asserted dominion over both of those groups and demanded their adherence to American laws, imposing the nation's authority over all people in (or near) its territory. The United States claimed that within its sovereign territory and along its border areas it had the right to deal with different categories of inhabitants as it saw fit. Domestically, U.S. military actions against Europeans, Indians, and African-heritage people helped define it as a nation. In fact, white Americans constructed their nation in relation to all three groups. The Seminole War advanced European Americans' vision of a racially and culturally defined national identity. Americans believed that legal line-drawing between Europeans and non-Europeans not only reinforced American nationhood but also rationalized slavery, Indian removal, and territorial expansion—practices that would be crucial for future growth of the Republic.

The American understanding of the laws of war in the 1810s was not created by the Seminole War. Rather, the war was an outgrowth of ideas and presumptions that had been percolating for some time but had not previously been presented as official doctrine. The timing and circumstances of the war provided an opportunity for Americans to articulate and defend those ideas openly and vigorously in public forums. The end of the War of 1812 and the

Napoleonic Wars gave the United States an auspicious occasion for affirming their nationhood in an assertive way. Placing at stake relationships with the Spanish, Creek and Seminole Indians, African-descended people, and the British, the Seminole War of 1816–1818 offered the United States a valuable opportunity to refashion law in order to accomplish short- and long-term objectives.

This book is a case study of how the early Republic implemented doctrines of law in practice. It shows where the government's position stood in relation to the evolution of domestic constitutional law and the law of nations as described by Europeans. It analyzes how law shaped military conduct and how the United States used doctrines of law to rationalize actions that the government deemed to be in the national interest. The book shows how the United States established in the late 1810s that it was a member of the law-abiding community of nations while at the same time successfully contending that law did not restrain its conduct in Florida.

Because the goal of the book is to examine how the United States used the occasion of the Seminole War to advance its own vision of its national identity and approach to law, the focus is on official rationales and public debate in the United States. Unfortunately, following the final invasion of 1818, there was scarcely any public commentary on the topic by African-descended, Seminole, Creek, or other American Indian contemporaries. Where their perspectives entered the public realm, they are included in this book because they would have been part of the debate that consolidated an American approach to the borders of law. The situation is different with regard to Spanish and British people of the time, who left a written record of commentary on topics relating to the Florida campaigns. Their perspectives, too, are included only to the extent that they were available to Americans at the time and therefore might have played a role in the American debate about legal borders.[16]

Occurring at the midpoint between Thomas Jefferson's and Andrew Jackson's presidencies—a decade after Jefferson left office, and a decade before Jackson became president—the Seminole War came at an important moment in political, legal, and social developments of the early national period. The debate about the war, which provided an opportunity to express core American values, marked an important stage in the transition from revolutionary to Jacksonian America. The defense of U.S. conduct presaged later Jacksonian Democratic positions on constitutional powers, state sovereignty, blacks and slavery, Indians, rule of law, military power, and nationhood. Moreover, on some issues the debate evinces the early emergence of important ideals that are normally associated with the end of the nineteenth century. The discourse of the time shows that the transition to a late nineteenth-century paradigm of constitutional and international law doctrine—ideas that would buttress the United States' imperial ventures overseas—was already under way in the 1810s. Most important, the debate about the Florida campaigns reveals the role of law in defining the boundaries of nationhood during the decades between the American Revolution and the Civil War.

CHAPTER ONE

U.S.-Spanish Relations and the Florida Campaigns

In the 1810s, the United States charged Spanish officials in Florida with sheltering and aiding "outlaws" who conspired against the Republic and "banditti" who crossed the border to attack Americans. Mirroring the American claims, Spanish authorities accused the United States of harboring "desperadoes," "pirates," and "enemies of all social order" who plotted insurgency against Spain and fostered violence in Florida.[1] Such accusations reflected the disorderly condition of the border region. The undefined and porous boundary between the United States and Spanish Florida created disquiet for both nations.

For years after the founding of the United States, the two countries jockeyed for the upper hand in negotiations over Florida. Despite Spain's assertion of a superior historical and legal claim, pragmatic facts on the ground ultimately decided the issue in favor of the United States: the spring 1818 military invasion forced Spain to abandon its abstract legal argument and agree to cede the territory, thus ending the conflict. Before and during that invasion, the United States introduced legal arguments that would later become central to the defense of the Florida campaigns and would provide a foundation for the ideas of the Monroe Doctrine, as well as for future U.S. expansionist efforts. Spain countered the American position, contending that the expeditions were unlawful. The arguments presented through the end of the war in May 1818 began the debate about the Florida campaigns, a debate in which the United States claimed its rights as a sovereign nation and asserted its position in the world.

Border Negotiations

Acquiring Florida was an important U.S. policy goal in the first two decades of the nineteenth century. Control of the Gulf Coast east of New Orleans was essential for transporting cotton and other products by water. Numerous rivers from U.S. territory only accessed the sea through Florida. Originating in Georgia and the Mississippi Territory, those American rivers flowed into West and East Florida's Pearl, Mobile, Perdido, Escambia, Choctawhatchee, Apalachicola, Ochlockonee, and Suwannee Rivers and then into the Gulf of Mexico. Without access to those Florida rivers, the United States lacked convenient outlets on the Gulf Coast. Moreover, Americans were concerned that leaving Florida in Spanish hands—and, even more, risking a British takeover of the territory—threatened American security interests. They were particularly troubled that New Orleans would always be vulnerable to attack as long as a foreign navy could find a base along the Gulf. From Florida, the British would also control trade in the Gulf of Mexico. Additionally, Americans protested, despite the United States and Spain's mutual treaty obligation to restrain Indian inhabitants from attacking each other's citizens or subjects, hostile Creeks and Seminoles freely launched cross-border attacks on frontier dwellers from Florida. Furthermore, Georgia's plantation owners complained that Spanish Florida served as a haven that lured fugitive slaves. Not only security and economic interests but also national pride drove the quest for Florida. Many wanted the United States to acquire Florida simply because they saw the Gulf of Mexico as the United States' "natural and proper" southeastern border.[2]

The United States had reason to doubt the solidity and durability of Spanish control of Florida for four reasons.[3] First of all, Spain had not retained continuous possession of the territory. Spain had ceded Florida to Britain in 1763, at the end of the Seven Years' War. After twenty years as part of the British Empire, Florida—by this point divided into West Florida and East Florida—returned to Spain in 1783, at the end of the American Revolution.

Second, the northern and western boundaries of Florida were persistently contested and ambiguous. The United States insisted that the northern border of West Florida followed the 31st parallel, which was the pre-1763 border. However, Spain claimed title to West Florida up to the mouth of the Yazoo River, as delimited by the British in 1767.[4] (See Map 1.1.[5]) Negotiations finally led to resolution of the dispute about the northern boundary of West

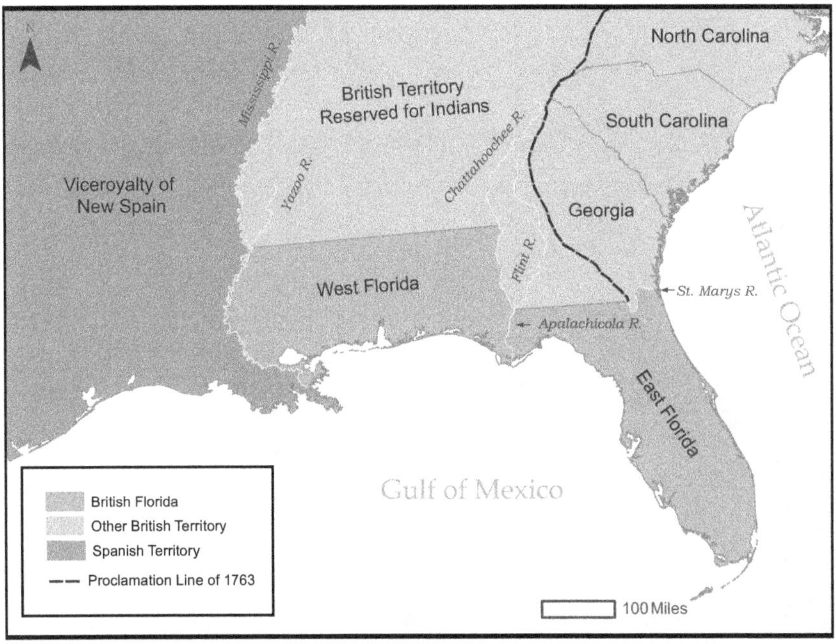

MAP 1.1 *British West and East Florida, 1767.*

Florida in 1795. In Pinckney's Treaty, Spain and the United States set the border at 31°, as the United States had wanted.[6] Though clearly defined, however, the northern West Florida boundary was still easily and frequently breached.

Meanwhile, the territory's western boundary remained a major source of contention between the United States and Spain in the years leading up to the Seminole War. The persistent question was whether the border between Louisiana and West Florida was at the Mississippi River (as Spain claimed) or further east at the Perdido River (as the United States claimed). The treaty by which the United States purchased Louisiana in 1803 did not specify the boundaries of the territory. To maximize the size of its acquisition and minimize the dimensions of neighboring Spanish West Florida, the United States based its asserted rights on the extent of pre-1763 French Louisiana, which had extended east to the Perdido. Spain, which naturally had the opposite goal, premised its claim on the boundaries of post-1763 British Florida, which had extended west to the Mississippi. (Map 1.2 shows the disputed area.)

Third, Spanish control of Florida had been challenged numerous times both by private actors and by the British and U.S. governments. In the seventeenth and early eighteenth centuries, English settlers in the nearby

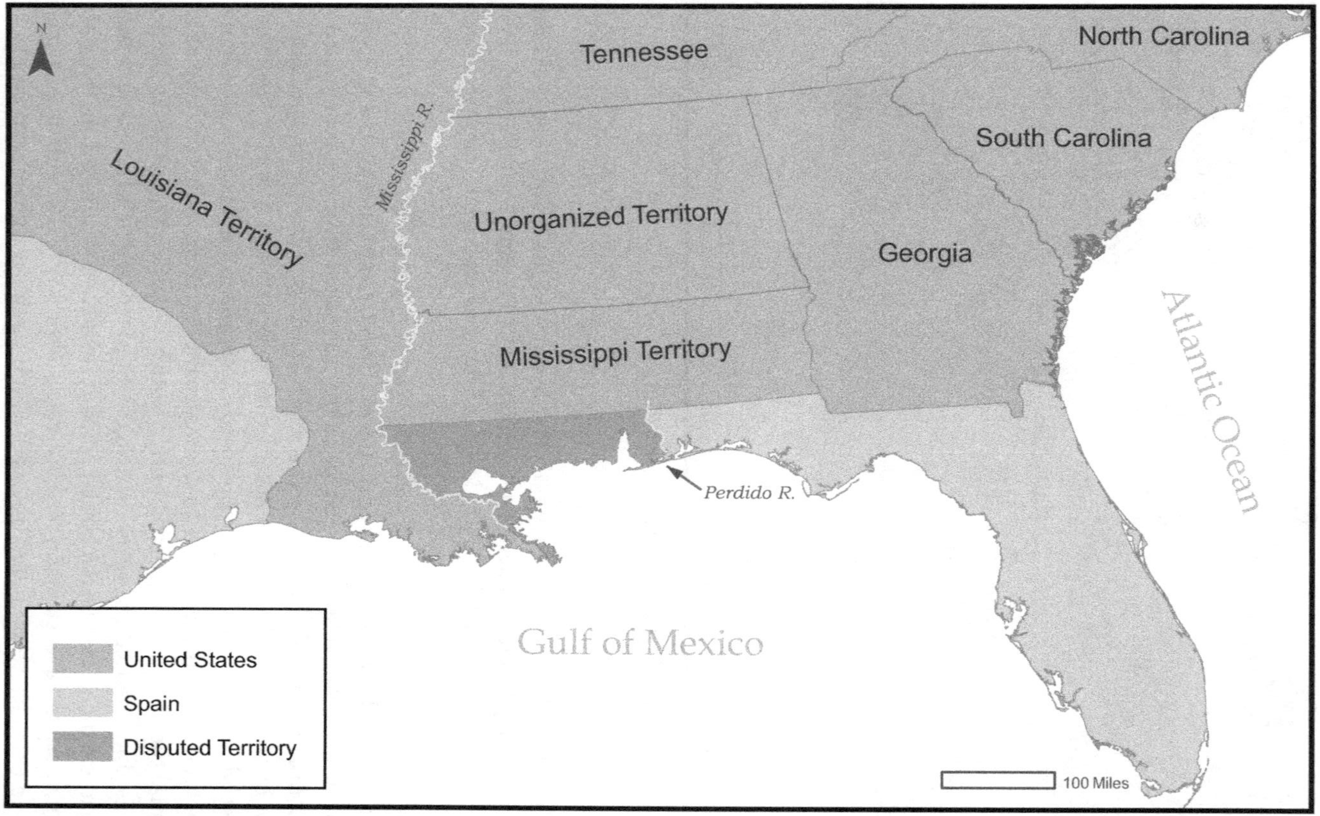

MAP 1.2 *Territory claimed by the United States and Spain, 1803.*

colonies of the Carolinas and Georgia repeatedly encroached on the Spanish territory from the north, leading to a number of military skirmishes. Florida had also been the focus of numerous filibustering efforts and revolts that sought to create independent nations. Between the 1780s and the early 1800s, West and East Florida remained highly unstable, as they experienced Anglo-American filibustering efforts and revolts, including rebellions by Richard Lang and other settlers in East Florida in 1795, by adventurer William Augustus Bowles in West Florida between 1788 and 1803, and by Reuben, Samuel, and Nathan Kemper in West Florida in 1804.

Additionally, the United States government sponsored efforts to gradually take possession of Florida without resorting to war. The turmoil in Europe during the Napoleonic Wars opened up an opportunity for the United States to pursue this tactic. From 1808—when France forced Spanish king Ferdinand VII to abdicate in favor of Napoleon's brother, Joseph Bonaparte—until 1814—when Ferdinand returned to the throne—the absence of strong Spanish leadership at the top made Spain's authority susceptible to challenge. There were disadvantages to Spanish weakness, since it permitted the British army to return to the Gulf Coast area during the War of 1812 and make free use of Florida territory to build forts, train soldiers, and launch attacks against the United States. However, the U.S. government also found that there were advantages to Spain's lack of full control in Florida, as it allowed the United States to encourage agitation among American residents of the territory. In 1810, settlers in the Baton Rouge area led a successful rebellion against the Spanish and declared an independent Republic of West Florida extending along the Gulf Coast from the Mississippi to the Perdido River. By 1812, the United States had claimed that land, incorporating the western portion into the new state of Louisiana and adding the eastern portion to the Mississippi Territory, as shown on Map 1.3. Success in West Florida was not matched in East Florida, however. An 1812 attempt by American agents to acquire East Florida in a similar way—by fostering a local rebellion and seizing Amelia Island—unfolded clumsily, and President James Madison disavowed the agents' actions and relinquished the island back to Spain in 1813. In any case, Americans sought more than just de facto possession of West and East Florida. They wanted European acknowledgement of the U.S. right to the territory. During and after the War of 1812, Americans remained frustrated that Spain would neither recognize U.S. claims to West Florida nor relinquish control of East Florida.

Fourth, Spanish-American independence movements were challenging Spanish rule throughout the Americas during the first two decades of the nineteenth century. By the time Jackson led troops into Florida in 1818, there had been rebellions in Spanish-American colonies for over a decade, juntas

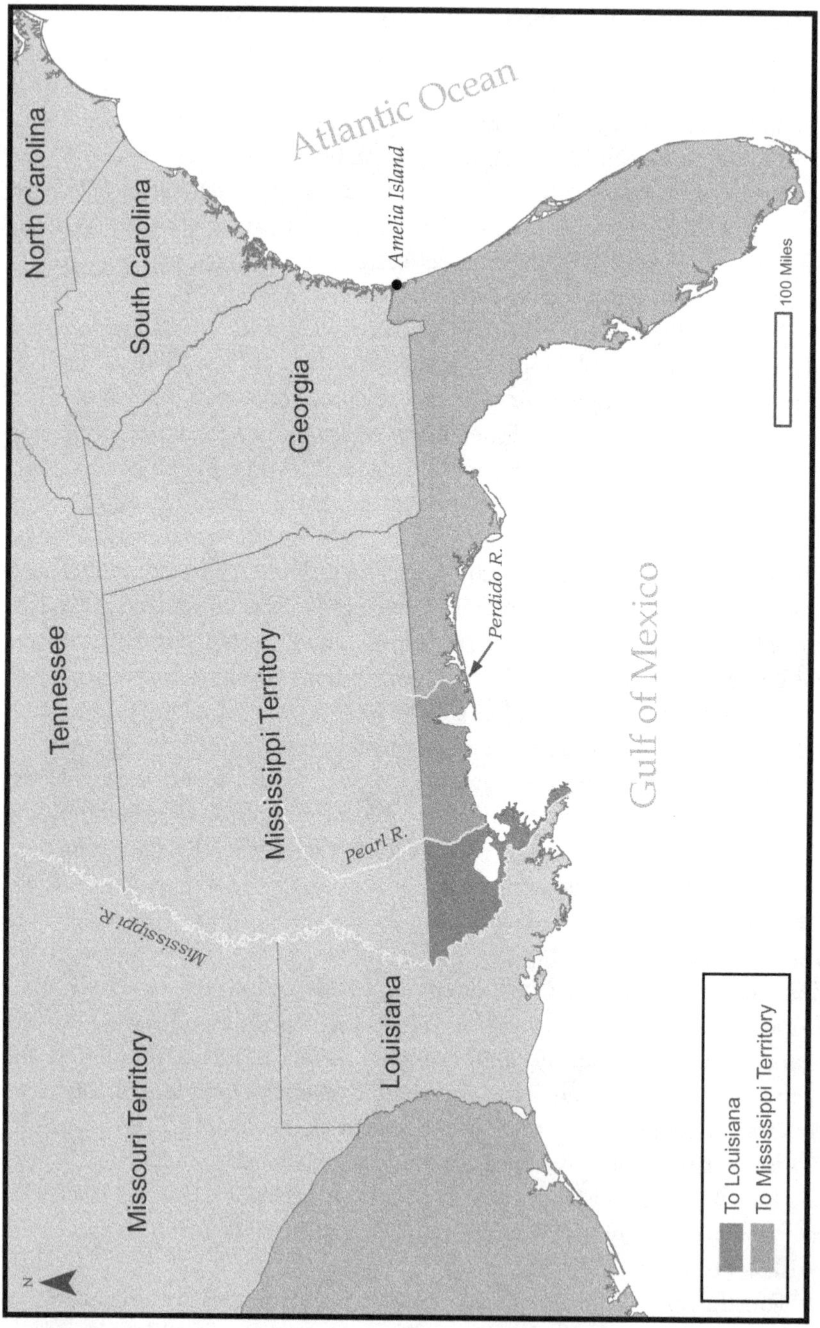

MAP 1.3 *United States claims to West Florida, 1812.*

had been established in a number of places, and several Latin American countries were de facto independent. Thus, the larger geopolitical context of American activity in Florida was a power vacuum in Spanish America and international competition to secure the best advantage from the imminent collapse of the Spanish Empire.[7]

Following the restoration of diplomatic relations between the United States and Spain in December 1815, Florida was a major subject of correspondence and consultations both in Washington (between Spain's envoy to the United States, Luis de Onís, and successive American secretaries of state James Monroe and John Quincy Adams) and in Madrid (between U.S. envoy George W. Erving and successive Spanish foreign ministers Pedro Cevallos Guerra, José García de León y Pizarro, and Carlos Martínez de Irujo y Tacón).[8] Much of the correspondence was later provided to Congress and published in newspapers. It became part of the public record discussed in the Seminole War debate, and it informed the positions of both supporters and critics of the campaigns.

Initiating discussion of U.S.-Spanish relations in a December 30, 1815, letter to Monroe, Luis de Onís demanded that the United States return West Florida to Spain. Restoration of Spanish territory was crucial for restoring matters to the way they stood in 1808, when diplomatic relations ruptured, he claimed.[9] As the United States and Spain continued to contest the Florida boundary over the next two years, Onís persistently emphasized the three-hundred-year historical foundation of Spain's right to West Florida. Describing Florida's history in minute detail, he admonished U.S. officials that they could not simply ignore such extensive evidence in Spain's favor. His long letters expounded on the exact chronology and geography of Spain's, France's, and England's exploration, settlement, and exchanges of territory in the Americas. In 1817, Onís further elaborated on the subject in a fifty-two-page pamphlet published in Philadelphia. In his letters and pamphlet, Onís declared that the facts were clear-cut and Spain's rights to the territory it claimed were based on immutable truth, reason, and justice. In contrast, he characterized the American territorial claim as groundless and arbitrary. In the pamphlet, he observed that "if the same reasoning were resorted to by Spain, she might ask from the United States a cession of any territory she might wish to acquire, and in exchange, renounce her rights to the state of Ohio, part of Georgia, Kentucky and Tennessee." Such a claim would be no more plausible than the imaginary right the U.S. government was asserting, he wrote. Onís protested that the United States could not stubbornly maintain that, having stated its positions on the subject, it would refuse to consider contrary documentary proof and would never alter its stance.[10]

In reply, Monroe asserted that West Florida was part of the Louisiana Purchase Lands, to which the United States had lawful title. He rejected the Spanish demand for a U.S. cession of the disputed area as a precondition to negotiations, and he complained that since 1803 Spain had refused to act cooperatively to resolve differences over Louisiana's borders in the West Florida area. The secretary of state declined to repeatedly rehash arguments based on early colonial history that the parties had thoroughly discussed during negotiations in 1804–1805. Monroe and his successor, Adams, brushed aside Onís's detailed description of distant history, instead urging Spain to accept a practical solution based on present conditions. Monroe and Adams each devoted just one letter to a thorough review of the territorial history. Though Onís tried to pursue the detailed historical analysis further, they told him it would be useless to repeat the old debates.[11]

With frustration, Spanish foreign minister Pizarro acknowledged that American officials deemed it "superfluous" to discuss the foundations of Spain's territorial rights and desired a settlement that took into account only "considerations of mutual convenience." He nonetheless pressed Onís to continue to insist on an examination of the historical facts so that "we, our Governments, and the world, can determine upon the propriety or impropriety" of any proposed settlement.[12] American diplomats disagreed with Spain's proposed framework for resolving the two nations' dispute over Florida, and negotiations remained at an impasse. However, between 1816 and 1818, U.S. military operations changed the situation on the ground in Florida. The new reality made evident by the American use of force would lead Spanish officials to shift their approach in early 1819. U.S. military pressure trumped whatever territorial claims Spain might have based on history and law.

Onís's prewar focus on the weight of historical facts and just resolution was mirrored by postwar American critics, who challenged the U.S. government's factual foundation for its legal claims and expressed concern about issues of justice. Meanwhile, Monroe's and Adams's prewar utilitarian arguments became a crucial element in the position taken by postwar defenders of the Florida campaigns.

Notably, Onís's comments also provided model legal arguments for supporters of military action. In his December 1815 letter, Onís explained that Spain was concerned not only about violations of its Florida territory but also about American support for men violently challenging Spain's authority elsewhere in the Americas. He charged that "insurgents and incendiaries" were recruiting and arming troops within the United States to assist revolutionaries in the king's dominions and that anti-Spanish pirates were using American ports to outfit their vessels and sell their plunder. Onís asserted that the law of nations required the United States to act against such "banditti," who recognized no law. He demanded that the United States prosecute insurgents making war on New Spain from U.S. territory and exclude from American ports any ship flying the flag of a rebelling colony.[13] Onís's arguments about alleged anti-Spanish banditti were in fact strikingly similar to claims later made by Monroe, Adams, and Jackson in 1816, in 1817, and again in 1818–1819 as they defended U.S. incursions into Florida.

In response to Onís's 1815 letter, Monroe denied that any anti-Spanish insurgents gathered anywhere within reach of American laws and assured Onís that the United States prohibited its citizens from taking part in Spanish-American wars and barred foreigners from recruiting Americans in the United States for that purpose. However, he pointed out that the law of nations did not obligate or empower the United States to punish inhabitants of Spanish colonies for acts committed outside the United States. He further noted that U.S. policy of receiving vessels of all countries into its ports was consistent with principles of neutrality.[14]

Interestingly, while U.S. officials denied any American responsibility for dealing with anti-Spanish insurgents acting within or from the United States, they also admonished Spain for failing to control anti-American British and Indian fighters located in Florida. Several members of the administration objected that Spain had permitted America's enemies to operate out of bases in Florida during and since the War of 1812. Not only did Spanish aid to British troops contravene the principles of neutrality, but Spanish support for Creek and Seminole Indians violated Pinckney's Treaty, they claimed. That treaty between the United States and Spain obliged both nations to restrain Indian inhabitants from attacking the other party's citizens or subjects. For these breaches, Americans primarily blamed Mateo González Manrique, the Pensacola-based governor of West Florida from 1813 to 1815. Although Onís claimed that Manrique had "uniformly observed the most scrupulous neutrality" during the war and had "employed every . . . practicable means" to prevent Indian hostilities on Americans, American officials saw the situation very differently. As Secretary of State Adams later explained in detail, the Spanish governor had permitted British Major Edward Nicolls and his men to take possession of Pensacola in the summer of 1814. For months, British troops, agents, and Indian allies operated freely out of the Florida post, preparing for action against the United States. After American general Andrew Jackson evicted the British from Pensacola in the fall of 1814, Adams noted, Nicolls and his men moved to another fort, located along the Apalachicola River on Prospect Bluff, about fifteen miles north of the Gulf of Mexico and roughly sixty miles from the Georgia border. The British invited "runaway negroes" and "savage Indians" to the Prospect Bluff fort in order to launch war against the United States, Adams charged. The secretary of state complained that "[t]he fort had been built upon Spanish territory, under the sufferance of Spanish authorities, by British officers, during the war, for annoyance against the United States."[15] In short, the U.S. government protested that Spanish officials permitted British agents to instigate blacks and Indians to attack the United States from Florida. This claim would be central to the U.S. defense of armed hostilities conducted in the period from 1816 to 1818.

Prospect Bluff and Amelia Island

While negotiations between the United States and Spain languished in 1816 and 1817, the United States sent troops to deal with two small, isolated areas that were ostensibly within Spanish territory but had been taken over by people deemed to be threatening to the United States. (See Map 1.4.)

The first of the two American military operations targeted the Prospect Bluff fort built in 1814 under the direction of British naval officers Edward Nicolls and George Woodbine. Many Americans called for the destruction of the garrison. Nevertheless, the fort still stood when the War of 1812 ended. Even following the Treaty of Ghent, the British continued to offer shelter to blacks and Indians there. After Nicolls sailed back to England in the summer of 1815, hundreds of African-heritage men, women, and children remained at Prospect Bluff and in settlements stretching for miles along the river outside the garrison.[16]

Southern planters became increasingly agitated about the outpost they now called the "Negro Fort," and Major General Andrew Jackson, commander of the Seventh Military District (Tennessee, Louisiana, and the Mississippi Territory), agreed that the garrison had to be destroyed. In April 1816, he made his intentions bluntly clear: he wrote to the new West Florida governor, Mauricio de Zúñiga, demanding that the Spanish dislodge the "banditti" from the Prospect Bluff fort. If Spain failed to do so, Jackson warned, the United States would be compelled to take care of it. Placing his warning within principles of the law of nations, Jackson informed Zúñiga that a U.S. attack on the fort would be justified as a matter of self-defense. In his May 1816 response, the Spanish governor agreed with Jackson that Spanish troops should occupy or destroy the fort and deliver its "negro" residents to "their lawful owners." However, he was both unauthorized and unable to do so immediately; he needed both military reinforcements and authorization from his superior before he could proceed. In the meantime, Zúñiga hoped that Jackson and the American government would take no steps "which may

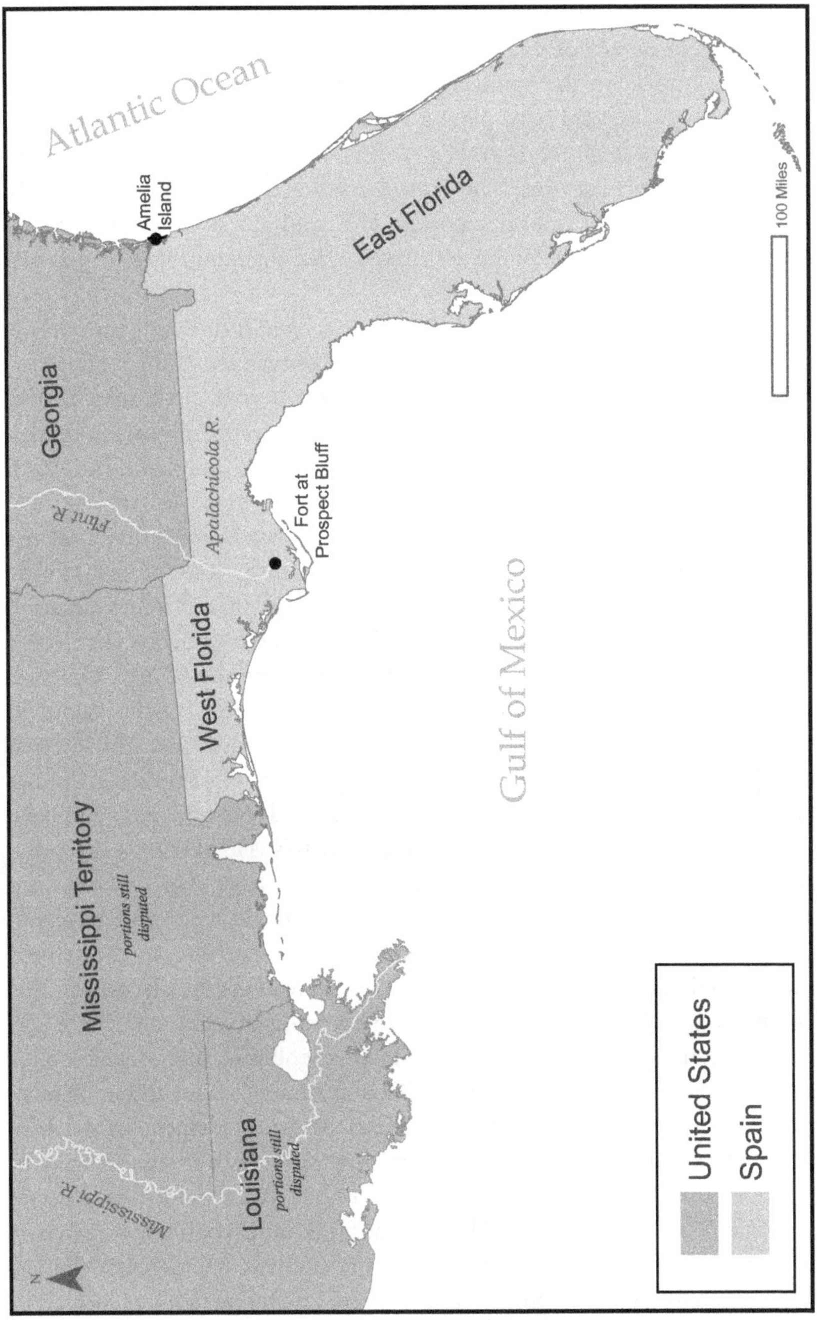

MAP 1.4 *Prospect Bluff and Amelia Island, 1816.*

be prejudicial to the sovereignty of the king . . . or the district of Apalachicola, which is a dependency of this government."[17]

Two months later, the Spanish government still had not acted, and the United States proceeded with plans to demolish the fort. On July 27, 1816, U.S. gunboats successfully destroyed the garrison with a hot cannon ball to the central powder magazine. The explosion killed dozens of the fort's inhabitants. Afterward, participants reported, U.S. and allied Creek troops captured other black residents of the area and carried them into slavery north of the border.[18]

The destruction of the Prospect Bluff fort evoked little comment internationally or domestically. Spain expressed little concern about the matter, presumably because the United States did not retain control of any Spanish territory, and, in any case, the demolition also served Spain's own interests. Moreover, the Madison administration did not publicly condemn the attack on the bastion, and Congress did not assert its authority to declare war.

The second American military action against Spanish Florida after the War of 1812 focused on Amelia Island, which lay off the coast of East Florida just south of the Georgia border. A center of smuggling, the island attracted a variety of people involved in illegal trading. In June 1817, Scotsman Gregor MacGregor, claiming authority under the United Provinces of New Granada and Venezuela, seized the island. After MacGregor left Amelia Island in September, his associate Louis-Michel Aury assumed leadership and declared a republic. In a special message to Congress in January 1818, President Monroe characterized Aury and his men as unauthorized adventurers who had been using the island as a base for smuggling activities. He acknowledged that Spain was unable to prevent injuries to Americans from Amelia Island but warned that "[h]er territory however ought not to be made instrumental, through her inability to defend it, to purposes so injurious to the United States." Providing legal context for the American intervention, he added: "To a country over which she fails to maintain her authority, and which she permits to be converted to the annoyance of her neighbours, her jurisdiction for the time, necessarily ceases to exist." This argument about feeble Spanish sovereignty in Florida would reappear later as a key element in the U.S. defense of its extraterritorial activities. In 1817, Monroe ordered the army to "suppress" the "establishment" on Amelia Island. Accordingly, on December 23, 1817, U.S. troops led by Major General Edmund P. Gaines moved in to take control of the island. In the January 1818 address to Congress, Monroe spoke indirectly to the lawfulness of the United States' actions, pointing out that "[i]n expelling these adventurers from these posts, it was not intended to make any conquest from Spain."[19] This, too, was a legal argument that the

United States would later elaborate on to explain why the laws of war did not apply to the Florida campaigns.

In contrast to the lack of protest after the 1816 attack on the Prospect Bluff fort, the U.S. seizure of Amelia Island the following year drew an objection from Spain. As it turned out, discussion about Amelia Island served as a rehearsal for arguments made after the 1818 invasion. Spanish envoy Onís protested that the United States had used military force against a friendly nation during peacetime. He demanded immediate restoration of the island to Spain. Secretary of State Adams replied that if Spain had taken care of the smugglers, pirates, and adventurers on Amelia Island the United States would have been spared the responsibility of dealing with the problem. Defending the legality of the intervention under the law of nations, he observed that the U.S. action was not intended to conquer the island from Spain but simply arose from a duty to protect the commercial interests of the United States and its allies, including Spain itself. Finally, Adams concluded by noting that the United States could not "permit that the adjoining territories of Spain should be misused by others for purposes of annoyance" to the United States. On the domestic front, there was little challenge to the military occupation of Amelia Island. Congress did not dispute the appropriateness of the military operation, convinced that it was both necessary and legal. A January 1818 House committee report concluded that military action was necessary to thwart a hostile occupation of Florida by foreign adventurers who interfered with commercial shipping and illegally imported slaves and other goods into the United States through Amelia Island. Moreover, most congressmen apparently were convinced that the president had a form of congressional authorization for the occupation in a secret "No Transfer Resolution" passed by Congress in January 1811 at President James Madison's request. The resolution authorized the president to take possession of East Florida if a foreign power threatened to occupy it. Whatever the reason for their lack of concern about Amelia Island, Congress deferred to the president in this foreign policy matter, and the United States did not return the island to Spain.[20]

Frustrated by the continuing conflict between the United States and Spain, Luis de Onís suggested submitting the two nations' disputes to British mediation. The U.S. government rejected the idea, using nationalism and American exceptionalism as the main rationales. During and immediately following the War of 1812, nationalistic enthusiasm led Americans to highlight the differences between the Old World and the New, and they were eager to assert the distinct identity of the Americas whenever possible. Thomas Jefferson commented on the separation of the hemispheres in an 1813 letter to Prussian naturalist Alexander von Humboldt. In the midst of his observations about the upheaval in the Spanish-American colonies, he predicted that whatever form of government the liberated nations chose, they would be "*American* governments," outside of the constant turmoil experienced among European countries. More broadly, Jefferson observed, "the European nations constitute a separate division of the globe; their localities make them part of a distinct system; they have a set of interests of their own in which it is our business never to engage ourselves." In fact, he wrote boldly, "America has a hemisphere to itself[;] it must have it's [*sic*] separate system of interests, which must not be subordinated to those of Europe." In 1816, an essay in the *National Register* proclaimed that North and South America were destined to be "one vast republic, affording to man an asylum from persecution, and a shelter from oppression," as well as freedom from "the thraldom and tyranny of European despotism." Also in 1816, an essay in the *Aurora* asserted that the New World was "provided by Providence to preserve liberty against the tyranny of the old world." The following year, a newspaper writer commented that there was "a common American continental interest, in opposition to an European interest." The writer went on to call for "[t]he independence of America from Europe." The author was ostensibly focusing on South Americans, but the implications for North America were evident: Americans, not Europeans, should direct the destiny of the New World. In the House of Representatives, Henry Clay predicted that, once liberated, South American nations would become part of the separate and unique American system of the New World, "in contradistinction to that of Europe."[21]

Building on such sentiments, Secretary of State Adams informed the Spanish envoy that the United States would not agree to any European mediation. In a statement that presaged the Monroe Doctrine, he explained that

> it has hitherto been the policy, both of Europe and of the United States, to keep aloof from the general federative system of each other. The European states are combined together, and connected with one another by a multitude of important interests and relations with which the United States have no concern, with which they have always manifested the determination not to interfere, and of which, no communication being made to them by the Governments of Europe, they have not information competent to enable them to estimate their extent and bearings. The United States, in justice to themselves, in justice to that harmony which they earnestly desire to cultivate with all the Powers of Europe, in justice to that fundamental system of policy which forbids them from entering the labyrinth of European politics, must decline soliciting or acceding to the interference of any other Government of Europe for the settlement of their differences with Spain.[22]

Onís would propose mediation again in the fall of 1818. At that time, he suggested that the United States and Spain refer their disputes to the monarchs and foreign ministers who were then meeting at Aix-la-Chapelle (Aachen), Prussia. The Congress of Aix-la-Chapelle included delegates from Britain, Russia, Prussia, and Austria. The group, convened primarily to discuss troops' withdrawal from their occupation of France, dealt with a variety of other European grievances and governance issues. Adams expressed surprise that Onís would persist in suggesting European arbitration. He declined the suggestion, referring Onís to the reasons already explained in the March 12 letter.[23] The United States' refusal to accept European mediation in 1818 was an important assertion not only of the distinction between Europe and the Americas but also of the United States' full sovereignty, rejection of foreign interference, and nascent hope for continental or even hemispheric dominance.

Meanwhile, Spanish and American grievances, as articulated by Onís and Monroe in their December 1815 and January 1816 correspondence, continued to simmer throughout 1816 and 1817 and into 1818. The two nations' accusations significantly paralleled each other. Each felt mounting uneasiness about the other party's perceived failure to maintain neutrality. Increasingly worried about the Spanish-American rebellions, Spain became even more vocal in protesting that the United States violated neutrality by permitting its citizens to aid insurgents and allowing vessels of Spain's enemies to prepare for war against Spain while docked in U.S. ports. U.S. officials denied that Americans were providing material support to anti-Spanish revolutionaries and claimed the United States was doing everything possible to prevent military enterprises against Mexico or other Spanish colonies. American complaints focused on Florida. Diplomatic and military leaders continued to complain that local Spanish officers—especially José Masot (governor of West Florida, 1816–1818) and Francisco Caso y Luengo, the commandant at Fort St. Marks (San Marcos de Apalache)—were neglecting the obligations of neutrality by allowing British agents to act freely in Spanish territory, permitting fugitive slaves to take refuge in Florida, and aiding and abetting Indians who were hostile to the United States.[24]

The Spanish government responded by denying American allegations against its officers in Florida. Onís wrote a vigorous defense on March 27, 1818. He observed that Americans had not notified Spanish officers of any complaints against Indians. If the governor had received such information, Onís wrote, he would have used forcible means to restrain the Indians, but he could not be expected to use force in the absence of evidence of a problem. He firmly stated that Spain maintained adequate garrisons in Florida and had always fulfilled its obligations under the treaty with the United States. Onís further said it was the responsibility of the United States to inform the Spanish government if local officials acted wrongfully. In the absence of notification, Spain could not act to punish officers who disobeyed the king's mandate. He enclosed a letter from José Coppinger (governor of East Florida, based in St. Augustine, 1816–1821), in which Coppinger stated that he had observed strict neutrality and adhered to treaty obligations, received no American complaints, denied British officer George Woodbine permission to bring troops to Florida for the purpose of attacking the United States, and urged Seminole chief Boleck to act peacefully with Americans and to turn away fugitive slaves from the United States. The Spanish had been peacemakers, not instigators of hostility, Coppinger wrote. Thus, Onís declared, Spanish officials had met all of their obligations with regard to the United States.[25] Later, American critics of the Seminole War would draw on some of these same factual arguments.

The 1818 Invasion of Florida

Notwithstanding the vigor of his defense of Spanish authorities in Florida, Onís anticipated a full-scale American invasion of Florida. As early as mid-1816, Onís reported to Foreign Minister Cevallos that the United States might attack Florida—and he was not referring to U.S. destruction of the Prospect Bluff fort. In March 1817, he warned Cevallos's successor, Pizarro, that he expected hostile U.S. action within six months. Again in January 1818, Onís warned Pizarro about a possible American military attack on Florida. That same month the British representative in Washington, Charles Bagot, likewise expressed his expectation that the United States would occupy Florida. In Madrid, U.S. envoy George Erving stressed to Pizarro that a failure to proceed with genuine negotiations might result in war. Evidently taking seriously the possibility of invasion, Pizarro's April 1818 instructions to Onís advised him to make concessions on the western boundary question if there was danger of war. Apparently quite alarmed in late March 1818, Onís warned Adams that he would protest strongly if U.S. troops violated Spanish territory in Florida.[26]

Onís had reason to worry. His claim that Spanish officials acted in a neutral fashion did not convince Americans. They blamed Spanish indulgence of the Seminoles—their collective name for all Indians in Florida—for the violence occurring on the frontier, and in the spring of 1818 government officials did not hide the possibility that U.S. troops might enter Florida in pursuit of Indians. In late March 1818, when Onís issued his assertive defense of Florida officials, the United States was already at war with the Seminoles. Americans viewed the "Seminole War" as having begun at least as early as

September 1817, and perhaps as early as the Creek War of 1813–1814, after which surviving Creeks fled to Florida and joined forces with Seminoles to resist American encroachments. In January 1818, the Senate mentioned ongoing military operations against the Seminoles when it requested a presidential report on how the military was supplying American troops participating in those operations. The House of Representatives, too, publicly showed awareness of the conflict. On April 3, 1818, the House approved a resolution directing the Committee on Military Affairs to consider an increase in pay for soldiers in the Seminole War. Subsequently a law providing that salaries and benefits for American militiamen who had been fighting the Seminole Indians since September 1, 1817, be equal to those offered to U.S. soldiers in the War of 1812 passed the House on April 10 and the Senate on April 18 and was signed by the president on April 20, 1818. (The specific dates would later be pertinent.) Furthermore, in March 1818 both the president and members of Congress publicly commented that fighting the Seminoles might require entry into Florida. On March 25, 1818, Monroe informed Congress that he had ordered Andrew Jackson—who was now in command of the United States' southern military district—to go to the frontier to deal with the hostile Seminoles. Monroe assured Congress that administration officials had instructed Jackson "not to enter Florida, unless it be in pursuit of the enemy, and in that case, to respect the Spanish authority, wherever it is maintained." With his message, Monroe released copies of instructions sent to Generals Gaines and Jackson by the secretary of war in late 1817.[27]

In the House of Representatives, the possibility of war with Spain came up in a context not directly pertaining to Florida. The issue arose in a debate about whether the United States should recognize South American nations that had declared independence from Spain. During the March 24–28 debate about Henry Clay's proposal to appropriate $18,000 to pay a U.S. minister to Buenos Aires, Clay said he was opposed to the United States commencing war with Spain even though the United States had just cause. If the United States were to end up at war with Spain, he explained, it would be better if that war were triggered by the United States taking a principled stand in support of South American republics rather than by the United States expropriating adjoining Spanish territory. If the United States were to seize Florida now, he said, it would only reinforce Europeans' perception that Americans had "inordinate ambition" and sought to "aggrandize ourselves by an extension, on all sides, of our limits." Clay concluded: "[I]f we are to be involved in war with Spain, let us have the credit of disinterestedness; let us put her yet more in the wrong." John Forsyth, chairman of the Committee on Foreign Relations, strongly disagreed. Why, he asked, should the United States risk war by advancing South Americans' interests when it had its own interests to assert and defend? Spain had inflicted injuries and losses on American citizens but for years had refused to provide compensation. The United States should simply seize Florida to "place the means of indemnity in our possession," Forsyth declared. A few other members of the House also took a position on whether the United States should take Florida. Forsyth even brought to the Foreign Relations Committee a motion to authorize the president to take possession of East Florida. A majority of the committee disapproved of the motion, so Forsyth decided not to pursue it. Later, critics of the Seminole War who said the invasion lacked congressional authority would point to this discussion as evidence that the House had expressed its opposition to seizing East Florida and also to initiating war with Spain. At the time, though, several newspapers took Forsyth's comments as a hint that there was a "rupture" in U.S.-Spanish relations and that an American invasion of Florida was imminent.[28]

Within the United States, especially in the South, the press increasingly expressed anti-Spanish sentiments and called for U.S. military action to seize Florida. Accounts of the Spanish attack on the U.S.S. *Firebrand* in the Gulf of Mexico, stories of alleged Spanish atrocities in the South American conflicts, and reports of frontier settlers' bloody conflicts with Seminoles near the Spanish border stoked Americans' hostility toward Spain. Since Spanish authorities had allowed Florida to become a dangerous neighbor, newspaper editorials proclaimed, the United States should occupy the territory. After thirteen years of waiting for peaceful resolution of American grievances, it was time to act decisively and, with force of arms, take possession of Florida. In mid-April 1818 (before hearing news of Jackson's invasion), the *Boston Patriot* declared that the necessity of U.S. occupation of Florida became clearer every day. The newspaper said Spain had been too weak to keep the British out of Pensacola during the War of 1812, eject Aury from Amelia Island, or restrain the Seminoles as required by treaty. Consequently, Spain must give up Florida to the United States. "[W]e want it and we must have it," the paper declared.[29]

In the winter and spring of 1818, many American newspapers not only called for but expected U.S. troops to enter Florida. The invasion should not have come as a surprise to anyone. In February, *Niles' Weekly Register* noted that Jackson's pursuit of the Seminoles "will not be limitted by the Florida line," while a report from Mobile that same month speculated that Congress had probably already ordered an attack on hostile Indians and blacks who were trying to hide out beyond the U.S. border. In late March, the *Alexandria Gazette's* Washington correspondent announced a rumor that U.S. troops had been ordered to occupy Florida, adding that "[t]he people here are all elated at the prospect of a war with Spain."[30]

Although Monroe administration officials apparently had not in fact ordered an occupation of Florida, months earlier they had set into motion the events that, in the spring of 1818, would extend the Seminole War into the Spanish territory and even into Spanish forts. In December 1817, Secretary of War John C. Calhoun ordered General Jackson to Fort Scott in southwestern Georgia to assume command of American military forces in the area and "to adopt the necessary measures to terminate" the conflict with the Seminole Indians.[31] During the previous month, there had been two deadly assaults near the fort: the November 21 American attack on Fowltown and the November 30 Indian attack on an American supply boat in Florida. When the Creek residents of Fowltown, fifteen miles from Fort Scott, refused to recognize American land claims under the 1814 U.S.-Creek treaty, the American commander at the fort sent an expedition that burned down the town, killed some residents, and dispersed the rest. A week and a half later, a party of Indians responded by killing Lieutenant Richard W. Scott and dozens of Americans in his supply ship traveling up the Apalachicola River toward Fort Scott. The latter incident became a rallying cry for frontier people and military leaders who demanded a more aggressive defense against Indians, and, later, Americans would point to the massacre as a prime justification for invading Florida. Then, in February, Seminoles murdered a woman and her two young children in southeastern Georgia near the Florida border. The slaughter of the Garrett family, a cross-border killing of noncombatants, would later be an oft-cited fact contributing to the United States' legal defense of its 1818 invasion. In the winter of 1818, southerners in the United States were eager for a vigorous American military response to these Indian attacks.[32]

War Department instructions regarding the southwest Georgia border shifted in December 1817. In letters sent October 30 and December 2, 1817, Acting Secretary of War George Graham had made it clear to Edmund P. Gaines, Fort Scott's commander in late 1817, that to avoid disrupting ongoing negotiations with Spain and good relations with other European countries he should not cross the Florida line to attack the Seminoles on Spanish territory. However, when new Secretary of War Calhoun took up his post, he immediately authorized Gaines to cross into Florida. If the Seminoles refused to make reparations for their depredations, he wrote on December 16, "it is the wish of the President that you consider yourself at liberty to march across the Florida line and to attack them within its limits, should it be found necessary, unless they should shelter themselves under a Spanish post. In the last event, you will immediately notify this Department." Critics would later accuse Gaines's successor at Fort Scott, Andrew Jackson, of violating the last part of these critical instructions.[33]

Jackson had long urged an aggressive policy with Indians, even if it meant acting in Spanish territory. Spain's recent provisioning and sheltering of anti-American Creeks, along with its inability to prevent Florida-based Indians from committing depredations in Georgia and Alabama, had prepared Jackson to dislodge the Spanish from the territory. On December 16, 1817, before he was sent to Georgia—and before American troops received permission to cross the border—he had written the War Department that he did not believe the frontier would be safe unless American troops struck the Seminoles in Florida. A few weeks later, on January 6, 1818, Jackson wrote to President Monroe, suggesting that the United States should take possession of Florida—and promising that he could accomplish the task in sixty days. Monroe did not respond to the letter but told Calhoun to instruct Jackson "not to attack any post occupied by Spanish troops." Calhoun apparently never forwarded the order to Jackson, even though the administration had already instructed Jackson to replace Gaines at Fort Scott while Gaines was on the east coast of Florida securing Amelia Island for the United States. Although Jackson had copies of Gaines's earlier orders, the Monroe administration apparently never officially imposed on Jackson the prohibition on entering Spanish posts. In any case, Jackson went ahead with plans for a military operation in Florida. In addition to subduing the Seminoles, Jackson was eager to act decisively against British agents in the border area, retrieve fugitive slaves using Florida as a haven, and supplant Spanish rule in the territory. Calhoun repeated more than once the injunction that Jackson pacify the frontier as speedily as possible in a way that would permanently settle the conflict with the Seminoles, and to Gaines he made explicit the correlation between carrying the war into Florida and achieving a "speedy and effectual termination." That Calhoun intended American troops to enter Florida was further evidenced by his December 26 orders to Gaines, which he also relayed to Jackson. After Gaines secured Amelia Island, if he could spare troops for "offensive operations" he was authorized to proceed through Florida to the Seminole towns, where he was to help Jackson subdue the Indians.[34]

Jackson arrived at Fort Scott on March 9; within a week, he had entered Florida and reached Prospect Bluff, where he built a new fort on the site of the garrison destroyed in 1816. (See Map 1.5 for the locations of forts and towns involved in Jackson's 1818 expedition.) From the new Fort Gadsden, he informed Calhoun on March 25, 1818, that the next day he intended to proceed toward the Spanish post at St. Marks and that he would "take possession of the garrison." Confident of success, he had sent his supplies ahead to St. Marks in a naval ship captained by Isaac McKeever and anticipated that he would send his next communication to Calhoun from St. Marks. In his March 25 letter, he also reported that, because he had found it difficult to get

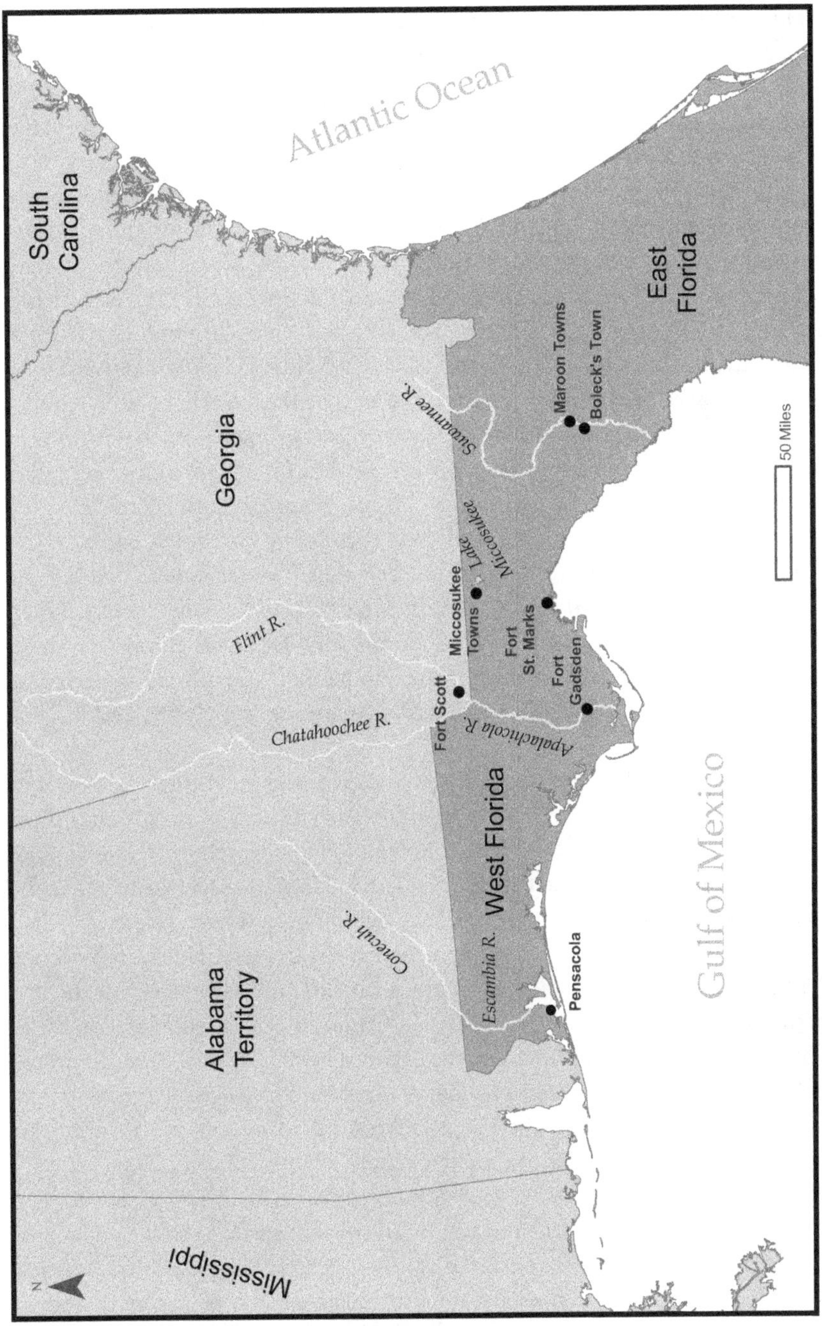

MAP 1.5 *Forts and towns of Jackson's military expedition, 1818.*

supplies to Fort Scott by land, he had ordered the supplies by water through Florida. The general informed Calhoun that he had warned the governor of Pensacola that if he interfered with the American transport of supplies during the Seminole War, Jackson would "view it as aiding our enemy, and treat it as an act of hostility."[35]

On April 7, Jackson's forces captured the Spanish fort at St. Marks. Showing awareness of the laws of war in his dispatch to Washington, Jackson justified the seizure of the fort on the grounds that hostile Indians threatened the garrison, the Spaniards were too weak to defend it, and the Americans needed it as a supply depot during the war. As American and allied Creek troops made their way through Florida, they burned down hundreds of Seminoles' and blacks' homes along Lake Miccosukee, on the eastern bank of the Apalachicola River, and especially in maroon towns on the Suwannee River, where some four hundred blacks lived. The troops indiscriminately killed and apprehended a number of blacks, Seminoles, and Creeks. They captured and summarily executed two prominent Creek prisoners, Hillis Hadjo and Homathlemico. Jackson alleged that Homathlemico had led the group of Indians who slaughtered Scott's party, and he called the two men "the prime instigators of this war." Additionally, Jackson's troops captured, tried, and executed two British men, Alexander Arbuthnot and Robert Christie Ambrister, whom they charged with aiding, supplying, and inciting the Seminoles.[36]

Jackson's dispatches of April 8, 9, 20, and 26 suggested that the war was almost over. However, on May 5 the general reported a rumor that there were hundreds of Seminole warriors in Pensacola, using the city as a base for launching murderous attacks into Alabama. He had also learned that the Spaniards were aiding and supplying the Seminoles in Pensacola, as they had been in St. Marks. If the rumors were true, he wrote, he would have to occupy Pensacola, the capital of West Florida. In his final military report at the end of the war, on June 2, Jackson informed Calhoun that as soon as American troops had passed over the Escambia River, Governor Masot had protested Jackson's aggressions in West Florida, ordered him to leave the territory, and threatened to use force in the event Jackson failed to comply. Treating the communication as hostile, Jackson occupied Pensacola on May 21. Subsequently, he forcibly took nearby Fort Barrancas, required Masot to sign articles of capitulation, and put the Spanish officers on a ship to Havana. Finally, on June 2, Jackson declared the end of the Seminole War. All measures Jackson adopted followed Calhoun's instructions, he asserted, and all were necessary to secure "peace and security to the southern frontier of Georgia." The general's dispatches to Calhoun reported his successes: the Indians no longer had "the power, if the will remain, of again annoying our frontier," the executions of the two Britons sent a clear warning to Europeans not to incite Indians against the United States, and American troops in several forts along the Gulf of Mexico provided protection until Spain could provide an adequate military force to control Indians and foreign agents in the future.[37]

Response to the Invasion

Southern newspapers began reporting on Jackson's invasion a week after it began. On April 14, Georgia papers reported that the United States had entered Florida and launched an expedition against Indians there. A few days later, readers learned about the occupation of St. Marks, the capture of Arbuthnot, the hanging of Hillis Hadjo and Homathlemico, the destruction of Miccosukee towns, and the deadly skirmishes with Indians and blacks. Articles from the southern press began appearing as reprints in northern papers within just a few weeks.[38] Subsequently, during the summer of 1818 and continuing into early 1819, the press throughout the country extensively covered the war, the executions, the congressional debate, and the larger legal issues relating to the United States' actions in Florida.

Secretary of State Adams and other administration officials appear to have learned about Jackson's capture of St. Marks when they received the general's earliest dispatches on May 4. Around June 18, they heard about Jackson's occupation of Pensacola. Only on July 7 did they receive Jackson's June 2 letter informing them about Pensacola, explaining the general's rationale for his actions in Florida, and providing a packet of supporting documents. After heated debate in cabinet meetings in July, the administration resolved that it would not condemn Jackson but would offer to withdraw from the Spanish forts when Spain could defend them. Administration officials also launched a public relations offensive to persuade Americans and Europeans that the United States had acted appropriately.[39]

In November 1818, James Monroe commented on the war in his State of the Union address to Congress, and both houses referred the president's comments to special committees. Thus, Andrew Jackson's invasion of Florida, seizure of Spanish forts, and treatment of prisoners occasioned the first major investigation by Congress, as well as the lengthiest debate engaged in by the House of Representatives up to that date. In the winter of 1819, House and Senate committees investigated the matter and issued reports summarizing their findings. The House committee's report—delivered to the full House on Tuesday, January 12—was highly critical of Jackson and was accompanied by a proposed resolution condemning the trials and executions of the two

Britons. At the urging of Representative Thomas W. Cobb, who pointed out that the Seminole War involved important questions pertaining to the law of nations and the Constitution, the house agreed to begin debating the report as a committee of the whole on Monday, January 18. At the start of the debate, Cobb proposed three additional resolutions. Two of them related to the occupation of Spanish posts: the first stated that the House "disapproves of the seizure of the posts of St. Marks and Pensacola, and the fortress of Barrancas, contrary to orders, and in violation of the Constitution." The second called on the Committee on Military Affairs to prepare a bill "prohibiting the march of the Army of the United States, or any corps thereof, into any foreign territory, without the previous authorization of Congress, except it be in the case of fresh pursuit of a defeated enemy of the United States, taking refuge within such foreign territory." The full House of Representatives vigorously debated the resolutions, along with other issues raised by Jackson's actions in the Seminole War, for three weeks, from January 18 to February 8, 1819. In the end, the House rejected all of the proposed resolutions, voicing strong support for Jackson's actions and the Monroe administration's policies. The Senate committee did not deliver its report until February 22, by which time developments in the United States' relations with Spain had changed so dramatically that the full Senate declined to debate the issues.[40]

The shift in U.S.-Spanish relations began soon after Jackson's spring 1818 invasion of Florida. The Spanish minister to the United States, Onís, heard rumors of the Florida expedition in May 1818 but could not confirm the events until he received Governor Masot's letters in June and July. The Spanish foreign secretary in Madrid, Pizarro, heard about the Florida invasion and capture of St. Marks sometime in mid-July and learned of the taking of Pensacola in early August. Onís and Pizarro protested Jackson's invasion of Florida, seizure of Spanish forts, capture and deportation of Spanish officers, and execution of two British men on Spanish soil. They demanded that the U.S. government return the forts, indemnify the Spanish for damages and injuries, and disavow the general's actions.[41]

Onís complained that the American invasion of Spanish territory violated peaceful U.S.-Spanish relations and trampled on Spain's rights. He claimed that Jackson had acted "as if war had been declared between the two nations." Further, the United States had used the war against the Seminoles as "a pretext for General Jackson to fall, as a conqueror, upon the Spanish provinces . . . for the purpose of establishing therein the dominion of [the United States] upon the odious basis of violence and bloodshed." Onís argued that any cruelties Indians might have committed along the American frontier were nothing in comparison to the atrocities committed by banditti and pirates launching expeditions from American soil against Spanish ships and provinces. He pointed out that even though South American rebels had taken refuge in the United States, Spain had not pursued them onto American soil. Civilized nations did not enter foreign territory to seize people who have taken asylum there, much less take possession of such territory, as Jackson did. In response to Adams's July 23, 1818, defense of Jackson, Onís accused the American administration of glossing over Jackson's "specious motives" and trying to exonerate the United States from all responsibility for the "outrages" committed.[42]

After Jackson's 1818 military operation, Onís again refuted American complaints against Spanish officials. As he had done before the invasion, he fervently denied that Spanish authorities acted wrongfully in their relationship with the Indians in Florida. Onís argued that Spanish officials' failure to demolish the Prospect Bluff fort as Jackson demanded in 1816 did not justify the American general's actions in 1818. Other than the complaint about the Prospect Bluff fort, he noted, American officials did not convey grievances against the Seminole Indians to Spanish authorities or request that they punish Indians for allegedly committing aggressive acts against Americans. The 1795 treaty only obligated Spain to act against Indians when there was real evidence of wrongdoing. It would have been unjust to punish the Seminoles in the absence of specific, plausible information against them, Onís maintained. The situation was complicated, especially given that the Spanish governors of Florida had heard numerous Seminole complaints of Americans' violent acts against them. Onís further denied both that Spanish officials had wrongfully sheltered or supplied Florida Indians and that they had illegally barred the passage through Florida of provisions to the American fort to the north. In any case, if the Americans had complaints about Spanish authorities, they should have submitted those complaints to the Spanish government, rather than taking military action.[43]

Meanwhile, Foreign Minister Pizarro characterized Jackson's conduct as "repugnant to the laws of nations, and the principles which regulate the conduct of all civilized Powers." He acknowledged that there had been previous small-scale acts of injustice by both Spaniards and Americans but argued that this operation was far worse because Jackson acted "with all the apparatus of war"; the invasion and occupation of Florida was an official, armed, military action against a friendly power during a time of peace. There was not even a plausible pretext to justify an American invasion—no claim to the territory, no rebellion of the inhabitants, and no aggressions by "banditti" from the territory. "[I]t appears," Pizarro concluded, "that a forcible occupation was preferred to a peaceful acquisition."[44] These arguments by Onís and Pizarro provided part of the foundation for the American critics' position that coalesced months later.

In the summer and fall of 1818, Secretary of State Adams launched a forceful defense of Jackson's conduct in Florida, arguing that it was both necessary and entirely defensive in nature. Americans living on the frontier had been repeated victims of depredations and murders "by Seminole Indians, and by a banditti of negroes sallying from within the Spanish border, and retreating to it again with the horrid fruits of their crimes," he observed. Adams demanded that the Spanish government conduct an inquiry into the conduct of Governor Masot and Commander Luengo, who had contributed to such violence, and that it punish them for failing to fulfill their obligations. However, he also made clear that he did not impute to Spain the failures of its officers and that he was willing to continue to negotiate toward a treaty with Spain. Moreover, Adams also reported to Onís that the president had ordered both Pensacola and St. Marks returned to responsible Spanish officials when Spain could properly defend the posts.[45]

Adams laid out his most aggressive legal arguments in letters posted between October 31 and November 30, especially in a November 28 letter to the American envoy in Madrid, George Erving. Those letters—which were quickly released to the American press—profoundly influenced the domestic debate about Jackson's conduct, but in fact they had little impact on negotiations with Spain. Although in August 1818 King Ferdinand VII ordered a suspension of negotiations, within less than two months a new foreign minister authorized Onís to resume formal discussions. Pizarro drafted those instructions in September 1818, and his successor, Irujo, modified and finalized them in October—well before the Spanish government had received Adams's forceful "great gun" letter in support of Jackson.[46] It was Jackson's assertive action in Florida, not Adams's spirited legal arguments, that pushed Spain to greater flexibility in the negotiations.

During the summer of 1818, President Monroe's private letters expressed confidence that the Florida invasion put pressure on Spain and would strengthen the American bargaining position. In July, Monroe wrote that "[t]here is much reason to presume that this act will furnish a strong inducement to Spain to cede the territory." He added, "Should it take place, I have no doubt that it will be due principally to the late pressure in Florida." In dealing with the repercussions of Jackson's invasion, one of Monroe's main goals was "to turn it to the best account of the country." In private correspondence, Monroe explained why he would not punish Jackson. If he were to rebuke Jackson for exceeding his orders, it would effectively exculpate the Spanish officers and "confirm [Spain] in the disposition not to cede Florida." Later, after both parties signed the treaty, Monroe looked back with satisfaction, noting that if he had censured Jackson, the United States would not have obtained the cession of territory.[47]

Jackson's foray into Florida made it apparent to Spanish officials that the United States could seize Florida at any time and that therefore Spanish arguments about historical rights were fruitless. Onís never doubted that his detailed historical analysis, backed by thorough documentary substantiation, had indisputably proven the legal validity of Spanish territorial claims—as well as the absence of evidentiary support for any U.S. claims. However, he came to see the irrelevance of that analysis in the face of practical realities. Adams made it clear that the United States would not enter into "any examination of the historical disquisition concerning the original pretensions of Spain to all the territories bordering on the Gulf of Mexico, and the whole country included in the French colony of Louisiana." The secretary of state also declined to examine more historical documents that Onís claimed would prove Spain's case. As soon as Onís received new instructions that gave him full power to negotiate a treaty, the Spanish envoy capitulated to the American refusal to discuss historical evidence or allow such evidence to determine the matter: "[A]s you [Adams] have intimated to me that it is useless to pursue the discussion any further," he wrote, "I acquiesce with you therein." He gave up on the argument based on rights and agreed the two nations should work out a pragmatic agreement. Specifically, he agreed to "[keep] out of view the rights which either Power may have to the territory in dispute." Instead, he conceded that he and Adams could "confine ourselves to the settlement of those points which may be for the mutual interest and convenience of both [countries]." Three weeks later, after years of disagreement and negotiation, the two nations settled on a treaty.[48]

Although previous administrations had asserted a broad claim to territory covered by the Louisiana Purchase, they had been reluctant to use military force against Spain to secure that territory, even when negotiations stagnated. Like Thomas Jefferson and James Madison, President Monroe hesitated to openly send troops to seize Florida. However, once Andrew Jackson committed the deed, President Monroe and Secretary of State Adams supported the general and took diplomatic advantage of the military operation. Jackson's occupation of Florida gave Adams the leverage he needed to press the Spanish government to conclude treaty negotiations. Although the parties had discussed possible cession of Florida since 1817, Jackson's actions secured the cession and also helped the United States obtain additional western territory in the final treaty. After Jackson's occupation of Florida, Adams ratcheted up the United States' demand: he proposed extending the United States all the way to the Pacific Ocean, not just west to the Mississippi River. In response, the Spanish envoy pointed out that the proposed line exceeded "by its magnitude and its transcendency, all former demands and pretensions started by the United States." By early January, however, having

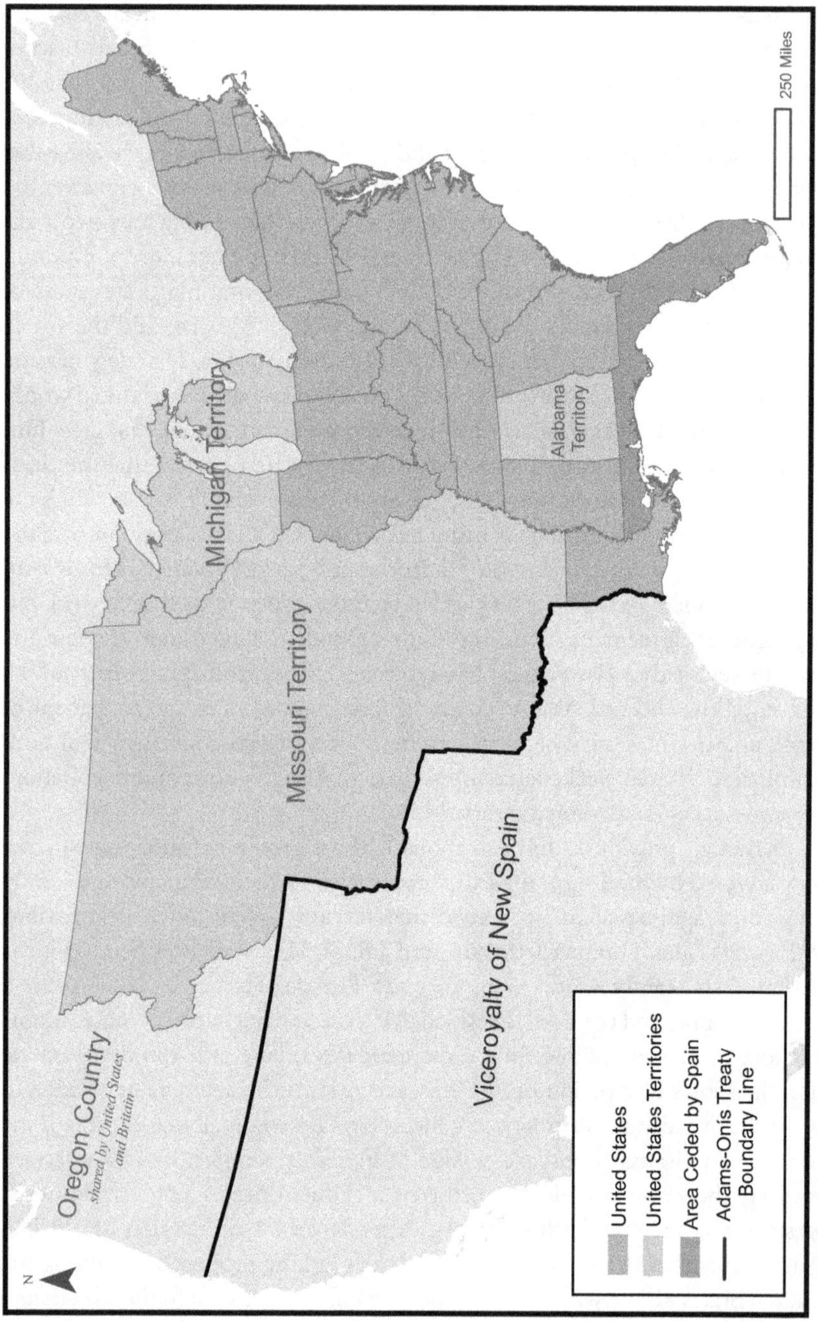

MAP 1.6 *Adams-Onís Treaty line, February 1819.*

just received new instructions that his government had sent in October, Onís agreed to a boundary that extended to the Pacific coast. Negotiations quickly solved the remaining boundary issues. Adams and Onís signed the treaty on February 22, 1819.[49] (See Map 1.6.)

While awaiting King Ferdinand's ratification of the treaty, John Quincy Adams expressed an optimistic and expansive view of America's future. Some months after he and Onís signed the treaty, his diary revealed his vision for the nation. He mentioned Secretary of the Treasury (and former Secretary of War) William Crawford's observation that the United States ought to demonstrate moderation in its foreign policy in order to counter Europeans' impression that Americans were an "ambitious and encroaching people." Adams rejected the advice. Europeans had to change their understanding; they had to become "familiarized with the idea of considering our proper domain to be the continent of North America." It was simply "a law of nature" that the United States would expand into the whole of North America; it was "unavoidable that the remainder of the continent should ultimately be ours." Although Spain and Britain possessed territory immediately adjacent to United States, it was only a matter of time before the United States would annex those territories. "[N]ot that any spirit of encroachment or ambition on our part renders it necessary," Adams clarified, "but because it is a physical, moral, and political absurdity that such fragments of territory, with sovereigns at fifteen hundred miles beyond sea, worthless and burdensome to their owners, should exist permanently contiguous to a great, powerful, enterprising, and rapidly-growing nation."[50]

In Adams's vision, the Florida campaigns made it possible for the United States to realize its proper place in the world. Before that achievement could be solidified, though, the Monroe administration, Jackson, and their political allies had to win the battle at home to define American collective identity, national goals, and status in the world, as well as the place of law, expansionism, military power, and executive authority in the United States. That battle, which would unfold publicly in Congress and in the press in 1818 and 1819, would conclude with a resounding victory for the slate of ideas that justified the Florida expeditions. The consequences for nineteenth-century American history were enormous.

CHAPTER TWO

Rules of War and American Nation-Building

IN THEIR DIPLOMATIC and legal defense of the Florida campaigns, Americans sought to bolster U.S. nationhood. Even after ratification of the Constitution in 1788, Americans had only a weak sense of national consciousness and were content to leave control over most domestic matters to local and state governments rather than centralizing authority in the federal government. However, in the realm of foreign policy and international relations, the United States took strides in building a nation. The events of the Seminole War jolted Americans, prompting politicians and journalists to publicly explain their positions on important issues of law and nationhood. The extensive record of those public comments reveals how Americans viewed territorial boundaries, national identity, and sovereign rights in the early nineteenth century.

The United States sought to further its nation-building interests through its public legal defense of armed hostilities in Florida as they involved Spain. Andrew Jackson's supporters framed their arguments regarding Spain in order to advance American nationhood in several ways: promoting U.S. integration into the European diplomatic community, enhancing the nation's standing, claiming the nation's natural southeastern territorial boundary, asserting control over inhabitants and subjects of the United States, reshaping international law doctrines to suit national interests, supplanting European nations from the United States' regional sphere, and asserting itself as the predominant continental power.

American Nationalism and the Seminole War Debate

As Susan-Mary Grant, Peter Parish, and Don H. Doyle and Marco Antonio Pamplona have observed, leading social science scholars of nationalism typically fail to include significant discussion of the United States. Most notably, the prominent works of Ernest Gellner, Benedict Anderson, Eric Hobsbawm, and Anthony Smith marginalize the American experience with nation-building. The early United States did not fit the theoretical mold of European nationhood in any obvious way. For some scholars, common ethnicity is the primal bond that unites a nation. Such writers have difficulty fitting the early American Republic into their theoretical models because it lacked a homogeneous population with common origins and could not fit the paradigm of ethnic nationalism the way European nations could. Those who take the correlated view that defines nationhood by pointing to shared cultural features—such as language, literature, and religion—that are distinct from other nations' also find the early United States incompatible with their theories. Additionally, for scholars who associate nationalism with centralized power, the federalism concept leads to a different theoretical problem with early nineteenth-century American nationhood. In the early Republic, full sovereignty did not lie in a single level of government; the American commitment to dual sovereignty made it unclear whether the decentralized United States was a true nation or a confederacy of smaller nations.[1]

Despite the ambiguous applicability of social scientists' theoretical models to the United States, historians have studied early American nationhood. Typically portraying it as a constructed rather than a natural entity, most scholars eschew the framework of ethnic or cultural nationalism and concentrate instead on civic ideals, ceremonial rituals of nationalism, or institutional and constitutional developments.[2] Fewer works examine how the evolution of American political or legal discourse over the early decades following independence contributed to constructing the American nation.

Of the older historical studies, Clinton Rossiter's *The American Quest, 1790–1860* (1971) provides the most relevant analysis for this book because Rossiter is particularly systematic about evaluating American progress toward nationhood between 1790 and 1860. Rossiter identifies four goals of nationhood, coupled with four goals of modernity (which he views as a necessary characteristic of an established nation): independence, territorial integrity, popular cohesion, and self-identity, along with political efficacy, economic viability, social integration, and cultural maturity. Of particular note for the Seminole War debate is Rossiter's view that territorial integrity ideally means having "a set of boundaries that are geographically sensible, politically stable, diplomatically viable, militarily defensible . . . , and demographically both inclusive and exclusive." Rossiter concludes that in the case of the United States geographic expansion through conquest was part of the nation-building process because land acquisition was important for achieving the external stability necessary for attaining territorial integrity. Moreover, he acknowledges not only that territorial integrity might entail conquest of adjoining land to ensure national security from outside threats but also that coercion of inhabitants is often needed to further internal unity. At the same time, he notes that when nations do not have a homogeneous population, it is important that they meaningfully incorporate diverse peoples to strengthen popular cohesion. Finally, he observes that "[t]o *be* a nation [the people] must *think* they are a nation." Shared history, mutual interests, consensus about basic values, a sense of distinctiveness in comparison to other nations, and commitment to a common mission can reinforce national self-identity.[3] *Border Law* utilizes some of the same criteria for nationhood that Rossiter lists but focuses especially on law, which was an additional venue for modernization and the construction of the United States as a nation.

Among more recent books, the most valuable exemplar of historical scholarship on American nation-building is Eliga Gould, *Among the Powers of the Earth: The American Revolution and the Making of a New World Empire,* which focuses on the seven decades between the French and Indian War in the 1750s and the Monroe Doctrine of the early 1820s. Gould highlights the prominence of the law of nations in the U.S. effort to be recognized as a "treaty-worthy" nation.[4] In examining legal factors in nation-building, I build on Eliga Gould's fresh approach to the study of early American nationhood. Indeed, analysis of the U.S. defense of the 1810s Florida campaigns provides insights into rarely studied aspects of the development of American nationhood in the early Republic.

The debate about the Florida expeditions shows that the lack of ethnic and cultural homogeneity in the United States did not preclude the development of a form of ethnic nationalism. The arguments relating to Creeks, Seminoles, and African-descended people aimed to strengthen European Americans' sense of national self-consciousness by excluding nonwhites from the community of rights-bearing inhabitants. Restricting the full protections of both the law of nations and the U.S. Constitution exclusively to European-descended people reinforced racial, ethnic, and cultural borders of nationhood. This was, in effect, a kind of ethnic nationalism, though it was not as narrowly tailored as was the European version.

The Seminole War arguments also make it evident that the federalism structure was not a barrier to nationalism. In the early nineteenth century, Americans not only developed a sense of national pride but also willingly delegated substantial authority to the central government in matters pertaining to national security, relations with other countries, and problems in territory outside U.S. borders.

Additionally, the language used to defend U.S. military conduct as it affected Spaniards and Britons helped construct the American nation in ways that went beyond racial identity and strong national government. Many of the arguments relating to Spain and Britain were outward-focused, intended to bolster U.S. nation-building by fortifying its international position and its status on the North American continent. Yet those arguments vis-à-vis European powers also had an internal dimension. The Florida expeditions and justifications for them boosted white Americans' national pride by reinforcing the perception that their country assertively defended its national rights against European interference and was entitled to act militarily to protect its territorial integrity against border-crossing enemies. The language used to defend the campaigns further reinforced the domestic sense of nationhood by conveying that Americans enjoyed common ground as citizens of an exceptional missionary nation that was destined to spread a superior civilization.

Moreover, the United States' use of a legal framework for the defense of its armed hostilities reveals interesting connections between law and nationalism in early America. In the past, legal scholars have not paid adequate attention to that topic, other than in the contexts of the American Revolution, the Constitutional Convention, or the subsequent development of federalism. In particular, though there are excellent studies of the doctrines of the law of nations, there is scant examination of ways in which people implemented that law in practice or how they used the doctrines to advance nation-building goals. The Seminole War arguments provide instructive perspectives on international law and the construction of nations.

The debates about the Florida expeditions are also suggestive of ways in which power dynamics may affect legal interpretations. The United States appears to have responded to each of the four categories of opponents—Britons, Spaniards, Creeks and Seminoles, and blacks—in a measured way, according to an assessment of the United States' relative power vis-à-vis each class of adversary. The public debates focused overwhelmingly on potential legal problems with Spain and Britain, paying little attention to issues relating to Creeks and Seminoles or African-descended people. The United States treated Spain and Britain with a degree of respect (agreeing to return forts and providing court-martial proceedings for captives) that was not extended to other groups, specifically Red Sticks, Seminoles, and blacks (who were flagrantly subjected to summary executions of captives, other unrestrained violence, and massive property destruction).

Finally, the Seminole War arguments illustrate that borders were important to American nation-building, including both territorial and legal borders.

With regard to territorial borders, the United States claimed that its nationhood status entitled it to claim dominion over all of its "natural" territory, including all the lands it needed to ensure that it had secure boundaries, safe from external attack. The United States argued that its troops could act freely in Florida because it was part of the United States' natural domain, lacked any recognizable and meaningful alternative sovereign power, and contained categories of people over whom the United States claimed authority. The Seminole War debates provide a fruitful source for examining the history of these kinds of justifications for extraterritorial military action in early American history, a topic that has received little attention from scholars. With regard to legal borders, the United States constructed nationhood by redefining boundaries of law both internally and externally. The United States clarified the borders of its own legal community domestically by showing that only European-heritage people could be assured that they fell within the protections of American law. Reshaping legal geography vis-à-vis other political entities, the United States also claimed that it was part of the European family of the law of nations and that Indian polities were excluded from that family. Few studies of early American policy making bring together U.S. relations with both Europeans and non-Europeans, yet the debates about the Florida campaigns provide a rich opportunity for such study.

The discourse of the early nineteenth century was part of the extended process of constructing an American nation, a process that in some ways began before the Revolutionary War and continued even after the Civil War. The Seminole War of 1816–1818, by stimulating an extensive debate, provided an occasion for Americans to express their views in the public realm. The heated discussion about the Florida campaigns unfolded both in Congress and elsewhere in the American public sphere.[5] Extensive congressional discussion of the Seminole War and comprehensive newspaper coverage indicate that it was prominent and important to contemporaries. The president's 1818 annual address to Congress, the reports of the House and Senate select committees, the reports of the dissenting minorities on those committees, resolutions and speeches made in the House, and diplomatic and military documents released to Congress were all published by newspapers. As a result, the American people had access to a solid (though selective) basis of information and were exposed to vigorous arguments both in support of and opposed to U.S. armed hostilities in Florida. In some newspapers, the Seminole War debate attracted even more attention than the issue of Missouri's admission as a slave state. As the *Boston Intelligencer* observed, the public mind was "in a ferment" on the subject.[6]

Surprisingly, despite the fact that it provides an invaluable window into early nineteenth-century thinking about nationalism and nationhood, this debate has received little scholarly analysis. Though existing scholarship provides excellent accounts of the Seminole War and, separately, superb theoretical studies of nationalism, the laws of war, U.S. constitutional law, and due process, scholars have not yet adequately analyzed how law applied in practice in the Florida expeditions, how legal arguments were presented in order to advance American sovereignty and nationalism, or how ideas expressed at that time had a lasting impact on American and European legal doctrine.[7]

U.S. military activity in Florida was a particularly acute problem because it seemed to disregard Spain's sovereign territorial rights. Both the passage onto Spanish soil and the subsequent capture of Spanish forts raised the problem of extraterritorial aggression against an ally. Moreover, though there was precedent for armed hostilities against Indians within the United States, extending such actions outside the nation's borders without congressional authorization prompted questions about possible abuse of the war power. Administration officials, congressmen, and newspaper commentators alike focused on the lawfulness of U.S. armed hostilities in Florida. Neither supporters nor critics presented legal doctrine as autonomous or isolated from societal circumstances and values. Though commentators framed their arguments in legal terms, their different views of national interests, values, and morality influenced their interpretations of law.

The United States vigorously defended its attacks on forts and people within Spanish territory in Florida, contending that Spain had no cause for complaint under the law of nations. Americans argued that international legal constraints did not apply to this situation and, even if they were applicable, presented no impediment to Americans' freedom of action in Florida. Regarding constitutional matters, the Monroe administration contended that it had not violated the doctrine of separation of powers by going to war without congressional assent. Key to the government's defense with regard to both international and domestic legal mandates were the assertions that the armed hostilities did not constitute "war" with Spain, that everything the U.S. military did was legally justified as necessary for national self-defense, and that, ultimately, utilitarian national objectives carried more weight than abstract precepts of law.[8]

The Law of Nations

The Seminole War took place soon after the end of the Napoleonic Wars, on the cusp of a major theoretical change in the conception of international law. Though an older discourse based on natural law was still in circulation, some legal thinkers maintained that the law of nations was properly grounded in actual usages and agreements. The United States took emerging notions of law and made them the center of their defense of the Florida campaigns.

Americans made reference to legal principles both before and after armed hostilities. When proposing or demanding military action, they placed their justifications within the framework of the United States' international legal rights and obligations. Even more extensively, when reporting or defending military actions after the fact, they explicitly justified their conduct using international law doctrines. The meaning of the law of nations was not fixed, however. In defending U.S. conduct in Florida, Americans put forward their own legal interpretation, emphasizing ideas that best served national interests.

When Americans presented their interpretation of the law of nations during the Seminole War debate, they relied most heavily on a mid-eighteenth-century treatise by Swiss jurist Emer de Vattel, *The Law of Nations, or Principles of Natural Law, Applied to the Conduct and Affairs of Nations and Sovereigns.* Commentators on the Seminole War occasionally cited other legal writers, but Vattel's 1758 book provided the overwhelmingly dominant framework for understanding the doctrines of international law. Americans who were willing to consider the authority of any European jurists cited Vattel first and foremost.[9]

Interestingly, both proponents and opponents of U.S. policy in Florida cited that same jurisprudential work. Vattel's ideas were elastic enough to be useful to both sides of the debate over the Florida campaigns.[10] As sources of law, *The Law of Nations* recognized both the law of nature ("natural law") and also state practices and treaties ("positive law"). The latter, law created by governments, correlated with a more utilitarian or pragmatic approach that advanced state interests and separated law and morality, whereas the former was a set of inherent, moral ideals that were higher than state law, could constrain governments, and applied universally. Formally, Vattel based his influential treatise on natural law, explaining in his "preliminary" comments that the law of nations was the law of nature as applied to relations among nations. He also recognized that nations could supplement natural law through explicit or tacit agreements, though such treaties and usages were themselves closely tied to natural law: nations' treaties and usages were unlawful if they contravened the law of nature, and, moreover, it was the natural-law "duty of nations to fulfill their engagements" that gave agreements their "obligatory force."[11] Since the centuries preceding Vattel had been significantly shaped by a natural law perspective, while the nineteenth century became an era of increased reliance on positive law, Vattel could be seen as a bridge between the two approaches to law.[12]

More specifically pertaining to warfare, Vattel's treatise echoed older visions of the rules of war while also introducing new concepts that would take firmer hold over the course of the nineteenth century. During the medieval period, European writers had espoused a moral concept of "just war," which held that a nation could not lawfully resort to armed hostilities unless it had a just cause and undertook war for the purpose of achieving justice and peace rather than simply to further national interests or other selfish impulses. By the early modern era, what was recognized as a just cause of war differed somewhat from the medieval Christian view, but elements of the old doctrine persisted. Vattel, for instance, insisted that no nation should make war without a just cause. For the eighteenth-century jurist, "the foundation or cause of every just war is injury, either already done, or threatened." Specifically, he identified the following three "objects of a lawful war": "1. To recover what belongs to or is due to us. 2. To provide for our future safety by punishing the aggressor or offender. 3. To defend ourselves, or to protect ourselves from injury, by repelling unjust violence." However, Vattel warned that the mere existence of a just end did not sanctify the use of unjust means. Thus, although he emphasized the importance of having a just reason for going to war, he also stressed humanitarian strictures that limited both sides in the actual conduct of war. Violence could lawfully extend no further than necessity required. Vattel also identified specific illegal practices, such as killing noncombatants, using poison, and executing or enslaving enemy captives who had committed no war crimes. In setting limits on the conduct of war, Vattel moved the laws of war in a modern direction. By the end of the nineteenth century, writers' perspectives on law and war had shifted more decisively. Jurists and statesmen of the late nineteenth and early twentieth centuries expanded on Vattel's early ideas about limiting violence in war, creating multilateral agreements, such as the Hague Conventions of 1899 and 1907, that placed humanitarian constraints on warfare. At the same time, they moved even further away from a primary focus on examining just causes for going to war, coming to a "realist" view of war as an expression of a state's will and an instrumentalist tool for achieving a state's interests, rather than a moral quest to achieve justice.[13]

Supporters of U.S. military actions in Florida in the 1810s used the language in *The Law of Nations* that most strongly justified American belligerency, which, for the most part, was the language that anticipated the late nineteenth-century view of rules of war rather than ideas that reinforced the medieval perspective. The United States' firm rejection of natural law universalism and use of racial-cultural criteria to determine legal rights and obligations of Creeks and Seminoles were the most pronounced ways in which the nation moved beyond Vattel's ideas and presaged late nineteenth-century jurists' theoretical approach.[14] Also significant in anticipating later theories of international law were American interpretations of several subjects that were most salient in U.S. relations with Spain: the state of war, neutrality, self-defense, and military necessity. The United States' predominantly utilitarian approach on those issues leaned more toward the prevailing interpretation of the late nineteenth century than that of the earlier period. Nonetheless, supporters of the Florida campaigns found intellectual support for their position in principles asserted in Vattel's 1758 treatise. In fact, the Swiss jurist's principles of war turned out to be conveniently adaptable to the U.S. position in Florida.

In addition to his general observations about natural law, just cause, treaties, common usages, and prohibited practices, Vattel's description of the laws of war made other important points relevant to Seminole War hostilities as they related to the United States and Spain, and Americans eagerly seized on those points for support.

First, Vattel presumed that wartime was distinct from peacetime, and that different rules applied if there was a "state of war": violence against the enemy and the enemy's property was permitted during wartime. He also explained that not all armed actions created a state of war. In his explanations of other principles (such as neutrality and self-defense), the jurist made it evident that the entry of troops of one nation into another nation's territory did not necessarily produce a state of war against that nation. He also described uses of military force, such as reprisals or punitive measures, that did not automatically constitute war. Isolated violence that did not totally rupture friendly relations between two nations was not war.[15]

Second, Vattel discussed the issues of national self-defense and military necessity. Every nation was lawfully entitled to employ force to defend itself by repelling enemy violence, responding to injuries received, and countering violations of its national rights, Vattel asserted. National self-preservation was a fundamental right, one that the jurist reinforced repeatedly in his treatise. Every nation, he wrote, had "a right to prevent other nations from obstructing her preservation, her perfection, and happiness—that is, to preserve herself from all injuries." Elsewhere in the treatise he stated that every nation had "the right of a just defence," "the right of making use of force against whoever attacks her and her rights," "the right to obtain justice by force, if we cannot obtain it otherwise." As important as national self-preservation was, however, a nation could only undertake such actions as were "necessary" for achieving the lawful goals. As a general rule, he explained, "[t]he right of employing force, or making war, belongs to nations no farther than is necessary for their own defence and for the maintenance of their rights."[16]

Vattel pointed out that, although nations had the right to protect themselves from injury, the law generally discouraged preemptive strikes. Nations could use force only against those that had actually launched or were clearly threatening aggressive acts or injuries. The right of self-defense did not permit them to attack another state merely upon "vague and uncertain suspicions." However, nations did not have to sacrifice their existence while waiting for an attack. They had an obligation to try to work out their disputes in a peaceful manner before turning to armed force, but they did not have to continue to pursue conciliation if there was no realistic possibility of a remedy and if delay would expose the nation to "greater danger of being overpowered."[17]

The Swiss jurist also made it clear that the right of national self-preservation did not mean a nation had free rein to empower or extend itself without just cause. A fundamental component of Vattel's law of nations was the principle that nations must respect—and not interfere with—each other's sovereignty and territorial domain. Every nation should "refrain from usurping the territory of others" and should "abstain from every act contrary to the right of the sovereign," he wrote. The mere desire to extend the boundaries of the nation's domain did not justify taking other states' territory by force, nor did it justify conquering other people or expelling people from their land in order to settle it.[18]

Third, the *Law of Nations* addressed the issue of neutrality. "Neutral" nations must remain impartial toward belligerent parties in a war, neither favoring one side with special advantages nor providing a haven for troops retreating from loss, which could permit the enemy to prepare to attack again. The treatise also defined the term "associates" and explained how associates abandoned neutrality. Those who made common cause with an enemy or assisted the enemy—for example, by providing money and troops—became "associates" of the enemy and could be treated as enemies. However, there was room in Vattel's scheme for providing other kinds of assistance to belligerents while still retaining neutrality. For example, a nation did not forfeit its neutrality by continuing its customary trade with a nation at war, as long as it did not refuse to sell goods to the other belligerent party.[19]

The neutrality issue involved not only the obligations of a neutral state toward nations at war with each other but also the obligations of the belligerent nations toward neutral ones. Because territorial sovereignty was so important, Vattel declared, a nation had to meet a particularly high threshold before carrying warfare into the territory of a neutral country. As long as a neutral nation maintained its neutrality, a belligerent's entry into the neutral's territory to attack an enemy there was presumptively unlawful as "a violation of his rights of sovereignty and supreme dominion." A commander had to ask permission before taking his troops into neutral territory. Vattel explained, "The tranquillity . . . and the common safety of nations, require that each should be mistress of her own territory, and at liberty to refuse every foreign army an entrance." Exceptions to the rule against entering neutral territory without consent could be made only in the rare cases when the belligerent was in hot pursuit of a retreating enemy to whom the "neutral" had given refuge or in the event of "[u]rgent and absolute necessity." Thus, he specified, "[I]f you cannot otherwise deliver yourself from an imminent danger, if you have no other passage for procuring the means of life, or those of satisfying some other indispensible obligation, you may force a passage that is unjustly refused." As an example, Vattel described a situation in which an army was "exposed to imminent destruction" if it did not pass through the neutral territory. He added that although the general rule forbade occupying a neutral's property, extreme necessity could justify the "temporary seizure of a place" within neutral territory and the establishment of a garrison there, though the place had to be restored as soon as the danger passed.[20]

Americans made frequent reference to these Vattelian principles in arguing that U.S. military actions were lawful with regard to Spain. Repeatedly, however, they interpreted the *Law of Nations* treatise not for the purpose of acknowledging constraints on the conduct of war but in order to explain why the United States was exempt from such limits in Florida.

In defending its armed hostilities in Spanish territory, in Spanish forts, and against Spanish officials under the law of nations, the United States relied on two lines of reasoning that are discussed in depth below: the "state of war" argument—that U.S. military conduct did not create a state of war with Spain—and the "self-defense and necessity" argument—that everything U.S. troops did in Florida was justified by self-defense and necessary to repel invasion and advance American national interests. These two law of nations arguments contributed to American nation-building in several ways: first, integrating the United States into the European diplomatic community; second, enhancing the nation's standing, bolstering national sovereignty, and claiming control over territory and people; and, third, furthering the process of displacing European nations from the Americas and asserting the United States' position as the predominant power on the North American continent and, eventually, the Western Hemisphere.

The goal of integration required that the United States plausibly explain how it was abiding by Europe's international rules. Most essentially, the United States had to explain that it had not unlawfully initiated war against a European nation, Spain. Both the "state of war" and the "self-defense and necessity" arguments provided essential support for that claim.

Strengthening the national standing of the United States was not just a matter of winning respect from Europe and attaining the United States' proper place in the international hierarchy, though surely that was important to Americans. It was also a matter of securing a fuller form of sovereignty. Though the United States officially gained its independence in 1783, it still lacked complete sovereignty in the early nineteenth century. There are degrees of sovereignty; different nations enjoy larger or smaller portions of the full bundle of possible sovereign rights. By seeking to enhance its sovereignty both through integration into the European state system and through insulation from interference by Europeans at the same time, the United States took a distinctive approach.[21] In the 1810s, the United States sought not only protection from intrusion by European agents but also more secure territorial integrity and the exclusive right to control inhabitants as the government saw fit. The United States' legal arguments pertaining to Spain furthered this multifaceted goal both directly and indirectly. The withering criticism of Spanish officials that was part of the "self-defense and necessity" argument most directly addressed this purpose. Both the "state of war" and the "self-defense and necessity" arguments regarding Spain also indirectly supported the U.S. effort to subordinate and control Indians and African-heritage people, providing a rationale for such domination that allegedly did not violate U.S. responsibilities under the European law of nations. The legal arguments addressing Seminoles, Creeks, and African-descended people will be analyzed in depth later, but it is important to note here that the United States' legal position with regard to Spain provided an essential foundation for its demand for full control over the diverse range of people in or near its territory, including not only Europeans and European-descended people but also Indians and blacks.

Finally, while the United States recognized the power and authority of European nations in their own spheres, the new Republic maintained that it was the natural leading power in the North American continent, and even in the Americas as a whole. The United States thus sought to displace longtime regional powers—especially Britain and Spain—and to pave the way for asserting its appropriate position as the foremost continental power. The "self-defense and necessity" argument provided essential support for starting the United States on the way to achieving that goal.

Absence of State of War with Spain

In an age that called for respect for territorial sovereignty among European nations, the United States had to justify its entry onto claimed Spanish soil. It accomplished that goal by maintaining that the Spanish had no ground for complaint under the laws of war because U.S. military actions in Florida did not create a state of war with Spain. The United States made four arguments to support that contention.

First, supporters of U.S. actions pointed out that the United States acted without any intent to wage war against Spain and that neither the United States nor Spain regarded U.S. actions as creating a state of war. Jackson did not enter Florida or capture the forts out of hostility to Spain, and his purpose was not to disrupt Spanish political authority. Secretary of State John Quincy Adams, President James Monroe, and General Jackson disavowed all hostile intentions against Spain. In his widely disseminated November 28, 1818, letter to George Erving, Adams observed that Jackson's occupation of Spanish posts had not been ordered by the U.S. government, was not intended to wrest Florida from Spain, and had not been implemented in a spirit of enmity toward the Iberian nation. In his annual message delivered to Congress that same month, Monroe explicitly denied any unfriendly intent against Spain. Jackson himself insisted that destroying the Prospect Bluff fort in 1816 served Spanish as well as American interests and that in 1818 he had "entered the territory of Spain as a *friend,* to chastise an enemy of both nations." Members of Congress likewise argued that armed action did not automatically constitute war in the absence of hostile intent and official recognition of a state of war. They noted that if a nation neither ordered violence against another nation nor approved it after the fact, it was not war. Moreover, if, despite violence between individuals from different nations, government officials chose to continue peaceful relations, there was no war.[22]

In the diplomatic handling of the 1807 attack of the British ship *Leopard* on the U.S. frigate *Chesapeake,* several representatives found precedent for the principle that there was no war when nations opted to continue friendly relations after violent incidents. Representative Alexander Smyth also noted incidents in North America that had not created a state of war in the years immediately preceding the outbreak of the French and Indian War, specifically, a French attack on George Washington and his troops in a fort on the Ohio in 1754 and armed skirmishes between the English and the French in Nova Scotia in 1750. Representative George Poindexter cited other European precedents: French displacement of British subjects from Turks Island in the Caribbean in 1764, Spanish dispossession of British settlers on one of the Falkland Islands off the coast of South America in 1770, and Spanish seizure of English trading vessels and a settlement at Nootka Sound on the northwest coast of America in 1789. Poindexter pointed out that the European nations involved in these conflicts did not consider them to be "actual war," and they resolved the disputes peacefully through restoration and reparations.[23]

To further rationalize why Jackson's 1818 foray into Florida did not constitute war against Spain, commentators cited previous U.S. incursions in Florida. They said the recent expedition was not substantively different from previous activities in the Spanish territory that were not regarded as war against Spain: Madison's annexation of part of West Florida in 1810, the occupation of Amelia Island in 1812, the occupation of Pensacola to counter British forces in 1814, the destruction of the Prospect Bluff fort in 1816, and the occupation of Amelia Island in 1817 to break up a dangerous nest of brigands and pirates that Spain was unable to expel. In fact, Congress had just voted to reward Jairus Loomis $5,000 for blowing up the fort at Prospect Bluff, which lay in Spanish territory. It would be inconsistent, Representative Henry Baldwin said, to punish Jackson for entering Florida to pursue "a remnant of the same negroes and their Indian allies" who had retreated from Prospect Bluff to St. Marks in 1816. Representative George F. Strother declared, "When the present Administration treads in the footsteps of their predecessors, let them have the benefit of . . . your former reading of the law of nations."[24] As proof that in 1818 the United States did not intend to wage war against Spain and did not regard the two countries as being at war, both administration officials and congressmen emphasized that the United States had offered to return the temporarily occupied forts to Spain.[25]

The United States' second argument to support its assertion that there was no state of war with Spain was that, in accordance with Vattelian principles, it was legally entitled to pursue an enemy into a neutral country's territory without triggering a state of war with that country. The *Richmond Enquirer* observed that if the Seminoles "were already in Florida before hostilities were begun, we could not cross the line to *attack* them—but we had a right to *pursue* them beyond the line, if they sought refuge in a neutral country." The editor cited Cornelius van Bynkershoek and Emer de Vattel for the principle that "it is not lawful to *begin* force in the territory of a neutral, but if begun out of that territory, it is lawful to *continue* it there in the heat of action." Such pursuit was "not an act of war as to the neutral." In 1818, some said the American right to enter Florida was particularly compelling because portions of the territory that the Seminoles used, occupied, and controlled could legitimately be viewed as enemy territory—and therefore a "legitimate seat of war"—even though neutral Spain held ultimate title. John Quincy Adams argued in November 1818 that "[t]he necessity of crossing the line was indispensable; for it was from beyond the line that the Indians made their murderous incursions within that of the United States. It was there that they had their abode; and the territory belonged, in fact, to them, although within the borders of the Spanish jurisdiction." Adams also pointed out that although Florida was Spanish territory, it "was the territory also of the savage enemy." In particular, "St. Mark's had, in substance, become an Indian fort under a Spanish standard." The *Democratic Press* insisted that "as between the Americans and their Indian invaders, lawful repulsion has no territorial bounds." Any nation had the right to pursue an enemy into the enemy's own territory, and the unusual status of Indian tribes did not deprive the United States of that right. Though there was no analogous situation in Europe, the singular circumstances in the Americas required this practical variation on the law of nations.[26]

Third, the United States argued that it had not interfered with Spain's territorial sovereignty because Spain failed to exercise meaningful sovereignty in Florida. In an 1812 case, the United States Supreme Court had expressed strong commitment to the inviolable territorial sovereignty of nation-states, proclaiming definitively that every sovereign had the right to exclude other states from acting on its territory. To explain why the invasion of Florida did not contravene that important doctrine, the United States argued that the principle was inapplicable where there was no effective sovereign power. Showing that Spain did not manifest meaningful sovereignty in the territory was critical for establishing the lawfulness of American actions. Supporters of American policy underscored the dangers presented by Spain's lack of effective control over Seminoles, blacks, and European foreigners in Florida. They referred to Florida as a "derelict sovereignty" where Spain had only "nominal" jurisdiction and "almost extinct" authority. Representative Baldwin declared, "The war would be endless if [Jackson] was bound to respect an authority that did not exist—a sovereignty that was not asserted or exercised." Spain's feeble hold on Florida nullified its right to exclude Americans from the territory. As Representative Smyth explained, "The right of a sovereign Power to exclusive jurisdiction within a territory, is founded on the engagement to govern the inhabitants, and restrain them from injuring other nations." It was absurd to suggest that because Spain could not restrain the Indians the United States must accept the fact that they would simply remain unchecked, congressmen maintained. When government "impotence" made it unable to restrain its own inhabitants from injuring people in another nation, that other nation had the right to attack the neighbor's inhabitants without its constituting war against the neighbor. Since Spain was either too weak or unwilling to prevent Indians who were enemies of the United States from taking sanctuary in Florida and committing depredations against Americans, it had no right to protest that the United States entered Florida in order to restrain them. Its citizens threatened with violence, the United States was compelled to do what Spain could not. Spain's weak authority in Florida and failure to restrain the inhabitants warranted U.S. military action on soil claimed by Spain.[27]

The fourth argument, which focused on Florida officials' misconduct, was multifaceted. Addressing the fact that Jackson's forces had not only attacked Creeks and Seminoles but also displaced Spanish officers from their forts, Americans argued that the United States did not create a state of war with Spain when it punished individual Spanish officers who acted without sovereign authority and allied themselves with America's enemies. Commentators avoided alleging that King Ferdinand himself promoted Indian incursions or committed belligerent acts. Though a number of commentators referred to the king's "imbecility" in dealing with Florida, they did not claim that he had acted willfully against the United States. Rather, they emphasized that the local authorities had behaved in a hostile manner and had been complicit with Florida Indians in their antagonism against the United States. As Representative Baldwin said, Jackson "did not war against Spain, but repelled the wanton and disavowed hostilities of her officers."[28] The United States explained that individual Spanish officials had committed three kinds of unauthorized inimical acts: they had breached Spanish neutrality, allied with U.S. enemies, and violated treaty provisions.

On the neutrality issue, supporters of U.S. actions claimed that Spanish authorities' hostile acts contradicted Spain's neutral stance. According to Vattel, they noted, a neutral country was obligated to be impartial and not to favor one of two warring parties. If officers of that country refused a privilege to one of the parties that had been granted the other, force was warranted. Commentators explained how Spanish officials in Florida showed partiality toward America's enemies: those officials allowed U.S. foes to use Florida territory, forts, and rivers but denied the same opportunity to Americans. More specifically, Spaniards were complacent when fugitive slaves, banditti, and hostile Indians escaped to Florida and then used it as a base for attacking the United States, they acquiesced when British commander Edward Nicolls erected the Prospect Bluff fort on Spanish territory to facilitate strikes on the United States, and yet they protested when the United States entered Florida forts to suppress enemy attacks. Additionally, they actively supplied these enemies of the United States, yet they refused to allow American supply vessels to use a Florida river to provision troops. By granting benefits to U.S. enemies that they denied to the United States, Spanish officials violated Vattel's principles of the law of nations and thereby forfeited their own status as citizens of a neutral country. It was legitimate for the United States both to punish the individual disloyal officials and to demand equal benefits as those received by its enemies without creating a state of war with Spain.[29]

Further, the United States argued, by supplying, sheltering, advising, and supporting belligerent Indians and blacks, Spanish officials made themselves "associates" or "auxiliaries" of the Seminoles in the war. In laying out his complaints against individual Spanish officers in Florida in postwar diplomatic dispatches, John Quincy Adams forcefully repeated his prewar accusations against Florida officials and also brought additional charges against Governor José Masot and St. Marks commandant Francisco Caso y Luengo.

He claimed that Masot encouraged Indians to make war on the United States, gave them shelter, furnished them with arms and ammunition, purchased their plunder stolen from American citizens across the border, and refused to turn over Indians accused of murdering Americans. Additionally, he accused Masot of improperly permitting Alexander Arbuthnot, a British Indian trader, and Robert Ambrister, a former royal marine, to come to Florida and act as incendiaries. Rather than arresting or deporting the Britons, he pointed out, Masot had permitted Arbuthnot to incite Seminoles and Creeks to wage war on the United States and allowed Ambrister to conduct anti-U.S. military operations with black and Indian allies. During the Seminole War, he alleged, Masot threatened General Jackson, obstructed the transport of necessary American military supplies, and allowed Indians to escape Pensacola before Jackson's arrival. Adams also itemized wrongful acts committed by Commandant Luengo, charging him with supplying America's enemies with provisions and munitions of war, allowing them to hold councils of war in the commandant's quarters at St. Marks, encouraging them to commit acts of murder in the United States, permitting the use of the garrison as a base of operations and a depot for stolen booty, and agreeing to purchase cattle and other property the Indians had taken from Georgians. Moreover, he claimed that Luengo approved the power of attorney Arbuthnot received from Florida Indian chiefs, allowed the Briton to use St. Marks as a base for his "intrigues" with the Indians, and warned him of the approach of American troops.[30]

Other commentators agreed. As Representative Strother explained, Masot's and Luengo's alliance with Seminoles meant the U.S. army had "the same right to operate against the Spanish authorities as [against] the belligerent Indians." Echoing that concept, a writer in the *Albany Argus* declared, "No principle is better established in the law of nations, than that a belligerent has a right to treat as enemies all the powers who lend assistance to the enemy, from whatever motive or in consequence of whatever treaty." The *Genius of Liberty* concurred: in Florida the Spanish authorities had acted as belligerents and could be treated as such. The United States had the right to occupy Luengo's and Masot's posts. President Monroe made it clear that the United States did not ascribe to Spain the misconduct of its officers in Florida. "As there was reason to believe that the commanders of these posts had violated their instructions," he said in November 1818, "there was no disposition to impute to their Government a conduct so unprovoked and hostile." However, Jackson's supporters argued that it was perfectly legitimate for the United States to punish individual Spaniards who were associates of its enemies.[31]

Finally, Spanish governors egregiously neglected Spain's obligations under Pinckney's Treaty, the United States asserted. In Article V of the 1795 treaty, the two parties agreed "to restrain by force all hostilities on the part of the Indian Nations living within their boundaries." Thus, Spain specifically agreed not to let its Indian inhabitants attack U.S. citizens. Representative Smyth observed that as to the United States and Spain, the treaty was "a written law of nations." Yet, rather than restraining Indians, Luengo and Masot facilitated their plundering invasions into the United States. American commentators claimed that the United States had respected the lawful authority of Spain in Florida, but when the fort commanders were not defending their posts from America's enemies in accordance with their treaty obligations, U.S. troops were legally entitled to enter the garrisons to provide that defense. In fact, because Luengo and Masot violated the treaty without authority from their sovereign, Congressman John Rhea explained, they "put themselves out of the protection of their own Government." Rhea analogized Luengo and Masot's legal status to that of Alexander Arbuthnot and Robert Ambrister. Like the Spaniards, the two British men had withdrawn themselves from the protection of their home government by aiding and abetting enemies of the United States. By making this analogy, Rhea implied that, just as the Britons' execution was not an attack on Britain, the displacement of Luengo and Masot from their forts was not an attack on Spain itself. Thus, the United States presented its actions as simply opposing the actions of a few disloyal Spaniards, rather than creating a state of war with Spain.[32]

In sum, Jackson's supporters argued that the laws of war did not apply because there was no state of war with Spain. The Florida expeditions did not constitute war with Spain because the United States was not hostile to Spain and was not challenging Spanish authority in Florida. Instead, the United States argued, it acted lawfully in Florida when it pursued non-state actors—Indians—as part of an ongoing conflict and when it punished irresponsible and disloyal Spanish officers who had individually contravened Spain's national legal obligations. Armed hostilities targeted Seminoles, blacks, and their European allies in Florida. There was no war with Spain.

Self-Defense and Military Necessity

The United States maintained that even if American actions in Florida constituted war against Spain, those actions were justified by self-defense and were necessary to repel invasion and advance American national interests. The Florida Indians commenced the conflict; the United States was merely defending itself. As one newspaper author declared regarding the start of the Seminole War, "We were invaded, an unprovoked war was waged against us." Like other nations, the United States had a preeminent right of national self-preservation that justified American troops' entrance into Florida and occupation of forts there. One congressman declared the right of self-defense to be "paramount to all other law," while a prominent newspaper linked to the administration proclaimed, "Self-preservation is the first dictate of nature; and there is nothing in the law of nations, most rigorously construed, which requires a nation to prostrate any part of its population at the mercy of an infuriated and savage enemy." Likewise, Representative Strother referred to the principle of self-preservation as "a law written by the finger of nature upon all animated creation," while Secretary of State Adams called self-defense "the first law of nature." The United States maintained that Creeks and Seminoles were the aggressors, and the United States had given them no provocation. The American nation had always followed a mild and just policy toward Indians, had extended into Indian territory only by agreement with the tribes, and had not committed offensive acts of aggression against Indians, including Creeks and Seminoles. Congressman Richard M. Johnson—who had gained fame fighting against Indians during the War of 1812—claimed nobody could prove "any act of aggression on [the Indians], except those alleged to have been committed in our territory, which we conquered, and which was ceded to the United States, and over which, therefore, the Indians had no jurisdiction." In short, U.S. actions in Florida were purely defensive in character and were therefore legal under the law of nations.[33]

It was necessary for the United States to destroy the Prospect Bluff fort in Spanish Florida in 1816 because blacks and Indians in the garrison were a deadly threat to the United States. The United States had notified Spanish officials about the problem and then waited for months for them to clear out the post. The Spaniards' failure to act had forced the United States to destroy the fort. "The danger was imminent," Representative Baldwin said, and "the emergency required immediate action."[34]

Crossing the border into Florida in 1818 was necessary, the United States claimed, because the danger to U.S. citizens along the southeastern boundary was certain and imminent. For years the Seminoles, with their Creek, Spanish, British, and black allies, had regularly attacked American settlers living along the border, committing acts of murder, arson, and robbery against them. Most recently, they had slaughtered Mrs. Garrett and her children in Georgia and had massacred dozens of members of the Scott supply boat party on the Apalachicola River. One newspaper claimed that southeastern border violence permitted by Spanish authorities had killed twenty thousand Americans. Moreover, hostile predators in Florida bases clearly were planning further acts of war against the young republic. The United States was entitled to pursue the marauders across the border. The Seminoles could not have been defeated if American troops had not crossed the Florida boundary, the United States argued. It was impossible to prevent Indians' violent depredations in the United States if they could find shelter from pursuit and punishment the moment they crossed over the borderline. Americans questioned why the Indians should be allowed to use the border as a "safeguard" and why U.S. troops should be confined by an "artificial boundary." Since the Indians moved freely back and forth across the border, others argued, the existence of a mere "mathematical line" or "ideal line" between the United States and Spanish Florida should not automatically constrain the United States from fighting Seminoles on either side of the line. As President Monroe said to Congress, "In pursuing these savages to an imaginary line in the woods it would have been the height of folly to have suffered that line to protect them." The only way to remedy the problem of Indian violence was to traverse the border that the Indians did not respect. In order to protect its citizens against cross-border violence, the government had the right—even the duty—to eliminate the threat, and if its troops could not otherwise remove the imminent danger, they could enter neighboring territory to do so. Pro-Jackson congressmen Strother and Smyth asserted that the United States "had an absolute right to security from depredation on her frontier" and had "a right not to suffer any other to obstruct its preservation". If we can't go into Spain now, Representative James Ervin asked rhetorically, under what conditions could we? "[D]o gentlemen require our whole Southern frontier to be laid waste with fire and sword before the necessity would be sufficient to justify our marching into neutral territory to put down savages there sheltered, and who have murdered our citizens?" Jackson's supporters denied that the United States was powerless to respond when a neighboring territory was serving as an asylum for predatory banditti. Rather, as Representative Smyth put it, "the Government, being bound to preserve the people, has a right to all the means necessary to preserve the people." As Representative Richard M. Johnson concluded in his minority report for the House Committee on Military Affairs, Jackson's actions were prompted by "dire necessity, to protect from the tomahawk and scalping-knife of the most ruthless savages our peaceful frontier settlers."[35]

Spanish inaction had made the American invasion necessary, the United States contended. For years the government had complained to local Spanish authorities about the border troubles, but they failed to remedy the problem, instead encouraging and assisting depredations. By 1818, it would have been pointless to attempt to negotiate with Spain about the problem because Spanish officials had been openly violating neutrality for years. Representative Ervin argued that it would be "extremely ungracious . . . for Spain to require the United States to spend several months in begging her to perform a solemn treaty, and, in the meantime, to leave her citizens exposed to the bloody vengeance of infuriated barbarians." Given the urgency of the situation, it was unrealistic—even ridiculous—to argue that the United States was required to make a formal request to the Spanish court in Madrid and await permission before entering Florida. Once the United States had commenced military action, Congressman Strother asked, why should it have paused that action "until a messenger had crossed the Atlantic to call the attention of Ferdinand to the condition of his subjects—to awaken him to a sense of duty, and to ask him to reassume the sovereignty of the Floridas, which he had carelessly lost"? Jackson agreed that there was no time for consultations and that any delay would have destroyed the military mission. After the expedition was over, he observed that if he had halted his operation at the border and waited for orders from the War Department, the entire campaign would have failed. Thus, it was necessary that he continue his military operation into Spanish territory without pausing to consult with Spanish authorities.[36]

Capturing Spanish forts was also necessary for self-defense, the United States argued. With regard to the seizure of St. Marks, Spain's admitted inability to defend the garrison in the face of a serious and imminent threat from Indians and blacks—five hundred of whom were beginning to march toward the fort to take it—justified Jackson's preemptive occupation of the post. The Seminoles had both the inclination and the ability to take St. Marks and, some argued, Pensacola as well. Representative Joseph Hopkinson of Pennsylvania pointed out that under the law of nations, when belligerents are about to seize a fort and use it against another party, the endangered party may preemptively take the garrison in self-defense, even on neutral soil. Hopkinson analogized the seizure of St. Marks to a man in a fight with another man taking a sword from a passing stranger if the sword otherwise might be used by the other man. The threat of an enemy taking a neutral fort constituted "extreme necessity," justifying a preemptive seizure by the threatened nation. A number of commentators observed that Jackson had to respond to previously unknown facts on the ground as they emerged in the theater of battle, such as the fact that the Spanish officers were auxiliaries of the Indians in war and that there were hundreds of hostile Indians in Pensacola. In Congress, Representative Baldwin declared that "the emergency required immediate action." In the diplomatic sphere, John Quincy Adams explained to Spanish envoy Luis de Onís that Jackson's occupation of Spanish forts was an "indispensably necessary" response to "unforeseen emergencies."[37]

Thus, the United States asserted that it had faced an emergency situation along the border and within Florida. Marching troops into the Spanish territory and seizing St. Marks and Pensacola were necessary for the nation's self-preservation and therefore could not be unlawful. Moreover, because all of the United States' military actions in Florida were necessary for self-defense, they were not subject to legal limitations under the laws of war. Military necessity and self-defense in an emergency situation trumped the constraints of law.

Finally, supporters of U.S. military actions said they were necessary for advancing the national interest in obtaining possession of Florida. Like any other sovereign nation, the United States argued, it was entitled to pursue its national aspirations, including its economic and security objectives. This was an era when polities around the world were defining clear, solid territorial borders, and the United States needed to do the same in order to secure its place in the world of nation-states. Historian Lisa Ford observes that in the years immediately following the end of the Napoleonic Wars—a time when "the whole world began to tidy its peripheries by parceling them into neat and recognizable systems of jurisdiction"—the United States tried to establish perfect territorial settler sovereignty, especially by clarifying its sovereignty over Indians and territory inhabited by Indians. Elizabeth Cobbs Hoffman likewise notes that "[t]he competitive world system in which the United States came to maturity demanded that states solidify their borders against other potential contenders for land. To fail to do so was to risk destruction."[38]

In addition, many Americans argued that they had a right—perhaps even a duty—to expand throughout the North American continent, and that it was both desirable and inevitable that they do so. Those who went beyond a focus on national security interests left it ambiguous whether they saw themselves as making an argument founded in the law of nations or one based outside of the law of nations. Some of their comments suggest that they viewed Vattel's definition of sovereignty and perspective on the proper cultivation of land as justifications for territorial expansion. However, other comments indicate that they saw U.S. expansion as outside regular European norms under the law of nations and instead viewed it as a natural right or special entitlement grounded in the United States' particular mission in the New World. Either way, in the Seminole War debate the United States lay the groundwork for the Monroe Doctrine by asserting that the region was the United States' sphere and Europeans would not be allowed to interfere. That principle was crucial not only to the United States' diplomatic and legal place in the world but also to American national identity.[39]

In the months following the occupation of Florida, the pro-Jackson press pushed for permanent U.S. control of the territory. "The Floridas must be ours," the *Savannah Republican* declared in mid-July. During the congressional debate the following January, Representative Strother took a similar line: "The high destiny of this growing empire demands the acquirement of Florida; the peace and tranquility of a large extent of population depends upon its possession." Jackson's conduct helped further that goal. In contrast, supporters warned, every denunciation of the Monroe administration and Jackson strengthened the hand of the Spanish minister in negotiations with the United States. In short, while diplomatic discussions were under way, it was not in the interest of the United States to portray the recent hostilities in Florida as an offensive war.[40]

After Adams and Onís signed the treaty on February 22, 1819, newspapers celebrated Spain's cession, which they attributed to Jackson's assertive military operation. The *National Intelligencer* applauded the fact that the treaty "rounds off our southern possessions." "Jackson has acted as a powerful mediator," *Niles' Weekly Register* proclaimed five days after the signing. The United States was destined to acquire the Floridas, and, the paper declared, it had long been clear that the United States "would possess them by fair or foul means—by treaty or by force." Two months later, the same paper declared that the Floridas "as naturally belong to us as the county of Cornwall does to England."[41]

Although supporters of the Florida expeditions were insistent that the United States' armed actions were both more justified and more humane than previous British territorial acquisitions, some of them cited those British acquisitions as precedent. They pointed out that American occupation of parts of Florida was comparable to British seizure of territory in "Indostan" (India), Spanish Trinidad, Dutch South America (Essequibo, Demerara, and Berbice, later united as British Guyana), the Cape of Good Hope, and Malta. In fact, they emphasized, those new British possessions were much more immense than the United States', resulting in vast swaths of territory and large numbers of people falling under British dominion.[42] Leaving their allegations vague and generalized, American commentators did not specify exactly how British actions were analogous to their own. Although Americans did not analyze the British precedents in any depth, however, they strongly asserted that those prior practices paralleled U.S. conduct.[43]

The United States should not relinquish Florida, Americans argued, because it had just as much right to acquire territory as other sovereign nations did. If foreign powers were not demanding that Britain give up the territories it had seized in South America, Africa, and South Asia, they should not demand that the United States give up Florida. The United States, like any sovereign nation, had the right not only to occupy Florida but also to conduct its military operations as it deemed necessary. Passage of congressional resolutions that proposed to condemn or restrict the activities of the U.S. army would weaken American sovereignty and abrogate American rights, thereby seriously harming national interests. If Congress approved Representative Thomas W. Cobb's proposals for legislation to limit the

United States' execution of captives and extraterritorial military action, Congressman Poindexter warned, the effect would be "to divest this nation of some of the most essential attributes of sovereignty." Such self-denial on the national level would be "a voluntary degradation, below the rank of other sovereignties, to which no American ought ever to submit." Americans should refuse to limit the nation's military options and should firmly resist any weakening of the sovereign rights to which the nation was entitled. The *City of Washington Gazette* summed up the sovereignty argument effectively: the United States should be free to "regulate its own concerns in a fair way" without foreign interference or criticism.[44]

Supporters of the Florida campaigns expressed confidence that the forceful military action increased European respect for the United States. To provide "proof" that Europeans regarded the United States as a stronger nation, American newspapers reprinted selected articles from London papers that expressed newfound admiration for the United States in the wake of the Seminole War. An American newspaper reported that *Bell's Messenger*, a London publication, had commented on the "increasing power, civilization, . . . and independent spirit" of the United States and also noted that the United States was "fulfilling the great purpose of Providence, in bringing the world by degrees . . . into order & law." According to another American newspaper, the *London Morning Chronicle* had described American military action in Florida and then commented with admiration that the United States had recently "become one of the most powerful nations of the world."[45] In actuality, many more British newspapers criticized the United States than praised it. Nonetheless, the lack of tangible evidence did not stop commentators from claiming greater American prestige abroad.

Supporters of the Florida campaigns boasted that the United States' decisive, muscular action bolstered its image in the world. An essay in the *Rhode-Island American* mentioned the nation's "becoming pride" about "the imposing attitude which the country now presents to the world." Under the pen name "Hampden," a writer in the *New-York Columbian* pointed out that "the courts of Europe" viewed the United States much differently than they had just a few years previously. Yesterday "the American Republic was like a little star of inferior magnitude, hanging on the skirts of the western horizon," but today "she is like the sun, rolling on in strength and glory, irradiating the mountains, lighting up the vallies, and sending forth her beams to the remotest corners of the globe." The jingoistic author commented on the United States' "rising importance in the scale of empires" and observed that "a new competitor [the United States] has entered the lists for national greatness, with the older powers of the earth." Warning England to "beware of interrupting our progress," he declared that "[w]e are on our march to national grandeur."[46]

Constitutional Issues

The "state of war" and "self-defense" arguments did double duty, supporting the United States with regard to domestic constitutional law as well as the law of nations. In response to the accusation that it had acted unconstitutionally by invading Florida without a congressional declaration of war, the Monroe administration argued that there was no need for such a declaration because Jackson's activities in Florida did not constitute war. Several commentators pointed out that Congress had never declared war against an Indian tribe because those wars had always been defensive and thus had been left to the president's authority. For example, they noted, George Washington had ordered military actions against Indians for many years without any express authorization from Congress, and nobody questioned the constitutionality of his doing so. The administration further contended that Congress's war power applied only to offensive war, and there was no need for congressional approval for defensive action to repel aggression, as in the case of the Seminole War. Repelling Indian invasion was within the president's constitutional powers, they argued (mostly ignoring the fact that the Indians in this case were outside of U.S. borders).[47] The United States presented the same evidence to support these two constitutional assertions as it used to rationalize parallel claims under the law of nations.

The administration mustered additional arguments in defense of its constitutional position as well: First, the Constitution required no fresh declaration from Congress for the Seminole War because a 1795 federal law gave the president standing authority to repel invasions or to act preemptively when there was imminent danger of invasion. Second, the Seminole War was just a continuation of a war that Congress had previously authorized—either a continuation of the War of 1812 or, alternatively, a continuation of a perpetual war against Indians. Third, in the spring of 1818, Congress had tacitly authorized the Seminole War by voting to supply the troops fighting the Seminoles and by failing to object when President Monroe informed Congress that he had sent soldiers to the border with instructions to pursue the Seminoles into Florida. Fourth, the administration claimed Monroe had not interfered with the congressional power to declare war because he had neither ordered nor authorized the incursions into Florida; Jackson had acted on his own initiative.[48]

Finally, many argued that practical utility and necessity negated the requirement of congressional authorization: this was an emergency situation that required preemptive action. It was obvious that Spanish officials had allowed Indians to butcher Americans and only U.S. occupation of Florida would prevent future depredations, so Jackson's military actions were justified and did not require explicit congressional approval. Because everything Jackson did in Florida was necessary to defend the nation and advanced national interests, neither he nor the president had exceeded his constitutional powers. Moreover, Jackson had not gone beyond his orders since everything he did was vital for accomplishing his assigned mission to terminate the Seminole War. Jackson's supporters explained why the general had to disregard the administration's order that he respect the Spanish forts: the order had been based on the assumption that Spanish officers would fulfill Spain's obligations as a neutral nation, an assumption that proved false once Jackson was in Florida. Jackson had to act in accordance with the newly revealed urgent facts, which meant seizing St. Marks and Pensacola to protect American interests. Jackson's supporters dismissed concerns about the threat of military power undermining civil authority. They denied that the general's actions raised any warranted concern about abuse of military power. If military action served the national interest, then it was legitimate and not dangerous to Americans. As one commentator wrote, "Military despotism! What is it! Is it military despotism to fight and beat the enemies of your country?"[49]

It was important that Jackson acted resolutely in the national interest, without getting bogged down with legal technicalities, supporters maintained. One newspaper commented admiringly that the general would not let "flimsy, wire-drawn, sophistical arguments" deter him from decisively protecting American frontier dwellers.[50]

Thus, in responding to constitutional challenges, the Monroe administration took a broad view of executive power, accompanied by a narrow view of congressional power. They circumvented the mandate that only Congress could declare war, finding rationales for allowing a general to pursue hostilities on his own initiative or pursuant to instructions from the executive branch. The fact that Jackson's actions served the U.S. national interest provided sufficient justification for what he did, and his supporters did not want to acknowledge any principles that might have challenged those actions on legal grounds.

United States Arguments, Sources of Law, and Contemporary Legal Theory

Most of the rationale for U.S. armed hostilities drew heavily from a developing modern understanding of both international law and the Constitution, though Jackson's supporters sometimes implicitly borrowed from an older theoretical perspective on war. The supporters rationalized their actions on the basis of four different legal sources—Vattel's principles, treaties, past practices, and notions of justice—but in actuality their core argument was that everything U.S. troops did in Florida was warranted and lawful because it advanced the national interest.

Backers of the Florida campaigns used a Vattelian approach to the law of nations when they discussed the state of war, neutrality, self-defense, and military necessity. When making its legal arguments, the United States used the most advantageous interpretation of both the facts of the Seminole War and legal theories. The U.S. argument that the United States and Spain were not at war because neither country perceived there to be a state of war related to—but did not directly cite—Vattel's statements that war was a state or a condition distinct from peacetime and that intruding on another nation's territory did not necessarily initiate war. The pro-Jackson argument on the issue of neutrality drew explicitly from Vattelian ideas about both appropriate conduct by neutral nations and lawful action by a belligerent power within the territory of a neutral state. Finally, the U.S. argument relied very heavily on Vattel's strong support for the right of self-defense and his adherence to the principle that military conduct was permitted to the extent that it was necessary. They used those concepts to support a broad doctrine of emergency action.

Supporters also used the two sources of law that were central to modern positivism, treaties and past practices. Positivism was a principal hallmark of late nineteenth-century legal thought. For positivists, law between sovereign nations was based on the will and consent of states as expressed in treaties and actual practices. Though the leading American international law jurist, Henry Wheaton, would not formalize this perspective for another two decades, it was already evident prior to the 1810s and gained widespread expression during the Seminole War debates.[51] Pro-Jackson commentators found it advantageous to make positivist arguments to justify the Florida campaigns. When Representative Smyth observed that, as to the United States and Spain, Pinckney's Treaty was "a written law of nations," he was clearly asserting the treaty as a source of positive law binding on both parties. To Americans, Spanish officials' failure to uphold the treaty provided an important justification for U.S. military action in Spanish territory. Likewise, the American reliance on precedents reflected a pragmatic, positivistic approach. As early as March 1818, Congressman Smyth explicitly contended that past practices defined the law of nations: "[J]ustice is not always the law of nations. The law of nations is the usage of nations." To justify the campaigns, supporters identified a number of precedents, including the United States' own previous military actions in Florida and also various analogous European occupations.[52]

Americans' use of positive law was consistent with broader political developments in the United States at the time. The rising concept of popular sovereignty posed a challenge to the foundations of natural law. Although Americans expressed the concept of popular sovereignty in the 1770s as a fundamental principle of the Revolution, it was not immediately implemented in practice. It took a few decades for the United States to shift from a monarchy to a republic and then to begin the process of developing a democracy. In the early nineteenth century, states across the country expanded the suffrage by eliminating property requirements. Although this process began in the 1790s, it accelerated in the wake of the War of 1812.[53] By the time of the Seminole War, a large proportion of white male Americans were voting citizens. To them, it was important that the legislatures they elected had significant power to establish law. They did not want elitist judges or legal theorists to claim abstract natural law principles to be higher than the will of the people as expressed through legislatures. Statutes and codes, more than judicial decisions, expressed Jacksonians' notion of the popular will. The rise of democracy in the United States undermined support for natural law and boosted support for positivism. It is unsurprising that the United States, a leader in the development of democracy, would also be among the earliest adherents of positive law.[54]

In the emerging Jacksonian era, however, Americans' view of law was not confined to mandates that were formalized in statutes and treaties. Their use of law was more complex than that. In their view, law included unwritten expressions of the popular will. If "the people" supported a government or military action, then, with regard to American laws, it was legitimate. The people's commonsense, instinctual understanding of justice could override formal written law. When they called for freedom from certain kinds of governmental restraints and regulations, Jacksonians themselves sometimes referred to their natural right to liberty and self-defense.[55] This was not the same as medieval or Enlightenment-era natural law, which was theoretically grounded in transcendental, universal, moral principles that applied to everyone equally. Nonetheless, when applied to armed conflicts, the Jacksonian approach drew on elements that hinted at the old doctrine of just war.

Supporters of the Florida expeditions argued that the campaigns furthered principles of justice that had broad support in American society. Most especially, they said, the United States' armed response furthered such high principles as national self-defense and national self-preservation, as well as the mission to spread American values. On that basis, some pro-Jackson commentators argued that the United States was "justified" in resorting to armed hostilities or asserted that the nation had a "just" reason for armed action. Such language shifted the focus from the conduct of the war to the righteousness of the cause. Premodern theory held that wartime conduct in pursuit of a just cause was legal as long as it was necessary for achieving that cause, while violence by a party lacking just cause was illegal. When "justice" was at stake, the need to take a humanitarian approach to war could seem less compelling.[56] Portraying the United States as acting defensively and with good cause, and depicting the nation's enemies in Florida as acting offensively and without cause, Jackson's supporters suggested that American troops were not required to restrain their violence in Florida. As a result, Enlightenment-era legal precepts that were intended to prevent excessive violence and cruelty had little effect in constraining American military actions in Florida.

In another important way, too, the United States declined to mechanically follow European theories and past practices. Many Americans refused to rely on European rules because they viewed the American situation as quite distinct. The principle of different regional legal norms that some commentators relied on did not fit comfortably within European usages and principles. Some advocates for the Florida expeditions openly stated that they did not view the United States as constrained by European normative rules or European practices. Instead, they contended that the occupation of Florida and the displacement of Europeans there was warranted because, as a legal space, the New World was in some regards distinct from the Old World and could apply its own, specially tailored rules. Moreover, they said, the United States, not any European nation, was the natural dominant power in the hemisphere. A few years after the Seminole War, these ideas led to the articulation of the Monroe Doctrine.

One could argue that the right of self-preservation under the law of nations justified the ways in which the United States implemented the nascent ideas that would soon become the Monroe Doctrine. It does seem that some contemporary Americans viewed it that way. They argued that self-defense justified not only expulsion of European colonizers and troublemakers but also expansion of U.S. territorial dominion. Yet it is doubtful that such an interpretation was consistent with the European vision of the law of nations, and it seems that Americans who made that argument understood that. Often, Americans portrayed the Americas as a place of superior moral and political values, implicitly suggesting that armed efforts to expel Europeans served a righteous purpose that was higher than positive law. The idea of a distinct New World sphere of law was inconsistent with the old European presumption of universally applicable legal principles and also incompatible with the enduring European concept of international law that applied throughout the entire family of civilized nations. It was an innovation. Additionally, although the United States maintained that it had a natural right to expand, the American concept of continentalism was inconsistent with the principle of territorial sovereignty as embodied in the law of nations. In short, neither the United States' claim of a separate legal and geopolitical sphere nor its assertion of a right to expand across the continent was reasonably a part of the law of nations as Europeans defined it at the time.[57] The United States asserted those principles as higher than rules derived from jurists' treatises, treaties, or Europe's customary practices.

In some regards, the idea of a separate hemispheric legal sphere gained some acceptance outside the United States in the late nineteenth and early twentieth centuries. In that era, some Latin American jurists, such as Chilean Alejandro Alvarez, supported the idea that the Western Hemisphere had its own principles of international law that paralleled and, within the Americas, had higher standing than European ideas of international law, though they did not accept that the United States would unilaterally establish those principles. Moreover, despite the fact that the League of Nations was designed to create a global community of nations based on commonly agreed-upon law, the organization's founding Covenant seemingly accepted the idea of separate regional law in Article 21, which stated: "Nothing in this Covenant shall be deemed to affect the validity of international engagements, such as treaties of arbitration or regional understandings like the Monroe doctrine, for securing the maintenance of peace." However, others in that era, such as British jurist John Westlake (1828–1913), were clear that the Monroe Doctrine was merely U.S. policy, equivalent, for example, to British or Russian policies regarding Central Asia. Such policies were not part of or enforceable by international law. As far as territorial expansion is concerned, late nineteenth- and early twentieth-century U.S. and European imperialism made use of some of the Seminole War justifications for occupying territory inhabited by nonsovereign, "uncivilized" people. In this way, some aspects of American ideas of expansionism later gained greater acceptance in Europe, as they came to serve European purposes. John Westlake, for example, described how, under certain circumstances, civilized states could acquire title to sovereignty in extra-European territory through effective occupation.[58]

Regardless of specific legal reasoning, at their core, arguments in support of the Florida campaigns were grounded in the premise that the belligerent actions furthered national interests. That position was consistent with the emerging nineteenth-century vision of war as a utilitarian instrument of policy and an expression of a state's will. Realists assumed that each state would pursue its own national interest, and war was a tool for doing so.[59] In

1818, stagnating negotiations with Spain about Florida had long failed to address American grievances and policy goals. Andrew Jackson took the initiative in giving up on negotiation. As an alternative path to solving the problems with Florida, he turned to military action. In doing so, he boldly asserted that, under the law of nations, a sovereign nation had the right to utilize its armed forces extraterritorially to achieve its national goals.

The Florida campaigns asserted a parallel point about constitutional law. Utilitarianism was blatantly evident in the argument that a good result justified Jackson's actions—that is, that the successful acquisition of Florida justified the flexible construction of separation of powers doctrine. This was hardly the first or the last time when the nation engaged in belligerent action without a formal declaration of war by Congress or hailed a general's victory that was achieved through somewhat irregular means. Because the occupation of Florida had beneficial consequences for the United States, supporters of the campaigns muted any concerns about possible abuse of executive power and intrusion into the constitutional authority of Congress. In fact, their lack of concern about potential abuse of military power was consistent with a broader shift in national values since the American Revolution. While Jefferson and other leaders of the revolutionary generation had been deeply anxious that standing armies and abuse of power threatened liberty, by 1819 the majority of political leaders and voters no longer worried that the army would crush civil government. Instead of fearing a strong army, many Americans believed that aggressive military action protected national security, advanced national sovereignty, and helped build national pride and solidarity.[60]

In constitutional considerations, as in the arena of international law, the United States interpreted legal texts and concepts in the way that best advanced what they perceived to be national interests. As a newspaper commentator warned, legal technicalities should not be allowed to obstruct national objectives. There are times, the writer observed, when "a too scrupulous adherence to established terms may jeopardize the national safety."[61]

THUS, IN THE Seminole War debate, the United States interpreted both constitutional and international law to support its campaigns in Spanish territory, to foster the solidification of American nationhood, and to demonstrate that the United States was as fully sovereign as any European nation. Postrevolutionary U.S. citizens presumed that although their territory lay outside of Europe, the country had joined the community of refined nations that were bound together under the law of nations, committed to the rule of law, and entitled to equal national rights. As Representative Joseph Hopkinson of Pennsylvania noted during the congressional debate on the Seminole War, although the United States was geographically removed from the rest of the civilized world, it nevertheless belonged to "the family of civilized nations."[62]

The United States asserted that it was entitled to all the powers that any independent government had to pursue its foreign relations and ensure its self-preservation. Within the American governmental structure, those powers were in the hands of the federal executive branch. As a matter of practice, the Constitution would not be a barrier to presidential authority in international or military matters. Nor would the Constitution be interpreted to stifle military actions deemed necessary for protecting the United States, even when a general's authority to act was ambiguous. Defenders of the Florida campaigns argued that the solidity and survival of the nation required such a constitutional arrangement. Likewise, when it came to international law, full sovereignty meant the United States had the right to defend the borders of its territory as it saw fit and to prevent interference by foreigners. As Representative Strother declared during the congressional debate, the American people, "when they assumed a stand amongst the Powers of the earth, became entitled to the benefit of all the law of nations." By acting boldly in Florida, the United States claimed its position in the world as an equal to European sovereigns.

CHAPTER THREE

Challenges and Conflicts

The government's legal justifications for entering Spanish territory and occupying Spanish forts gained widespread public support, but they were not uncontested. A forceful domestic critique challenged some of the United States' basic premises. American critics of the Florida campaigns contended that U.S. armed hostilities in Spanish Florida violated international and constitutional law. Citing Emer de Vattel and other jurists, critics charged that the United States had contravened the law of nations by initiating armed hostilities against Spain without any just cause. Moreover, they accused Jackson and the Monroe administration of flouting the Constitution and endangering civil government by waging war without congressional authorization. Characterizing Andrew Jackson as a dangerous military despot who had no respect for international or domestic legal principles, they feared that his heroic image and the tangible benefits potentially accruing to the nation as a result of the general's actions might blind Americans to the high principles at stake. Though they shared the government's desire that the United States gain acceptance into the European family of nations, they disagreed on the appropriate means of achieving that goal. They insisted that Europe would accept the United States in its diplomatic community only if the Republic obeyed the law of nations and otherwise acted in a just and moral manner. Moreover, they warned that American republican values were at risk if the nation allowed a military chieftain to override civilian authority.[1]

State of War

The central premise of the critics' law of nations argument was that Jackson's conduct constituted offensive war against Spain. They contended that using military force to take possession of Spain's territory during peacetime amounted to waging war. As one newspaper essay bluntly concluded, Jackson made "a direct attack on Spain[,] . . . an act of plain and palpable WAR."[2] Other commentators came to the same conclusion. Pseudonymous writer Algernon Sidney itemized the tangible evidence that Jackson himself viewed his actions as war: the general's statement to West Florida governor José Masot that the Spaniards in Pensacola would be prisoners of war, his later reference to the Spaniards as "a conquered enemy," his report that Masot had agreed to cede his portion of Florida, and Jackson's decision to establish a substitute government for Pensacola. "With respect to Spain, this was not only war but conquest," the writer concluded. In Congress, Jackson's most outspoken critics likewise argued that the general's invasion of Florida and seizure of territory, towns, and forts constituted acts of offensive war against Spain.[3]

The key issue was that American troops entered the territory of a neutral country and occupied its forts without permission. To Jackson's critics, it was self-evident that Spain was an American ally and a neutral party in the U.S. conflict with the Seminoles. Before crossing the line into Florida in 1816 and in 1818, critics said, the government should have contacted Spanish authorities to request a right of passage for its troops. Representative Timothy Fuller noted that since Spain owned the land on both sides of the Apalachicola River and the right to navigate rivers "belongs only to the nation whose territories encompass them," American gunboats had no right to travel on the Apalachicola River through Spanish territory toward the Prospect Bluff fort in 1816 without asking permission from Spain. Likewise, in 1818 U.S. troops had no right to travel through West or East Florida, and no right to enter Spanish garrisons, without Spain's approval.[4] In the absence of Spanish consent, U.S. entry into Florida and the Spanish forts was tantamount to offensive war.

Critics further pointed out that the United States had not seriously worked with Spain to find a peaceful solution. Diplomacy, not military action, was the appropriate approach for dealing with alleged Indian hostilities, they said. It was Spain's proper role, not the United States', to handle Indians living on sovereign Spanish territory. If the United States had complaints about the Florida Indians, it should have demanded that Spanish officials restrain the Indians. Those officials had not been uncooperative, and the possibility still remained that they would voluntarily assist the United States once they learned of the problems. Armed hostilities on Spanish soil would have been justified only if the United States had demanded that the Spanish restrain the Indians and the Spaniards had refused to act. Critics pointed out that, according to Spanish envoy Luis de Onís, Spanish officers had received no communication from the United States containing complaints about Indian violence. Newspaper commentator Algernon Sidney pointed out that Vattel scorned those who, when faced with a problem, needlessly turn to armed force as "the scourges of the human race, barbarians, enemies to society, and rebels to the law of nature." In the absence of a request and refusal, the United States had no legal justification for entering Spanish territory. Moreover, Commander Francisco Caso y Luengo of St. Marks had responded to Jackson's requests in a cooperative manner, saying he would seek instructions from a higher authority. It was possible that the Spanish commander would have allowed Jackson access to the fort voluntarily. If Jackson had not been so impatient, he might not have had to resort to military action, critics contended. Marching into Florida and seizing the forts therefore initiated offensive war against Spain.[5]

The United States' unlawful entry and armed hostilities in Spanish territory created a state of war against neutral Spain, critics insisted. Lacking just cause for initiating such a war, the United States had violated the law of nations.

Self-Defense and Military Necessity

Critics also mounted a detailed and systematic challenge to U.S. claims of self-defense and military necessity. They challenged the factual foundation of the American claim that invading and seizing forts in neutral Florida was necessary for self-defense. The law of nations forbade a belligerent to enter a neutral country to attack an enemy unless there was no alternative means of preserving and defending the nation. Critics denied that the conditions in Florida legally warranted American military action according to principles explicated by Emer de Vattel and other jurists.

Neither entry into Spanish territory nor seizure of forts there in 1816 and 1818 was necessary for defending the United States, critics claimed. In actuality, they said, American hostilities in Florida were active aggressions, not commenced in self-defense at all. They accused the government of distorting the facts to make its case. Vis-à-vis Spain, anti-Jackson commentators said the military incursions were neither defensive in nature nor necessary because the United States had not been attacked by Spain and was not in imminent danger of being attacked by that nation. Nor did Spain's friendly relations with Florida Indians justify American offensive action in Spanish territory, critics maintained. Those friendly relations did not make Spain an "associate" of the Creeks and Seminoles under the laws of war. Continued normal commercial and friendly relationships between Florida Indians and Spanish officials in St. Marks and Pensacola did not make Spain an enemy of the United States, even if the Indians were the United States' enemies. The acts of Spanish commanders in supplying Indians did not constitute war against the United States. If all people and nations involved in international commerce were legal associates of each of their trading partners, such a situation would multiply and spread wars, critics said. Even Spain's obligations in Pinckney's Treaty of 1795 did not make it a legitimate target. Although a treaty provision required Spain to restrain the Indians, this referred only to the Indians' offensive deeds, not their defensive actions. The provision did not obligate Spain to ally itself with the United States against Indians in Florida nor to disarm the Indians and thereby prevent them from defending themselves.[6]

In addition to these general observations, commentators separately addressed the different American military actions in Florida, explaining how the actual facts of each situation did not support a self-defense justification. They contended that it had not been necessary to destroy the Prospect Bluff fort in 1816, to cross the line into Florida in 1818, or to seize St. Marks or Pensacola.

With regard to the 1816 attack on the Prospect Bluff fort, critics rejected the U.S. argument that it was justified in blowing up the stronghold on the Apalachicola River because men in the fort fired on American gunboats. Rather, the armed Americans on the gunboats were acting in a hostile manner as they approached the post, and it was natural for the men on the bluff to act defensively. Prior to the gunboat attack, the Gulf Coast area, including Prospect Bluff, had been calm and peaceful. Since the fort's occupants were not a threat to the United States, there was no necessity for American troops to demolish the garrison and kill its inhabitants.[7]

Marching U.S. troops over the southeastern border into Spanish Florida in 1818 was likewise unjustified by self-defense or military necessity. The Florida Indians posed no significant threat, critics maintained. In fact, violence along the Florida border was mostly the result of American aggression, rather than Indian violence. Far from being threatening assailants, the Seminole Indians were trying to live in peace in Florida and simply defended themselves when attacked. The argument that the massacre of the Scott party in the military supply ship on the Apalachicola River in November 1817 justified U.S. self-defense in Florida was without foundation, since those killings took place outside of U.S. territory and were justified as self-defense on the part of the Indians. In fact, it had been the Americans who first broke the peace in 1817—a week and a half before the Scott incident—by destroying the Indian village at Fowltown. The claim that the subsequent 1818 invasion was justified by "alarming necessity" was particularly implausible when the supposed danger came from people previously described as wretched fugitives and savages—hardly constituting a threatening military force. Given the lack of any serious danger, the United States could not argue that the invasion of Spanish Florida was necessary to defend and protect the United States. The United States acted offensively in entering Florida, not in self-defense.[8]

Moreover, the U.S. seizure of St. Marks was unwarranted as American self-defense because Indians were unlikely to seize the fort and their doing so would not have constituted a significant danger to the United States. Representative Thomas S. Williams noted that the facts did not meet the requirement described by Dutch jurist Hugo Grotius that there be a "certain (not only imaginary) danger" that would result in "irreparable mischief." The danger from the Indians was far from "certain." Williams's colleague, Congressman John Tyler, observed that Jackson's only legitimate justification for capturing St. Marks would have been if it had been necessary "to save his army, or to guard the post against the imminent hazard of falling into the hands of his enemy." There was no proof of such necessity. Jackson's justification focused on past aid and comfort provided to Indians in the garrison, rather than on the expectation and prevention of future danger. In fact, Representative Charles F. Mercer noted, St. Marks was 104 miles from the main object of Jackson's campaign, the Suwannee towns, so it was implausible that military necessity demanded the fort's capture. Moreover, critics argued, at the time when Jackson took the garrison, there was no real threat. There was no evidence that Seminoles were capable of seizing the fort and no reason to think they actually planned to do so. The Indians had already been defeated and had scattered into the swamps. Moreover, even if they had taken the fort, that could not have endangered the American army or done other irreparable harm. The Indian force in the vicinity of St. Marks was so small and weak that Jackson—with roughly 2,360 American troops plus 1,500 Indian auxiliaries—could easily have recaptured the fort from them. It was not necessary for Jackson to preemptively seize St. Marks. Therefore, the U.S. capture of the fort violated Spain's rights under the law of nations.[9]

Likewise, the argument for self-defense with regard to Pensacola was baseless. Since there was no imminent danger to the United States from either Spaniards or Indians in Pensacola, seizure of the city was unnecessary. With regard to the Spanish, Jackson's assertion that the governor of West Florida had acted in a hostile manner by threatening him could not support a claim of self-defense. One day before the attack on Pensacola, when the American army was just a few miles away, the governor ordered Jackson and his troops to leave Spanish territory and threatened force if Jackson did not comply. The logical meaning of the governor's statement was that if Jackson attacked Pensacola, the Spanish would resist with force. Such a position was a reasonable response to Jackson's approaching troops and did not constitute an act of hostility that legally justified Jackson's attack on the city. In fact, some critics believed the "irascible" Jackson only took Pensacola because he was angry that the governor would presume to obstruct his wishes. Jackson acted because of a personal affront, not military necessity, they said.[10]

Nor was taking Pensacola necessary for self-defense against Indians. Critics noted that seizing the city did not advance the American defense against Indians in any way. The United States did not find Indians in Pensacola to kill or capture, so clearly Indians did not already occupy Pensacola. Under such circumstances, commentators noted, for an Indian threat to necessitate the capture of Pensacola under the law of nations, three conditions had to be met: that the enemy Indians meant to attack the town, that the neutral power (Spain) could not or would not defend it, and that its occupation would be dangerous to the very existence of the United States. Jackson's critics found no proof that any of the three conditions was met. There was no genuine possibility that Indians sought to occupy Pensacola or the nearby garrison at Barrancas. The Indians who had been defeated along the Suwannee had fled south into the peninsula or to St. Augustine, not to Pensacola, which was 150 miles away. Furthermore, there was no evidence that Spain could not defend Pensacola or that Indian occupation would be a serious threat to the United States. In fact, before Jackson headed to Pensacola, he had already declared the war effectively over. In an April 16 letter, critics noted, Jackson wrote that the Indians had been defeated and would no longer bother frontier people, and ten days later he wrote that his "presence in this country can be no longer necessary." If his presence was not necessary on April 26, critics inquired, why was it necessary in early May? Additionally, Congressman Mercer doubted Jackson's assertion that he had to take Pensacola in order to use the Escambia River to supply Fort Scott with provisions from the Gulf. He pointed out that that fort, which was only fifty miles from one American river or, alternatively, twenty-five miles from another, shallower waterway, could easily have been supplied by land. Moreover, prior to Jackson's seizure of Pensacola, the governor granted the United States free transit through Florida to supply the fort. So, he concluded, the United States could not argue that it was necessary to attack Spanish posts in Florida in order to facilitate the supplying of American forts.[11]

Moreover, commentators asked, if it was necessary to capture Pensacola and St. Marks in April and May 1818, what changed to make it no longer necessary to hold the town and the fort a few months later when the Monroe administration committed to return them to Spain? That nothing had changed with regard to either the Spanish or the Seminoles suggested that even the president knew the seizure was unnecessary and therefore unlawful. The promised restoration of St. Marks and Pensacola to Spain was an admission of wrongdoing by the U.S. government, critics argued. If the garrisons could so quickly be returned to Spain, it was clear that there was no serious danger to U.S. security warranting Jackson's occupation of the posts.[12]

Thus, to the critics, none of the allegations against Spain—the Pensacola governor's alleged threats, denial of passage through territory, trading with an enemy, and refusal to ally with the United States against Indians—constituted just cause for war or justified the self-defense claim. In the application of a self-defense argument, they said, there was no principled distinction between Jackson's actions in Florida and a potential broader attempt to dispossess Spain from North America completely. The former was just as much a violation of the law of nations as the latter would be, the critics said.[13] In short, Spain had not actually or virtually threatened the United States nor provoked a need for the United States to defend itself. The United States could not lawfully attack Spanish territory and forts based on self-defense.

In support of their arguments, opponents of the war frequently referenced European jurists' treatises. They relied primarily on Emer de Vattel's rendering of the rules of war, though occasionally they also quoted or cited passages from juridical texts by Hugo Grotius, Georg Friedrich von Martens, and Cornelius Bynkershoek. Essays by pseudonymous author Algernon Sidney cited Vattel numerous times. Congressional critics citing Vattel included Charles F. Mercer, James Johnson, and Thomas W. Cobb. Jackson critics citing other jurists on the law of nations included Representatives Williams (citing Puffendorf's discussion of Grotius) and William Henry Harrison (citing Bynkershoek). Harrison—who found Jackson's capture of Pensacola and the Barrancas fort unjustified by the law of nations but declined to vote for the censure—referred to two passages from Bynkershoek. He quoted the jurist: "But he who commits hostilities upon the territories of a friend to both parties, makes war upon the sovereign who governs them." And he described the author's principle that a conqueror may pursue a conquered enemy into the territory of a neutral, but he should avoid damage to the fortresses and injury to the ally. Additionally, Representative Cobb cited American author Alexander Macomb's treatise on martial law and courts-martial.[14]

Based on their understanding of the laws of war, critics of the Florida expeditions dismissed the entire self-defense justification, calling it a subterfuge, a "strange perversion of language." They viewed Jackson's "necessity" argument as a mere pretext to justify seizing St. Marks and Pensacola. They concluded that Jackson did not capture those posts in order to avoid their seizure by Indians nor because control of the posts was necessary for the safety or provisioning of the army. Rather, they claimed, Jackson intended to take possession of Florida for the United States from the very beginning of his expedition. They explained that Jackson's actual purpose was not to defend the United States against Indians but rather to strengthen the American claim to Florida. At the very least, they alleged, the government intended the invasion to increase American leverage in negotiations by showing Spain that the United States could acquire Florida without a treaty. As the *National Messenger* observed after the invasion, "Spain might be tempted to accept any price, when 'practically convinced,' that the sword could do the office of the treasury." Other critics went further, arguing that Jackson's intention was to conquer Florida and add to American territory. The obvious context of Jackson's invasion was the United States' persistent efforts to obtain Florida, first by seizing a large portion of West Florida, then by occupying Amelia Island, and subsequently in 1818 by taking most of East Florida. As specific evidence, congressmen pointed to Jackson's June 2, 1818, letter to the secretary of war, in which he described the agreement with Governor José Masot as a "complete cession to the United States" of the territory governed by Masot and referred to Florida as "this important territorial addition to our Republic." Jackson further revealed his motives in his May 5 letter to Secretary of War John C. Calhoun, which said the United States could not be secure on its southern border without a "cordon . . . of posts along the seashore" of the Gulf of Mexico. Thus, critics argued, in the Seminole War the United States was not defending itself. Rather, it was actually trying to conquer Florida, which was not a lawful goal justifying offensive war. Because the United States acted offensively, not defensively, when it entered Spanish Florida and captured or destroyed forts in 1816 and 1818, the invasions were not legally justified as self-defense. In short, critics asserted, the United States lacked just cause for its war against Spain.[15]

Opponents of the Florida campaigns highlighted the dangerous international precedents set by the nation's military actions and rationales. If Jackson's conduct went unchallenged, they said, it would set a terrible precedent for the future. If allowed, his actions could lawfully be repeated. More specifically, they warned, there were potentially perilous consequences to Jackson's doctrine of preemptive action—justifying his capture of a Spanish fort not based on Indians having taken the town but in anticipation that Indians might possibly take it. Some commentators objected to the whole concept of preemptive strikes. The doctrine that individuals' aiding and supplying an enemy justified war was even more frightening, critics said. As Representative Williams pointed out, Spain's grievances against the United

States could potentially justify Spanish troops' entrance into U.S. territory. Spain claimed that Americans were providing arms and ammunition to Latin American rebels and were fitting out privateers to attack Spanish shipping. Applying Jackson's logic, Spain could take possession of U.S. ports where anti-Spanish privateers docked and also U.S. cities where supplies were prepared to send to rebels. The United States would never accept such an invasion as lawful, Williams declared. Congressman James Johnson pointed out that the United States would never allow France's European enemies to pursue Frenchmen who had fled to the United States—or to make war on the United States if the nation refused to surrender the Frenchmen. Representative Henry R. Storrs of New York raised the specter of a Canadian army following Jackson's example by marching into New York State to conduct hostile actions against Indian tribes residing there. "Will it be tolerated," he asked, that such an army "could lawfully exercise the power of marching across that State—prostrating her sovereignty, and subjecting her citizens to all the horrors of war in pursuit of those tribes?" Of course not, he answered. The proper course of action would be to request that the United States handle the problem within its own territory. More broadly, Storrs noted, one nation could not enter another's territory in pursuit of criminals. Law required that the first nation request that the other country deliver up the criminals rather than chasing them down in foreign territory. The law of nations provided no authority "for one Government, at its own pleasure, to pursue banditti, outlaws, renegadoes, or even its own felons, into the territories of another."[16] The United States had violated the law by entering Spanish territory and capturing Spanish posts without justification.

National Honor

Critics of the Florida invasions further argued that they damaged the United States' reputation as an honorable, law-abiding nation. In the past, they noted, the United States had shown admirable restraint in dealing with international conflicts, rather than rashly turning to military action to deal with a problem: the United States did not rush to violence in response to Britain's retention of western forts after the Revolutionary War, French spoliations on American commerce in the 1790s, Spain's withdrawal of the right of deposit at New Orleans, or Britain's attack on the *Chesapeake*. In fact, Americans had criticized other nations that had committed unjustifiable acts against neutral countries. For example, a number of commentators noted that in 1807 Americans had expressed outrage when Britain seized the Danish fleet at Copenhagen in order to prevent it from falling into Napoleon's hands. The odious preemptive nature of that attack was analogous to Jackson's invasion of Florida, critics argued. In fact, Henry Clay explained, Jackson had even less justification for his actions: Britain had captured the Danish fleet at a time when she was "struggling for her existence" and "was combating, single-handed, the most enormous military Power that the world has ever known" and was trying to prevent that power from gaining control of the Danish fleet, whereas in Florida Jackson was merely facing "a few half-starved, half-clothed, wretched Indians and fugitive slaves." Rather than following the example of Britain, the republican United States should adhere to the highest standards, he said.[17]

In addition to noting the United States' dignified precedent of showing moderation in the face of violence, some commentators pointed to the nation's previous noble pattern of taking principled positions on the law of nations. The *Richmond Enquirer* pointed out that Americans had outspokenly revered and upheld the law of nations in the past, even when Europeans trampled it. In particular, the United States had always been a strong advocate for the rights of neutral powers. But now, the editor lamented, many people seemed to forget the law of nations in their rush to rationalize the American acquisition of Florida. The argument formerly brought against European princes seemed altered "because it is convenient for us to 'round off our territory' with Florida." Though a genuine national security threat would justify armed hostilities, he insisted, mere desire to acquire territory was not a legitimate goal for war.[18]

Abandoning past approaches to foreign policy that adhered to law and tried to avoid recourse to war would only compromise American virtue and honor, critics maintained. National character mattered as a foundation not only for a proud national self-image but also for the country's global standing. Externally, Europe's opinions mattered most, since the United States sought acknowledgement as a member of the European family of civilized nations. For Jackson's opponents, the United States could only gain such acceptance if it showed the highest character and honor. Americans assumed that Europeans were watching them and judging their worthiness. Lamenting that Jackson's conduct was "disgraceful to our reputation as a civilized and enlightened nation," the *New-York Evening Post* proclaimed just before the congressional debate that "[t]he character of the American nation is at stake; the eyes of Europe are turned towards us." Similarly, Representative Fuller admonished the House: "[L]et us remember that the eyes of European nations are upon all our measures. Republican America must expect a strict scrutiny of her policy and her principles."[19]

Those who challenged Jackson's invasion warned that it had seriously harmed the nation's reputation, though they disagreed as to whether there was any way to mitigate the damage. While some said the return of the Spanish forts nullified potential illegalities and allowed the United States to continue treaty negotiations with "clean hands," others viewed the damage as lasting and irremediable. Making the latter argument, the *National Messenger* stated: "We should like to know what system of ethics teaches that having committed a violent wrong, the mere abandonment of our error, purifies us from its original stain. In common life, it would be no atonement, we suspect, for knocking a man down, and rifling his pockets, that we afterwards picked him up, wiped his clothes and returned his money, and placed him 'as far as we could in status quo.'" Others saw hope of a remedy. Though the editor of the *Richmond Enquirer* believed that returning the Spanish forts would in fact "wipe away the wrong *which has been done,*" he agreed with the *National Messenger* about the importance of upholding the nation's sterling reputation. Restoration of the posts was crucial for allowing Americans to "maintain that national honor which forms the brightest halo around our head," he wrote. If the United States were to use the Indian threat as a pretext or trick to take Florida, it would bring "disgrace upon the American name." Though the United States had an interest in acquiring Spanish territory, he opined in June and July 1818 editorials, "[o]ur national character" and "[t]he honor of the American nation" were "more precious than a hundred Floridas."[20]

Others, too, persistently raised the principle of national character and honor. Representative Joseph Hopkinson reminded his colleagues that the issues under debate in Congress reflected on "the character of our country." Although the United States was "removed far from the rest of the civilized world," he said, "we belong to the family of civilized nations, and . . . [must] be most forward to prove our devotion to those rules of conduct" that govern such nations. Manifest adherence to the law of nations was essential for demonstrating the United States' elevated character and worthiness as a member of the civilized community, he believed. Henry Clay said the United States should be careful about departing from "established laws and usages" precisely because "we hold a proud and lofty station, among the first nations of the world." On the eve of the congressional debate, the *Connecticut Journal* expressed the hope that, "for the honor of our country," Congress would take measures to "to wipe off the foul blot which ha[d] been cast upon the American character" by Jackson's actions, especially the military executions. As the *Northern Whig* stated when the House began its deliberations, "Nothing less than our character in the eyes of the world for national justice is at stake." The American people should refuse to approve "measures so derogatory to their high character."[21]

Critics' Arguments and Contemporary Theory on the Law of Nations

On the subject of Spain, critics of U.S. policy used a different framework of analysis than that relied on by the administration and its defenders. To support their opposition to belligerency in Florida, critics of the invasion borrowed from the concept of just war, questioning whether the United States had a just cause for resorting to war. Although a few critics also questioned whether American troops fought the war in a humane way, overall the criticism focused more on justice than on humanitarianism.

During the congressional debate about the Seminole War, two critics, Thomas M. Nelson and Joseph Hopkinson, explicitly used the term "just cause," and other critics repeatedly employed the words "morality" and "justice" and unequivocally valued national "character" and "honor." Most notable was the critics' refusal to treat benefits to national interest alone as lawful goals of war absent any other legitimate reason for resorting to armed hostilities.[22]

Key to critics' view that there was no legitimate purpose for war was their rejection of the military necessity and self-defense arguments. Their speeches and articles addressed this issue extensively and repeatedly. They forcefully refuted the assertion that circumstances in Florida created an emergency situation that demanded a military response. Contrary to Jackson's allegations, they argued, the United States did not face imminent danger nor could it plausibly claim that it crossed the border in "hot pursuit" of enemies. Moreover, once U.S. troops were in Florida, their actions went well beyond acts of necessity at each stage of the war—at Prospect Bluff, Miccosukee, St. Marks, Suwannee, Pensacola, and Barrancas. Critics contended that the United States' main objective was not to defend the United States against imminent threat of foreign attack but to press Spain to relinquish Florida. Rather than justifiable emergency actions, Jackson's incursions were an attempt to force Spain to bend to American will. In fighting the Seminole War, the United States was motivated by the ambitious desire for conquest, territorial expansion, and national power, they alleged.

Once critics had—in their view—demolished the necessity argument on factual grounds, they attacked the utility argument based on legal principles. They did not dispute whether the acquisition of Florida might benefit the United States. Rather, they argued that, under the law of nations, it was not a legitimate purpose for initiating armed hostilities. The mere usefulness of war against Spain did not justify it, nor was it a valid reason to waive legal limitations on state violence. Thus, they did not agree with the United States' characterization of its goals in Florida, nor did they concur that the utility of armed hostilities was the best measure of their lawfulness. Intended to further national interests rather than to defend the nation from injury or to promote high moral principles, the Seminole War was unlawful.

Constitutional Issues

In addition to their concern about the United States' violations of the law of nations, critics also maintained that the Florida campaigns contravened the U.S. Constitution. The central premise of their constitutional argument was the same as that based on the law of nations: that the general's conduct constituted offensive war against Spain. By going to war without proper authorization, they maintained, Jackson violated the Constitution. Although the constitutional war powers violation was not the determinative factor for most critics—since even with congressional consent the war against Spain would have been unlawful because of the lack of justification—anti-Jackson newspaper editors and essayists had far more to say about constitutional issues than they had on the law of nations.

The primary constitutional challenge was straightforward: under Article I, section 8 of the Constitution, only Congress had authority to declare war.[23] Whether Jackson acted to fulfill President James Monroe's orders or invaded Florida on his own initiative, he proceeded without lawful authority because Congress never declared war against Spain. Spanish officers' alleged acts and omissions did not extend a general's power. It was up to the people's representatives, not a general or even the president, to decide how to respond to wrongs committed by one nation against another. It was possible that Spanish instigation and supplying of the enemy might be just cause for war, but assessing those factors and deciding to respond with military action was the responsibility of Congress, not of an individual general in the field. Even if Jackson's rationalizations might justify Congress in declaring war, they did not validate the general's own actions. He had wrested from Congress the authority to decide what constituted legitimate causes of war and the power to declare war.[24]

The same principles that governed war with Spain also applied to war with Seminoles in Florida. Congress had authority to decide upon war with Indian tribes just as it did war with other sovereigns. Even if Indian activity might justifiably trigger military action in the national self-defense, that was Congress's decision, not a general's. Arguing that Jackson's actions were merely an extension of other Indian wars could not constitutionally justify them. Previous Indian wars had occurred within U.S. territory, so the army's activities had been aimed at suppressing an internal enemy rather than waging war outside the nation's borders. In contrast, Jackson's invasion constituted foreign war and therefore required congressional authorization. By waging war against Seminoles in Spanish territory, the general had usurped the constitutional powers of Congress.[25]

Nor was there an urgent situation requiring an immediate response in the field. A Vermont newspaper article pointed out that if, as Jackson alleged, the Seminoles' atrocities had extended over two years, there had been plenty of time for Congress to respond if it so chose. Even after the start of the military operation, occupying the posts without authorization was not necessary because there was an alternative that equally protected Americans, the critics explained. Rather than seizing St. Marks and Pensacola, Jackson could have had his troops surround the posts to cut them off from the enemy, notified his superiors, and awaited fresh instructions from the government. Neither garrison was under Indian control and neither was seriously threatened, so there was time for Jackson to get proper authorization.[26]

The critics refused to treat as a congressional declaration of war the federal statute providing support for widows and orphans of troops killed in service against the Seminoles, as was argued by some of Jackson's supporters. The *New-York Daily Advertiser* challenged that "dangerous" assumption. The paper pointed out that if that doctrine were accepted, then the president could commence a war at any time on his own initiative. Any subsequent federal statute that incidentally mentioned the existence of the war could be interpreted as a declaration of war even in the absence of real congressional sanction. The Constitution demanded more than that. In the case of the Seminole War, critics noted, the statute cited by Representative Alexander Smyth and others, passed by the House on April 10 and the Senate on April 18, became law on April 20, 1818—thirteen days after Jackson occupied St. Marks on April 7. Much of the war had already taken place before Congress passed the law that supposedly authorized it. "If a retrospective and implied declaration of war is all that the constitution requires," the *Daily Advertiser* warned, "a back-handed vote of both houses, on a collateral subject, and without any reference to the legality of the war, would operate as a complete indemnity to the chief magistrate who had undertaken it on his own authority, and would forever save him harmless for an act of the most aggravated and dangerous usurpation."[27]

In fact, some commentators pointed out, rather than declare war in Florida, Congress had explicitly taken a position against a military seizure of the Spanish territory. In March 1818, Georgia representative John Forsyth had proposed that Congress authorize the president to take possession of

Florida, but the Committee on Foreign Relations and the House as a whole had opposed the idea. Nothing of significance had changed since that time, critics pointed out. During the congressional debate in early 1819, Representative William Lowndes of South Carolina asked, "[W]ho could have foreseen that the very circumstances which in March last were insufficient to give the sanction, even of political expediency, to the occupation of Florida, were soon after to be the principal constituents of a military necessity, which would justify a General in taking what the Congress of the United States had determined not to take?" Jackson's opponents condemned him for doing on his own initiative what Congress had refused to approve.[28]

A few commentators wondered whether Monroe had authorized Jackson's seizure of Spanish posts, thereby intruding on the war power. Algernon Sidney warned that if the war power fell into the hands of the executive, the American president would be akin to a monarch. Most commentators, however, believed that Jackson acted beyond orders from the executive branch, which raised the problem of abuse of military authority. Critics emphasized that Jackson's instructions did not authorize him to cross the border into Florida under the circumstances. The December 1817 letters from the secretary of war to Jackson and to his military predecessor in Georgia, General Edmund P. Gaines, said the generals could enter Florida only if the Indians committed hostilities within the United States (December 9) and only if the army was pursuing invaders or punishing depredation (December 26). Critics pointed out that there were no such hostilities, invaders, or depredation in the United States (the attack on Scott's party having taken place outside the United States). The president's message to Congress on March 25, 1818—three months after the December 26 letter to Jackson—also made it clear that the administration had ordered Jackson "not to enter Florida, unless it be in pursuit of the enemy, and in that case to respect the Spanish authority wherever it is maintained." The general did not enter Florida in pursuit of the enemy. Further, even if the entry into Florida was justified, his instructions specifically ordered him to report to the president if the Indians took shelter in a Spanish fort. He was not to pursue the Indians into the garrisons. He should have consulted the War Department before seizing St. Marks and Pensacola. The limits on Jackson were clear, his orders were not unlimited, and he defied and disobeyed his instructions, critics maintained.[29]

Anti-Jackson commentators said there were important reasons for leaving the war power to the representatives of the people rather than to a military commander. The *New-York Daily Advertiser* explained that "[b]y entrusting Congress exclusively with the power of declaring war, the framers of the constitution intended to secure the nation against wars of injustice, ambition, and conquest—to save us from the expenses as well as the miseries of war, the dangers to which it exposes nations, and especially free nations, and the sacrifices which it too often forces a people to make of their prosperity and happiness." More specifically, essays in the *Georgia Journal* and the *Union* pointed out that by declaring war in Florida Jackson single-handedly exposed the United States to all the dangers of war with Spain, including threats to America's oceanic trade from predation by privateers holding Spanish commissions, risks of jeopardizing the United States' relations with European nations, and damage to ongoing negotiations with Spain. Representative Tyler warned that countenancing Jackson's conduct would mean that again in the future the United States could be led into war without consultation with "the Representatives of the people." Tyler asked rhetorically what would happen if the United States were at war with northern Indians who fled to a fort in Canada and were protected there. Would a general be entitled to take that fort by storm as Jackson had in Florida? If so, he warned, the result could be a massive war with England, without the approval of Congress. The rule should not be different when dealing with a weak nation (Spain) than when dealing with a strong one (Britain), he concluded.[30]

Algernon Sidney was particularly vocal in objecting that government officials were not reining in Jackson. In the *Richmond Enquirer,* the pseudonymous author wrote that Jackson had "inflicted a vital wound upon the constitution of my country." In another essay he lamented: "[I]n vain have the people and the states confided their peace and honor to the keeping of their representatives, in vain has the constitution ordained, that Congress alone shall have the power of declaring war; if a military officer may wage war according to his own judgment of necessity or propriety, and if, the approbation of the executive be sufficient to justify the act." In a third publication he claimed that "in General Jackson's opinion, whenever he is at the head of an army, all the powers of every branch of our governments, state and federal, are suspended or transferred to him."[31]

Sidney asserted that Monroe should have explicitly condemned Jackson's conduct in Florida and ordered that Jackson stand trial before a court-martial, or at least appointed a court of inquiry to examine Jackson's conduct in Florida. The writer expressed outrage that the president had condoned Jackson's flouting of military orders, asking: "Why has this officer been permitted to transcend his instructions? to counteract the declared policy of the executive? to take measures on the strength of his own judgment alone, that directly affect the peace of the nation? measures, which the government expressly told him, it did not intend to place within his discretion?" Most of all, Sidney asked, "Why has [Jackson] not been punished? Why has he been countenanced, justified, applauded?" Sidney alleged that excessive violence, deliberate disobedience of military orders, violation of the federal and state constitutions, and offences against the law of nations had marked Jackson's whole military career. Moreover, itemizing Jackson's wrongful conduct during the War of 1812 and the Creek War (1813–1814), Sidney said the capture of St. Marks and Pensacola was "not the first instance in which he has of his own independent, sovereign authority, declared and waged war against a nation with which his country was at peace." It was long past time to rein in the dangerous general. Sidney warned that "the government, which tolerates open disobedience, in effect relinquishes its authority, and the soldier, who may violate his orders with impunity, soon comes to dictate orders to his superiors."[32]

In March 1819, the *Rhode-Island American and General Advertiser* praised Algernon Sidney as "one among the few who have stood forward to defend their country against the reproach of countenancing military despotism, as sanguinary and horrible as any that ever stained the records of history." A number of other newspapers likewise warned of the dangers of military tyranny. A pseudonymous essay in the Boston newspaper *Repertory* proclaimed the importance of keeping the military subordinate to the civil power in a democracy. An editorial in the *Richmond Enquirer* declared that the American constitutional system would be endangered if an individual military officer—or even the president—could make war. Another essay in the same paper warned: "Watch the military arm; put it in strict subordination to the civil power; guard the powers of the people's representatives; or our liberties may yet tremble." Sharing these publications' concern about military despotism, House Speaker Henry Clay referred to Jackson as a "military chieftain." The armed forces must be accountable to the public, Clay said, warning that if Congress praised and reinforced Jackson's conduct, it would "be a triumph of the principle of subordination—a triumph of the military over the civil authority" and might also end up being "a triumph over the liberties of the people." Encroachments on the Constitution were particularly dangerous when committed by military chiefs, Representative Lewis Williams wrote in a strongly worded report printed in a North Carolina newspaper. That Jackson apparently acted without orders from Monroe meant that "[t]he peace and welfare of this country [were] subject to the control of, and jeopardised by, a self willed military commander!" wrote one newspaper commentator. Another accused Jackson of seizing for himself the "most important prerogative" of government "and wield[ing it] with all the rigour of oriental despotism." Jackson's critics warned that the general's actions set a dangerous precedent for relations between the military and civil branches of government. If Congress countenanced Jackson's conduct, they argued, the United States could get involved in war at a general's whim, without any consultation with Congress.[33]

Many commentators complained that Jackson did not seem to think he had to follow the law and found it acceptable to impose his will and power as he wished. Though his worst offense was waging war and conquering territory on his own initiative, they said, he also violated other constitutional principles. For example, he exercised legislative and executive powers in Pensacola,[34] violated states' rights by supplanting Georgia governor William Rabun's authority to appoint state militia officers,[35] and raised troops in an illegal manner.[36]

The administration permitted Jackson to act beyond and outside the law, critics objected. Calling for a military inquiry into Jackson's activities, the *Richmond Enquirer* noted that in the American system all men were subject to law: "[N]o man, however great, . . . is great enough to be above the laws of this land." Yet after the House rejected all of the proposed resolutions, the paper observed that the administration and Congress seemed inclined to let Jackson do whatever he wanted, regardless of law. An essay in the *Georgia Journal* protested that law was being subordinated to Jackson's will: "At the altar of *his* opinions, and *his* actions, the Executive, the laws of humanity and of nations, state sovereignty, nay, the *Federal Constitution itself,* must bow in humble reverence," the writer lamented. To the extent that Jackson had "the *power* of enforcing his *wishes,*" the author warned, "*laws* of *no kind* will be any restraint."[37]

To the critics, obedience to the Constitution's distribution of power was crucial for the United States' long-term survival as a republic. Military despotism and other abuses of power threatened core components of the United States' national identity. Americans were united by the nation's high ideals, and destruction of those principles threatened the bonds of nationhood. This argument perhaps was particularly important to critics because the United States lacked ethnic, cultural, linguistic, and religious homogeneity, which were markers of national identity elsewhere, and therefore shared republican ideals were a central feature of Americans' national self-image. Steady adherence to constitutional principles and correlated core values would solidify and strengthen the nation. Raw, lawless exercise of power and violence undermined the nation's most glorious strengths.

Moreover, a failure to preserve the United States' high character would have global consequences, critics argued. The United States was a model for other nations, a noble example of liberty and republican government. "We are fighting . . . a great moral battle for the benefit, not only of our country, but of all mankind," Henry Clay declared. "The eyes of the whole world are in fixed attention upon us."[38] Americans' pride in their national exceptionalism was a key component of their internal national identity. Just as important, the United States' standing abroad mattered because the United States eagerly sought European recognition of its worthiness to be a member of the European family of civilized nations.

The Persuasiveness of Supporters' and Critics' Arguments

Assessing the persuasiveness of critics' and supporters' use of sources of law available at the time does not prove which side was "right" or "wrong." Rather, it is an attempt to place contemporaries' arguments in terms of what Vattel actually wrote, what the customary practices of nations were, and what treaties and the Constitution actually said.

On the surface, supporters of the Florida campaigns seemed to apply Vattel's principles plausibly, but their version of the underlying facts is dubious. The critics' challenge to the supporters' factual assertions is persuasive. As a result, it is doubtful whether, under Vattelian principles, the United States could lawfully claim that when it seized Spanish posts at St. Marks, Pensacola, and Barrancas in 1818 it was lawfully acting out of "necessity" and in reasonable "self-defense" as an emergency action. The fact that the Monroe administration agreed to return the posts as soon as Spain could properly defend them suggests that it was aware of—and to some extent trying to demonstrate adherence to—Vattel's rules about seizing property in neutral territory, which provided that a nation could temporarily occupy such property but had to restore it once the dangerous situation had subsided. An additional legal problem was raised by American treatment of Spanish officers in St. Marks, Pensacola, and Barrancas. The Spaniards had not made common cause with the Indians but instead continued their friendly trading relationships with them. Therefore, the U.S. claim that Spanish authorities in Florida were "associates" of the Creeks and Seminoles who had forfeited their neutrality seems unsubstantiated by Vattel's definitions of the concepts of "associates" and "neutrality."[39]

As measured by Vattel's treatise, the legality of American troops' entry into Florida is a closer issue, but overall the U.S. claim still seems questionable. On the one hand, the jurist permitted a nation to pursue an enemy into a neutral's territory if the neutral nation allowed the enemy "to remain in his territories on the watch for a convenient opportunity to attack me a-new." On the other hand, he also discouraged preemptive attacks and cautioned against entering neutral territory in nonexigent situations. The United States' application of a doctrine of emergency action does not seem to have factual justification. It does not seem that U.S. passage into Spanish territory was a matter of "[u]rgent and absolute necessity" either on the ground that the American army would otherwise be "exposed to imminent destruction" or on the ground that the nation faced an equivalent imminent danger. Since the facts do not support a claim that Jackson's soldiers were actually in hot pursuit of men who had attacked Americans within the United States, on the whole the entry into Florida does not seem to have been legally justified.[40]

However, Spain probably would have had no basis for complaining that the earlier destruction of the Prospect Bluff fort in Spanish territory violated Vattel's principles because the attack seemed to have Spanish support and tacit consent. The Prospect Bluff attack of 1816 raised legal issues with regard to other parties, however. Its lawfulness with regard to the African-descended people and Indians in the fort is a separate question, one that is addressed later.

With regard to customary practices of nations on the issues of neutrality, extraterritorial armed hostilities, territorial sovereignty, occupation of territory and forts, and preemptive strikes, backers of the Florida campaigns mentioned both prior U.S. practices in Florida and previous British usages overseas. As precedent for its intrusion onto neutral Spanish territory, the United States' main argument was weak because it focused primarily on specific prior military activity of the United States in Florida. Americans' own previous actions in the same theater do not provide adequate evidence of the broader customs of nations. A somewhat stronger analogy was to British precedent. A handful of commentators referred to British acquisition of territory in various places around the world—such as India, Trinidad, Guyana, the Cape Colony, and Malta—as precedent for the U.S. occupation of Florida and seizure of forts there. British imperial activity could be plausible evidence of international practices of the time if the situations were analogous. To some extent, British acquisitions of dominion over people and territory in South America, Africa, and South Asia were different from the United States' occupation of Florida because they took place in the course of acknowledged wars with France and other European nations: Britain acquired Trinidad, Guyana, the Cape Colony, and Malta during the Napoleonic Wars, and the British East India Company gained control over significant portions of India during the War of the Austrian Succession and the Seven Years' War. In contrast, the United States itself declared that it was not at war with Spain when it occupied Spanish territory and seized or destroyed Spanish forts in the late 1810s. Territorial acquisitions that might be justified during wartime would not have the same justification during peacetime. Another distinction to consider is that European extraterritorial activities had different goals and outcomes: while Europeans sought to establish special enclaves or colonies overseas to exploit resources and bolster global commercial connections, the United States sought to incorporate contiguous continental territory fully into the nation.

Regardless of these distinctions, it is possible to see similarities between European and American occupation of territory. Parallel to the situation in Florida, some of the territories that became part of the British Empire before 1818 had previously been claimed, colonized, or occupied by other European powers or entities whose control was too weak to resist conquest by a third power (France) that was a threat to Britain: Trinidad had been claimed by the Spanish, Guyana and the Cape Colony by the Dutch, Malta by the Knights of Malta, and parts of India by various European nations' trading companies.

In short, early modern laws of war did not deter Europeans from conquest, enslavement, and extreme violence against peoples in Africa, Asia, and the Americas prior to the U.S. expeditions in Florida. Despite strident commitment to the ideal of territorial sovereignty, both the United States and European nations acted extraterritorially against weaker polities when it was expedient and advantageous to do so.[41] Like European actions overseas, American actions in Spanish Florida, too, were shaped more by relative power than by legal dictates. Though the young Republic lacked the robust army and navy it would need to confront European nations on their own turf or on the ocean, in Florida in the late 1810s the United States was a relatively strong power because neither Spain nor Britain allocated significant military resources to the distant territory, indigenous people of the region had lost their earlier military advantage over the European-descended populace, and African-heritage inhabitants were outgunned and vulnerable. The United States had the power to cross the southern borderline, occupy Spanish forts, and displace Spanish officials, and they argued that important national interests—along with Spain's lack of meaningful sovereignty in Florida—justified their actions, just as such factors provided the basis for British acquisitions around the world.

Finally, the United States' interpretation of treaties and the Constitution was selective and self-serving. It is difficult to reconcile the inconsistency between the U.S. claim that the Florida incursions did not require a congressional declaration of war because they were part of an ongoing war with Creeks and Seminoles and the U.S. insistence that an 1814 treaty ended warfare with the same Indians. If the claim about the treaty was true, then the expedition violated the Constitution's war powers provisions. Moreover, if the Indians were acting defensively rather than offensively, as seems to have been the case, then Jackson's supporters' interpretation of Pinckney's Treaty of 1795 was unwarranted. The treaty did not obligate Spain to prevent the

Creeks and Seminoles from defending themselves. The United States' arguments vis-à-vis the Constitution were similarly self-serving. U.S. initiation of war in Florida clearly violated the Constitution by circumventing congressional authorization. The Constitution gives Congress the power to declare war, yet the Monroe administration did not obtain such a declaration before sending Jackson to resolve the problems with Creeks and Indians in Florida. Overall, therefore, the supporters' reading of treaties and the Constitution did not comport comfortably with the actual language of those documents.

Regardless of how one might view the supporters' and critics' arguments today, though, contemporaries found the supporters' position convincing. The language, symbols, and images used by Jackson's supporters resonated with many Americans. Focusing in particular on John Quincy Adams's vigorous defense of Jackson, historian William Earl Weeks observes that by framing his argument in terms of "basic American myths of virtue, mission, and destiny," Adams made it difficult for anti-Jackson challenges to succeed. Weeks further points out that "[c]ritics did not realize that Adams's narrative of American courage and patriotism contrasted with foreign duplicity and depravity would render all facts to the contrary irrelevant." In fact, he writes, "Adams understood that the rhetoric of American empire would trump rational discourse in the theater of American politics."[42]

In the House of Representatives, critics of the Seminole War proposed a number of resolutions condemning various aspects of the campaigns, but their argument did not convince enough congressmen to support the anti-Jackson resolutions. The House rejected proposed resolutions that would have disapproved of the seizure of Pensacola and the fort at Barrancas as unconstitutional (by a roll call vote of 70 yeas and 100 nays), condemned the trial and execution of Alexander Arbuthnot (by a roll call vote of 62 to 108), condemned the trial and execution of Robert Ambrister (by a roll call vote of 63 to 107), prohibited U.S. troops from entering foreign territory without congressional authorization unless they were in fresh pursuit of an enemy (rejected with only 42 yeas and an unspecified number of nays), banned the execution of prisoners in peacetime or during Indian wars without the president's approval (by a vote of 57 to 98), and provided that white men who instigated or fought with Indians against the United States could be punished as spies (rejected "by a large majority").[43]

It is difficult to identify specific electoral consequences for members of the House based on their speeches or their votes on the Seminole War, because only a quarter of the 15th Congress (as it was composed in February 1819) also served in the 17th Congress, which is the first Congress that was elected after the debate. Moreover, there were several other important issues that could have influenced voters' decisions in the fall of 1820, so one cannot isolate the Seminole War as a factor in the elections. However, there is a suggestive pattern when one examines the three Seminole War resolutions for which there was a roll call vote: those relating to Pensacola, Arbuthnot, and Ambrister. Notably, of the forty-six overlapping members of the 15th and 17th Congresses, thirty took the pro-Jackson position on the resolutions in 1819, twelve voted anti-Jackson, three opted for a mixed vote, and one did not vote. Thus, of those members of the 17th Congress who took a clear position on the Seminole War in 1819, 71 percent voted to support Jackson. This does not necessarily mean that constituents favored incumbents solely because of their Seminole War votes, but it may reinforce the interpretation that the pro-Jackson view of expansionism was popular.[44]

Tactical Use of Legal Arguments

It is important to consider what motivated the legal arguments made by critics and supporters during the debate on the Seminole War. It matters whether commentators were genuinely committed to the legal principles they expressed and whether their main goal was to shape legal doctrine. It is also significant if, instead, they used legal arguments tactically to achieve other goals.

Admittedly, it is not always easy to discern true motives underlying idealistic language in the realm of foreign policy and war, but it seems that personal political ambition, especially a desire to undermine Andrew Jackson, determined some commentators' positions. In the late 1810s, underlying political rivalries led some people to use legal arguments opportunistically in order to advance their individual political careers by either defending or attacking Jackson and the Monroe administration. Allegations to that effect arose at the time: some supporters of the campaigns openly alleged that crass politics motivated the opponents, while critics responded by denying that their positions were prompted by political ambitions. Some commentators expressed unease about Jackson's rising popularity. The enthusiastic feasts held for Jackson around the country to celebrate his victory caused palpable concern that he was rousing the "passions of the people," concern that the feastings "were in the nature of an appeal from the constituted authorities, to the undefined sensations of the community."[45] The resolutions put forward in Congress proposed no punishment for Andrew Jackson; in fact, they did not even mention the general. Nonetheless, passage of the resolutions would have been an implicit condemnation of Jackson. The general himself was outraged about members of Congress questioning his conduct, seeing their criticisms as an effort to tarnish his reputation, his accomplishments, and his honor. Critics of Jackson would naturally have thought that the resolutions would discredit him and dampen his popularity. Some politicians' resentment of Jackson's celebrity and their perception that he was a political threat thus seemingly affected the positions they took on the war.

For example, in the congressional debate the Georgia representatives who opposed the war appeared to be siding with their state comrades, Governor William Rabun and Secretary of the Treasury William Crawford, both of whom had strained relationships with Jackson. Henry Clay, another political rival of Jackson's—who was also resentful that Monroe had not appointed him secretary of state—strongly condemned the general and the president for the 1818 U.S. invasion of Florida even though he had previously supported the idea of occupying West Florida. Among the supporters of the campaigns, Secretary of State John Quincy Adams is the most prominent example. The assertiveness of Adams's defense of Andrew Jackson in diplomatic correspondence masked his underlying doubts, his real audience, and his primary motives. Adams's diary reveals his disapproval of some of Jackson's conduct, as well as his recognition that his own legal argument was overstated. The diary further verifies that Adams's aggressive defense of Jackson aimed to shield the administration from criticism, gain leverage in negotiations with Spain, and enhance Adams's reputation as a possible future presidential candidate.[46] As it turned out, in the 1824 election Jackson, Adams, Clay, and Crawford would compete as candidates for president. Thus, self-interest evidently affected the legal positions that some commentators took on the Seminole War.

At the opposite end of the spectrum, some commentators were genuinely motivated by legal issues. They were deeply alarmed by Jackson's apparent disrespect for law. Critics were particularly concerned about the lack of due process afforded to Alexander Arbuthnot and Robert Ambrister before their execution on Jackson's orders. The general's claim that the rules of war did not protect the two British men because they were "outlaws" was troubling, as were the procedural irregularities and the brutal, hasty punishment. Jackson's apparent disregard for law in the Arbuthnot/Ambrister matter fed broader concerns about his tendency to impose his own will rather than respect legal and constitutional mandates. Some critics were profoundly concerned that, in the invasions of Spanish Florida, Jackson exceeded his orders, overrode civil authority, abused his power, and waged war on his own initiative. Rule of law was a fundamental principle that sincerely motivated the positions expressed by these opponents of the Seminole War. Certainly, their vision of rule of law was severely limited by their own racial-cultural biases, and they sometimes exaggerated the extent of their concern about law to maximize the force and breadth of their attack on Jackson. Nonetheless they were authentic in their concern about legal process and legal principles.

Most commentators' views fell somewhere between the self-serving pretense of the first group and the genuine concern about law expressed by the second. Clearly, most men who expressed legal opinions in the debate borrowed from theoretical foundations that best fit their end goals, using law as a tool to support their views. However, their assessments of the Florida campaigns were not merely political postures of convenience, and the debate was not purely a matter of cloaking pro- and anti-Jackson political positions in the language of law. Underneath considerations of self-interest lay principled ideological divisions and genuine differences in outlook, mentality, and policy positions. Sincere opinion about what was in the national interest determined most commentators' views on the Florida campaigns. In portions of the debate that related to Spain, commentators promoted their authentic political and diplomatic positions regarding U.S. expansionism, national security, national destiny, military power, states' rights, and relations with Europeans. Likewise, in parts of the debate that pertained to non-Europeans, commentators expressed their underlying views on race, slavery, and the status of blacks and Indians.

Supporters of the Florida expeditions genuinely believed that the United States' end goals justified the means it used. They placed the highest value on protecting national security along the southeastern border. For them, the United States' success as a nation required that it decisively terminate the ability of Indians to attack Americans from Florida, expel Europeans from a region in which the United States claimed primacy, and expand the nation's territorial borders. Because they viewed the achievement of those goals as a matter of self-defense, they found it easy to conclude that everything they did in Florida had to be legally justifiable. To supporters, the U.S. claim that the defense of its borders necessitated military action in Florida provided an absolutely justifiable cause for belligerency. Therefore, in defending the expeditions, supporters interpreted the law of nations to permit wide leeway for military action. They took full advantage of the elasticity of the terms "necessity" and "self-defense," juristic loopholes that could override customary limits on wartime violence and bans on military action in neutral territory. A nation's self-preservation, after all, was one of the most fundamental principles of the law of nations as reflected in accepted usages and Vattel's treatise. With regard to the Constitution, supporters seemed convinced that, when it came to defending the nation, the fundamental law allowed—perhaps even required—the executive branch and the military to do what was necessary. The supporters believed that the law of nations and the Constitution had to permit a nation to defend itself. Furthermore, the United States claimed that as a sovereign state it was as entitled as any nation to defend itself and to interpret the rules as it deemed fit. A firm, aggressive assertion of power in the national self-defense was necessary for the United States to demonstrate its sovereignty and thereby gain full acceptance into the European family of nations.

Most critics of the Seminole War genuinely opposed the military hostilities, even though they shared some of the supporters' goals. Opponents of the campaigns, like supporters, cared about furthering national interests. However, they believed that the United States' interests were better served if the army acted with calm moderation than if it acted aggressively in Florida. They believed that honorable restraint and strict adherence to international law would prove the United States worthy of membership in the civilized family of nations. The executions of Arbuthnot and Ambrister caused them particular uneasiness. They feared that the executions tarnished the United States' international reputation as a law-abiding nation. In addition to their different perception of the United States' interests (and, for some, different view of rule of law), critics also diverged from supporters in their interpretation of the factual circumstances underlying the Seminole War, which led them to apply the rules of war in a different way. As described above, they did not share many of the factual premises of the supporters' argument, such as the seriousness of the potential threat to the United States from St. Marks or Pensacola. They also felt less threatened by the disorder in Florida, felt confident that ongoing negotiations with Spain would result in a peaceful acquisition of Florida, and were less eager to support territorial expansion for its own sake. Consequently, they were not convinced of the urgent and exceptional circumstances alleged by supporters. Because the belligerent actions did not seem necessary for self-defense, critics concluded that the armed hostilities were not warranted in Florida. The critics' concerns and goals differed significantly from those of the supporters.

For the most part, the supporters' and critics' underlying policy positions were sincere. The genuineness of the sharp disagreements about which policies best served the national interest is indicated by the fact that divisions were apparent not just in the Seminole War debate but also in discussions of other issues. In 1819, challenges to the old ideas of Federalism were evident in the reaction against the Bank of the United States, which was blamed for the Panic of 1819, as well as in the reaction against Chief Justice John Marshall's Supreme Court decisions that supported a strong national government with expansive powers *(McCulloch v. Maryland)* and respect for property rights against state interference (the *Dartmouth College* case).[47] The future sectional divide over slavery was apparent in 1819–1820 debates about the admission of

Missouri to the Union (though it should be noted that during the Seminole War debate Congress actually did not divide cleanly along sectional lines). Just as it would be a mistake to brand as "mere partisanship" the strong statements made on these political disputes about the authority of the federal government, states' rights, and slavery, it would be wrong to presume that there were no principled differences underlying the discussion about Jackson's expeditions in Florida. Over the succeeding twenty years, those genuine differences would become magnified. A decade after the Seminole War, the nation's deep cultural rift manifested itself in the bitter presidential election of 1828, in which the candidates' supporters divided sharply over such issues as the role of morality in government, the rule of law, and constitutional interpretation. Subsequently, the very different mentalities of Democrats and Whigs made evident a profound division among Americans over fundamental political, economic, moral, religious, social, and legal issues. In sum, the political culture was not monolithic. Citizens of the early Republic did not all share the same outlook, were not just driven by partisan interests, and did not always have ulterior motives for expressing fundamental ideas. As a whole, critics and supporters of the Florida expeditions genuinely held different conceptions about the issues raised by the campaigns.

However, commentators' genuine differences about policy issues did not mean that they necessarily were committed to the abstract legal principles they used to support their positions in the debate. Many commentators used law as a tool, employing whichever legal arguments offered the best support.

That the United States was not fully committed to abstract legal principles considered in isolation from particular national interests is evidenced by the fact that later adherence to the tenets articulated during the Seminole War debate depended on the circumstances. When national interests seemed to require it, the United States shifted its legal interpretation. After the Florida campaigns, the United States took a similar legal position in later conflicts on the Mexican border but took a different position when conflicts occurred on the Canadian border. For example, American officials repeatedly supported incursions into Mexico to attack Indians in the 1830s, 1850s, and 1870s; finally in 1882 Mexico and the United States signed a treaty formalizing the right of each party to pursue Indians across the border. On the other hand, although in the Seminole War Americans argued that necessity might justify preemptive extraterritorial acts, they objected in 1837 when their own territory was invaded by the British to destroy the ship *Caroline,* which was being used by American supporters of Canadian insurgents to support rebellion in Upper Canada.[48] Varying later U.S. positions in similar situations suggest that, at least to some extent, the American legal stance depended on whether it was perceived as advancing or harming the national interest.

In fact, for most commentators on both sides of the Seminole War debate, the main purpose of the legal arguments was to further their other goals, not to establish the legal principles on their own merit. Shaping the provisions of international law was not the primary goal of the supporters nor even of most of the critics in the Seminole War debate. Rather, their underlying goals were political and diplomatic. In the Florida campaigns and the ensuing debate, the United States was less concerned about shaping the law of nations than it was about securing territory that was important for strategic and economic interests, policing the southern border, gaining control over Seminoles and Creeks, eliminating refuges for fugitive slaves, avoiding war with European nations, and asserting itself as a formidable, sovereign nation.

However, that did not mean the discussion of law was peripheral or unimportant. The fact that American officials did not regard the law of nations as prohibiting any of the actions it took in Florida does not mean that they did not care about the law of nations. They did care—had they not, they would not have gone to such lengths to explain how their actions were consistent with internationally recognized principles of law. Americans believed that to be recognized as a member of the European family of nations, the United States had to demonstrate that it was a "civilized" nation. The civilized nations were those that had a European-style government, culture, and religion and that adhered to the law of nations, especially the rules of war. The United States had expressed commitment to restraint in warfare during the War of 1812, which ended just a year and a half before the United States destroyed the Prospect Bluff fort at the beginning of the Seminole War: in 1813, Congress authorized the president to cause retaliation against the British in the event of "any violations of the laws and usages of war, among civilized nations," and in 1814 a congressional committee issued a report itemizing British violations of the rules of war. Several years after the Seminole War, American jurist James Kent succinctly articulated the American view of the law of nations: "The faithful observance of this law is essential to national character," and any nation that violated the law of nations would be subjected to "reproach and disgrace."[49] Since Americans of the early Republic believed that demonstrated adherence to the law of nations was a characteristic of all civilized nations, the United States framed its actions so as manifest their obedience to the principles of that law.

Thus, defenders of the Florida campaigns made long speeches and wrote numerous articles explaining how their actions in Spanish territory and against Spanish officials obeyed the laws of war. The fact that they framed their arguments in terms of the law of nations means that they knew that Americans cared about the law of nations—and cared especially about being seen as adhering to the laws of war. Although Jacksonians tended to distrust legal mandates that interfered with their liberties or that seemed inconsistent with their instincts about what was right, they did not reject or ignore law. They used it to justify their actions. They used it to make their actions look both legitimate and rational. Because law is perceived as neutral, the argument that the United States followed the law of nations showed that the American Republic was not arbitrary, as a monarchy might be. American officials employed rhetorical tools aggressively and effectively to defend the United States from possible criticism. They also presented the facts and the meaning of treaties in the best light, to support their claim that they acted within accepted legal principles. It was important to the American image abroad and at home that the United States be perceived as acting in accordance with law. Using the law of nations to justify U.S. actions against Spanish interests in Florida was an important part of the United States' strategy for asserting itself as a member of the European community of civilized nations. In the wake of the Seminole War, American officials used their apparent adherence to legal principles as a way of both asserting the United States' claim to Florida and protecting the nation's international reputation as law-abiding.[50]

IN 1819, THE critics' factual and theoretical arguments lost out to the pro-Jackson government position on the Seminole War. The debate that emerged in the wake of the war gave Americans the opportunity to reflect on the nation's character and image, and they were not persuaded by the critics' vision. The discussion was a battle over how to define American national identity, how to advance American interests, how to maximize the United States' reputation abroad, and how best to ensure acceptance of the United States into the European diplomatic community. Supporters and opponents of the Florida expeditions disagreed on these issues. Despite all the challenges grounded in international and constitutional law, critics of U.S. military actions were unable to convince most Americans that those actions were illegal, immoral, or against the national interest. In the end, the supporters and their slate of ideas, policies, and interpretations emerged victorious. The public debate leaned heavily in favor of the pro-Jackson position supporting expansionism and robust military action. Supporters' legal positions, emphasizing utilitarianism and power, remained popular over the long term and continued to dominate later in the nineteenth century as Americans became even more firmly devoted to asserting the United States' natural primacy in North America by eliminating threats posed by Indians and Europeans.

In the late 1810s, champions of U.S. military actions in Florida dismissively swept aside all criticism, claiming that the anti-Jackson men were basing their entire case on "imaginary grounds." Supporters of the administration mocked opponents' "spongy, pompous" speeches as "full of sound and fury signifying nothing; and, as usual, sugared over with piety [and] humanity."[51] Most Americans apparently were inclined to agree. They appreciated the tangible benefits of the Florida campaign. Jackson's actions in Florida allowed the United States to assert itself as a strong, sovereign nation, a triumph that overrode the critics' petty legalistic arguments. Rather than concurring with the condemnations of Andrew Jackson, most Americans who participated in the public debate were grateful for his accomplishments. On the question of the legality of hostilities conducted on Spanish soil against Spanish forts and Spanish officials, Representative Richard M. Johnson asserted the bottom line: Jackson's feats would help give the United States the "military fame" it needed to "secure us respect in Europe." Americans regarded that accomplishment as essential for American nation-building. Rather than questioning Jackson's—or the United States'—authority to act, Americans applauded the end results. In Representative Poindexter's words, the nation was thankful to Jackson for giving "glory and renown to the arms of your country throughout the civilized world" and for teaching "the tyrants of the earth the salutary lesson, that, in the defence of their soil and independence, freemen are invincible."[52] To most Americans of the 1810s, that was an unassailable achievement.

CHAPTER FOUR

Creeks, Seminoles, and Indian Wars

FROM THE PERSPECTIVE of the United States, Creek and Seminole legal status differed significantly from that of Spain. Both international rules of war and domestic American legal principles applied differently to indigenous people than to Europeans. Consequently, the United States argued, its legal obligations to Florida Indians in the Seminole War were quite unlike its lawful duties to Spain. The rhetoric used to support U.S. hostilities against Creeks and Seminoles in Florida illuminates American attitudes regarding the status of Indians, U.S. sovereignty and power, borders of law, and national identity.

During the debate of 1818–1819, Americans explicitly and intensively addressed the issue of Indians' status in war as never before. The question became one of widespread public debate. The issue was not entirely new; treatment of Indian combatants during the Revolutionary War and the War of 1812 had also raised questions. However, the Seminole War provided a unique occasion for in-depth public discussion of the rules of war. Strong American support for the invasion of Florida and the summary executions of Creek captives Hillis Hadjo and Homathlemico revealed white Americans' belief in Indian difference and also their conviction that they could exclude Indians from protections of law. The fact that Andrew Jackson's actions in Florida were not just tolerated but praised and endorsed signified what the broader status of Indians was to be in relation to white Americans.[1]

Creeks and Seminoles

In the eighteenth century, present-day Florida and central Georgia and Alabama contained a number of semiautonomous towns occupied by Hitchitis, Alabamas, Yuchis, Natchez, Okchais, Cowetas, Shawnees, and other Native groups. The residents' primary allegiance was to their own town and kin, though there was some sense of a common bond among the towns. Colonial Anglo-Americans categorized these southeastern Indians collectively as "Creeks," distinguishing them from Cherokees who lived farther north and Choctaws and Chickasaws to the west. Sometime before the American Revolution, the designations became more geographically specific: "Upper Creeks" were Indians living on the Alabama River and its tributaries, the Coosa and Tallapoosa Rivers; "Lower Creeks" were those residing along the Chattahoochee River; and "Seminoles" were those Creeks who had migrated to Florida. Communities in all three locations included not only a range of Indian ethnic groups but also people of African and European descent.[2]

Scholar J. Leitch Wright, Jr., notes that at the end of the eighteenth century the Creeks and Seminoles were "the most numerous and powerful of Indian people on the white frontier." He concludes that they numbered at least forty thousand. Approximately five thousand of them—the "Seminoles"—lived in Florida. Their largest town was Miccosukee, on the shores of Lake Miccosukee, just a few miles south of the U.S.-Florida border (near present-day Tallahassee). Other clusters of substantial settlements were located along the Suwannee River (Boleck's Town, Payne's Prairie, and Aluchua, near present-day Gainesville) and also along the Apalachicola River.[3]

From 1783 to 1795, most Creeks/Seminoles lived on land claimed by Spain under the terms of the Treaty of Paris. However, Pinckney's Treaty between Spain and the United States (1795) brought a significant amount of Creek territory into the American orbit by moving the United States' southern border south to the 31st parallel in the area adjacent to West Florida.[4] Over the next two decades the United States used a variety of tactics to try to gain control over the rest of the region, including the entire Gulf Coast.

In the late eighteenth and early nineteenth centuries, even though the Creeks were not tightly unified politically and Florida Indians were becoming increasingly independent, Creek negotiators who dominated the national council claimed to be acting on behalf of all Creeks. Eager to work with a centralized authority, the United States accepted the national council as representative of all Creeks, including those who lived in Spanish Florida or who otherwise regarded themselves as politically separate from Creek negotiators, had different interests than those at the treaty table, or refused to consent to bargaining over land. The U.S. assumption that U.S.-Creek treaties applied to Florida Indians was particularly important because those agreements not only ceded land to the United States but acknowledged U.S. sovereignty. As stated in Article 2 of the 1790 Treaty of New York, the Creek signatories agreed that "all parts of the Creek Nation within the limits of the United States . . . [were] under the protection of the United States of America, and of no other sovereign whosoever." Article 1's inclusion of Seminoles among those covered by the treaty, combined with American claims to sovereignty over West Florida, provided a foundation for the United States' later reliance on this statement of authority over all Creeks to justify its extraterritorial actions against Indians in Florida. Yet only the 1790 Treaty of New York explicitly included the Seminoles. The later treaties—signed in 1796, 1802, and 1805—did not specify the extent of the "Creek nation"; those other treaties gave no hint as to whether the Creek nation included the Seminoles, and the question of their membership remained ambiguous. Historian Claudio Saunt notes that by 1812 the Seminoles opposed Creek national council policies and resisted the council's authority, and council leaders acknowledged that in practice they did not govern the Seminoles. However, ethnologist William Sturtevant concludes that only the Seminole War firmly established Seminole independence of the Creeks. Not until 1823 would the United States negotiate a separate treaty with the Seminoles.[5]

Even among Creeks living within U.S. borders, not all supported national council policies. Under the leadership of William McIntosh, Lower Creeks were receptive to the civilization program run by U.S. Indian agent Benjamin Hawkins, but many Upper Creeks firmly opposed American acculturation and expansion policies. In the early 1810s, some Upper Creeks, known as Red Sticks, were inspired by Tecumseh and his brother Tenskwatawa, the Shawnee Prophet. The two Shawnees advocated for a pan-Indian religious and cultural revival to counter American civilization efforts and urged military resistance to American territorial expansion. The Red Stick Hillis Hadjo (also known as Josiah Francis or the Prophet Francis) was particularly drawn to Tecumseh and Tenskwatawa's message. A trader and silversmith from Autauga (near present-day Montgomery, Alabama), Hillis Hadjo became a spiritual leader and close comrade of Tecumseh. As reported by an American observer, during a fall 1811 visit to Creek country Tecumseh urged Creeks to regain their lost nobility and fight against the Americans.[6] The Red Sticks resisted American efforts to "civilize" Creeks, advocating for retention of traditional Creek culture and religion. They also defied American encroachment on Creek territory, opposed Lower Creek land cessions to the United States, and allied with British officers and traders who encouraged Indian unity. During the War of 1812, many Red Sticks joined with the British against the United States. Some three thousand of them received military training and arms from the British, including both Hillis Hadjo and Autosse chief Homathlemico. Some of them, including Hillis Hadjo, also obtained weapons from the Spanish and British at Pensacola.[7]

Tensions among the Creeks intensified in April 1813, when Lower Creek chiefs executed a group of Red Sticks who had killed American settlers. By spring, there was an ongoing civil war within the Creek community, with William McIntosh leading the Lower Creeks in their conflict with Hillis Hadjo, Homathlemico, and the other Red Sticks. Historians have proposed a variety of causes of the war, including tensions over land cessions, centralization efforts, new notions of property, stratification of wealth, the American civilization program, religious revival, and the pan-Indian movement, as well as deep-rooted ethnic divisions among the Creeks and stresses resulting from American, British, and Spanish activities in the Gulf Coast region before and during the War of 1812.[8]

In the summer of 1813, U.S. troops led by General Andrew Jackson got involved in the Creek War on the side of the Lower Creeks. Two years earlier, Jackson had made clear his chilling vision for the Indian tribes, writing that Indians were barbarians and banditti who "ought to be swept from the face of the earth." Historian Leonard Sadosky emphasizes Jackson's importance in establishing a new relationship between the United States and Indian nations. The "Jackson Doctrine" called for the United States to solidify its own sovereignty and security by undermining Indians' independence and isolating them from potential European allies. Once Indians were left without British or other European support, the United States would be able to exert firmer control over them. In the Creek War, Sadosky writes, Jackson saw an "opportunity to change the geopolitics of the North American interior and place the interactions between the United States and the polities on its western borders on an entirely new footing." On the battlefield and in treaty negotiations, Jackson was successful in achieving that goal.[9]

In 1814, Jackson's American soldiers and McIntosh's Lower Creek troops killed hundreds of Red Stick fighters at the Battle of Horseshoe Bend, decisively defeating them. Led by Hillis Hadjo, Homathlemico, and Peter McQueen, surviving Red Sticks fled to Spanish Florida, setting up bases near Pensacola and the Apalachicola River. There they joined with the Seminoles and continued to resist American intrusions into Indian territory.[10]

Meanwhile, Jackson forced the remaining Creek chiefs—all but one of whom had been U.S. allies—to sign the Treaty of Fort Jackson on August 9, 1814. The treaty's preamble stated that the United States had, "in conformity with principles of national justice and honorable warfare," repelled the "unprovoked, inhuman, and sanguinary war, waged by the hostile Creeks." It specified that though the United States had in good faith fulfilled all of its commitments to the Creeks, the hostile Creeks had committed "numberless aggressions . . . against the peace, the property, and the lives of citizens of the United States," contrary to Creek obligations under the 1790 Treaty of New York "between the two nations." In the substantive provisions of the Treaty of Fort Jackson, the United States demanded that the Creek nation "cease to hold any intercourse with any British or Spanish post, garrison, or town; and that they shall not admit among them, any agent or trader" who was not licensed by the United States. Furthermore, as reimbursement for its military expenses incurred in the war, the United States required the Creeks to cede twenty-three million acres of their land lying in the present-day states of Alabama and Georgia, as shown on Map 4.1. Despite Lower Creek protests, the cession included not only Upper Creek territory but also a significant amount of the Lower Creeks' land, even though they had fought as allies of the United States. The treaty was signed by three dozen Creek leaders, but not by Hillis Hadjo, Homathlemico, or Peter McQueen. Nor did Seminole leaders sign the treaty.[11]

Even though no Seminoles and only one Upper Creek had signed the Treaty of Fort Jackson, the United States presumed that the treaty bound all of the Creeks, including those in Florida, and that it brought the war to an end for all parties involved. The nonsignatory Creeks had a different perspective. They maintained that the war was not over because Lower Creek men were not authorized to sign on behalf of Upper Creeks and Seminoles. This different perception of the treaty's application became particularly pertinent a few months later, when the United States and Britain signed the Treaty of Ghent to end the War of 1812. In Article 9 of that treaty, the United States committed "to put an end . . . to hostilities with all the tribes or nations of Indians with whom they may be at war at the time of such ratification; and forthwith to restore to such tribes or nations, respectively, all the possessions, rights, and privileges, which they may have enjoyed or been entitled to in [1811], previous to such hostilities."[12] The Red Sticks and Seminoles argued that because they were still at war with the United States at the time of ratification of the Treaty of Ghent, the United States had to return to them the land that they had held in 1811, including any such land ostensibly ceded in the Treaty of Fort Jackson. In short, they maintained, the Treaty of Ghent nullified the land cession provision of the Treaty of Fort Jackson.

Red Stick and Seminole chiefs protested that the United States violated the Treaty of Ghent by refusing to acknowledge that it made the earlier Creek land cession inoperative. In petitions sent to British and Spanish officials

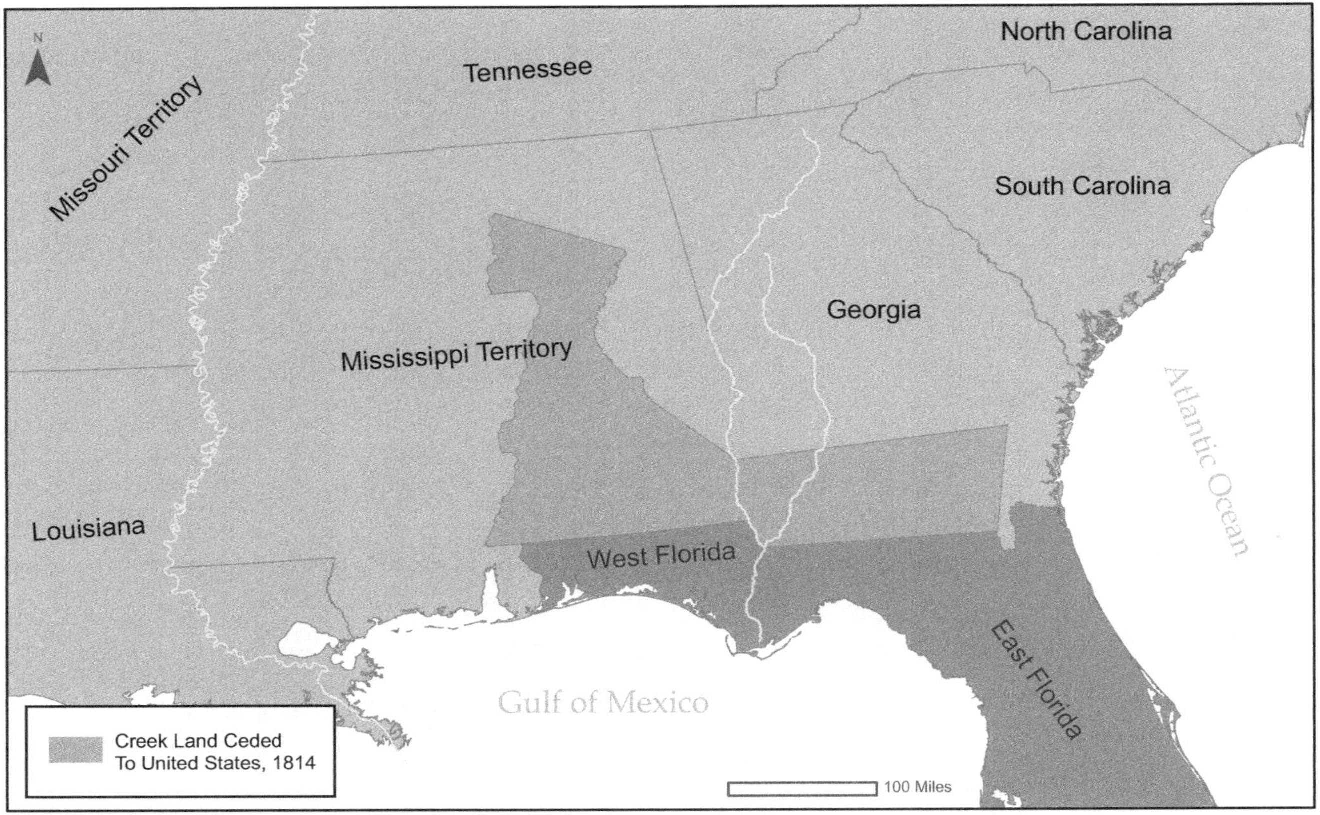

MAP 4.1 *Creek land cession in Treaty of Fort Jackson, 1814.*

between 1815 and 1817 (and later made public in the United States), the chiefs objected that the United States was illegally building roads and forts on Creek territory and that hundreds of Americans were swarming into Creek soil. The chiefs disavowed cession agreements signed by McIntosh and others who lacked authorization to convey Creek land. They worried about an imminent American attack on the main Creek towns in Florida, Miccosukee and Suwannee, and requested British military assistance. Red Sticks and Seminoles emphasized that they had refrained from offensive acts of violence against Americans. Since the Treaty of Ghent made land restoration contingent on Indian tribes' desisting from all hostilities against the United States and its citizens, the Red Stick and Seminole assurances of their peacefulness could counter potential American allegations that Indian violence nullified the obligation to return the land. Creeks and Seminoles claimed that any hostile actions of their own were solely defensive in nature, and any skirmishes between Americans and Gulf Coast Indians after the Treaty of Ghent were solely the Americans' fault.

Prominent among Creek petitions was an 1815 letter from Hillis Hadjo and twenty-nine other chiefs to the king of England. The petition expressed enmity toward Americans, the Creeks' "inveterate and never-to-be-satisfied foe," who had been told "to keep out of this nation." The document is "signed" using the mark, rather than a signature, of each chief. Apparently, neither Hillis Hadjo nor any of the other chiefs could write or sign his name. In a later letter, one chief explained that "the impossibility of finding a person to write an answer" was the reason for the delay in his responding to a letter from East Florida's Governor José Coppinger. Thus, it is likely that the documents were written or transcribed by British and Spanish men—such as Scottish trader Alexander Arbuthnot—on behalf of the Indians.[13] Nonetheless, such documents are the closest we can get today to determining the contemporary views of the Creeks and Seminoles themselves in the period leading up to the Seminole War.[14] Since the U.S. government later made the Creek and Seminole petitions and letters public, they were available to Americans as they deliberated on the lawfulness of the troops' conduct in Florida.

Another petition, from Creek chiefs to Bahamas governor Charles Cameron, warned that if the British did not supply troops and ammunition to repel an American attack, the Creeks would "soon be driven from the land we inherited from our forefathers." The chiefs declared that they "cannot submit to [American] shackles, and will rather die in defence of our country."[15] Red Sticks hoped Britain would feel both a moral impetus to help Indians who had aided them in the War of 1812 and a legal obligation to ensure fulfillment of the terms of the Treaty of Ghent. Uninterested in undertaking another war against the United States, however, British officials in London declined to promise military support.

The Seminoles sent protests authored by Chiefs Boleck and Kinache. In May and November 1816, Boleck wrote to Governor Coppinger to protest American encroachments and aggressions in the face of peaceful behavior by the Creeks. In November 1816, Kinache joined with Red Stick Peter McQueen and others in a protest letter to Charles Bagot, the British minister in the United States. Less than a year later, Kinache wrote to U.S. general Edmund P. Gaines to explain that border violence was the fault not of Seminoles but of "lawless freebooters" from the United States. Soon after, Kinache and Boleck jointly wrote to Bahamas governor Cameron, expressing fear that Gaines and Jackson planned to bring troops and settlers into Creek and Seminole territory to drive the Indians from their lands. They denounced the Americans as "lawless invaders of our soil." Finally, Kinache and two other chiefs tried to sign on to the Treaty of Ghent: in a document titled "Accession of Muscogee Indians to the Treaty of Peace of 1814," they agreed to Article 9 of the treaty and confirmed that they had ordered their people to desist from hostilities against Americans, in accordance with that treaty.[16]

Americans bluntly denied that the Treaty of Ghent had any relevance to implementation of the Treaty of Fort Jackson. Although initially some thought the Madison administration would be willing to apply the Treaty of Ghent to the Creeks, in July 1815 Secretary of State James Monroe officially asserted on behalf of the government that Article 9 had no bearing with regard to Creek lands because the Treaty of Fort Jackson was concluded before the Treaty of Ghent. Two years after the signing of the latter treaty, when Monroe took over the presidency, the United States continued its firm stance. When, at the Creek chiefs' request, Arbuthnot demanded that U.S. officers at Fort Gaines explain why Americans were descending the Chattahoochee River and taking possession of Indian homes and fields, an American provided a straightforward answer: "[I]n right of, and conformably to, [the Treaty of Fort Jackson]; for this part of the territory was ceded to us as a compensation for expenses and aid furnished and incurred by the friendly Creek Indians, against McQueen and his party; not having any reference or touching any article or part of the [Treaty of Ghent]."[17]

With the United States insisting that the Treaty of Ghent had no impact on execution of the treaty with the Creeks, tensions between Florida Indians and American settlers and soldiers continued. Americans rushed to establish themselves on the territory acquired under the Treaty of Fort Jackson, the U.S. military built several forts there, and the federal government included ceded land in the jurisdiction of the Mississippi Territory. Violence escalated in 1816 and 1817. Feeling threatened by African-descended people and Indians who controlled the Prospect Bluff fort overlooking the Apalachicola River after the 1815 departure of the British, the United States—with assistance from Lower Creek leader McIntosh—destroyed the outpost in July 1816. In

November 1817, American soldiers attacked the Creek village of Fowltown in southeastern Georgia, an action that Alexander Arbuthnot characterized as an offensive act of war. Soon after, a party of Indians attacked a boat containing forty American soldiers and family members as they traveled up the Apalachicola River toward a new American fort in southeastern Georgia, Camp Crawford (later known as Fort Scott). Most of Lieutenant Richard W. Scott's party died in the ambush. Three months later, Seminoles murdered three members of the Garrett family, including a woman and her two young children, in southeastern Georgia near the Florida border.[18]

In late 1817 and early 1818, Americans claimed that Red Sticks, Seminoles, and allied blacks were preparing for war against them. In a November 1817 letter to Jackson from Fort Scott, General Gaines estimated that there were more than two thousand Red Stick and four hundred black soldiers prepared to fight the United States, and that George Woodbine of the Corps of Colonial Marines had promised them British assistance. A week later, following the attack on the Scott party, Gaines warned the secretary of war that the security of the frontier depended on strong retaliation by the Americans for such outrages committed by the Indians. Although the president had previously prohibited striking Indians "below the line" (i.e., south of the border), Gaines wrote that attacks like that on the Scott party changed the legal situation. Apparently aware of the rules of war, Gaines justified the incursion into Florida in advance. The Scott massacre legally justified an American response because "self-defence is sanctioned by the privilege of self-preservation," he wrote. Two days later Gaines followed up with more forceful language suggesting that the United States was not bound by the usual rules of international law when dealing with uncivilized people. "The savage must be taught and compelled to do that which is right, and to abstain from doing that which is wrong," he declared. "The poisonous cup of barbarism cannot be taken from the lips of the savage by the mild voice of reason alone; the strong mandate of justice must be resorted to and enforced." He added: "[I]t is a melancholy truth, that in no Indian nation within my knowledge, (the Chickasaws excepted,) has the scalping knife been laid aside for any considerable length of time, until their every hope of using it with impunity had been defeated."[19]

Likewise, Andrew Jackson advocated strong action against Florida Indians, characterizing them as uncivilized and beast-like. In mid-December, he informed the acting secretary of war that if the hostility of "the savages" continued, "the protection of our citizens will require that the wolf be struck in his den." Successful handling of the Indian problem along the southeastern border would require U.S. troops to attack Seminole bases within Florida, he wrote. In January 1818, in a circular seeking to raise troops, Jackson declared, "The Seminole Indians have raised the war hatchet. They have stained our land with the blood of our citizens: their war spirit must be put down, and they taught to know that their safety depends upon the friendship and protection of the United States."[20]

On March 20, 1818, former royal marine Robert Ambrister wrote an urgent letter to Governor Cameron warning that "[t]here is now a very large body of Americans and Indians, which I expect will attack us every day." At the request of Hillis Hadjo and other Creek chiefs, he pressed the British government to supply Creeks with weapons and ammunition so they could defend themselves. The Americans had commenced hostilities two years previously and were making steady progress toward taking over the entire territory, he explained. Without British aid, they would have to surrender.[21]

By the time Ambrister wrote his letter on March 20, American troops were already positioned in Florida at Prospect Bluff, secure in newly built Fort Gadsden. Within a week, 2,800 Americans under Andrew Jackson, accompanied by 1,400 Creeks under William McIntosh, began their sweep through Florida, with the professed goal of decisively ending the ongoing border conflict with the hostile Red Sticks and Seminoles. They destroyed the Seminole towns around Lake Miccosukee on March 31 and April 1, seized St. Marks on April 7, burned Seminole and black towns along the Suwannee River over a few days in mid-April, and took Pensacola on May 23. Along the way, they killed or captured dozens of Seminoles and Red Sticks.[22]

On April 3, 1818, near the Spanish fort at St. Marks, an American naval commander in the waters near the fort lured Red Stick leaders Hillis Hadjo and Homathlemico onto his warship by flying a British flag. Learning about the two prisoners after he seized St. Marks on April 7, Jackson ordered Hillis Hadjo and Homathlemico to be summarily hanged on April 8. Jackson alleged that Homathlemico had led the group of Indians who slaughtered Scott's party, and he called the two men "the prime instigators of this war."[23]

As Jackson conducted the Seminole War, he framed his actions so as to explain their lawfulness. His reports to the secretary of war stated that his actions were necessary for American self-defense and characterized the Indians and blacks as savage and uncivilized. Jackson's reports, along with other prewar and wartime military and diplomatic correspondence, which was made public, provided the documentary foundation for American legal arguments made after the war.

Aftermath and Reactions

Unfortunately, surviving documents do not reveal Seminole and Creek reactions to the executions of the two Red Stick prisoners, the killing and capturing of other Indians, or the destruction of Seminole towns. Nor is there evidence of responses by other Indian tribes. Probably because of difficulty finding someone to present Florida Indians' views in English after mid-1818, there are far fewer documents from them in the period immediately after the executions as compared with the few years immediately preceding the 1818 invasion. Moreover, efforts to create a strong pan-Indian movement weakened after the War of 1812, lessening the chances of a unified, vocal response to the executions from Indians outside of Florida. Most notably, the Red Sticks' ally and inspiration, Tecumseh, had been killed by U.S. forces under General William Henry Harrison in the Battle of the Thames in 1813.[24]

Internal conflicts within the Creek nation—between McIntosh's Lower Creeks and the Red Sticks—continued after 1818. Red Stick animosity toward McIntosh, already intense because of his military role at Horseshoe Bend in 1814 and Prospect Bluff fort in 1816, intensified further because of his active participation in Jackson's 1818 invasion. Red Sticks also resented McIntosh's role in agreeing to land cessions. He had been a leading signatory of the Treaty of Fort Jackson. In secret, McIntosh profited handsomely from bribes paid in connection with the 1814 treaty, as well as other treaties that he negotiated or signed. Eleven years after the Treaty of Fort Jackson, he negotiated the Treaty of Indian Springs, under which the Creeks ceded to Georgia all of their lands east of the Chattahoochee River and agreed to move west of the Mississippi River. Other leading Creeks denounced the treaty and ordered McIntosh's execution. Two months after McIntosh signed the treaty, Red Stick leader Menawa—who had fought against McIntosh and the Americans at Horseshoe Bend—led a group of incensed Creeks who assassinated McIntosh at his home. Later, Congress ruled that the Treaty of Indian Springs was fraudulent. The Creeks negotiated a new treaty with the United States. Nonetheless, they still had to surrender most of their land, and by the end of the 1820s the United States had moved most Creeks to Indian Territory west of the Mississippi River.[25]

The Seminoles signed a separate treaty with the United States a few years after Spain ceded Florida. In the 1823 Treaty of Moultrie Creek, the Seminoles agreed to "continue under . . . the protection of the United States." They also promised to relocate to a four-million-acre reservation in central Florida, give up other land claims in Florida, and apprehend and return fugitive slaves.[26] White southerners were dissatisfied and called for the removal of the Seminoles out of Florida. After Andrew Jackson became president of the United States and pushed the Indian Removal Act through Congress in 1830, the United States pressed the Seminoles to sign the 1832 Treaty of Payne's Landing, which provided for the Seminoles to move to Creek territory west of the Mississippi River and to be "re-admitted" as members of the Creek nation.[27] Some chiefs signed and some Seminoles moved west, but others resisted. The Second Seminole War erupted in 1835, when Seminoles refused to acquiesce with the removal. When the bloody war ended seven years later, the United States had succeeded in moving thousands of the Seminoles, but hundreds still remained in Florida. Indeed, today's Seminole Tribe of Florida has chosen to print the slogan "Voice of the Unconquered" beneath the masthead of their official newspaper, *The Seminole Tribune*. Other Seminoles survive as members of the Miccosukee Tribe of Indians of Florida and the Seminole Nation of Oklahoma.[28]

Among Americans, the treatment of Hillis Hadjo and Homathlemico was one of the subjects discussed during the congressional debate in the winter of 1819, and many newspapers commented on the executions in 1818 and 1819. Because Americans had fashioned a lower threshold for unlawful treatment of Indians than of Europeans, they were less concerned about the fate of Hillis Hadjo, Homathlemico, and other Creeks and Seminoles than that of Spaniards and Britons in Florida.[29] There was widespread consensus among congressmen and also in newspaper publications that neither the military operation against the Red Sticks and Seminoles nor the summary executions of Hillis Hadjo and Homathlemico violated U.S. law or the international rules of war. In January 1819, an essay in the *Albany Argus* declared confidently that nobody denied Jackson's right to execute any Indians he captured.[30] Indeed, the debate in the House of Representatives seemed to take for granted that the "Seminoles"—congressmen's common designation for all Indians in Florida, including Red Sticks—could expect no legal protection.

American Indians and the Law of Nations

Scholars of the history of international law describe two major phases of legal development between the medieval period and the early twentieth century. From the thirteenth to the eighteenth centuries, jurists expressed a universalistic approach that assumed all humans had the same natural rights and all nations had an obligation to provide the protections of fundamental law universally. Then, a shift occurred in the late nineteenth century. In contrast to the earlier view, late nineteenth century international law provided a positivist legal order that was specific to "civilized" nations, as defined by the Europeans who viewed themselves as not only the creators of international law but also the exemplars of civilization. This new version of international law was a particularist body of doctrine that applied by mutual agreement among European and European-heritage states. It did not apply equally to or protect people in non-European, nonsovereign polities, which were perceived as existing in a "distinct legal universe."[31] Writings from the thirteenth century through the early twentieth century provide substantial evidence of these two different theoretical approaches to law and of the transformation that occurred in the late nineteenth century.

However, this broad account of legal developments omits the Americas. When the history of laws governing relations between peoples includes Natives of the Western Hemisphere and other non-Europeans, it is evident that medieval and early modern European writers qualified their concept of "universal" natural law. During early European colonization of the Americas, jurists continued to rely in principle on the medieval natural law foundation that claimed universal application but also found ways to justify the European practice of applying different rules to indigenous peoples. In reality, Europe's "universalist" natural law in that era was limited by Eurocentric and Christian-centric conceptions.[32]

A schematic history of Europeans' perspective on the applicability of the European law of nations to non-Europeans should highlight four (not just two) different periods. In the medieval era, there was an automatic legal line between Christians and "infidels"; Christian Europeans argued that they had the right to conquer Muslim territory during the Crusades because infidels could not be sovereign and divine law entitled Christians to dominion over Muslim lands and peoples. In the sixteenth century, European jurists' new framework rejected the idea that Christians automatically had the right to dominate non-Christians but nonetheless justified asserting dominion over Native Americans based on the tenet that the Natives' natural rights were dependent on their behaving a certain way. In the third period, which prevailed roughly from the eighteenth century to the mid-nineteenth century, a new view maintained that Europeans had no right of dominion over non-Europeans regardless of whether or not they followed European norms of behavior. Finally, the last few decades of the nineteenth century witnessed another theoretical shift. Legal writers in this fourth period contended that "civilized" (European-heritage) people automatically had the right to assert dominion over "uncivilized" (non-European) people and their territory. Uncivilized people could not have sovereignty. The late nineteenth-century ("civilized") European claim of entitlement to ("uncivilized") non-Europeans' lands paralleled the medieval (Christian) European claim of entitlement to (non-Christian) non-Europeans' lands.

The U.S. defense of the Seminole War took place during the third period of development but anticipated the ideas of the fourth period—ideas that would not dominate European international law theory until the late nineteenth-century.

When the young Republic had the opportunity in the 1810s to articulate its vision of how the law of nations applied to its own actions in North America, it made differences between peoples a central factor. While medieval and early modern European scholars apparently had not perceived their peripheral comments about non-Europeans as contradicting the basic premise of natural law universalism, white Americans, who had people of non-European heritage within their midst, had to confront the issue of difference more directly. In the Seminole War debate, they bluntly articulated a racial-cultural line defining the law's applicability. Although the United States' approach to the law of nations added new elements and made difference an acknowledged and pivotal factor, it had roots in the exceptions suggested in earlier European theories. To understand how Americans' view of their obligations toward Indians under the law of nations grew out of but also modified European ideas, it is important to examine in depth what Europeans wrote about the legal status of Native peoples of the Americas in the sixteenth, seventeenth, and eighteenth centuries.

Both Catholic and Protestant jurisprudential scholars of the Renaissance era provided a legal rationale for exemptions from the usual standards of universal application of law. In the sixteenth century, the most influential Spanish theorist of legal doctrine governing relations with American Indians was Francisco de Vitoria (1483–1546), a Dominican scholar at the University of Salamanca. Vitoria's theory had roots in theologically oriented medieval rationales for the Crusades, which justified Christians' conquest of infidels' lands, but he modified that older theory. Although his famous 1539 lecture, "On the American Indians," recognized the indigenous peoples of the Americas as human beings entitled to the same natural rights as Europeans, he also said that Spaniards could wage just war against Indians who diverged from what Europeans considered to be rational, universal norms. If Indians refused to welcome Spanish missionaries into their communities, hindered missionaries' conversion efforts, declined to engage in trade with Spaniards, or engaged in human sacrifice, the Spanish were entitled to use armed force against them. Under such circumstances, Spaniards could conquer the Indians, coerce their conversion, enslave them, and seize their property as a way both to protect Spanish rights and to teach Indians to be rational, civilized people. Additionally, Vitoria said that Indians' lack of laws, magistrates, systematic agriculture, manufacture, literature, arts and crafts, and civilized food might justify the Spaniards' exercising guardianship over them as a matter of charity. In fact, he concluded, since the barbarian Indians appeared "little different from brute animals," it might be fitting to govern them as slaves.[33]

Protestant writers built upon the Spanish discourse of colonialism and conquest. In *De Iure belli* (On the law of war), published in three volumes in the late 1590s, Oxford professor Alberico Gentili (1552–1608) agreed with Vitoria that Europeans had the right to wage war against people who violated natural law. Though Gentili denied that mere Indian resistance to hearing the Gospel justified European violence, he maintained that Europeans could make just war on Indians who were "destitute of any religious belief," "practiced abominable lewdness," or committed other sins that were "contrary to human nature." Indians' nonconformity with European notions of normal, moral behavior made them the "common foes of mankind" who were justly subject to violent punishment and conquest.[34]

England employed such doctrines as legal rationales when it colonized Virginia in the seventeenth century. Legal scholar Robert A. Williams, Jr., identifies several examples of such discourse: The Virginia Company's instructions permitted the use of coercion—even deadly coercion—against Indians who engaged in idolatry and devil worship. A 1609 sermon by Puritan preacher Robert Gray proclaimed that the English could lawfully make war on the Indians because of their "barbarous kinds of life," their "brutish manners," and their lack of real government. In 1622, the Virginia Company voided a land grant that had been conditioned on approval by the Indian emperor Opechancanough, on the ground that an infidel could not have sovereign authority over land. Lawyer Edward Waterhouse declared that, under the law of nations, the 1622 Indian assault on the Virginia settlements provided the English with a just cause for war against the "wicked infidels." A 1625 publication by Puritan preacher Samuel Purchas concluded that the Virginia Indians' 1622 massacre had made them "Outlaws of Humanity" who had forfeited their natural rights under the law of nations.[35]

At a time when Europeans expressed ideas that excepted indigenous people from natural law doctrine, it is unsurprising that their practices of warfare against Indians would be unconventional. Focusing on English colonies in the lands that later became the United States, historian John Grenier has provided a scathing history of frontiersmen's irregular tactics used against Indians, especially killing civilians and destroying enemy crops and homes. He particularly notes the frequent execution of enemy captives. Specifically, he describes many instances in which frontiersmen killed prisoners, turned a blind eye to Indian allies' killing of enemy prisoners, offered bounties for enemy scalps, and slaughtered enemy combatants and noncombatants who could have been captured alive instead. Grenier describes such behavior by frontier fighters in extirpative colonial wars against the Powhatans in Virginia (including the execution of the captive chief Opechancanough), against the Tuscaroras and Yamasees in the Carolinas, and against the Pequots,

Wampanoags, Narragansetts, and Abenakis in New England. He points out that such behavior continued to be evident against enemy Iroquois tribes and the Delawares during the Seven Years' War. Grenier points out that Europeans in America blanketly branded Indian warfare as savage but tended to categorize their own style of warfare as civilized even though they engaged in the same kind of brutalities that they charged to Indians.[36] Other historians, too, have described the violence of white-Indian relations throughout the colonial period. Notably, both sides executed captives in wartime, including both combatants and civilians.[37] The history of past usages in warfare with Indians was replete with unrestrained violence. The laws of war, which were supposed to provide humanitarian constraints on the conduct of warfare, rarely prevented such violence in practice. Relations between whites and Indians in colonial North America stubbornly resisted adherence to formal European theories of international law.

Those European theories took another turn near the end of the British colonial period in mainland North America. Enlightenment ideas, which led jurists to shift their view of the applicability of the law of nations, had the potential to change how the rules of war applied in conflicts with Indians. Now legal scholars rejected both the notion that Christians automatically had the right of dominion over non-Christians and also the idea that Europeans could acquire the right of dominion over non-Europeans who did not adhere to European cultural norms of behavior. Mid-eighteenth-century authors such as Christian Wolff (1679–1754) and Emer de Vattel (1714–1767) declared that non-European peoples were equal to European peoples, and the latter had no right to dominate the former. Yet even these Enlightenment thinkers had difficulty equally accommodating people whom they saw as culturally different.

Vattel, author of the influential 1758 treatise *The Law of Nations,* condemned "usurpers" who imposed their rule on American Indians. "Those ambitious Europeans who attacked the American nations, and subjected them to their greedy dominion, in order, as they pretended, to civilise them, and cause them to be instructed in the true religion," he wrote, "grounded themselves on a pretext equally unjust and ridiculous." He asserted the general position that it is wrong for one nation to use force to impose a religion on another. Additionally, he condemned nations that used violence to expand the boundaries of their own territory. He explained that "no nation has a right to expel another people from the country they inhabit, in order to settle in it herself." In fact, whenever a nation has subdued another people and seized "all the rights of the nation, and of the sovereign," its acts are unjust even if the nation does not expel the other people from their land or destroy their property. "[T]he least encroachment on the territory of another is an act of injustice," he declared. Even "wandering" people were entitled to the land they used, and Europeans could not justly deprive them of that land.[38]

However, the Swiss jurist also articulated some principles that either directly or indirectly supported the idea that it was legal to treat American Indians differently than Europeans. Notably, at several points in his treatise he referred to Indians as "savages." His use of that term established the foundation for a line between "civilized" and "uncivilized" people, which had the effect of dehumanizing non-Europeans. In wars between Europeans and Native people, Vattel thus made it easier to dispense with the usual rules.[39] Although *The Law of Nations* presented standards for dealing with prisoners and noncombatants in a neutral manner, its reference to Indians as "savages" reinforced Americans' propensity to use perceived cultural differences to justify evading humanitarian constraints on violent conduct during war. Moreover, Vattel's description of the principle of retaliation provided a potential legal justification for executing Indian prisoners of war: if an enemy officer had killed captives, the jurist wrote, a nation had the right to retaliate by doing the same to an equal number of the prisoners it held.[40]

Vattel did not just imply that the law of nations regarded Europeans and non-Europeans differently; he explicitly described cultural differences and explained the legal consequences of those differences. With regard to the impact on American Indians, the most devastating Vattelian position was his judgment about what constituted a meaningful use of land. At several points in the treatise, he emphasized that humans were obligated to cultivate the soil. In fact, because "[t]he earth . . . belongs to mankind in general, and was designed to furnish them with subsistence," the law of nature required every nation to make its own land productive. Those who subsisted by raising livestock and hunting did not actually own their "extensive tracts" because they did not use them responsibly. They "ranged through rather than inhabited" their territory; "[t]heir unsettled habitation in those immense regions cannot be accounted a true and legal possession." Wandering tribes "cannot exclusively appropriate to themselves more land than they . . . are able to settle and cultivate," he wrote. Because they obstructed a fuller use of the land that would feed more people, they were usurping more territory than they needed or were entitled to. Consequently, they would have "no reason to complain, if other nations, more industrious, and too closely confined, come to take possession of a part of those lands." On this basis, European settlements in North America might, "on confining themselves within just bounds, be extremely lawful." Later in the treatise, Vattel elaborated: "The savages of North America had no right to appropriate all that vast continent to themselves: and since they were unable to inhabit the whole of those regions, other nations might without injustice settle in some parts of them, provided they left the natives with a sufficiency of land." Thus, he justified Europeans' taking possession of American Indians' lands on the ground that they were nomadic people who were not fully utilizing the land and did not need all of it.[41] This argument later served as a fundamental premise for the American concept of manifest destiny.

Cultural differences between Indians and Europeans could also warrant different treatment of Indians' property, Vattel said. Though the rules of war normally prohibited destruction of enemy towns, the jurist made an exception when such mass destruction of towns was necessary for "chastising an unjust and barbarous nation, of checking her brutality, and preserving ourselves from her depredations." It was also permissible to "ravage a country and render it un-inhabitable, in order to make it serve us as a barrier, and to cover our frontier against an enemy whose incursions we are unable to check by any other means." Both of these tenets were potentially pertinent in the Florida campaigns.[42]

Finally, Vattel's definitions of what constituted lawful war were biased against the Native people of the Americas. He explained that the laws of war pertained to "public war," that is, war "which takes place between nations or sovereigns, and which is carried on in the name of the public power, and by its order." Only a sovereign power had the authority to make war. Private war between individuals did not fall under the rubric of the law of nations. Vattel defined "nations" or states as "bodies politic, societies of men united together for the purpose of promoting their mutual safety and advantage by the joint efforts of their combined strength."[43] These statements could provide support for assertions that the law of nations applied only to relations between sovereign nations and that Indian polities were not sovereign nations.

Thus, Vattel was an Enlightenment thinker who viewed natural law as the governing precept of the law of nations, asserted the equality of all individuals and all nations, condemned states that conquered other peoples, and denied that Europeans were entitled to impose their dominion on non-Europeans. His doctrines could have provided strong support for the rights of American Indians. Yet his ideas about sovereign nationhood, the obligation to cultivate land, and the right of retaliation had the potential to negate the positive impact his views might have had on Native peoples. Vattel was the predominant authority on the law of nations at the time when the United States declared its independence, and Americans relied frequently on his treatise to explain their international law positions.

As conflict between Britain and the American colonies intensified in the 1760s and 1770s, the colonists drew significantly from Enlightenment discourse. They emphasized natural law principles and expressed the new theoretical position on the legal status of Indians. Natural law doctrine provided a useful framework for challenging positive law emanating from Parliament and the king. Higher-law arguments provided a credible foundation for challenging imperial policy not only on such issues as taxation, representation, standing armies, and jury trials but also on the subject of Indian relations. The British effort to prevent colonists' settlement and land purchases in Indian country west of the Appalachians, especially as expressed in the Royal Proclamation of 1763, provoked vociferous American protests. To bolster their own interests, colonists who had purchased (or wanted to purchase) land directly from Indian tribes claimed not only that they had a natural law right to acquire property without government interference but also that Indians had a natural law right to sell their land. In this vision, indigenous people were not outlaws but were instead eligible beneficiaries of universal natural law. In a 1781 pamphlet, *Public Good,* Samuel Wharton explained that this modern, enlightened view of Indians had replaced an older view expressed in "more ignorant and superstitious ages."[44]

Yet, even if revolutionary leaders formally recognized Indians' natural rights, they also believed that Indians, typically categorized together as an indistinguishable group, could easily forfeit those rights through savage behavior. One of the grievances listed in the Declaration of Independence—blaming Britain for instigating frontier attacks by "the merciless Indian savages, whose known rule of warfare is an undistinguished destruction of all ages, sexes, and conditions"—characterized Indians collectively as not following the rules of war. Scholars who have studied Native American rules of warfare have found that they did not subscribe to the same rules of war as those proclaimed by European-descended people. They had their own rules. Because of the deep cultural differences between the two groups—because they were not following the same rulebook—each side misunderstood, abhorred, and distrusted the other. The result was heightened brutality in warfare, especially notable in the atrocious treatment of prisoners.[45] Thus, even during a period when European Americans said they respected Indians' natural rights, they did not feel obliged to adhere to their own laws of war when dealing with Indians who did not fight in a European style or follow the European customs of warfare.

Historian John Grenier points out that, during the Revolutionary War and the early Republic, Americans continued the pattern of colonial-era warfare against Indians. During the war Americans exhibited brutal behavior against Shawnees, Cherokees, Delawares, Chickamaugas, Mohawks, and Senecas, and then in the years following independence they engaged in irregular warfare against Chickamaugas and Creeks in the Old Southwest and against Shawnees in the Old Northwest. Given the events that unfolded during the Seminole War, an American officer's 1779 execution of four pro-British Indian prisoners as a way of pressuring the British to surrender Fort Sackville is a telling example of American warfare tactics during the Revolution.[46] Thus, although during the Revolutionary War era Americans sometimes supported Natives' natural rights, in practice they did not usually apply "universal" principles of law to Indians.

In any case, once Americans secured their independence, they deemed an exclusionary conception of law to be more advantageous, and they abandoned the pretense of a commitment to Indians' natural law rights. Where they had previously argued that Indians had a natural law right to sell their land to colonists, they now contended that ultimate sovereignty over Indian soil lay not with Indian tribes but with the U.S. government, by devolution from the British Crown.[47] Thus, after the Revolution, Americans carried on most elements of the basic European theoretical construct. They adopted a savage-civilized distinction, identifying themselves and Europeans as civilized and others as savage. They viewed the laws of war as binding them only when they were fighting Europeans, that is, fellow members of the "civilized" world. Increasingly in the early national period, a presumption of racial inferiority reinforced a dehumanized view of Indians, making it even easier to treat them brutally in wartime. Perceived racial distinctions compounded the cultural differences that had long been at the heart of European Americans' conviction that the rules of war did not limit them in their battles with presumed savage people, such as Indians. In wars with Native peoples, European Americans denied that they had to obey natural or customary practices that normally applied between nations. As a result, in such wars Americans' conduct was "unrestrained."[48]

The Seminole War fit the pattern of warfare that had been evident in British North America since the sixteenth century. In the wake of the war, for the first time the United States had an extensive public debate about Indian warfare. In justifying the Florida campaigns of the late 1810s, Americans framed their practices in terms that would become familiar in European treatises of the late nineteenth century—which also had similarities to the ways in which European jurists had justified the Crusades in the medieval period.

Specifically, during the Seminole War and in the subsequent debate about the war, Americans claimed their automatic superior claim to Indian lands. They might have ceded their claim to Spain if that European country had exerted actual control over Florida. From the U.S. perspective, meaningful Spanish sovereignty in Florida was absent, and the territory was actually in the possession of Creeks and Seminoles. To white Americans, that was not a tolerable situation. They believed that Providence entitled them to dominion in Indian lands, and therefore they had a right to impose that dominion. By asserting in the 1810s that as civilized people they had an automatic claim to the land of uncivilized people, Americans articulated the principles of long-standing practice in North America and also anticipated the legal theory normally associated with the late nineteenth century.

Moreover, the Seminole War debate made it evident that Americans also added another element that usually went unstated in published treatises on law: race. They conflated all Indians together into a single group, attributing to all the perceived "uncivilized" behaviors of some members of the group. They did not believe it necessary to assess the degree of civilization of any particular community of Indians but presumed that every polity made up of people who were racially classified as Indian lacked civilization, regardless of the group's actual cultural practices. Presumed to be uncivilized people, Indian polities necessarily lacked sovereignty in Americans' eyes. In practice, that was also how European imperialist ventures worked in the late nineteenth century: nonwhite people were categorically presumed to be "uncivilized" and to lack sovereignty, thus warranting their exclusion from the protections of international law.

The Seminole War debate shows that the shift from eighteenth- to nineteenth-century legal doctrine was not as abrupt and total as usually described. Elements of late nineteenth-century legal doctrine—especially the racially inflected civilized/savage and sovereign/nonsovereign distinctions—did not appear suddenly during the "age of imperialism." Rather, there was considerable precedent well before that time, including ideas manifested during the Florida campaigns. The principles expressed in the Seminole War debate articulated the reality of white-Indian relations, a reality that went counter to formal legal theory, and at the same time it also augured late nineteenth-century European jurists' views of the applicability of law to non-Europeans.

CHAPTER FIVE

Civilization and Nationhood

For those who endorsed armed hostilities against Creeks and Seminoles, both the constitutional rationale and the justifications based on treaty obligations, precedent, self-defense, and military necessity echoed arguments presented in support of Andrew Jackson's treatment of Spanish officials. However, other legal explanations for treatment of the Florida Indians had no counterpart in the rationale for entering Spanish territory and forts. Beyond the reasoning applied to Spain, the United States made additional arguments that were specific to Hillis Hadjo and Homathlemico, to Red Sticks and Seminoles, or to all Indians aggregated into a single category. The latter arguments drew on perceived distinctions between "civilized" and "barbaric" people as assessed from a Eurocentric perspective. In making these claims, government officials and military officers relied on the principle that the law of nations applied only to "civilized" people who were constituted as "nations." They presumed that Red Sticks and Seminoles failed to meet those standards on the ground that they were members of a group that was inferior culturally, racially, and politically. Americans concluded that because the law of nations did not apply to Florida Indians, the United States did not have to obey the laws of war in dealing with them. As will be seen, such arguments were at the forefront of broader intellectual developments in the field of international law and played a significant role in American nation-building.

The Constitution and the State of War Issue

As previously discussed, possible abuse of power was a significant issue in the debate about U.S. military actions in Florida. The leading constitutional objection to the Seminole War was that a military general had waged war against Spain and against Indians without congressional authorization. Because this war extended outside of U.S. borders, some said, it was distinguishable from internal Indian wars and required congressional authorization. If the president had approved Jackson's invasion, then he had unconstitutionally extended executive authority and intruded on Congress's sphere of power. If the president had not sanctioned the invasion, then Jackson himself had sidestepped legislative authority. Either way, the invasion infringed on Congress's exclusive constitutional authority to declare war, critics claimed.

The Monroe administration responded that Jackson's actions did not constitute "war" against Indians, so Congress's power to declare war was irrelevant. Supporters claimed there could be no such thing as a war between the United States and Indians because, in their view, Indians were not independent of the United States and therefore were not foreign enemies. The United States had never before considered it necessary or appropriate to require a formal congressional declaration of war with Indians, they said. Since fighting an Indian enemy was not war, Jackson and Monroe did not violate the Constitution by circumventing Congress.[1]

Others acknowledged that Jackson had conducted war but claimed that the Constitution required no fresh declaration from Congress because the Seminole War was a continuation of both the Creek War and also "the war which the Seminoles and other Creek Indians carried on against the frontiers of Georgia in the year 1812, and afterwards." Alternatively, some argued, no fresh declaration of war was required because the Seminole War was a continuation of perpetual war against Indians generally. Having a "standing declaration of defensive war against the Indians," there was no need to get congressional authorization for each separate engagement in that war. Pro-Jackson commentators apparently were not troubled by the conflict between alleging a state of continuing or perpetual war and contending that the war with the Creeks and Seminoles ended with the Treaty of Fort Jackson. The contradictory assertions were intended to serve different purposes: the claim of perpetual war was to justify military action without a congressional declaration of war, while the claim that the state of war ended in 1814 was to counter Creek claims to land that was not returned to them after the Treaty of Ghent.[2]

In relation to U.S. military measures against Creeks and Seminoles, more pressing than domestic constitutional issues was how those actions fit into the laws of war. Some of the issues paralleled legal arguments raised in connection with Spain. Particularly notable are U.S. justifications for American military actions based on interpretations of treaty obligations, past practices, and Emer de Vattel's concepts of self-defense and military necessity.

Treaty Obligations and Customary Practices

For positivists, explicit agreements between nations and actual practices were the best sources of international law. In 1818 and 1819, the United States avowed its respect for law as embodied in formal agreements, including treaties with Indian tribes. In contrast to England and Spain's reliance on "the law of force" in their relations with Indians, Americans boasted, the United States had always acted in accordance with agreements with Indian tribes. It had not extended into Indian territory except as permitted by treaties and with fair exchange. It had abided by the terms of all treaties with the Creeks. Yet the Red Sticks and Seminoles had violated the terms of the 1790 Treaty of New York, the 1814 Treaty of Fort Jackson, and other treaties. In the American view of law, an enemy's failure to abide by treaty provisions warranted a nation's resort to arms in response.[3]

The United States presumed that the Creek signatories could bind dissident Creeks and Seminoles, even if they were in Spanish Florida. Congressman John Rhea addressed this issue most directly. "The Seminoles, a part of the Creek nation, were party to the treaty of 1790," he said, and they had benefited from later treaties with the Creeks. The Red Sticks, too, were bound by the agreements. Obligated by the Creek treaties of 1790, 1796, 1802, and 1805 but failing to abide by them, the Red Sticks and Seminoles forfeited any claims they might have had under those treaties, Rhea said. They had lost their right to land that the treaties "allotted to them . . . to live and hunt on." It did not matter that they might have been led by British incendiaries to believe that the United States had wrongfully taken land from them in the 1814 Treaty of Fort Jackson. That treaty was entirely valid. It was a fair consequence of Indian aggression, and it legally and properly ceded the Creek territory to the United States. Because the Indians had violated earlier treaty terms in going to war against the United States in 1813 and 1814, "it was therefore just to take a large part of the country and to sell it, to defray the expense of that war." The treaty provisions bound them. Even if the treaty triggered Creeks' and Seminoles' dissatisfaction and hostilities, Rhea and other commentators pointed out, that did not change the offensive nature of their deeds and the defensive character of U.S. actions in the period from 1816 to 1818. Furthermore, the U.S. argument assumed that the Treaty of Fort Jackson ended the state of war with all Creeks and Seminoles. Therefore, government officials flatly rejected the argument that Article 9 of the Treaty of Ghent nullified the land cession agreed to in the Treaty of Fort Jackson. Consequently, Creek and Seminole resistance was illegal. Moreover, even if the Treaty of Ghent had been applicable to the Creeks, by its terms that treaty did not offer anything to tribes that failed to desist from hostilities against Americans. Since the Seminoles had not refrained from continuing attacks on Americans, they would not be eligible for any benefits under the Treaty of Ghent in any event.[4]

Thus, Jackson's supporters pointed to U.S.-Creek treaties as sources of law that validated American conduct. Brushing aside any questions about the legitimacy of the Treaty of Fort Jackson or about its application to Red Sticks and Seminoles, they strictly interpreted the language of the treaty to conclude that it ended war with the Creeks. Conveniently ignoring claims that the United States had violated previous treaties with Indian tribes, Americans insisted that the Creeks had to meticulously obey the terms of the 1814 treaty. The United States then strictly interpreted the terms of Article 9 of the Treaty of Ghent and found it inapplicable to the Creek territory because there was (they surmised) no ongoing war with the Creeks at the time of ratification. Based on those premises, the treaty agreements seemingly compelled several conclusions: that the Creeks had no claim to the territory in question, that their violent resistance to American use of the land was illegal, that the United States held a lawful claim to Creek territory, and that Americans were justified in asserting that claim by any means. As sources of law, treaties established the illegality of Indian violence and the lawfulness of American military action.

Not everyone agreed with the government's interpretation. In commenting on the legality of American hostilities during the Seminole War, opponents of U.S. policy did not accept rationales based on a narrow interpretation of Creeks' treaty obligations. They presented a counterargument that went beyond treaty language to consider the fairness and reasonableness of treaty provisions. They questioned the legitimacy of the Treaty of Fort Jackson on three grounds: The terms of indemnity were "exorbitant" because the land was worth ten or twenty times the expense of the Creek War to the United States. The United States forced the treaty on the Creeks by "duress" and "military coercion." Finally, only a minority of the Creek nation agreed to the treaty and therefore it was "void . . . [as] a national compact." Not having been signed by most of the hostile Creeks, it did not end the war with them. Since the Treaty of Fort Jackson was both harsh and invalid as to the enemy combatants, critics argued, the Creeks and Seminoles had an understandable basis for hostile reaction to American intruders, as well as a legitimate claim for restoration of their land under Article 9 of the Treaty of Ghent.[5] However, most commentators rejected the critics' approach to interpreting treaties.

In addition to treaties, the United States also regarded the customary practices of warfare as an important source of law. Ignoring general practices engaged in among European nations, Americans focused on specific practices evident in previous clashes between non-Europeans and Europeans. They allowed past deviation from the laws of war to justify present violations. Supporters of U.S. military actions in Florida pointed out that the unrestrained fighting against Creeks and Seminoles and the executions of Hillis Hadjo and Homathlemico were consistent with longtime practices during Indian wars. In the late 1810s, the United States had plenty of precedent on which to rely. Supporters of U.S. military action during the Seminole War drew from the long history of past conflicts between Europeans and Indians to justify American violence against Creeks and Seminoles. They maintained that the violence against Seminoles and Red Sticks and the executions of Hillis Hadjo and Homathlemico were consistent with previous European American encounters with Indians. As additional precedent, a few supporters mentioned Europe's practices in Asia and Africa. For example, during the congressional debate of 1819, Representative Rhea made the connection between U.S. relations with indigenous peoples in the Americas and European interactions with indigenous inhabitants of their imperial domains elsewhere in the world. Justifying the absence of any declaration of war against the Creeks and Seminoles, Rhea pointed out that Britain likewise had not declared war against "any of the powerful potentates of Asia, who have been overthrown and put down by Great Britain."[6] Backers of the Florida campaigns also portrayed British occupation of territory in India, Spanish Trinidad, Dutch South America, the Cape of Good Hope, and Malta as precedent for the principle that European-heritage nations, including the United States, had a right to occupy land inhabited by non-Europeans.

Interestingly, critics of the Seminole War did not question the relevance of past modes of warfare. Instead, they focused on a factual challenge, arguing that Americans' past practices had never included the execution of Indian prisoners. Consequently, they said, the executions of the two Red Sticks did not conform with customary usages and was unlawful.[7]

In any case, disregarding any qualms that a few critics expressed, the United States used positive law (treaties and customs) as sources of law to rationalize its armed hostilities against Creeks and Seminoles under international law. Pro-Jackson commentators' use of positive law to advance their case did not mean they were full-blown positivists, since they were not consistent in leaning on positive law sources. Although Jackson's defenders made good use of treaties and customs, they ignored alternative arguments—also based on treaties and prior practices—that weighed against U.S. actions. For example, as previously noted, supporters of the campaigns refused to take seriously critics' argument that the Treaty of Ghent nullified the land cession of the Treaty of Fort Jackson. They also disregarded evidence of a contrary prior practice from 1793, when President George Washington refused to approve the seizure of a Canadian military post that was supplying Indians with provisions and munitions of war, even though the fort was located within U.S. borders.[8] Moreover, their standard of past practices was inappropriately narrow, not taking into account common usages in previous wars among Europeans but only prior wars against various Indian nations and against people in Asia and Africa. The United States took a tougher, narrower approach when it interpreted treaties and past practices applicable to Creeks and Seminoles than when it assessed the mandates of treaties and prior usages deemed applicable to the Spanish.

Self-Defense and Military Necessity

As a source of law, the United States also relied on the laws of war as described in Emer de Vattel's 1758 treatise. The United States contended that Jackson's actions in Florida, including the executions of Hillis Hadjo and Homathlemico, were lawful under Vattelian tenets because they were necessary for self-defense. Red Sticks and Seminoles threatened the security and territorial integrity of the nation, government supporters argued. In the debate that followed the invasion, commentators pointed out that every nation had a right to protect itself. The Seminoles and Creeks had started the war through repeated, unprovoked aggressions against Georgia, they maintained. Hostile Creeks and Seminoles used Pensacola and other locations in Florida as bases from which to launch murderous attacks on American citizens—and as refuges to escape to after such attacks. Most recently, the killing of the Garrett family in Georgia and Richard W. Scott's supply party on the Apalachicola River constituted tangible acts of war. Those killings were particularly significant because they involved lethal violence against noncombatant women and children, a flagrant violation of civilized principles of war. Moreover, the Indians continued to be a threat. Imminently, they were on the verge of occupying the St. Marks fort, and they were still a strong force: most of their leaders remained, and they had three thousand men under their command to fight against the United States. The United States had a right to defend itself against the Indians, supporters of the Florida campaigns argued. The nation acted defensively, not offensively. In this way, the United States used Vattel's descriptions of the laws of war as evidence that the warfare tactics used by Creeks and Seminoles did not meet the standards of civilized nations, rather than using Vattel's principles to limit the United States' own conduct.[9]

The self-defense argument reinforced the comforting national self-perception that neither American intrusions on Indian lands nor American violation of treaty terms caused frontier violence. In particular, the executions of two Creek men and their two British allies forcefully made the point that others—specifically, Indians instigated by Europeans—were responsible for border troubles. Thus, the executions fortified Americans' positive self-image by asserting both national honor and national innocence.

One newspaper, noting that the situation on the southeastern border called for a practical response, dismissed those who would present legalistic principles in opposition to American troops' defense of the frontier: "We may expect to see Vattel, Martyns & Co. quoted at large, and the laws of nations ransacked for legal opinions on the subject in question; but still there is a higher authority—self defence." The frontier would not be secure as long as Indians were free to wage war there. Southern whites thought that Jackson's actions made them more secure by eliminating Florida's role as a base for Indian raids. Indeed, many Americans saw the Florida expeditions as bringing significant benefits without any negative effects.[10] Thus, the United States employed a very modern theoretical perspective on international law: utilitarianism.

However, critics of the Florida campaigns rejected the utilitarianism argument. They denied the alleged necessity of military action for self-defense, and they used the language of fairness and morality to buttress their arguments. Critics maintained that American actions were not warranted as self-defense. They insisted that Red Sticks and Seminoles were not a genuine threat to the United States. National self-defense did not necessitate destroying or occupying the Prospect Bluff fort, St. Marks, Pensacola, Miccosukee, or the Suwannee towns. In reality, the Indian forces were weak; well before Jackson headed to Pensacola, they had already been defeated.[11]

In fact, critics argued, it was Indians, not Americans, who had acted reasonably in self-defense. Americans had been the ones to initiate violent acts against Creeks and Seminoles. They had murdered Indians and stolen their cattle. They had destroyed the Prospect Bluff fort in 1816 and Fowltown in 1817, killing many people. Creeks and Seminoles had shown great restraint in reaction to American belligerence, and when they finally reacted, it was a natural response to American aggression. A month before the start of the congressional debate, the editors of the *Massachusetts Spy* pointed out that if "it appears, that, in consequence of our invasion of their territory, pillaging their castle, and murdering their inhabitants, they were driven to forcible measures in self-defence, however *uncivilized* may be their mode of warfare, it does not lie in our mouths to complain of it." The article continued with an analogy: "It would be but a ridiculous complaint in a highwayman, who, failing in his nefarious design, should have his ears cut off, or his eyes torn out, by the person he attempted to rob, that the laws did not authorize this mode of punishment—the reply would be, do justice yourself before you require it at the hands of others." In short, when Florida Indians took up arms, they were simply responding to "atrocities and encroachments" by whites. Like the United States, Creeks and Seminoles had a right of self-defense. Their attack on the Scott party—their ostensible act of war that justified the American invasion—was an understandable exercise of their right of self-defense provoked by armed American soldiers traveling through their territory outside the United States a week after the assault on Fowltown. As Congressman Timothy Fuller declared, "Is it not manifest that we have been the aggressors in this war—very much the aggressors?"[12] Thus, critics asserted that the United States had acted offensively rather than defensively, and they contended that U.S. hostilities were unjustified because Seminoles and Creeks had not provoked war.

In addition to challenging the justice of the United States' cause, critics also protested the United States' failure to conduct the war against Creeks and Seminoles in a humanitarian fashion. Critics were particularly concerned that American conduct in Florida vis-à-vis Creeks and Seminoles did not reflect well on the nation. As a model to the world, they said, the United States should take the lead in mitigating the horrors of war, showing mercy even in the absence of a technical legal obligation to do so. Representative Fuller asserted this position eloquently during the congressional debate. He objected that American troops' violence against Indians in Florida was not fitting for an enlightened republic. Protecting the rights of humanity would more properly reflect the nation's high character. Demonstrating forbearance and mercy in interactions with oppressed and conquered people would be a potent symbol of Americans' "republican virtue." Humanitarianism promoted national glory more than military prowess did. "Though yet in her infancy," he said, "America has exerted her influence among the nations, in behalf of insulted and oppressed humanity." Continuing that mission by treating Indians humanely would reinforce Americans' national pride and would enhance the nation's standing abroad.[13]

However, few American commentators agreed that the nation would gain more from showing restraint than from exerting power. Instead, most believed that vigorous action in defense of U.S. interests was important both for Americans' self-image and for the nation's reputation in Europe. Rejecting the contention that gentle treatment of Indians strengthened U.S. nationhood by boosting its status as a civilized nation, supporters of the Florida campaign made the opposite argument: that firm and forceful action against Indians in Florida advanced the United States' national interests and helped build its standing as a sovereign nation. Likewise, arguments against the legality of U.S. armed hostilities in Florida failed to win over many of the pundits. Most analysts concluded that with regard to Creeks and Seminoles, just as with regard to Spaniards, treaties and past practices were legitimate sources of governing law. Moreover, they believed that military action against Creeks and Seminoles—as also against Spanish officials in Florida—was legally justified because it was necessary for protecting and advancing U.S. national interests. Arguments based on self-defense and military necessity prioritized utilitarian national interests over considerations of morality and justness. Though actual application of the principles had a harsher impact on Indians than on Europeans because bias affected both past practices and treaty interpretations, these kinds of legal arguments made about Indians paralleled those presented about Spaniards.

Beyond reasoning that pertained similarly to Spaniards and Indians, the United States also had broader rationales for recognizing fewer constitutional constraints, procedural requirements, and international regulations when engaged in hostilities with Indians than when fighting a European nation. Those rationales focused on perceived distinctions between savagery and civilization and between sovereign and nonsovereign polities.

Savagery versus Civilization

The United States asserted that the rules of war did not constrain American soldiers in their armed conflict with Seminoles and Red Sticks because the Florida Indians were too uncivilized to follow the rules themselves. Some commentators made generalized negative observations about all Indians as part of an undifferentiated racial-cultural group that tacitly included Red Sticks and Seminoles. Others made points that were specific to Seminoles (their typical catchall name for Indians in Florida, including Red Sticks). At the heart of this argument was Americans' use of Indians' (or Seminoles') alleged war crimes to serve as a marker between "civilized" and "uncivilized" people. Commentators explained their savage-versus-civilized argument in newspapers, as well as in publicly available diplomatic correspondence and congressional debates.

Many commentators freely conflated all Native people together, attributing to all the alleged conduct of some. Thus, they argued that it was well known and established that "the Indians" did not fight honorably, that the Indian way of war was "indiscriminate murder," and that Indians killed prisoners. For example, Secretary of State John Quincy Adams observed that killing of captives "without discrimination of age or sex" was one of the "ordinary characteristics of Indian warfare." Some only made such comments about alleged Indian savagery in the context of explaining the United States' self-defense argument. Others used general observations about past patterns of Indians' alleged cruel acts and savage behavior as a rationale for the inapplicability of the protections of the laws of war to Florida Indians and as a justification for unrestrained violence against them. Like politicians, newspapers also took this approach, arguing that force, rather than law, was the appropriate means of dealing with lawless Indian savages who, writers alleged, engaged in scalping, burning, and pillaging. In the *City of Washington Gazette,* a writer argued that retaliation for barbaric actions was sometimes the only way to force savage people to adhere to civilized rules. The author explained that "[w]hen a nation, whether civilized or savage, so far forgets the rights and offices of humanity as to violate the usages of civilized warfare, it is not only permitted, but it becomes necessary, to make the offending nation respect the laws of humanity." An essay in the *Albany Register* noted that because "Indians give no quarters in warfare; of course they are entitled to none." In fact, the author asserted more broadly, the law of nations only applied to civilized people, not to Indian savages. "There is no propriety in appealing to the law of nations in a case of this kind," he wrote; "as well might you think of squaring your conduct by that law when you are at war with bears and wolves." The *Nashville Whig and Tennessee Advertiser* explained that the law of nations did not apply to savages because they "know nothing either of law or reason," they "satiate their vengeance indiscriminately on the aged and young," and "[w]ith them a treaty has no binding obligation." Instead, the writer asserted, "[s]avages, in war, are to be brought to submission only through fear."[14]

Other commentators focused on conduct of the Seminoles and Red Sticks themselves rather than on alleged past actions by other Indians. Congressmen Richard C. Anderson, John Holmes, and Henry Baldwin identified specific brutal behavior by Florida Indians as a rationale for the inapplicability of legal protections to them. They viewed those Indians as murdering savages whose mode of war was "indiscriminate massacre." The Seminoles had violated the normal rules of war that applied between civilized nations by committing vicious acts against white settlers and soldiers, such as slaughtering the Garrett family and the Scott party. Especially important was the allegation that in these two incidents Florida Indians had murdered women and children, a war crime that was considered a key marker of uncivilized warfare. Pertinent as well was the charge that they had killed prisoners, which also violated the rules of war. To reinforce the popular representation of barbaric acts against civilians by Hillis Hadjo's Red Stick Indians, a Boston printer published a prominent captivity narrative in 1818. Allegedly penned by "Eunice Barber," it told a gruesome story of how the Indians had murdered her husband and seven children in southeastern Georgia and subsequently held Barber captive for six weeks. The narrative testified to the ultimate war crimes by Red Sticks: slaughtering children and torturing and killing prisoners. The title page included a note to the reader: "It may be a gratification to the reader, to learn that the said tribe of SAVAGES have been since exterminated by the Brave and Intrepid GEN. JACKSON, And the Troops under his command." Such literary propaganda likely played at least as important a role as did political speeches in persuading people of Red Stick and Seminole savagery and building support for U.S. policy in Florida.[15]

Supporters of the Florida campaigns argued that the law of nations was reciprocal. A country was not bound by humanitarian strictures of the rules of law when dealing with an enemy that failed to adhere to those strictures itself. Combatants who refused to submit to moral constraints on warfare were outside the compact of civilized warfare and could claim no benefits or immunities from it. Addressing the reciprocity issue, the *Boston Patriot and Daily Chronicle* asked rhetorically: "Can it be reasonable that we should be bound by laws which our enemy despises?" Other newspapers freely answered the question. An essay in the *National Advocate* came right to the point, explaining that the rules of war "are not binding upon one party, if disregarded by the other." Here, too, commentators sometimes attributed to Seminoles and Red Sticks alleged past conduct by other Indians. The *Maryland Censor* declared "that Indians . . . cannot be judged by any laws of nations; they have no claim to such protection; they do not treat others by such laws; they do not expect their benefit themselves." Indians as a whole, Representative James Barbour proclaimed, were "without the pale of the compact" that reciprocally constrained warfare between civilized peoples and could "claim no benefit from it." Other commentators based their argument on the Florida Indians' own conduct. To Americans, the Seminoles' refusal to follow the rules of civilized warfare absolved the United States from the requirements of those rules when dealing with them.[16]

Not everyone agreed with the claim that humanitarian constraints on warfare were categorically inapplicable to Indians based on the savagery argument. Their challenge focused primarily on alleged factual errors made by defenders of the Florida campaigns, though a few also challenged the

United States' doctrinal misunderstandings. Congressmen Timothy Fuller and Charles Mercer denied that Indians routinely executed captives, questioned the characterization of the Seminoles as aggressors, and argued that defending one's own people against attack is not a crime. Consequently, they said, Indian prisoners were entitled to the same treatment as white captives, and the executions of Hillis Hadjo and Homathlemico were wrong. Representative Mercer said that a distinction between Indian and white prisoners had never been made in the past and was not warranted in the present. As for the Florida Indians specifically, Mercer noted, those Indians were "at peace" with the United States at the time of the 1816 American invasion of their territory to attack the Prospect Bluff fort. They had not invaded the United States. They did not retaliate after the destruction of the fort, and only responded violently after the aggressive American attack on Fowltown. They were entitled to resist American aggression and American intrusion on their territory. They directed their hostility against Americans who were traveling in Seminole areas of Florida, not in the United States. Mercer went on to criticize the U.S. assertion that it was legitimate for the nation to attack a fort outside the United States simply because it contained fugitive slaves and "disaffected" Indians. The mere disaffection of Indians who owed the United States no allegiance was no cause to attack them in Florida, he declared. Representatives Fuller and John Tyler went beyond factual challenges to dispute the underlying legal doctrine. "[T]he rightful laws of war are immutable," Fuller said; "they are the same between the most ferocious as between the most humane nations." Similarly, Tyler observed that the "new code that had been adopted by civilized nations . . . provides the mode of conducting war even against barbarians." Thus, Fuller and Tyler explicitly rejected the savage/civilized distinction for the application of the rules of war.[17]

However, critics were in the minority on this issue. Most commentators felt comfortable with the concept of a divide between civilized and savage societies and maintained that Indian—or, more specifically, Creek and Seminole—savagery absolved the United States from conducting warfare against Florida Indians in a humanitarian way in accordance with the rules of war.

Nationhood and Sovereignty

In addition to ardently arguing that protective rules of war did not apply to Seminoles and Red Sticks because they were uncivilized and lawless, political commentators also addressed a second reason that the law of nations did not apply to the Seminoles and Red Sticks: they were not a "nation." Only sovereign nations were entitled to wage war, the United States insisted. The Florida Indians were not a nation and consequently their war against the United States was unlawful. Although pro-Jackson commentators gave different explanations for that position, they all concluded that the rules of war did not apply.

In Congress, a few representatives explained the Florida Indians' lack of sovereignty by pointing to specific characteristics of the Seminoles and Red Sticks. One position was that the Red Sticks and Seminoles were merely fragments of the Creek Nation and could not lawfully act independently of their sovereign government. Only Representatives Rhea and Baldwin mentioned this argument. Rhea explained that in the 1790 Treaty of New York the Creeks had acknowledged themselves to be "under the protection of the United States, and of no other sovereign." The Seminoles were a party to that treaty and had benefited from its provisions, as well as from later treaties with the Creeks, he asserted. Rhea criticized the Seminoles and Red Sticks for violating the 1790 treaty and also for refusing to attend the treaty negotiations at Fort Jackson in 1814 and choosing instead to carry on the war from Florida. Although Rhea never said so explicitly, he seems to have been suggesting that the Seminoles and Red Sticks were not an independent nation because they were really just a renegade portion of the Creek Nation. The implication could be that, in continuing hostilities against Americans, they acted against the policies and without the authority of their presumed home government, the Creek national council, and therefore waged an illegal private war. However, in his lengthy remarks on the floor of Congress, Rhea never actually spelled out such arguments, focusing instead on violent acts inconsistent with treaty obligations.[18]

Representative Baldwin, too, mentioned that Seminoles and Red Sticks were members of the Creek Nation, but he also gave a second reason for their not constituting a nation: they had combined with African-descended people. When the Florida Indians joined with blacks, they could not claim national status because they were a mixed group of people who lacked a common, shared history as a community. Baldwin highlighted the absurdity of calling "a gregarious collection of . . . outlawed Indians and runaway negroes a nation." He argued, "A better or more appropriate name could not be given to them as a mass, or as individuals, than outlaws and pirates." Similarly, Tennessee congressman Francis Jones explained that the "tri-colored party" of Seminoles with their fugitive Red Stick, black, and British allies did not constitute a "nation" but rather were "the refuse of villany."[19] This perspective mirrored many white Americans' assumption that U.S. nationhood itself required racial homogeneity, which in turn served as a rationale for excluding Indians and blacks from the national polity.

Theoretically, these arguments by Rhea, Baldwin, and Jones could have left open the possibility that some Indian polities could be sovereign. If supporters of the Florida campaigns had denied Seminoles status as an independent nation because they were a racially mixed group or because they really were fugitive members of the Creek Nation, then the U.S. argument would not have constituted a significant attack on tribal sovereignty. To the contrary, it could be viewed as supportive of the Creek Nation's sovereignty.

However, these three congressmen did not affirmatively support tribal sovereignty, and, in fact, while Jones was ambiguous on that issue, Rhea's and Baldwin's other comments seem to foreclose the potential for tribal sovereignty. Jones hinted at a possible distinction between Indians who fought for their "country" and those who committed murders as individuals, yet he also made numerous generalized statements about the savage and cruel nature of Indian warfare and he never identified the Red Sticks or Seminoles as insubordinate members of the Creek Nation. Moreover, at one point he left open the question of whether an Indian polity was a nation: when distinguishing between Creeks who fought against or with the United States, he said that "many of the citizens of the [Creek] nation, (if it may be so called) rallied round their [the United States'] standard." Rhea argued that the peace treaty with Britain at the end of the American Revolution made the U.S. sovereign over all territory within its borders and voided Indian rights or claims to any such land. Moreover, the treaty left the Indian nations completely subject to the mercy of the United States. Subsequently, numerous tribes had made treaties with the United States in which they acknowledged themselves under U.S. protection. Thus, Rhea appeared to reject the notion of tribal nationhood autonomous of the United States. Likewise, Baldwin's other comments during the congressional debate suggest that his argument about lack of nationhood was not limited only to the Seminoles and Red Sticks but applied more broadly to all Indian tribes. Baldwin made generalized observations about the distinctive features of "Indian wars" that did not differentiate between recognized Indian tribes and other, mixed communities of Indians. Because Indians were unlike European nations, he said, Indian wars were distinguishable from European-style wars. "An Indian war is like no other," the congressman observed. "It is not a war on the nation, but [on] individuals. Their [Indians'] object is murder and plunder. In guarding against the attacks of a civilized force, you watch the movements of their armies; but in terminating an Indian war, the incursions of individuals must be stopped." In the Seminole War, he said, the Indian force "would not meet our army in battle, and thus end the war. They were scattered through the whole country in small parties." Consequently, they had to be treated differently than one would treat a normal army. Finally, Baldwin made a point of observing that Spain did not recognize Indian tribes as "having any attributes of a national character" and did not make treaties with them.[20]

Moreover, the two pro-Jackson congressmen who did acknowledge Seminole sovereignty—James Tallmadge, Jr., and James Barbour—only recognized the principle as applicable in foreign territory, not within U.S. borders. They could acknowledge an Indian polity as sovereign in Florida only because Spain had such a feeble hold on the territory, and they only put forward the argument in order to justify U.S. extraterritorial action there.[21]

Other commentators who raised the nationhood issue conveyed that no Indian tribe could assert itself as an independent nation. This was a broad argument, not limited only to the specific make-up of the community of Red Sticks and Seminoles. As an essayist in the *Rhode-Island American* observed, because "the Indians" had acknowledged U.S. sovereignty and put themselves under U.S. protection, they were vassals, not independent nations. Consequently, they could not lawfully wage war on the United States. Congressmen taking the same position included Representatives Alexander Smyth, John Floyd, Richard M. Johnson, and George F. Strother. Smyth argued that the Seminoles and Red Sticks were subjects of the United States even when they were located outside the country's borders. He concluded that since the Seminoles were not independent of the United States, "there can be no such thing as a war . . . between [the United States] and a tribe of American savages." Since an Indian tribe could not be a nation and could not make war on the United States, during the Seminole War the United States did not have to follow the usual rules that it would normally observe with foreign nations.[22] Thus, the Seminole War debate conveyed a pointed rejection of the whole concept of Indian tribal sovereignty and nationhood.

When presenting their position on Creeks and Seminoles, Jackson's supporters tried to avoid overreliance on principles articulated by Vattel and other jurists, preferring to cut their own legal path based on the singularity of conditions in the Americas. The status of the Seminoles and Red Sticks, pundits said, was "anomalous" and "peculiar." The normal rules of war could not apply to Indian wars, including the Seminole War. Foreign jurisprudential works were irrelevant, because this was a situation unknown to European authors of legal treatises on the law of nations, some American commentators observed. They distinguished between European and American legal spaces, conveying that Europeans could not provide answers to American conflicts, nor did European rules automatically apply to such conflicts. During the congressional debate, Representative Tallmadge contended that the law of nations, which was "established by common consent of mankind, as a rule of action between free, separate, and independent Governments, has no application to the present case. The history of Europe," he explained, "affords no parallel to the present circumstances and could not be expected to have provided a rule for the present case." Representative Baldwin likewise noted that "[i]n the history of civilized nations, we find nothing analogous to the situation of the Indians inhabiting this country, and cannot expect to find, in their usages or intercourse with each other, any principles adopted, which will apply to this case, which is strictly one *sui generis,* and to be governed by its own rules." Some newspapers also denied that legal treatises determined rights of combatants in a war with Indians. Many Americans seemed to share the sentiment of a pseudonymous essay by "Junius Brutus," which rejected the notion that rules governing warfare between civilized nations were relevant to Americans' battles with Indians. "This is not a case that can be determined by European authors," Junius Brutus opined, since "no such case ever existed in Europe." Likewise, the *Nashville Whig and Tennessee Advertiser* argued that legal treatises did not apply on the frontier, since they could not possibly provide any solution to the problem of people who "scalped and butchered."[23]

Few of Jackson's allies cited specific authorities to support their arguments. While Alexander Smyth and a few other pro-Jackson commentators relied on Vattel and other European authors, some were unwilling to acknowledge the relevance of the foreigners' writings. For example, Baldwin pointedly refused to use European jurisprudential writings to bolster his case for Jackson. At one point—when he was focusing on Jackson's occupation of St. Marks and Pensacola—Baldwin explicitly pointed out that he had not mentioned any writers on the law of nations, because he did not deem them relevant to the Seminole War.[24]

Some critics of the United States' conduct in Florida challenged the "lack of nationhood" argument, though their protest was weaker on this issue than on the savagery argument. To contest the "lack of nationhood" claim, Congressman Mercer contended that Indian tribes were separate, sovereign nations. The United States could not treat the Florida Seminoles and Creeks as stateless people. "Man has a natural right to live somewhere on the earth," he asserted, and Florida was their home. At the time of the U.S. attack on the Prospect Bluff fort, the Florida Seminoles and Creeks "were beyond the limits of the United States, occupying towards us the relation of an independent people—the relation under which we had treated with them for peace, at New York and Colerain." Henry Clay also implicitly recognized that Indian tribes were nations when he acknowledged that, because the Florida Indians were "capable of maintaining the relations of peace and war," their hostilities were not "private war." However, even among Jackson's critics, few others expressed commitment to Indian sovereignty and independence. For example, anti-Jackson congressman Henry R. Storrs explicitly rejected the notion that the Seminoles were an independent nation. He explained, "[A]ll rights over the countries which they [Indians] occupy are subordinate to the sovereignties of those governments within whose jurisdiction they reside. The common consent and universal convention of European Powers has settled this question—our own Constitution has recognised and established the adoption of this principle into the code of public law."[25]

The critics' argument was weakly presented and apparently convinced few white Americans. The dominant interpretation of the situation in Florida was that the rules of war did not constrain American soldiers in their conflict with Florida Indians. It was up to Jackson to deal with Seminoles and Red Sticks however he saw fit. They were outside the safeguards of law.

Even with regard to European allies of Indians, the law of nations did not apply equivalently in accordance with the European ideal, the U.S. government contended. International law could not require the United States to recognize the legality of individual Spaniards' and Britons' unauthorized alliance with Seminoles and Red Sticks. Individual Europeans' actions in the Seminole War would only have been legitimate, American analysts argued, if they had been attached to a lawful combatant nation—as the Marquis de Lafayette had been allied with the United States during the Revolutionary War. Since the Seminoles and Red Sticks were not a lawful combatant nation, their unlawful status carried over to their European allies, who could be executed or exiled at will. The executions of Alexander Arbuthnot and Robert Ambrister, as well as the exile of some of Florida's Spanish officials, illustrate that it was not only racial and cultural factors that determined whether someone could be treated as outside normal legal constraints. In special circumstances, other European-descended people, too, were treated in a way that paralleled the treatment of Indians during the early modern period. A prominent example is the Acadians, French Catholic settlers in Nova Scotia and nearby maritime areas, whom the British deported to other colonies beginning in 1755. The Acadians appeared to lack clear membership in a recognized sovereign nation, since their attempt to stay neutral between France and Britain left both countries questioning their allegiance. Moreover, they had at times allied with the Mi'kmaq. Their apparent lack of sovereignty and affiliation with a First Nations people may explain why they were subjected to harsh violence and removal.[26] Similarly, in 1818 Florida Indians' European allies were denied the usual protections of the laws of war. In the Seminole War, the executions of Hillis Hadjo and Homathlemico, and the punishment of their British and Spanish supporters, clearly conveyed the message that Indian tribes were not sovereign nations that could lawfully declare war or legitimize the actions of individual European allies.

The Seminoles' perceived lack of sovereignty in turn justified U.S. occupation of their land, according to Jackson's supporters. Though Spain had ultimate ownership of Florida soil, portions of Florida were enemy country rather than neutral territory because they were effectively used, occupied, and controlled by the Seminoles. Therefore, that territory was a "legitimate seat of war." The United States had the right to enter those areas to pursue and suppress the Seminoles. Defenders of the Florida campaigns concluded that "as between the Americans and their Indian invaders, lawful repulsion has no territorial bounds." This assertion should be assessed within the context of an era of supposedly strict territoriality. Prior to the rise of the nation-state the law of nations assumed that a ruler had personal jurisdiction over all of his or her people, wherever they were. After the emergence of the nation-state, a sovereign polity had jurisdiction over all of the people within its defined territorial borders but needed special arrangements to retain jurisdiction over its subjects who were abroad. In this context, the United States' extension of jurisdiction over Indians and African-descended people in Florida seemed to echo the older notion of personal jurisdiction at a time when notions of territorial sovereignty reigned.[27] Regardless of potential theoretical inconsistencies, in the 1810s the United States contended that it had the right to act extraterritorially against Creeks and Seminoles and to occupy the land they inhabited outside the United States.

Outlaws

Defenders of U.S. troops' violence against Indians in Florida made ambiguous use of the term "outlaws" to describe Indians in Florida. A contemporary newspaper described "out-laws" as "men whom no laws could restrain, and therefore men whom no law will protect."[28] Designation as outlaws—people outside the protection of law—had serious consequences in early America. In the 1810s, there was extensive precedent for the principle that outlaws had no legal rights and could even be killed on sight. To the U.S. government, the Red Sticks' and Seminoles' status as outlaws not only justified violence against them but also provided a crucial foundation for classifying their British allies as outlaws who were devoid of legal rights. Therefore, defenders of the Florida campaigns should have provided a clear and persuasive explanation for classifying the Florida Indians as outlaws, but instead they were vague about their reasoning.

In the 1810s, the Red Sticks' political status was a major rationale for an explicit outlaw classification, especially in Secretary of State Adams's and General Jackson's early justifications for the 1818 invasion. Adams referred to the Red Sticks as "fugitive outlaws from the Creek nation" and, elsewhere, as "fugitive outlaws from the United States." In both instances, Adams referred separately to "the Indians of Florida," indicating that he viewed the Seminoles as distinct from the Red Sticks. In a military dispatch, Andrew Jackson also referred to "the outlaws of the old Red Stick party," and in a message to the West Florida governor he characterized the Red Sticks as "[a] party of outlaws and refugees from the Creek nation" who had combined with fugitive slaves and Seminole Indians. However, Adams's and Jackson's political-status explanation for outlaw classification was insufficient, since they also treated Seminoles as outlaws without claiming that they, too, were refugee members of the Creek nation. Only Representative Baldwin included the Seminoles in his political-status justification for the outlaw label. Baldwin said both Red Sticks and Seminoles were "Creeks, who had been outlawed by their own people." Others seemed content to gloss over the question of how the Seminoles' political condition made them outlaws. Yet American commentators did not distinguish between Red Sticks' and Seminoles' rights under the law of nations. Instead, as they made their legal arguments they typically conflated the two groups, for example by referring generically to "Indian outlaws" in Florida (Adams). In their justification for U.S. military actions they distinguished between "friendly" Indians (allied Lower Creeks led by McIntosh) and "enemy" Indians (Seminoles and Red Sticks) rather than between Red Sticks and Seminoles. They consistently treated both Red Sticks and Seminoles as outside the sphere of legal protections and both groups as unable to convey legitimacy to their British allies Arbuthnot and Ambrister. That the United States repeatedly conflated the Red Sticks and the Seminoles suggests that their outlaw status actually derived less from their political position vis-à-vis the recognized Creek Nation than from the fact of their hostility to the United States, refusal to submit to U.S. authority, resistance to U.S. rule, and alleged depredations against Americans.[29]

There was precedent for outlawing unfriendly or allegedly violent Indians. Earlier in American history, colonial and state governments had enacted legislation that had the effect of outlawing such Indians. For example, a Virginia law of 1666, enacted in response to murders allegedly committed by Indians, provided that it was lawful for any Englishman to kill any Indian who crossed into the borders of the frontier county of Henrico. Later, a 1787 Georgia statute provided: "[F]rom and immediately after the passing of this act the Creek Indians shall be considered as without the protection of this

State, and it shall be lawful for the government and people of the same to put to death or capture the said Indians wherever they may be found within the limits of this State, except such tribes of said Indians which have not, or shall not hereafter commit hostilities against the people of this State."[30]

Although many commentators on the Seminole War treated the Creeks and Seminoles as outlaws, only one congressman, John Rhea, directly stated that Florida Indians' conduct warranted their outlaw status. After explaining that the Creek nation's treaties included and bound both Seminoles and Red Sticks, he claimed that members of both groups were outlaws because they disregarded treaty obligations. In the 1790 treaty, the Creek nation agreed to perpetual peace and friendship with the United States and acknowledged an obligation to refrain from violent acts against Americans. Rhea said that when the Seminoles and the hostile portion of the Creeks (the Red Sticks) waged war on the United States, they "put themselves out of the protection of the United States" and "made themselves outlaws."[31]

Hillis Hadjo and Homathlemico

Americans used the argument that the Seminoles and Red Sticks were savages and outlaws who did not legally constitute a nation to justify not only general unrestrained violence against the Florida Indians but also the execution of Hillis Hadjo and Homathlemico. Whatever rules might normally apply to prisoners of war, the United States claimed, they could not prohibit the Republic from summarily executing two Red Stick captives.

Some commentators used the "lack of nationhood" argument to defend the executions: as illegal combatants—not members of "nations"—captured Red Sticks and Seminoles were not entitled to protections mandated by the law of nations for prisoners of war. Because Indians could not be lawful combatants against the United States, the United States was not obligated to abide by the usual rules of war in the course of hostilities with them. Jackson was free to treat them as harshly as he wished. Since Hillis Hadjo and Homathlemico were not fighting lawfully for a sovereign nation, they were not covered by the shield of the laws of war, so Jackson could execute them if he deemed it expedient to do so.[32]

Defenders of the executions also used the savagery-versus-civilization divide as justification. They maintained that Indian savagery, and, more specifically, Red Stick and Seminole savagery, meant that the United States acted lawfully in executing Hillis Hadjo and Homathlemico. Junius Brutus, the pseudonymous *National Advocate* essayist, explained that "every hostile Indian may rightfully be put to death" in the Seminole War because the Florida

Indians had waged war in the "customary manner" of savages, "viz. by murdering all prisoners." Secretary of State Adams cited Vattel for the principle that when a nation was at war with "an inhuman enemy" that observes no rules, it could take the lives of prisoners. Even though the rules of war ordinarily required troops to spare the life of a captured enemy, Representative Richard M. Johnson pointed out, since Hillis Hadjo and Homathlemico were Indians, the law of nations did not constrain the United States. In fact, Johnson went further, connecting all Indians as a racial category. Referring to Hillis Hadjo and Homathlemico, he declared that "their color was sufficient evidence of their subjection to [Jackson's] right of disposing of them as justice required."[33] Johnson thus made explicit the unstated racial classification that underlay other commentators' melding of all Indians together. They viewed the Red Sticks and Seminoles as part of a larger racially defined group that shared the same legal status. Defenders of Jackson's actions collectively relegated all Indians to a sphere outside the protections of the laws of war.

At times analysts ambiguously conflated an argument that the restraints of the rules of war were binding only when the enemy itself followed those rules with an argument that the restraints were binding only to the extent that the enemy followed the rules. The former argument took the enemy completely outside of the law of nations, whereas the latter argument supported the principle of "retaliation" under those rules. Under the doctrine of retaliation, brutality was a lawful response to an enemy's viciousness, and forbearance was called for only "when a corresponding humanity is shown by your adversaries" (in Representative Anderson's words). Since Indians slaughtered their captives, pro-Jackson congressmen claimed (again lumping all "Indians" together into one undifferentiated category), Americans were entitled to put Indian prisoners to death. As a rationalization for such brutality, Kentuckian Joseph Desha argued that if you want an Indian to be peaceable, "you must make him fear you." Even if punishment and retaliation failed to "bring [Indians] to a sense of humanity," he said, "it would at least convince them of the necessity of acting less barbarously, for their own safety."[34] Whether arguing that Indian savagery nullified the laws of war or justified retaliation, the outcome was the same: it was lawful to execute Indian prisoners.

Some commentators went beyond general arguments about "Indian" or "Seminole" behavior to focus on Hillis Hadjo's and Homathlemico's own actions. They claimed that the United States lawfully executed the two men because of their individual war crimes. As Representative Jones pointed out, Hillis Hadjo and Homathlemico were not just any random Indians; they were Indians who had murdered Americans. Specifically, he charged, the two

Red Sticks had led the brutal assault on the Scott party. Congressmen Tallmadge, Strother, Rhea, and Desha likewise pointed to Hillis Hadjo's and Homathlemico's own offenses as justification for their execution. Because they had committed war crimes, they were not entitled to the usual protections given to prisoners of war. The *Kentucky Reporter* labeled the two Red Sticks "a couple of outlawed barbarians, who had forfeited every claim to be regarded as prisoners of war." The paper concluded that their executions violated neither the rules of war nor the rights of humanity but were instead "entirely justifiable and correct." The United States could lawfully punish the two men for their crimes.[35]

As evident in the *Kentucky Reporter* article, the "outlaw" designation was important. The United States characterized Hillis Hadjo and Homathlemico as members of a group of people who were outlaws for a mix of reasons. In part, it was because Indians were racially and culturally distinct from European Americans and could not be lawful combatants against the United States. To some extent, it was also because Red Sticks were Creeks who took themselves outside of Creek jurisdiction and governance. Additionally, it was because Red Sticks and Seminoles were hostile to the United States, failed to abide by the Treaty of Fort Jackson and other treaties with the United States, were a collection of individuals waging private war, and were savages who committed violent depredations against Americans and violated the rules of war. Moreover, the United States argued, even independent of their affiliations, Hillis Hadjo and Homathlemico were outlaws because they had committed war crimes. Once the two men and their community were set aside as outlaws, the executions became easy to rationalize.

Some critics of the Seminole War condemned the executions of Hillis Hadjo and Homathlemico as inhumane. Representative Fuller expressed the most concern. He said the United States should always try to protect "the rights of humanity," "meliorate the evils of war," and "inflict no useless cruelty." "Barbarous practices," he declared, "are . . . mere abuses of military power." The United States should lean toward "mercy," rather than exercising "the extreme rights of war." In particular, the nation should avoid the "intolerable barbarity" of killing women, children, and prisoners. Fuller scorned the executions of Hillis Hadjo and Homathlemico as "without necessity, and almost without pretext." He concluded that the proposed congressional resolution disapproving of the executions of Arbuthnot and Ambrister should also condemn the executions of the two Creek men.[36]

Other representatives also objected to the executions of the two Red Sticks on humanitarian grounds. John Tyler observed that modern rules of war prohibited executing prisoners, including Indian captives. He blamed Jackson for executing enemy men out of mere vengeance, totally outside legal constraints. He warned that when Americans killed prisoners or otherwise disobeyed the new humanitarian code of war, "we throw ourselves out of the pale of the law." Henry R. Storrs lamented that the executions were inconsistent with the new era of "humanity and benevolence" that had recently emerged "among the nations of the earth." Charles F. Mercer asserted that "[n]o man has a right . . . to practise cruelty or injustice; and all needless severity is both unjust and cruel." Executing Indian captives "in cold blood" constituted a departure from "the humane code of America." Henry Clay proclaimed that the U.S. military should adhere to "humane custom" and should consider precepts of "humanity" before retaliating against Indians.[37]

A few critics also raised procedural problems with the capture and execution of Hillis Hadjo and Homathlemico. Clay, along with Fuller and Mercer, disapproved of the way the two Red Sticks were deceived into boarding the American ship by the use of a British flag. With regard to the executions, Representative Mercer pointed out that the United States had not identified any legal charges against Hillis Hadjo and that the main charge against Homathlemico was completely without factual foundation; there was no proof at all that he had participated in the attack on the Scott party. A handful of commentators expressed concern that the lack of due process prior to the executions of the two Red Sticks violated American legal principles. Some commentary, such as the Senate Select Committee's report on the Seminole War, just took note of the fact that the men had been hanged without trial. Others expressed criticism more directly. For example, the *National Messenger* denounced the absence of a trial to determine whether Hillis Hadjo and Homathlemico were guilty of any crimes. Without any legal proceeding to examine the facts, Jackson acted with "bloody cruelty and high-handed tyranny," summarily ordering the two men executed, the writer lamented.[38]

Though only a few critics objected to the lack of a trial for the two Creeks, there was more support for a different sort of challenge to the executions: that they were not necessary for achieving the lawful purposes of the war. Some analysts pointed out that once Hillis Hadjo and Homathlemico were in military custody, they were not a threat to the safety of U.S. soldiers. Since simply detaining them would have achieved the same purposes as killing them, the executions were legally and morally indefensible, they contended.[39] But Jackson's allies soundly rejected that argument, claiming that the executions were in fact necessary as a form of retaliation: Indian viciousness would be answered with American brutality, in the hope of deterring future cruel acts by the Seminoles and Red Sticks.

Broad support for Jackson's summary executions of Hillis Hadjo and Homathlemico revealed that white Americans were comfortable viewing noncompliant Indians—or even all Indians—as outside the shield of law.

Jackson offered the two Creeks no hearing prior to their executions, in contrast to the court-martial proceedings provided for the two British prisoners. Nonetheless, Americans expressed far less concern about the process followed for the two Red Sticks than about the procedures used prior to the execution of the two Britons. Most commentators dismissed the notion that regular procedural requirements applied to Indians. A pseudonymous newspaper essay by "Phocion," which referred to Seminoles as "babe slaughtering scalpers . . . outlaws, exterminators, and man-roasters," proclaimed that it was "anti-social foppery" to put Jackson on trial for his military conduct against Seminoles and "absurd" to apply "the beautiful forms of civil liberty" to violent deeds by Indians.[40] The procedural distinction thus made between Indians and Britons indicated that the line of law followed racial-cultural boundaries.

Congressional debates and newspaper publications show that most white Americans who commented in the public sphere broadly agreed with Jackson's definition of what it meant to be civilized or uncivilized, shared his view of the position of Indians in that dichotomous classification, and approved of his interpretation of the consequences of a prisoner's being identified as savage. White Americans presumed that civilized people lived under a system of laws while uncivilized people were lawless, and they concluded that only the former were entitled to the protections of law and legal process. Moreover, white Americans considered themselves to be united with Europeans on the civilized, law-abiding side of the line and viewed Indians as uncivilized and lawless. As lawless people, they were viewed as unprotected by law. Consequently, commentators concluded, in its dealings with Indians, the United States was not restrained by any legal obligations. It was not bound to adhere to humanitarian limits on warfare presented in the law of nations nor to offer due process before executing prisoners.

The Seminole War Debate and International Law Doctrines

The Seminole War took place at the start of a century of transition in European and American attitudes toward colonization, imperialism, race, and the civilization-savagery divide. In debating the application of the law of nations to conflicts with Florida Indians in the late 1810s, the United States made a contribution to the evolving understanding of international law by articulating three legal principles that deviated from Enlightenment thought and universalistic versions of natural law theory: that there were racial-cultural boundaries to the application of the rules of war, that some nations had a right to conquer territory occupied by other peoples, and that "wartime" was not always a clearly delimited period of time.

First, the United States explicitly injected a racial-cultural line into international law theory. In the wake of the war, supporters expressed two critical distinctions: between civilized and savage people and between sovereign and nonsovereign entities. Coupled with those distinctions were the presumptions that nonwhite people were uncivilized, that uncivilized people could not be sovereign, and that nonsovereign political entities were not covered by the law of nations. Many commentators concluded, therefore, that, as a general rule, nonwhite people did not enjoy the protections of the rules of war. This set of concepts anticipated doctrines of international law that became dominant later in the nineteenth century.

At the time of the Florida campaigns, prevailing European legal doctrine was still formally based on universalist principles of natural law. However, some prominent jurists, such as Vattel, referred to "savages," leaving open the possibility that, because of their behavior, some people might not enjoy the full protections of the rules of war. Vattel and other Enlightenment-era writers also maintained that the law of nations applied only to relations between sovereign nations, which provided a theoretical framework for excluding from the usual rules of war any polities that were not nations and/or not sovereign.[41] The United States used these intellectual wedges to open up a sharp legal rift between white Americans and Native Americans.

The violence against Creeks and Seminoles during the Seminole War was not new. There was a long history of unrestrained violence by European-heritage people against American Indians. One factor that was new in the Seminole War was the full-fledged public debate about that violence and its formal validation under the law of nations. More important, what was new was the assertion of inherent differences, rather than religious beliefs or objectionable behavior by the particular enemy, as a justification for the violence. Some defenders of violence against Creeks and Seminoles mentioned crimes or atrocities that Hillis Hadjo, Homathlemico, or other Creeks and Seminoles allegedly had committed, but supporters of the U.S. campaigns in Florida mostly relied on a blanket racial-cultural categorization of all Indians. Such racial-cultural classification presumed that everyone in a particular racial group shared the same "uncivilized" culture. The presumed lack of civilization of that racial group in turn meant that none of its polities could be "sovereign" and therefore signified that none of its polities could be included in the family of nations covered by international law. By racializing sovereignty, the United States racialized international law, using racial-cultural lines to define legal status. At a time when the law of nations formally still stressed universalist doctrine and the rules of war had come to emphasize the importance of humane conduct, the United States forged an alternative approach that exempted it from the obligations of humanitarian warfare during conflicts with Indians. The United States asserted that the laws of war and other aspects of international law did not constrain European and European-heritage nations when they dealt with non-Europeans.

Second, the Americans' racial-cultural line had spatial implications. The United States asserted that it could act extraterritorially in an area that was under the effective control of uncivilized, nonsovereign people.

At the time of the Seminole War, international law was framed around independent nations with defined and mutually exclusive territorial boundaries. Theoretical and diplomatic commitment to territorial sovereignty was a fundamental principle of the law of nations, and, increasingly, conquest and annexation of one European nation by another was viewed as violating people's right of self-determination. Nonetheless, Enlightenment-era scholar Vattel indicated an exception to the general rule about not intruding on others' territory when he questioned whether people who were primarily hunters were entitled to resist occupation of their land by those who would use the land in a more productive way by cultivating the soil. Americans used Vattel's mildly phrased exception to justify territorial expansion into Florida and, subsequently, across the continent. The United States claimed that it had both a right and a responsibility to extend agricultural practices into underutilized land—and, more generally, to spread civilization into uncivilized areas. As Congressman George F. Strother observed during the Seminole War debate, "[T]he Western frontier is that portion of the world where civilization is making the most rapid and extensive conquest on the wilderness, carrying in its train the Christian religion, and all the social virtues. It is the point where the race of man is most progressive; establish but the principle, that the God of nature has limited your march in that direction—that the Indian is lord paramount of that wide domain, around which justice and religion have drawn a circle which you dare not pass—the progress of mankind is arrested, and you condemn one of the most beautiful and fertile tracts of the earth to perpetual sterility, as the hunting ground of a few savages."[42] Stopping the spread of civilization, Strother argued, would hinder the progress of mankind. Thus, the United States used European notions about optimal use of land to advance its interests in Florida.

Even more emphatically, the United States used its understanding of the concept of sovereignty to further its interests. It circumvented the tenet of territorial sovereignty by arguing that Florida was a zone of exception. To Americans, Spanish sovereignty in Florida was legally meaningless because it was "derelict" and "nominal." Moreover, the people who actually controlled Florida, Creeks and Seminoles, were not sovereign in Florida because they were part of a racial-cultural group that, because of their collective presumed inferiority and barbarity, could not be sovereign. Meanwhile, the United States' own sovereign status meant that it was entitled to use all necessary means to defend itself from threats to its national security coming from an "ungoverned," disorderly neighbor. Thus, the defense of the Florida campaigns diverged from the doctrine of territorial sovereignty by interpreting Seminole, Spanish, and American sovereignty, respectively, so as to justify the United States in breaching the territorial border with Florida. Though forceful acquisition of Indian land through conquest was not new, this multifaceted approach to sovereignty contributed a novel justification for such conquest. The United States argued that in Florida it did not have to deal with normal strictures on the acquisition of territory by occupation and conquest. Over the longer term, this basic principle of the Seminole War—that the United States could occupy territory that lacked any truly sovereign authority—became central to the American political ethos of continentalism and manifest destiny.

Although Americans typically framed justifications for expansionism in terms of religion (the United States' providential destiny to spread its values), efficient use of land (cultivation), and political inferiority (lack of sovereignty), fundamental racial-cultural assumptions underlay the expressed rationales. Since whites tended to presume that people's cultural status correlated automatically with their racial classification, the outcome was aggressive extension of U.S. territory based largely on perceived racial distinctions.

Third, in the Seminole War debate Americans introduced an alternative way of viewing "wartime." Some of the explanations for why there was no need for an American declaration of war presumed a perpetual state of war against Indians, suggesting that, in its relations with certain groups of people, there were no boundaries to wartime. Since the laws of war permitted certain acts of violence only during discretely defined periods of war, the existence of an open-ended war with Indians seemed to justify constant violence against them. Furthermore, to white Americans, the notion of ongoing war with "Indians" explained why they could attribute to all Indians the conduct of any Indians. In an unending war, past atrocities by any Indians could be attributed to the Creeks and Seminoles, justifying Americans' unrestrained violence against them.

Less than two decades after the Seminole War, Henry Wheaton's landmark treatise, *Elements of International Law,* formalized the United States' approach to international law as expressed in defense of the Florida campaigns. The influential 1836 work, which was the first American study devoted to international law, rejected universalist law, endorsing the exclusionary vision asserted by the United States in its defense of the Florida campaigns.

Wheaton described international law as applying only to civilized, Christian nations. He bluntly stated that there was "no universal, immutable law of nations, binding upon the whole human race." Instead, European states' public law—as well as that of nations built from "European stock"—was based on their own specific "customs, usages, and conventions." Such law was inapplicable to people or nations that did not share Europeans' culture and religion, he wrote.[43] Thus, the first American scholar of international law legitimated a system that allowed Americans to disregard the normal rules of war in conflicts with Indians.

In other ways, too, Wheaton's treatise endorsed rules that were bound to be used against the interests of Native people. He generally prohibited ravaging enemy territory but made an exception if such destruction of property was necessary in order to secure a nation's frontier. He prohibited the killing of civilians or prisoners but allowed exceptions to all his general humanitarian rules in cases of necessity. As he explained, "[T]he rights of war, in respect to the enemy, are to be measured by the object of the war. Until that object is attained, the belligerent has, strictly speaking, a right to use every means necessary to accomplish the end for which he has taken up arms." At the beginning of his discussion of war, Wheaton asserted that "[e]ach state is . . . entitled to judge for itself what are the nature and extent of the injuries which will justify" a resort to force. Thus, Wheaton's treatise gave the United States (as well as other nations) wide latitude to commence a war for any purpose it deemed desirable and then to use whatever means it deemed necessary for achieving that purpose.[44] This perspective echoed arguments made by American supporters of the Seminole War.

Wheaton's treatise also took a generous view of territorial expansion. He highlighted "[t]he exclusive right of every independent state to its territory" but clearly did not extend that right to the Native people of the Americas. He noted that European countries had acquired clear title to regions of the New World based originally on conquest and later ratified by compacts among European nations as well as by "the general consent of mankind." As a matter of law, he declared, the first Christian discoverer of lands not only asserted a claim superior to that of other European nations but also extinguished Indians' title. Any "primitive title" that the Native people might have held had to give way "as the progress of cultivation gradually compelled the savage tenant of the forest to yield to the superior power and skill of his civilized invader."[45]

Paying particular attention to American interests, Wheaton asserted "[t]he right of every independent state to increase its national dominions" through lawful means, including "the pacific acquisition of new territory [and] the discovery and settlement of new countries." What should be regarded as a "pacific" acquisition, and what constituted "new" countries," was ambiguous. However, Wheaton's presumption that it was lawful for Europeans to unilaterally displace Indian title and sovereignty provided legal support for U.S. expansion into Indian territories. Moreover, his description of the United States' special interest in "the American continents," where European powers should not interfere, suggests that he endorsed the spread of the United States into areas like Florida. Lacking already-existing strong European control, such regions could not lawfully be pulled into the European sphere but, rather, properly belonged in the American realm.[46]

Wheaton also suggested that he might accept the third concept put forward by American supporters of the Florida expeditions—the notion of perpetual war against Indians—though he did not take an explicit position. Although he seems to have envisioned the normal state of war as having a fairly distinct beginning and end, his description of Indians being "gradually compelled" to yield to Europeans and European Americans implies a more extended, less time-limited process. Additionally, his portrayal of Indian polities as inferior to European-heritage political entities raises questions about whether he considered the former to be treaty-worthy. Wheaton explained that a war usually ended with a peace treaty; once the treaty was in effect, all force and all hostilities ended. Yet his definition of a "sovereign state" as any nation or people "which governs itself independently of foreign powers" made it doubtful that he considered Indian polities to be sovereign bodies that could commit to mutually enforceable peace treaties. Therefore, it seems plausible that, in Wheaton's view, there might be no restoration of peacetime between whites and Indians. Instead, there would be perpetual war. Interestingly, while Wheaton approached the subject of wartime indirectly, in 1826 another prominent American jurist, James Kent, addressed the topic more directly. In *Commentaries on American Law,* Chancellor Kent wrote that for American Indians, "continual war" was the "natural instinct."[47]

Thus, in the debate about the conflict with the Florida Indians, the United States articulated a new approach consisting of three important legal principles. It used racial-cultural criteria to determine both the enemy's legal rights and the United States' legal obligations under the rules of war. It also justified the occupation of territory controlled by "uncivilized" people who lacked recognizable sovereignty. Finally, it envisioned the possibility of perpetual war. These American views, as expressed by the United States government and its supporters in the 1810s, and formalized in American international law scholarship by Wheaton in the 1830s, would become dogma in Europe by the end of the century. Wheaton's treatise, which appeared in numerous editions and was translated into French, Spanish, and Italian, was influential not only in the United States but also in Europe. In fact, the American approach would strengthen a crucial foundation for Europe's second-wave imperialist projects in Africa and Asia later in the century. American application of the rules of war in the 1810s provided a reinforced rationale for Europeans' late nineteenth-century approaches to imperialism, as both the United States and Europe used racialized savage/civilized and sovereignty/nonsovereignty distinctions to bolster their imperial ventures.[48]

American National Identity and U.S. Sovereignty

The United States' treatment of Creeks and Seminoles in the Seminole War strengthened national identity in two significant ways: it reinforced the United States' identity as a white nation and it bolstered the United States' confidence in its own sovereignty.

In order to assert its position as a member of the European family of civilized nations, the United States established clear legal borderlines between European-heritage people and Native and African-descended people. White Americans evidently believed that only by drawing clear lines excluding blacks and Indians from the American polity could the United States claim its identity as a European-descended nation, equal to European nations and worthy of inclusion in the European family of nations.[49] The American treatment of Red Sticks and Seminoles helped the young Republic demonstrate that white citizens had a separate identity from American Indians and African Americans, reinforcing that neither of the latter groups was part of the American polity. European Americans believed they needed a narrowly defined "shared civic identity."[50] That shared identity was based not only on culture but also on race. When European-descended people of this era distinguished themselves from Indians, they were drawing a racial-cultural line. The executions of the two Creek men in 1818 enhanced the shared cultural and racial connections between European-heritage people in Europe and the United States, as well as the common bond of whiteness among white Americans. The exclusion of Indians and their allies—relegating them to the other side of the line of law—fortified white Americans' overall sense of nationhood. Excluding Indians as savages boosted whites' sense of collective identity and shared values.[51]

The Seminole War also reinforced American national identity by enhancing the United States' faith in its own sovereignty. To a significant extent, by subjecting Creeks and Seminoles to unrestrained violence and summarily executing two Indian prisoners, the United States strengthened its exclusive authority over a defined territory and the inhabitants thereof, signaling that the Indians were not separate, independent nations protected by the rules of war. The disregard for tribal nationhood and sovereignty that Americans expressed in connection with the Seminole War redirected the country's stance on Indians for the rest of the century. Just five years after the war, the *Johnson v. McIntosh* case formalized as a part of U.S. law the legal boundaries created by the civilized-versus-savage distinction. Eight years later, the Supreme Court endorsed U.S. policy not to recognize full tribal sovereignty and nationhood, declaring that the Cherokee Nation was not a foreign state but instead had an extraconstitutional status as a "domestic dependent nation."[52]

The doctrine of territorial sovereignty served a dual function for the United States. Indian tribes' lack of exclusive control of their territory indicated that they were not "sovereign." At the same time, the United States claimed that its own territorial sovereignty meant it had exclusive, plenary power over all its inhabitants, including Indians—even Indians who had moved into adjacent, "ungoverned" land outside the United States. Although the United States flouted the principles of territorial sovereignty when it acted extraterritorially against Seminoles and Red Sticks, throughout the nineteenth century it used the doctrine to justify its authority over Indians and its immunity from international law in its dealings with Indian tribes. U.S.-Indian relations were made a purely internal matter. The concept of exclusive territorial sovereignty supported the notion that U.S.'s treatment of Indians within its borders fell outside the scope of international law. The doctrine thus buttressed U.S. claims that Indians could seek no protections from international law. The United States was free to act as it deemed appropriate, without having to answer to international standards.[53]

To Americans, fortified U.S. sovereignty meant they could integrate into the European community of nations on their own terms. Among other things, that meant they asserted the right to determine the scope of their political community and to define how law applied within their own territory, even if American rules differed from those of European nations. When Andrew Jackson "outlawed" Hillis Hadjo and Homathlemico and their allies, he made it clear that while the United States counted itself among the civilized nations governed by shared principles of law, it also reserved the distinctive right to limit the applicability of rule of law culturally and racially. That is, Americans demanded acceptance as a full and equal member of the family of nations bound by the law of nations, but they also claimed that some of the norms that applied among European-heritage people did not constrain white Americans' actions in America against Native people and blacks. They wanted European recognition of the United States as a civilized nation on the rule-bound—rather than the lawless—side of the line. However, they also wanted to be exempt from the requirements of the rule of law when dealing with certain categories of peoples. Though they proclaimed themselves a nation whose citizens could depend on the rule of law, and they expected the law of nations to apply to relations between Europeans and Americans, they wanted to be free to treat "savages" as outside law. By summarily executing Hillis Hadjo and Homathlemico and by engaging in unconstrained violence against other Creeks and Seminoles, the United States clearly conveyed that it could apply different rules to its conflicts with Indians than would be presumed in conflicts between European-heritage nations.[54]

In the House debate on the Seminole War, Congressman Baldwin's explanation of the rationale for following different precepts in the Americas than within Europe provides the starkest expression of Americans' desire to be equal to but also distinct from Europe. When Baldwin stated that "[c]ivilized nations govern themselves by the laws of humanity," he left no doubt that he included the United States in that category. And when he observed that Indian wars were different from European wars, it was obvious that the distinguishing feature was the presumed savagery of Indians.[55] These two points provided the foundation for the early nineteenth-century American definition of the boundaries of law: Law would govern U.S. relations with Europeans as well as white Americans' relations with each other. But Indians—as well as others deemed to be savage and lawless—were beyond the boundary of law, outside the shield of law. Americans used the savage-civilized line to justify violence against Indians while still claiming a place for themselves among the civilized community of nations.

Thus, the strengthening of U.S. sovereignty and Americans' increased confidence in their nation's equality with European states occurred concomitantly with an increased assertion of authority over Indians, a decline in respect for the sovereignty and rights of Indians, and a rejection of sources of law that might protect Indians. As Leonard Sadosky's history of early American diplomacy demonstrates, these developments were correlated. Sadosky concludes that in order to fully establish itself as a nation the United States needed to undermine the attributes of Indian sovereignty. He argues that the United States only gained full recognition and sovereignty as a nation after it successfully established that Indian nations were not fully sovereign. During the eighteenth century, Indian polities had participated in a "borderlands diplomatic regime" that required Americans to acknowledge Indian sovereignty. However, in the period from the 1810s to the 1830s—around the same time as the United States gained full acceptance into the Europe-centered Westphalian diplomatic system—the United States subordinated and marginalized Indian nations.[56] The Seminole War played an important role in that development.

The Seminole War as Precedent for Future Violence against Indians

The summary executions and unconstrained hostilities against Florida Indians made a strong statement that Hillis Hadjo and Homathlemico individually, Seminoles and Creeks collectively, and Indians generally were outside the safeguards of the law of nations. Their presumed status as outside the shield of law reinforced rationalizations for treating Indians differently from non-Indians not only during war but also outside of military contexts. The Florida events showed that Americans thought they lawfully could deal with Indian tribes in an arbitrary and violent manner, unhindered by generally applicable legal principles. The idea that Indians were in a distinct legal universe had broad ramifications for Indians within or near the United States.

The unbounded military actions against Creeks and Seminoles signaled that there would be few legal checks on private violence against Indians. Most especially, the U.S. claim that it could execute two Creek captives without any legal procedures because they were from an "uncivilized" group had serious repercussions. It reinforced the perception that Indians were especially dangerous, an insidious threat to innocent frontier settlers. Rejecting legal process as a means of handling frontier conflicts with Indians, many whites felt justified in turning to vigilante acts to deal with the apparent Indian menace. Thus, Americans often used private violence, rather than formal criminal law, to police Indians on the frontier in the nineteenth century.[57]

Moreover, treating Indians as a distinct and subordinate legal category in the Seminole War paved the way for arbitrary treatment by the federal government. Indians' resistance to civilizing efforts, and the supposed threat Indians posed, served as a justification for their forced removal from areas near white settlements. Incidents like the Seminole War executions nudged the United States toward a more explicit Indian removal policy.

In the 1830s and 1840s, critics of removal amplified the arguments previously used in opposition to the Seminole War: Whig Party members and Protestant evangelical groups even more strongly emphasized the role of morality and rule of law in public policy. While Jacksonians were willing to use the relatively strong American military to force southeastern Indians to vacate their lands in order to advance the economic and security interests of European Americans, opponents of Indian removal explicitly argued that might did not make right and the United States had an obligation to act in a moral and honorable way in its relations with weaker people. A minority view, this perspective lost out to the Jacksonian approach. Within a dozen years after the Seminole War, mass expulsions of Indians from the southeastern United States were under way. Following the Florida precedent of unbounded violence, the United States freely used aggressive coercion to implement Indian removal. Later in the nineteenth century, the United States went even further, applying the principles underlying its military actions in Florida to the western Indian wars both within and beyond U.S. borders. The justifications for extraterritorial hostilities against Creeks and Seminoles in the 1810s reappeared in the 1860s–1880s to support American troops' warfare against Indians in the Plains and the Southwest as well as their expeditions into Mexico to suppress cross-border raids by "lawless" Indian "thieves and robbers" who allegedly preyed on American citizens.[58]

By the late nineteenth century, the United States had contained many of the tribes on reservations, which were "zones of exclusion" from the American nation. The federal government not only physically separated tribes from white Americans but also targeted them with an aggressive acculturation program. Additionally, the United States placed Indians both on and off reservations under a different legal regime than non-Indians. Programs that ostensibly acknowledged the inclusion of Indians in the American nation actually continued their distinct and separate—though not autonomous—status. Late nineteenth-century assimilation programs that fostered Indian acculturation were premised on a lack of tribal sovereignty and demanded Indian acceptance of federal government guardianship and second-class status in American society. Moreover, the Seminole War debates, by asserting American dominion over indigenous people, also reinforced the individual states' claims of jurisdiction over Indians within their borders, as well as states' laws that treated Indians differently from other state residents. The presumption that Indians were subject to federal and state government rule yet were outside the protections of law made arbitrary government action—including Indian removal, reservations, Congress's plenary power over Indians, and discriminatory state laws—appear justified to many whites.

Legal Borderlands

By "outlawing" Hillis Hadjo and Homathlemico, the United States delineated boundaries of law. It identified the edges of the applicability of law in a way that differed from the theoretical ideal described as governing both the American colonies and early nineteenth-century European nations. Yet defining the two men as beyond the shield of law was not an aberration in

U.S. history. The rhetoric used to explain their status exemplifies how numerous people have been classified as outside law even in a nation that identifies rule of law to be a central defining principle.

The treatment of Creeks and Seminoles during the Florida campaigns not only presaged U.S. dealings with other Indian tribes but also influenced U.S. conduct toward other groups. The executions of Hillis Hadjo and Homathlemico reinforced a conceptual framework that justified violent and arbitrary treatment not only of Indians but also of other people believed to be uncivilized, whether at home or abroad, as the United States extended its empire to distant parts of the world. Other countries, too, have limited the coverage of law in their own ways. But because Americans tend to take pride in being a nation of laws, the disparity between the ideal and the practice is particularly significant.

A 2005 collection of essays in the *American Quarterly* about "legal borderlands" explores how the United States has historically defined certain places and people as beyond legal protection. The essays illustrate how the United States has suspended law for such groups as "coolies," immigrants, and African Americans and has governed without legal constraints in some territories it controls outside the United States, such as the Guano Islands and Guantánamo. The editors of the special issue point out that those spheres without law were "ideological gaps" that nonetheless allowed continued belief in the United States as a nation governed by rule of law.[59] For Hillis Hadjo and Homathlemico, Florida was such a place—a sphere without law, an ideological gap—during the Seminole War. Not protected by law, the men were treated as if they were stateless, which they were not.[60] Because of the rhetorical construction that justified this exceptional space, however, the United States was able to maintain the argument that it was the law-abiding party and that the executed prisoners were the ones who were lawless and took themselves out of the sphere of law. What happened to these men was not just a rare exception to consistent rule of law, however. It demonstrates how malleable the borders of law were. The United States defined legal borders broadly when it presumed to put the two British men, Alexander Arbuthnot and Robert Ambrister, on trial outside the United States. It also defined legal borders broadly when it claimed that Indians and African-descended people were subject to U.S. will even when they were located outside the nation's territorial borders. Yet the nation demarcated legal borders narrowly when it identified the scope of the protective shield of law in a way that excluded the two Creeks. Thus, the executions demonstrated the long potential reach of American authority, while at the same time the debate about Hillis Hadjo and Homathlemico was a model for rationalizing the creation of places and people who are outside the law.

CHAPTER SIX

Race and Territoriality

The violence against blacks in Florida during the Seminole War most starkly evidenced how the United States restricted the boundaries of law and nationhood. In some ways, the theoretical foundation for the treatment of African-heritage people drew from the same doctrines as were applied to Creeks and Seminoles. Most especially, European-descended Americans tended to categorize blacks and Indians as uncivilized and stateless and therefore excluded from the law of nations. Additionally, the United States justified its attacks on both groups on the grounds of national self-defense. Moreover, both tended to be viewed as lawless if they refused to obey white American mandates, and the government maintained it was not bound to adhere to law in dealing with lawless people. Americans also saw the exclusion of blacks and Indians from law and nationhood as essential to their own effort to build a nation that was plausibly European in descent, thus warranting the United States' admission to the European community of civilized nations and creating a sense of common identity among white citizens.

Although there are parallels in the theories applied to blacks and Indians, there are also significant differences. In the Seminole War era, perceived racial distinctions played an even larger role in shaping how whites treated blacks. In the legal realm, disregard for ostensibly universalist principles was still more flagrant in Americans' treatment of African-descended people than it was for Creeks and Seminoles. There were no treaties to provide even a hint of consent or constraint in relations between the United States and blacks in Florida, and the practices of race-based slavery provided the worst kind of precedent. In effect, U.S. military actions in Florida in 1816 and 1818 extended American domestic slave laws into foreign territory and treated African-heritage people as legal targets for unrestrained violence wherever they were. Few Americans publicly questioned the extraterritorial, brutal slaying and abduction of blacks in Florida. In truth, Americans paid little attention to blacks' participation in the Seminole War at the time, and, perhaps as a result, many later accounts of the war ignored their crucial role. A number of historians have revived the history of blacks in the Florida wars that was largely missing from contemporary accounts, though scholars have not yet provided in-depth analysis of how Americans interpreted the legality of military actions against people of African descent during the 1816–1818 Florida campaigns. It is important to examine the legal issues.[1]

Why did leading Americans feel free to ignore territorial boundaries when dealing with people assumed to be fugitive slaves? And why was there so little concern about the level of violence directed against presumed runaways in Florida? National self-defense provided a widely accepted justification for the Florida expeditions, and the concept of the "pirate" was used loosely to rationalize U.S. military conduct. The notion of fugitive slaves as "outlaws" served as justification for unrestrained violence.

Blacks in Florida

When eleven fugitive slaves from the Carolinas came to Spanish St. Augustine requesting sanctuary and baptism as Catholics in 1687, Governor Diego de Quiroga refused to return them despite English demands. Other groups of runaways arrived over the next few years. Soon, royal decrees declared such refugees free, establishing a sanctuary policy that (except during twenty years of British rule in Florida) would last until 1790. By the early nineteenth century, the free black population of Spanish Florida, which included not only escaped slaves from the north and their free-born descendants but also immigrants from Santo Domingo and other Caribbean islands, had expansive opportunities. They received land grants, became entrepreneurs, practiced a variety of occupations, owned guns, and served in the military. Hundreds settled in maroon communities near Seminole villages between the Apalachicola and Suwannee Rivers, lived in St. Augustine and Pensacola, or occupied a free black town at Fort Mose in the northeast corner of Florida near St. Augustine. Additionally, there were black slaves in Florida, including fugitives from American slavery unable to obtain full free status, as well as people transported directly from Africa or brought in by planter immigrants from the United States. Compared to Americans, both Spaniards and Seminoles granted slaves more autonomy, mobility, opportunities, and rights. Thus, Florida's early nineteenth-century black population was a diverse mix of free and slave, living in the cities, on plantations in the countryside, and in villages near Seminole settlements.[2]

Anglo-Americans in colonial South Carolina and Georgia felt threatened by the nearby black settlements in Florida. They were particularly concerned about the free-black community at Gracia Real de Santa Teresa de Mose, which was two miles north of St. Augustine. Anglo-Americans presumed that Fort Mose contained African Americans and served as a continuing magnet for fugitive slaves. Colonists under James Oglethorpe attacked and destroyed the garrison in 1740, during the War of Jenkin's Ear. After the war ended in 1748, Georgia and Carolina planters tried to get Spanish officials in Florida to voluntarily return American fugitives. In 1749, South Carolina governor James Glen protested to the lords commissioners for trade and plantations that "both in Peace and War" the Spanish in St. Augustine "receive and protect the Negroes that desert from this Province." He alerted the commissioners to "the Danger that attends this Province from the Protection that our runaway Slaves receive at Augustine" and requested that the British minister in Madrid intercede to encourage a more cooperative Spanish policy in Florida. The following year Glen sent an agent to St. Augustine "to demand the Restitution of such of our Slaves as had deserted since the peace; and also to propose an Agreement to be entered into for the mutually delivering up of all such as should desert from either side for the future." Despite the Americans' forceful arguments, Spanish officials refused to restore the alleged slaves and instead rebuilt Fort Mose in 1752. Only in 1763, when the Spanish lost Florida to the British, did black inhabitants relinquish the fort and evacuate to Cuba.[3]

During the revolutionary and early national periods, African Americans petitioned for equal rights and called for the abolition of slavery and the slave trade.[4] As legal scholar Henry J. Richardson III has pointed out, not only their words but also their actions challenged slavery and racial oppression: slaves' flight to Florida constituted a rejection of the legitimacy of American law and an appeal not only to Spanish and Seminole law but also to transcendental, universal principles of natural law. Thus, though there may be a lack of written documents from African-heritage people in Spanish Florida, their actions can be interpreted as expressions of their legal and political position.[5]

Though black and white activists successfully achieved the gradual end to slavery in the North and obtained a federal law banning the importation of slaves as of January 1, 1808, the institution of slavery became further entrenched and even more brutal in the South after the Revolution. Georgians and South Carolinians became even more determined to solidify their control over slaves. After Spain regained sovereignty over Florida in 1783, American planters once again sought an official solution to the problem of slaves escaping there. At the behest of state and federal governments, agent James Seagrove traveled to East Florida three times between 1787 and 1797 to negotiate an agreement regarding the mutual return of fugitive or stolen slaves, but his meetings failed to satisfactorily solve the conflict. Tensions between southern plantation owners and the Spanish on the subject of runaway slaves consequently continued unabated into the 1810s.[6]

In addition to the fugitive slave issue, many white Americans resented the important contributions black militias—including the one based at Fort Mose—played in defending Florida for the Spanish. Such militias were particularly important in protecting Florida against the English in the 1720s and 1740s and in defeating the U.S.-sponsored "Patriot Rebellion" of 1812. White American commanders expressed anger at Spaniards' use of black troops, fearing that it might encourage slave flight and rebellion in the United States. In 1814, when British naval officers Edward Nicolls and George Woodbine settled former slaves from West and East Florida, French and Spanish Caribbean islands, and the United States in a fort at Prospect Bluff on Florida's Apalachicola River, Americans understood the potential military impact of the black militia being trained there. Many demanded the destruction of the garrison, which was located about fifteen miles north of the mouth of the river on the Gulf of Mexico and roughly sixty miles from the Georgia border. But the fort still stood when the War of 1812 ended, and even after the Treaty of Ghent the British continued to offer escaped slaves freedom there. According to estimates by General Edmund P. Gaines, in May 1815 there were 450 armed blacks and 900 Indian "warriors" at the fort. The following winter, after Nicolls and his troops had sailed home, the United States estimated that there were between 250 and 300 black men, women, and children living in the garrison, possibly joined by a smaller number of Indians. In addition, hundreds of other people of African descent resided nearby, along the banks of the Apalachicola River.[7]

Southern planters became increasingly agitated about the outpost they now called the "Negro Fort." Historian Claudio Saunt observes that "[t]o white Americans, the Negro Fort was an affront, a place where racial boundaries between black, white, and red threatened to dissolve." Southern newspapers continued to call for its destruction. In June 1816, a Georgia editor, outraged by the existence of a sanctuary for American runaways and disturbed by the "mischief" allegedly done to whites by inhabitants of the fort, asked, "How long shall this evil, requiring immediate remedy, be permitted to exist?" The author went on to state that if the Spanish did not "disperse this horde of ruffians, and deliver up the slaves to their owners," the United States should send troops to eliminate the problem.[8] While southern newspaper essays demanded demolition of the fort and killing or capturing of its inhabitants and northern papers reprinted some of those essays, northern publications and politicians did not speak out strongly against such a preemptive assault. Since the first African American–owned newspaper, *Freedom's Journal,* would not be founded for a decade and black Americans had only limited opportunities to publish their views, there appears to have been no public African American protest in advance of (nor in the years immediately following) the attack on the fort at Prospect Bluff.

Official military and diplomatic correspondence later referred to the fort as a "receptacle for fugitive slaves," a "general rendezvous" and "asylum" for runaways, and "a stronghold where [fugitives] found arms and ammunition to protect themselves against their owners and the Government." In March 1816, Gaines warned the top U.S. commander in the Southeast, Andrew Jackson, that the "Negro Fort" was "likely to produce much evil among the blacks of Georgia, and the eastern part of the Mississippi territory." Gaines concluded his letter by asking Jackson for approval to "break up" the fort. Secretary of War William Crawford had told Jackson to wait for Spain to act and said he could attack the fort only if the president so ordered. Nonetheless, Jackson agreed with Gaines that the garrison "ought to be blown up regardless of the ground it stands on" and proceeded with plans to ensure its demolition. In late April, noting that the fort contained 250 "negroes" who had been "enticed" and "inveigled" from American masters, he threatened the governor of Pensacola that if the Spanish failed to return the "stolen" slaves, the United States would be compelled to take care of the situation. Two weeks before he wrote that letter, Jackson had already given Gaines permission to attack the fort.[9]

Rather than striking the stronghold openly, the United States intentionally provoked the inhabitants to fire first by sending a "supply convoy" accompanied by two gunboats up the river right past the bluff on July 27, 1816. As expected, the men in the fort fired on the convoy. U.S. gunboats then successfully destroyed the garrison with a hot cannon ball to the central powder magazine. Fort commander Garçon, a black carpenter from Pensacola, survived but was captured. Lieutenant Colonel Duncan Clinch, who led the American land force that entered the fort, turned Garçon over to allied Creeks for execution. The exact number of people killed or captured in the expedition is unknown. Some American witnesses reported that the attack killed 270 out of the 320 people inside the fort and that, in the garrison and along the Apalachicola, U.S. and allied Creek troops captured approximately

100 other black residents, who were then carried into slavery in either Spanish Florida or the United States. However, the accounts of other witnesses suggest that the number of casualties and captives might actually have been lower, since many of those who lived in and around the post successfully escaped and fled east to settle along the Suwannee River. In order to justify their actions—and to make it clear that they were not enslaving random prisoners of war contrary to normal European practice—the Americans alleged that all the African-heritage people that they seized in Florida and brought to the United States were fugitive slaves from Georgia, legally owned by American citizens, while those who were taken to Pensacola had all escaped from their masters in that city.[10]

Even though many residents of the Prospect Bluff area escaped, Commodore Daniel T. Patterson, the naval commander at New Orleans, enthusiastically reported to the secretary of the navy that the expedition had been a tremendous success. "The service rendered by the destruction of this fort, and the negroes who held it, and the country in its vicinity," he wrote, "is of great and manifest importance to the United States, and particularly those states bordering on the Creek nation; as it had become the general rendez-vous of runaway slaves, and disaffected Indians, an asylum where they were assured of being received; a strong hold, where they found arms and ammunition to protect themselves against their owners and the government. This hold being destroyed, they have no longer a place to fly to, and will not be so liable to abscond."[11] Despite Patterson's confident words, however, the presence of black refuges in Spanish territory continued to be a major concern for American plantation owners even after the destruction of the Prospect Bluff post. One southern newspaper explained that the destruction of the "formidable receptacle of lawless banditti" had brought a degree of temporary security but that the long-term security of the border required that the United States obtain full possession of Florida.[12]

The continuing border security problem was partially alleviated in December 1817 by the U.S. occupation of Amelia Island, a barrier island off the Florida coast near the Georgia border. Though the immediate trigger for U.S. action was the seizure of the island by Scottish adventurer Gregor MacGregor and French privateer-smuggler Louis-Michel Aury, Americans were also concerned about Amelia Island's potential as an asylum for fugitive slaves from the U.S. South. However, the seizure of Amelia Island did not address the border issue further west, and southerners demanded broader action against Florida. Finally, in March 1818 Andrew Jackson led his troops south from Georgia for a full-scale invasion of Florida. As a main focus of the mission, Americans and allied Creeks indiscriminately killed and apprehended a number of African-descended people and burned down hundreds of Seminole and black homes along Lake Miccosukee, along the eastern bank of the Apalachicola River, and especially along the Suwannee River, where some four hundred blacks lived. When confronted by a force much larger than theirs, the Suwannee blacks fought back fiercely, allowing most of the civilians to successfully evacuate into the swamps. Although Jackson reportedly demolished about four hundred black and Seminole homes, he failed to wipe out the African-heritage population of the territory since many blacks living in northern Florida, perhaps even a majority, simply moved farther south on the peninsula. Nonetheless, the general declared the campaign a success. And he made sure he profited in an immediately tangible way: at least one of the blacks seized at Suwannee—formerly owned by a Spaniard in St. Augustine but a free man since about 1812—ended up as a slave on Jackson's Tennessee plantation.[13]

Like the 1816 attack on the Prospect Bluff fort, the Florida invasion of 1818 attempted to eliminate safe havens for runaway slaves and put an end to cross-border raids by blacks and Seminoles. It was not a coincidence that it was Andrew Jackson who initiated both incursions. The attacks exemplify what a leading historian of lynching, Christopher Waldrep, has called Jackson's "mob law spirit." Waldrep notes that Jackson was "famous for boldly killing enemies of the public, members of despised populations, without according them due process of law."[14] Few were more feared and loathed by southerners in general and by Jackson in particular than the allegedly lawless and violent fugitive slave, especially if that slave was supposedly conspiring with enemy Indians and British agents. Jackson wrote that his invasion of Florida was necessitated by the combination of "a savage foe" with "a lawless band of negro brigands" who were waging war on the United States. The seizure of St. Marks was justified, he added, because "Indians and negroes viewed it as an asylum," and the destruction of the Suwannee towns was necessary to "[b]reak down the hostile savages & Negroes in this quarter & give peace to our frontier." Tellingly, the summer before the attack, Gaines, accusing the Seminole chiefs of harboring "a great many of my black people among you at Suwanee," promised the chiefs that "[i]f you give me leave to go by you against them, I shall not hurt anything belonging to you." Gaines thereby conveyed that the United States' main concern in Florida was fugitive slaves, not Seminoles or Red Sticks. Other documents also evince the importance of the slave issue. On April 2, 1818, as Jackson's troops moved through Florida, British trader and Seminole ally Alexander Arbuthnot warned his son John that "[t]he main drift of the Americans is to destroy the black population of Suwany." Eleven days later, William McIntosh, commander of the allied Creeks, reported to Indian agent David B. Mitchell that his troops had just joined with Jackson's in Florida and "we are going this morning to fight the Negroes together . . . at Suwannee."[15] Although the Florida incursions of the late 1810s were known as the "Seminole" War, it is clear that the perceived threat of Florida's blacks was a primary motivation for initiating hostilities. During the course of the 1818 invasion, U.S. soldiers led by General Andrew Jackson especially targeted the black inhabitants of Spanish Florida, killing, seizing, and enslaving an indeterminate number of them.

The political debates that followed the 1818 expedition ignored potential legal problems with the extraterritorial application of state slave laws that presumed blacks were slaves, put the burden on alleged slaves to prove free status, guaranteed the mobility of planters' property rights in slaves, equated slave flight and resistance with a nonslave felon's refusal to submit to law, and permitted the use of deadly violence against fugitives.[16] Such principles provided an essential foundation for capturing, killing, and enslaving blacks within state boundaries. Extending their application across the international border into Florida would seem to pose a jurisdictional problem. In other contexts—such as contracts, insurance, and crimes—early U.S. law endorsed the principle of territoriality, which limited legislative and judicial jurisdiction to the nation's home territory. The general rule was that laws were not enforceable extraterritorially. In an apparent contradiction of this rule, in Spanish Florida the United States applied southern American states' legal principles as they pertained to blacks. Yet this inconsistency attracted little attention in the debates about U.S. actions in Florida.

Congress's winter 1819 debate about the legality of Jackson's conduct focused primarily on possible encroachments on Spanish sovereignty and violations of British agents' individual rights. Congressmen also devoted significant attention to the Creeks and Seminoles. However, blacks received little notice. The record of the debate consumed more than five hundred pages in the *Annals of Congress* but addressed the attack on the Prospect Bluff fort only on a few pages. Only a handful of congressmen even mentioned the destruction of the fort. Jackson's critics did not dispute the right of U.S. troops to kill or seize former slaves or other phenotypically African people in Florida. During the debate, congressmen said nothing about the complete lack of process afforded those people—who were turned over to Georgia claimants without any hearing whatsoever. Two representatives expressed regret about the destruction of the Prospect Bluff fort: Representative Charles Mercer lamented the 270 "unoffending Negroes and Indians" who were reported killed in the explosion and referred to the event as a "wanton" and "savage" "massacre." Mercer asked the administration to provide documents relating to the attack on the fort because he viewed it as the start of the Seminole War. His colleague Timothy Fuller was ashamed and horrified that the United

States wreaked such "[t]errible revenge" by blowing up the fort and that it allowed two of the leaders who survived the explosion to be subjected to "instant butchery." However, neither congressman argued that blacks had been treated unlawfully. Newspapers described the attack on the fort but did not comment on its legality with regard to the victims. Likewise, congressmen, newspaper authors, and military reports ignored legal problems with the extraterritorial deadly violence against people of African descent during the 1818 invasion of Florida.[17]

Why did legal issues pertaining to African-descended people prompt almost no public comment? What was the context in which Americans interpreted the legality of the military's actions in 1816–1818 against blacks in Florida? Many white Americans were accustomed to the violence and extraterritorial practices that underlay the institution of slavery. The lack of strong criticism of the treatment of blacks in the Seminole War meant there was no need for the administration and its political allies to present a strong defense of its actions with regard to African-descended people. Apparently, Americans just presumed that the United States had free rein. Underlying that presumption were concepts of utilitarianism, racism, self-defense, and outlawry.

Extraterritorial Precedent

Ever since the rise of the nation-state in the seventeenth and eighteenth centuries, one of the central principles of the law of nations had been territorial sovereignty. In the early Republic, American judges firmly endorsed strict territorial sovereignty because, as a weak state, the United States needed to prevent Europeans' interventions on American soil. The United States was just as concerned about Europeans' intrusions on American ships, especially in the late eighteenth and early nineteenth centuries. One of the United States' most serious complaints about Britain was that it claimed the right to search neutral American ships and impress British-born American seamen, whose naturalized U.S. citizenship British law did not recognize. The United States firmly asserted that no nation could apply its laws outside its own territory. Applying U.S. laws regarding the status of African-descended people to inhabitants of Florida seems contrary to that tenet. U.S. actions in Florida were also inconsistent with the principles expounded by influential jurist Emer de Vattel, who clearly stated that every nation had jurisdiction within its own territory and had to respect other nations' jurisdiction in their territory. Even after the Seminole War, American jurist Henry Wheaton strongly rejected the notion that any nation could wield extraterritorial authority. Referring especially to England, he said that a nation could apply its own laws only within its own territory, not abroad. He added, "[N]o government thinks of controlling by its own laws, property of its subjects situated abroad; much less does any government think of entering the territory of another power for the purpose of seizing such property and applying it to its own uses."[18] Yet the attacks on the Prospect Bluff fort and on the Suwannee and other villages blatantly disregarded the general tenet of territoriality. Buttressing the institution of slavery in the southern United States by retrieving slaves who had escaped to Florida and destroying sanctuaries that lured fugitives was considered an essential goal that could not be derailed by abstract territorial legal principles.

The U.S. treatment of blacks during the Seminole War was an example of extreme utilitarianism. Utilitarian concerns have always shaped law regarding African Americans and had widespread support across white America in the early Republic. Even when ostensibly universalist natural law theory formally dominated legal doctrine in the seventeenth, eighteenth, and early nineteenth centuries, in practice governing officials presumed that it was acceptable to apply different standards of law to African Americans. During the Seminole War, white policy-makers, who plainly regarded blacks as a separate and distinct group, clearly did not believe that it would serve their own interests to apply ordinary legal protections to African-descended people in Florida or to subject themselves to the ordinary territorial limits of law. Nor did they feel compelled to treat blacks equally on the basis of humanitarianism or commitment to human rights. Few contemporaries were willing to challenge the government's commitment to supporting slavery by any means possible. Even Jackson's strongest critics evidently saw no political advantage, legal mandate, or moral obligation to publicly label Jackson's treatment of Florida blacks as unlawful.[19]

In fact, in the wake of the 1816 and 1818 incursions into Spanish Florida, there was little public debate about Americans' right to seize African-descended people outside U.S. borders. White Americans accepted the premise that slaves were chattels, that is, moveable property. Therefore, they argued, Spain had an obligation to restore them back to their rightful place on U.S. plantations. Early nineteenth-century planters would concur with the eighteenth-century South Carolina agent who reportedly asserted to Florida officials, "[S]laves should be handled as were English ships which ran aground in Florida waters—returned to their owners."[20] If Spain failed to restore American slaves, planters were entitled to assert their property rights in Florida, they claimed.

Americans seemed comfortable assuming that American laws followed former slaves outside of U.S. territory even though slaves were not recognized as U.S. citizens and one could not presume their allegiance to the

United States or voluntary submission to American rule. Neither citizen nor alien, slaves in southern states were considered perpetually subject to American law. In a territory under the weak authority of Spain, the United States did not even have to prove that the blacks they were enslaving had ever lived in the United States. Because of the paired presumptions that blacks were slaves and that slaves were property, all African-descended people in Florida were vulnerable to capture and rendition to the United States whether they had fled American owners or not.

Disregard for the territoriality principle in this context contradicted not only the dominant tenet of territorial sovereignty but also the standard applied to the two British captives, Alexander Arbuthnot and Robert Ambrister. In the case of the British men, the United States proceeded on the assumption that a nation's laws extended only as far as its territory. This assumption served as a justification for Arbuthnot's and Ambrister's trials by military tribunals: because the Britons in Florida were beyond the reach of American civil laws, the United States claimed, they had to be tried by the military. Yet the United States applied a different principle to blacks, presuming that they were subject to American law whether they were within American borders or outside the United States.[21] Thus the United States manipulated the rules of spatial legality to suit its interests. The extraterritorial abduction of alleged runaway slaves in the 1810s was consistent with the broader pattern that emerged by the end of the nineteenth century. As historian Daniel Margolies explains, in the last quarter of the century, the United States continued its rhetoric in support of territorial sovereignty yet also exerted its power extraterritorially in weaker states controlled by people it deemed to be uncivilized.[22]

Though the United States' extraterritorial action provided a precedent for the future, such action also had a strong foundation in the past. Jackson's attacks—intended to defend American slavery against a serious black challenge—were founded on legal presumptions that were central to the entire institution of slavery.

The longtime existence of extraterritorial models in the Southeast was one reason Americans felt free to ignore territorial boundaries when dealing with people presumed to be fugitive slaves. By the 1810s, they had ample precedent to rationalize their treatment of African-descended people in Spanish Florida. Domestically, though state law provided the foundation for slavery, plantation owners were accustomed to having the right to repossess slaves from outside their state's jurisdiction. Article IV, section 2, clause 3 of the U.S. Constitution required that slaves who escaped into another state be returned to their owners. A federal law of 1793 implemented the constitutional guarantee, providing that owners were empowered to "seize or arrest" slaves who had fled to other states. Although the statutory mechanism included a judicial examination before removal of the slave from a free state, in practice slave-catchers were known to take captured fugitives back to their home state without first going before a judge to prove ownership, and slave states were reluctant to punish them for kidnapping. Even legally free African Americans were vulnerable to kidnapping and subsequent enslavement.[23]

Slave owners extended the principle of interstate comity to the international context and felt entitled to retrieve runaways across the southern U.S. border just as they recovered fugitives from neighboring states. The colonial period offered strong official precedent for such a policy. Legislation enacted in the two English colonies closest to Florida, South Carolina and Georgia, actively promoted slave-stealing raids into the Spanish territory. When private individuals entered Florida to kidnap escaped slaves, their local home governments not only declined to prosecute them but even rewarded them. Eighteenth-century statutes officially specified the rewards, reserving the highest sums for slaves captured south of the St. Johns River. Then, as now, the entire length of the St. Johns River was located in Florida. Even the northernmost point of the river (near present-day Jacksonville) was in Spanish territory. The colonial South Carolina legislature, noting that "many disobedient and evil minded negroes and other slaves . . . have fled to St. Augustine and other places in Florida, in hopes of being there received and protected" and that "many other slaves have attempted to follow the same evil and pernicious example," offered a hefty reward of one hundred pounds to any white or Indian who brought back an adult runaway found south of the St. Johns River—or fifty pounds for the scalp of such a runaway. Lesser, but still substantial, rewards went to those who captured slaves north of the St. Johns but south of the Savannah River (which runs along the border between South Carolina and Georgia). Once returned, such runaways were subject to execution for deserting out of the colony. The Georgia legislature likewise noted that because of the encouragement given to runaways in St. Augustine, it was "much to be feared that many Negroes will be tempted to desert from their Masters and fly there in hopes of being received and Protected which if not prevented may be attended with Consequences fatal to many of the Inhabitants of this Colony." Therefore, any white or other free person who apprehended an adult male fugitive south of the St. Johns River would receive a fifteen-pound-sterling reward; a "Scalp with two ears" brought a thirty-shilling reward.[24] Thus, both British colonies rewarded people who seized alleged fugitives in Spanish Florida.

After the Revolution, there was a hint of a new policy, suggested by a 1797 opinion by U.S. Attorney General Charles Lee that American William Jones, who had used violence to retrieve fugitive slaves in Florida, should be extradited to Spain for punishment. "It is an offence against the laws of nations," Lee wrote, "for any persons . . . inhabiting within the limits of the United States, to go into the territory of Spain with intent to recover their property by their own strength." The United States would take the same legal position with regard to British territory in Upper and Lower Canada. As it turned out, however, although Lee's principle was effectively applied along the U.S.-Canadian border, it went mostly unenforced along the U.S.-Florida line. The difference between British and Spanish sovereignty in North America determined the reality of the northern and southern border situations for African-descended people in the early nineteenth century. Britain recognized the freedom of every person who reached Canadian soil, and it had the power to stand behind that principle. Consequently, instead of seeking a military solution or furtively retrieving their own slaves, American slave owners who wanted to recover their fugitives from the Canadas sought legal and diplomatic solutions: they sought remedies in Canadian courts and pressed the U.S. government to negotiate an extradition agreement. The situation on the southeastern U.S. border was different because Spain wielded less power in Florida than Britain did in the Canadas. In the Southeast, the failure of attempts in the 1790s to persuade the Spanish to return escapees convinced Georgian and South Carolinian planters that they had to continue to resort to self-help. During the first two decades of the nineteenth century, southern planters repeatedly entered Florida surreptitiously to recover (and steal) slaves.[25]

In addition to approving of individual slave-seeking ventures in Florida, many Americans supported the right of U.S. troops to seize fugitive slaves, analogizing the nation's rights with regard to blacks and Seminoles in Florida to other situations within the country's borders. The subject received attention in early 1819 during the congressional debate. Representative Alexander Smyth analogized the nation's rights to those of an individual property owner. "I may pursue and destroy on your land a noxious animal which I have started on my own," he declared. "If your house adjacent to mine is on fire, I may enter on your premises, and pull it down, for the preservation of mine." The U.S. military could act on behalf of the nation in parallel circumstances, he explained, because "[w]here the reason is the same, the law is the same." Similarly—though primarily with Seminoles in mind—Representative James Ervin proclaimed that since "a fort bears the same relation to a nation as a house does to an individual," to capture a criminal a government lawfully could send troops into a neighboring nation's garrisons just as it could send officers into a private home within U.S. territory.[26]

As noted earlier, in addition to slave-catching raids, Americans also entered Spanish Florida for other purposes. Many Americans viewed the territory as a natural extension of their country, were eager to make Florida a part of the United States, and resorted to a variety of tactics, ranging from diplomacy to filibustering, to accomplish that goal. Collective official and unofficial excursions intended to secure American dominion over Florida—which would have provided a long-term solution to the planters' fugitive slave problem there—provided precedent for the 1816 and 1818 forays.

Thus, not only had both South Carolina and Georgia long encouraged their citizens to cross the border to capture slaves, but many southerners supported the idea that the U.S. army could be used to catch runaways. Moreover, the federal government had incited or condoned several filibustering missions. Consequently, U.S. military actions in 1816 and 1818 were consistent with prior private and official acts that provided useful precedent. U.S. conduct in the 1810s continued the long-held notion that blacks' presumed status as property persisted even when they were in a foreign jurisdiction. Acting in accordance with established precedent, Jackson never explained the legal foundation for his extraterritorial abduction and killing of blacks in Florida—and evidently nobody demanded that he do so.

Self-Defense

The second reason few Americans raised the territoriality issue with regard to U.S. campaigns against black settlements in Spanish Florida is that they insisted such expeditions were necessary for national self-defense. Self-defense was a core principle of the law of nations. Before the Seminole War, many white Americans believed—or claimed to believe—that African-descended men in Florida had attacked white settlers in Georgia and Alabama and were preparing to launch more vicious attacks in the future. Though whites' biggest concern may actually have been the threat to the institution of slavery posed by the very presence of independent black refuges just over the border from Georgia, plantation owners' public remarks focused on the menace of cross-border violence. Prior to the Florida expeditions, they argued that it was essential for American troops to enter Florida in pursuit of blacks and their Seminole allies because the danger to U.S. citizens along the southeastern border was certain and imminent.[27]

Presenting the self-defense argument most forcefully in Congress after the Seminole War were Representatives Henry Baldwin, John Floyd, George F. Strother, and Alexander Smyth. In 1816, they contended, fugitive slaves in the Prospect Bluff fort threatened to wreak "a savage negro war" against the United States. The congressmen further claimed there was a large stash of arms in the outpost "manifestly destined to be used against the United States," and the fort's denizens had already killed sailors who had landed nearby seeking water. In 1818, Baldwin, Floyd, and Strother asserted, blacks in Florida were engaged in a slave insurrection; they were "assembled and armed for purposes hostile to the country." The congressmen noted that "rebellious slaves . . . observe no law, human or divine." Like their Seminole allies, they were "fiends" who were eager "to murder, indiscriminately, men women, and children, burn, plunder, and destroy, without distinction, without remorse." From their bases in Florida, the four congressmen warned, the black "banditti" were planning further vicious acts of war against the United States. "Is there any nation more interested in avoiding neighbors of a certain description than the United States?" Representative Smyth asked rhetorically. "Would it be safe to allow Florida to be revolutionized by black troops?" In order to protect its citizens against black violence, the men argued, the government had the right—even the duty—to eliminate the threat, and if they could not otherwise remove the imminent danger, they could enter neighboring territory to do so. Their House colleagues apparently agreed overwhelmingly. Congressmen based these shrill warnings largely on distorted and untrue factual assertions. Nonetheless, the frightening claims about the danger posed by people of African descent apparently resonated with many white southerners.[28]

The portrayal of Florida blacks preying on innocent frontier families implicitly validated the public perception that African-descended people along with Seminole allies had initiated "war" against the United States and that the United States was compelled to fight back. Since Florida's blacks posed a serious threat to the southern frontier and Spain was unable or unwilling to prevent their depredations, the government and its supporters argued, the United States was entitled to defend itself, even if it had to enter Spanish territory to do so. A nation's right to preserve itself took precedence over competing claims, they asserted, so self-defense justified American troops' killing and apprehension of African-descended people in Florida.

In the 1819 congressional debate, two lone representatives questioned whether self-defense actually required the 1816 destruction of the Prospect Bluff fort and the killing of so many people living there. U.S. troops had no right to fire on the garrison when its residents were merely trying to defend it against the Americans' clearly hostile intent, Representatives Charles F. Mercer and Timothy Fuller argued. However, rather than focusing on the legal rights of the fort's occupants, Mercer's and Fuller's arguments emphasized Spain's entitlements and Congress's constitutional prerogatives. Likewise with regard to Jackson's 1818 sweep through Florida, though Mercer and Fuller broadly criticized the foray as a violation of neutral relations with a European nation and an encroachment on Congress's powers, neither commented on the army's treatment of African-descended people there; they did not challenge the United States' legal justification for killing and enslaving blacks captured during that expedition.

During the debate, no other congressmen expressed concern about the legality of killing so many black civilians and militiamen in the Prospect Bluff fort. To the contrary, the House of Representatives voted to give the officers and crew of the gunboats a monetary reward for blowing up the fort.[29] Congressmen overwhelmingly supported U.S. actions against African-descended people in Florida on the ground of national self-defense.

Land Pirates and Extraterritoriality

The third rationale ostensibly permitting the hunting of people of African descent outside U.S. borders was that they were like "pirates," people who obeyed no nation's laws and who were subject to punishment by any nation wherever they were found. Typically, pirates committed their crimes and were captured on the ocean, outside any nation's exclusive territorial jurisdiction. The law of nations recognized universal jurisdiction over pirates, which meant any nation could prosecute them. In 1790, the United States officially asserted its jurisdiction over pirates its ships captured on the ocean, and federal law imposed the death penalty on people judged to be pirates. Although pirates normally were seafaring criminals, they did not have to be. In fact, during the early national period the popular definition was quite broad. As one writer pointed out in the *National Register,* there were "land pirates as well as water pirates." The black and Seminole "banditti" in Florida, who had committed extreme villainous acts on land, were land pirates, the author argued. Three years earlier, Andrew Jackson himself had referred to the inhabitants of the Prospect Bluff fort as "land-pirates."[30] Accordingly, they could be subject to summary extraterritorial punishment by the United States, just as a pirate on the ocean could be.

Indeed, to many southern whites, a black person's mere refusal to submit to slavery could make that person a "pirate" or "outlaw," most especially if the person had previously been a slave. During the congressional debate about the 1816 and 1818 incursions, Representative Baldwin asserted that, as a class, runaway slaves were "outlaws and pirates." Moreover, he added, their status did not change because they had gone to Florida. Americans could follow them into the Spanish territory and assert control over them.[31] The perception of fugitive slaves as land pirates, along with the self-defense argument and the extensive precedent for wide-ranging slave-catching operations, served as justification for the United States' extraterritorial conduct in Florida.

Violence against Outlaws

Explicitly and implicitly, the concept of the "pirate" or "outlaw" was an essential foundation to justify not only extraterritorial armed hostilities but also the use of deadly violence against people of African descent. When Congressman Baldwin claimed that African American fugitives found in Florida could be treated like runaway slaves who remained within the United States—that because of their refusal to obey the law they could be captured or killed by anyone they met—he was merely stating long-standing principles of American slavery.[32] The conception of fugitive slaves as outlaws, combined with the presumption that blacks had slave status unless they could prove otherwise, had deep historical roots in American history.[33] White Americans customarily treated fugitive slaves as outside the shield of law, and European Americans normally were not legally accountable for violence against disobedient or threatening African Americans. Southerners' tendency to categorize all runaways as rebels and outlaws—and their assumption that all blacks in Florida were fugitives from American plantations—made American troops' treatment of blacks in Florida seem natural, not unlawful. Normal legal protections were deemed irrelevant.[34]

Europeans had set precedents for labeling criminals as outside the law and for justifying unrestrained warfare against outlaws. Going back to the medieval era, Britain had an official outlawing process that targeted individual criminals who were declared outside the sphere of legal protection and could be killed with impunity. Under traditional English common law, an accused felon who refused to submit to legal process could be proclaimed an outlaw and would thereafter have *caput lupinum* (the head of a wolf). As jurist William Blackstone explained it, such a person was "put out of the protection of the law" and "might be knocked on the head like a wolf, by any one that should meet him; because, having renounced all law, he was to be dealt with as in a state of nature, when every one that should find him might slay him." By the time Blackstone wrote those words in the 1760s, he declared that England had discontinued the inhumane practice.[35] Yet, in the late eighteenth- and early nineteenth-century United States, where slaves were treated as property, recalcitrant fugitives were habitually treated like outlaws, killed even if they had committed no crime other than escaping slavery and resisting apprehension.

The precedent for presuming blacks' slave status and for treating fugitive slaves as outlaws was so well entrenched that it apparently did not occur to commentators to complain of any violation of blacks' rights in the massacre at the Prospect Bluff fort, the summary execution of the leader Garçon, or the killing and enslaving of black inhabitants of villages along the Suwannee and Apalachicola. In the past, Anglo-American colonists had rhetorically positioned all slaves outside the law. For example, South Carolina statutes of 1712 and 1722 explained that "negroes and other slaves . . . are of barbarous, wild, savage natures, and such as renders them wholly unqualified to be governed by the laws, customs, and practices of this Province." In the nineteenth century, a South Carolina judge asserted, "[i]n the very nature of things [a slave] is subject to despotism. Law to him is only a compact between his rulers."[36] Even free blacks were potentially vulnerable to being declared outside the protective sphere of law. Three years after the Declaration of Independence, Thomas Jefferson proposed a Virginia bill to outlaw certain categories of "negroes and mulattoes." The bill declared all emancipated slaves who did not depart the commonwealth within a year to be "out of the protection of the laws." Likewise, any "negroes or mulattoes" who came into Virginia "of their own accord" would be "out of the protection of the laws"; an exception was made only for seamen, who could remain for twenty-four hours before being outlawed.[37]

Though state statutes sometimes entitled slaves to criminal trials, the use of courts for slaves was rare. Southerners were accustomed to a system in which masters punished slaves on plantations outside formal law. Extralegal violence against slaves, without any concern for due process, was the norm. Historian Christopher Waldrep points out that such a system, which held people accountable to public opinion rather than law, fostered lynching and vigilantism. It was bad enough for slaves on a plantation, but runaways were subject to physical violence not only by their purported owners but also by strangers. They were systematically excluded from legal protections because they refused to submit to the laws that enslaved them. Southeastern colonies and states had a long history of applying the principles of outlawry to fugitives, allowing slave-catchers to take the lives of those who resisted capture. In short, killing and enslaving blacks in Florida in 1816–1818 raised no legal objections because southern Americans had long been accustomed to unrestrained violence against fugitive slaves and had laws in place to validate that practice.[38]

For over a century, Florida's neighbors in the Carolinas (settled 1670) and Georgia (1733) had provided for outlawing and killing fugitive slaves. Those laws, which were based on precedent established in earlier Virginia statutes, did not always use the term "outlaw," but their provisions were consistent with the traditional practice of outlawry. At least as early as 1715, North Carolina permitted the slaying of fugitive slaves against whom justices of the peace had issued a proclamation. Later laws explicitly referred to slaves "killed on outlawry." A late colonial statute that criminalized the willful murder of slaves exempted from punishment those who killed "any Slave outlawed by virtue of any Act of Assembly of this Province" (as well as any slave resisting his owner or dying in course of "moderate correction"). Closer to the Florida sanctuary, South Carolina and Georgia legislated even more extensively on the subject of runaway slaves. As early as 1691, South Carolina required militia captains to pursue fugitives and to bring them back "either alive or dead" and also provided that there was no penalty for taking the life of a slave who was caught stealing and resisted capture. Eighteenth-century statutes permitted anyone in the colony to apprehend a runaway slave. The laws also declared it lawful to beat, maim, or assault a defiant runaway and even to kill him if he refused to be taken. When Georgia legalized slavery, its legislature borrowed from South Carolina's laws. Both South Carolina and Georgia allowed whites to moderately correct slaves who refused "to submit to . . . examination" and to kill slaves who assaulted or struck whites. Both imposed the death penalty on slaves who ran away with the intent of leaving the colony, as well as on anyone who tried to entice slaves to escape "by specious pretence of promising them freedom in another country."[39]

England did not invalidate such statutes. The Court of King's Bench ruled in *Somerset v. Stewart* (1772) that holding slaves was illegal in England itself, but it did not prohibit slavery in the colonies, where local positive law could sustain the institution. Scholar Eliga Gould notes that in the 1760s and 1770s Britain was trying to end that "bifurcated geography" and to incorporate interior portions of America into "Europe's diplomatic republic."[40] However, the colonists resisted British efforts to impose metropolitan norms and reforms. The resulting American Revolution politically separated the United States from its former colonial power, leaving Americans even freer to forge their own legal path.

The ensuing U.S. Constitution did not force any positive change in the treatment of slaves. Colonial-era precedent guided practice in the early national period, when states continued to permit extreme violence against slaves who resisted by escaping their masters' control and refusing to submit to slave-catchers. Slave codes enacted during the colonial period, at the height of slave importation, became the lasting foundation for American slavery. Andrew Fede's thorough study of early national- and antebellum-era judicial opinions found that colonial-era statutory provisions pertaining to violence continued in effect in the nineteenth century. Although postrevolutionary legislatures enacted some new limits on white violence against slaves in the nineteenth century, the purpose was not to protect the lives and safety of slaves but to defend slave owners' property interests against poor whites' physical violence against slaves. Masters continued to enjoy substantial leeway in punishing their own slaves, and runaways were still exempted from prohibitions on excessive violence by strangers.[41]

Some states utilized a formal outlawry process well into the nineteenth century, while others abandoned official proclamations of outlawry but nonetheless considered themselves bound by no legal constraints in dealing with runaways. In North Carolina, for example, slaveholders often published justices' outlawry proclamations and offered rewards for the return of slaves—or their decapitated heads. Just a few months after Andrew Jackson's incursion into Florida, William P. Moore of New Bern, North Carolina, offered a twenty-five-dollar reward for the apprehension and delivery of his teenage slave, Charles Emery—or fifty dollars for Charles Emery's head. Moore also obtained a proclamation of outlawry from two justices of the peace. Dated September 17, 1818, and promptly published in local newspapers, the proclamation asserted that Charles Emery had "absented himself from his . . . master's service, and is lurking about in the county, committing acts of felony and other misdeeds." The proclamation commanded Emery to return home, required the county sheriff to search for the slave, and authorized the sheriff to raise a posse to assist him. Finally, the document declared that, in accordance with state law, if Charles Emery "doth not surrender himself and return home immediately after the publication of these presents, that any person may kill & destroy the said slave, by such means as he or they may think fit, without accusation or impeachment of any crime or offence for so doing, and without incurring any penalty and forfeiture thereby." Other North Carolina proclamations of the time period used the same formulaic language, with only slight variations.[42] These formal proclamations represent only a small proportion of runaways whom slave-catchers hunted down. Even in the absence of official designation as "outlaws," fugitive slaves were often treated as outlaws. As one newspaper essay pointed out, the term "outlaw" applied not only to "a man who is judicially proclaimed as such" but also to someone who, by his own action, made himself a "pirate" and thus who was the enemy of all nations even in the absence of any formal court declaration.[43]

There is ample verification that white Americans actually killed fugitive slaves. In response to the 1739 Stono Rebellion, in which eighty slaves tried to escape to Florida, South Carolinians killed forty-four fugitives during attempted apprehension, and they captured and decapitated the rest (and placed their heads on spikes to send a warning to other slaves). The South Carolina General Assembly granted immunity from prosecution for all of those killings. The legislature explained that "the exigence and danger the inhabitants at that time were in and exposed to, would not admit of the formality of a legal trial of such rebellious negroes, but for their own security, the said inhabitants were obliged to put such negroes to immediate death." Therefore, any killing of negroes was declared "lawful . . . as fully and amply as if such rebellious negroes had undergone a formal trial and condemnation."

Thus was the lack of due process retroactively excused. Likewise in situations that involved no "rebellion" against whites, deadly violence was used against runaways. The journal of the South Carolina Assembly lists a number of planters whom the government would compensate for their slaves killed by patrols. Among them was Reverend John McLeod, who received £250 in 1751 after a member of a slave patrol, "being in quest of some Run-away Negros, did surprize a Camp of them on the Marshes near New-Cut; and firing among them, one of the said Run-aways [the reverend's slave Ben] was killed upon the Spot." A 1787 joint expedition by Georgia and South Carolina militias against "the banditti of runaway slaves" who had set up an independent settlement at Patton's Swamp, Georgia, killed at least eight blacks, captured numerous others, and destroyed twenty-one houses. That many other fugitive slaves were slain in the eighteenth and nineteenth centuries is evident from newspapers and official records.[44] Well into the nineteenth century, fugitive slaves from Georgia and the Carolinas continued to have "heads like wolves."

The slaughter and taking of captives at the Prospect Bluff fort and along Florida's rivers during the 1810s must be seen in this historical context. The widespread classification of all African-descended people in Florida as fugitive slaves clearly conveyed that they could be treated like wolves. In fact, sometimes they were explicitly referred to as wolves. A prominent example occurred in June 1816, when Andrew Jackson referred to the Prospect Bluff fort as a "den of wolves."[45] Allegations that Florida blacks had engaged in cross-border depredations further reinforced the notion that they were "outlaws" and "banditti" and that therefore there were no constraints on white violence taken against them.

As previously noted, between the 1770s and the 1810s, African Americans actively petitioned for equal rights and called for the abolition of slavery and the slave trade. However, in that time period, before the rise of a strong abolitionist movement, few openly challenged the legitimacy of a process that—whether through formal proclamation or de facto practice—removed human beings from the protection of homicide laws. There were a few exceptions, such as a comment about North Carolina that appeared in the *New-York Daily Advertiser* about a month before Jackson took U.S. troops into Florida: "If the laws of that state admit of a process of outlawry, the effect of which is to reduce a man to the condition of a wild beast, that he may be hunted down as game by the first butcher that meets him, they are not only a disgrace to a civilized, but much more to a christian country." In later decades criticism of violence against fugitive slaves and other free blacks would become blunter. A particularly powerful example is an 1852 article in *Frederick Douglass' Paper* that resolutely supported blacks' right to resist enslavement by kidnappers by all means necessary. A Maryland slave owner had recently been killed while trying to capture four fugitive slaves in Christiana, Pennsylvania, and thirty-eight people had subsequently been arrested and charged with treason. The writer protested that by denying people the right to resist slavery the "government has virtually made every colored man in the land an outlaw, one who may be hunted by any villain who may think proper to do so." Under the American laws of slavery, a hunted man who defended himself was subject to capital punishment. The author exposed the absurdity of such laws, observing that since "[t]he basis of allegiance is protection," alleged slaves owed no allegiance to a government that "stript [them] of all legal protection." Under the law of nature, people were entitled to defend themselves by "shooting down" anyone who tried to reduce them "to the condition of a brute." Nobody had the right to enslave a person, nor to use deadly violence in an effort to take a captive, he argued. By the 1850s, antislavery advocates, both black and white, commonly used newspapers, pamphlets, and speeches to challenge the kidnapping of free blacks and deadly violence against fugitive slaves.[46] However, in the 1810s, the public forum heard few such vigorous public criticisms of violence against alleged fugitive slaves and free blacks.

Thus, at the time of the 1816–1818 killing and abduction of blacks in Florida, few Americans, black or white, openly challenged the lawfulness of the government's actions. Not many publicly contested the validity of a definition of "property" that included humans. Few argued that fugitive slaves could refuse to be bound by immoral fugitive slave laws and proclamations, or asserted that higher principles of natural law warranted slaves' escape and resistance to recapture. The legitimacy of laws that forced people to accept slave status or be murdered was not a prominent part of the public debate. The near absence of public challenge to the mode of capturing fugitives in the 1810s meant that participants took the process for granted. That many white southeasterners accepted the legality, propriety, and normality of hunting and slaying runaways allowed them to participate in Jackson's roundup and killing of African-descended people without questioning its lawfulness. Few openly challenged this aspect of Jackson's conduct in Florida.

Nationhood

The Seminole War provides an example of how racial ideology helped build American national identity, an identity based on "racial nationalism." The early Republic, an era of increasing populist democracy for white men, was a period of rising racial exclusion as free blacks increasingly were shut out of the American polity. Historian Robert J. Cottrol describes the ideological shift from the eighteenth century, when there was a "relative absence of racial exclusion," to the nineteenth century, when the racial climate became "less tolerant." Whereas the revolutionary generation had recognized that blacks could be citizens, the Jacksonians idealized the notion of a white republic and were unwilling to view free blacks as potential citizens. Cottrol notes that the "new ideological turn" toward white supremacy accelerated after 1815, leading to a "growing tendency in the Jacksonian era to read free Negroes out of the body politic and the term *the people*." The violent attacks on African-heritage people in the Florida campaigns occurred at exactly this time, when white Americans were becoming less willing to recognize blacks as fellow Americans and more likely to categorize free blacks with slaves. While some states still recognized that free blacks were members of the American community and included them as voting citizens, militiamen, and jurors, other states systematically excluded them from the most important rights of members of the civic polity. Some went even further, enacting legislation—the Negro Seamen Acts of the early 1820s—that imprisoned foreign black sailors when they were in U.S. ports, thus refusing to acknowledge that African-descended people could be citizens of other predominantly European-heritage nations. These developments coincided with a shift in the understanding of race. In the new "racial science" of the early national period, racial differences that had previously been presumed to be environmentally determined (and therefore malleable) came to be perceived as intrinsic, biologically determined, and unchangeable. This shift provided support for the view that blacks were too inherently different to be part of the American nation.[47]

Five months after the United States demolished the Prospect Bluff fort, a diverse mix of people formed the American Colonization Society, whose goal was to help blacks in the United States migrate to a new colony in Africa. Some white supporters acted from racist motives; they did not want Africans to be a part of the nation. Others saw themselves as benevolent reformers: Because it was impossible for blacks to assimilate into American society as equals, such advocates for colonization thought it was humane to help them move somewhere where they would be freer and more independent. In fact, some African-descended people, seeing persistent discrimination and violence against nonwhites, despaired of any future in the United States and initially supported the colonization movement as a way for blacks to achieve autonomous nationhood. To them, it seemed that blacks were a separate nation within the American nation. Establishing their own independent nation outside of U.S. borders was the only way they would ever significantly improve their condition. However, most blacks vigorously opposed the movement on the ground that they were part of the American nation. In January 1817, resolutions by James Forten, Richard Allen, and other "People of Colour" in Philadelphia declared opposition to the plan "to exile us from the land of our nativity." A decade later, with the founding of the first African American newspaper, *Freedom's Journal,* African Americans had more opportunity to express their views. In the first year of the newspaper's publication, Reverend Allen wrote, "This land which we have watered with our tears and our blood, is now our mother country." That same year, another writer asserted in the paper, "The free people of colour will never go to Africa." They "are as truly Americans, as the President of the United States," and their "rights to the country are equally as good as . . . any other citizens."[48]

At a time of debate about this issue within both the black and the white community, the Florida campaigns made a strong statement that African-descended people were neither Americans nor foreigners. They were subject to U.S. law but assured of no rights. Though white commentators on the Seminole War disagreed sharply on the legality of U.S. actions with regard to Spanish and British men's rights, there was almost no challenge to the country's actions as they affected blacks. Even those who contended that the U.S. entry into Spanish territory, seizure of Spanish forts, and execution of British subjects violated the laws of war apparently saw no problem with American hostilities toward African-heritage people in Florida. The expeditions' legal premise as it pertained to blacks—that they were outside the protections of both American law and the law of nations—was devastatingly uncontested. That legal premise both drew from and reinforced many whites' opinion that blacks in the United States neither were part of the American nation nor constituted their own independent nation. Only members of the American polity were entitled to constitutional rights and due process, and only people acting on behalf of sovereign nations got the benefit of the laws of war. The United States denied Florida blacks any legal status that could provide a foundation for claims based on law. The American treatment of blacks in the Florida expeditions conveyed the message that the Supreme Court would formally endorse four decades later in the *Dred Scott* case: African-descended people were not American citizens and had no rights that whites had to respect, yet they were subject to U.S. sovereignty.

Support for the Florida incursions thus implicitly conveyed that blacks were "foreign in a domestic sense." Legal scholar Devon Carbado applies this phrase, which originally appeared in a Supreme Court decision characterizing the status of Puerto Rico, to blacks in the United States. Mirroring the language of *Downes v. Bidwell,* Carbado explains that "under slavery, blacks were 'subject to the sovereignty of and . . . [were] owned by the United States.' Moreover, with respect to citizenship, blacks had 'not been incorporated into the United States, but . . . [were] merely appurtenant thereto as a possession.'" Blacks in America were not foreigners, nor were they citizens. Instead, they were subjects of—and owed allegiance to—the United States. They were "inferior beings that belonged to America," which governed them as a subordinate class. Thus, blacks in the United States faced an "inclusionary form of exclusion." The color line constituted an internal border within the American community.[49]

Thomas Jefferson and other European Americans of his era had spoken of blacks as a separate nation.[50] However, by 1818 the more dominant strain of thought viewed blacks as neither a separate nation nor a prospective separate nation. They were an intrinsic part of America, "foreign in a domestic sense." They were not aliens and not citizens but were a constant threat that needed to be controlled for national self-preservation.

The American treatment of African-descended people in the Florida campaigns helped define the United States as a nation by reinforcing the notion of European-heritage national identity, as well as the concept of subordinated racial groups fully subject to U.S. sovereignty. The violent, unrestrained treatment of Florida blacks signaled their inferiority and enhanced the common ties of whiteness among European Americans and also the sense of shared racial heritage of the United States and European nations.

Limits of Law

Adherence to statutory, constitutional, and judge-made law is not equivalent to honoring justice. U.S. military actions in Florida followed practices that had long found support in American legislation and the U.S. Constitution. Many federal and state laws incorporated racial distinctions or, in their application, failed to protect African Americans, and the Constitution supported a race-based institution of slavery. Since the Florida campaigns against blacks followed legal principles embodied in such enactments as customarily implemented, U.S. actions were seen as "lawful" in the narrowest way. However, a more expansive view of rule of law takes into account whether laws are just. The broader perspective further considers whether laws are applied equally, impartially, and universally, rather than merely serving the narrow self-interests of the people in power.[51] This vision of law is consistent with the ideals of natural law that provided a foundation for the law of nations in the late eighteenth and early nineteenth centuries. Clearly, by categorically excluding African-descended people from legal protections, the United States failed to abide by that idealized vision of law. Europeans had always articulated exceptions to the supposed universal application of law. However, American troops' completely unrestrained violence against blacks in the Florida campaigns was so extreme that it demolished the foundational premise of universal natural law, giving higher priority to positivist law as expressed in statutes and as evidenced by prior practices. The Seminole War version of law was particularist, rather than universalist, and it was applied so as to advance utilitarian interests. The treatment of blacks in the Seminole War reinforced the emerging racially inflected dividing lines in international law, the borders between civilized and savage and between sovereign and nonsovereign.[52]

The lack of significant public protest against U.S. troops' egregious actions against African-descended people in Florida in 1816 and 1818 indicates that most influential white Americans of the time did not contest the racial boundaries of law. Americans publicly expressed little or no concern about the level of violence directed against presumed runaways in Florida because they were accustomed to such violence within the United States. Most Americans apparently presumed that Jackson's actions were appropriate. Blatant biases and legal distortions were evident in discussions of the subject. American officials interpreted legal principles narrowly when blacks' fundamental welfare was at stake but broadly when white planters' property interests were threatened. While fugitive slaves were excluded from the shield of law, planters enjoyed dramatically expanded legal rights that extended not only throughout their home states but also into foreign territory. The southeastern U.S. border presented no insurmountable obstacle to implementation of state and federal policies regarding fugitive slaves and other people of African descent, and slaveholders benefited from the extraterritorial application of American racial presumptions and legalized violence in Florida.

In sum, Americans felt free to ignore territorial boundaries when dealing with people assumed to be fugitive slaves for several reasons. Slave owners presumed that, since they were entitled to possession of their property, American troops could capture fugitives wherever they were found, even outside the geographic boundaries of the country. Moreover, in the view of slave owners, because runaway slaves posed a serious danger to the United States, national self-defense justified Jackson's doing whatever was necessary to protect the country, even if it meant acting extraterritorially to deal with the problem. Finally, since fugitive slaves were viewed as outlaws, or even likened to pirates, the United States could act against them wherever they were. To many whites, the violent abduction and killing of people of African descent in Florida was defensible because runaway slaves were outlaws who refused to abide by the law. Rejecting law, they could not claim any legal protection. Allegations that fugitives in Florida had flagrantly preyed upon innocent white frontier families reinforced the belief that they were outlaws who had no rights that the military force had to respect.

In the 1810s, there was little public questioning of this version of law. Spain's cession of Florida to the United States soon after the 1818 invasion erased some of the problematic legal issues for future racial conflicts in

Florida. The eradication of the former international border obviated the question of extraterritorial application of American law, customs, and military force. Despite the fact that Florida was thereafter part of the United States, some ground for potential legal challenges remained when whites, blacks, and Seminoles next went to war in 1835. However, as in the earlier contest, Andrew Jackson, then president, had no intention of letting idealized visions of law and justice stand in his way.

CHAPTER SEVEN

Military Tribunals and Rule of Law

Andrew Jackson's capture and execution of two British allies of the Seminoles in April 1818 occasioned extensive debate in the United States. Some people condemned Jackson for his failure to provide proper legal process to the two Britons. Alexander Arbuthnot and Robert Ambrister were tried and convicted by a military tribunal, a process that these critics claimed undermined the principle of rule of law and violated the Constitution, federal statutes, and the laws of war. However, the U.S. government, along with many commentators, defended the general's decision to deny Arbuthnot and Ambrister the rights normally accorded to prisoners of war. They derided the critics as obsessed with meaningless legal technicalities and praised Jackson for having achieved important national goals through the executions. The debate about the two Britons asserted a new stance on the United States' place in the world.[1]

Arbuthnot, Ambrister, and U.S.-British Border Conflicts

Alexander Arbuthnot was a Scottish trader who had been based in the Bahamas before going to Spanish Florida to sell goods to the Seminoles. In Florida, he served as an advocate for the restoration of the Creeks' lands in Alabama and Georgia, which they had ceded to the United States in the 1814

Treaty of Fort Jackson. Arbuthnot obtained a power of attorney authorizing him to act for the Creek chiefs and subsequently wrote on their behalf to British minister to the United States Charles Bagot, Bahamas governor Charles Cameron, Cuba governor José Cienfuegos, and Indian agent David B. Mitchell. Robert Christie Ambrister, a native of the Bahamas, was a former naval officer who had served with the British marines against the United States during the War of 1812. After helping to train pro-British Creek and African-descended men to fight against the United States in 1814, Ambrister returned home at the end of the war. In 1818, he was back in Florida, resuming his work with Indians and blacks.[2]

Although neither Arbuthnot nor Ambrister acted in an official capacity for Britain in 1818, their activities in Florida resembled previous British practices in areas adjacent to the U.S. borders. Between 1783 and 1815, Britain had traded actively with North American Indians, encouraged Indian unity, developed alliances with Indian tribes, and worked to prevent U.S. expansion. In return for their support, British agents won the allegiance of many Indians. Britain had also developed an influential abolitionist movement and welcomed African-descended men, including former slaves, as allies in its North American wars. During the War of 1812, when the main body of British troops was battling Napoleon in Europe, Britain recruited Indians and blacks to join its fight against the United States. By the mid-1810s, Seminoles and Creeks in Spanish Florida were actively petitioning the British for help in resisting Americans' intrusions on their territory. Although the British government declined to endorse official action in support of Red Sticks or Seminoles, Arbuthnot continued to offer private assistance to the Florida Indians, and Ambrister persisted in training and arming both Indians and African-heritage men in Florida. Americans perceived Britain's alliance with blacks and Indians to be a significant threat to national security.[3]

Formerly, the United States had been in no position to effectively counter such activities, but the relationship between the United States and Britain shifted after the end of the War of 1812. In 1816, John Quincy Adams, the U.S. minister in Britain and lead treaty negotiator, wrote to the British foreign minister, protesting that British agents along the Gulf Coast endangered U.S.-British relations by aggressively putting themselves forward as protectors of Indians.[4] By 1818, General Andrew Jackson, commander of the southern military district, was ready to act decisively against Britons who remained along the southeastern U.S. border.

In the spring of 1818, Jackson invaded Florida with the stated goal of stopping the ongoing border conflict with the Indians but with the additional underlying objectives of ousting the Spanish from Florida and ending the territory's role as a sanctuary for fugitive slaves. During the conflict, Jackson's troops snared Alexander Arbuthnot at St. Marks on April 8 and caught

Robert Ambrister ten days later near the Suwannee River. Then, on April 26, Jackson convened a court of twelve officers, with General Edmund P. Gaines presiding, to hear the charges against the two Britons. Within two days the court found them guilty of aiding and supplying the enemy. Arbuthnot was also convicted of "exciting and stirring up the Creek Indians to war against the United States" and Ambrister of leading the Creeks in war against the United States. The officers initially sentenced both men to death but, upon reconsideration, reduced Ambrister's sentence to fifty lashes plus confinement for a year at hard labor. Jackson approved the death sentence for Arbuthnot but changed Ambrister's punishment to death by firing squad. On April 29, American troops shot Ambrister and hanged Arbuthnot from the yardarm of his ship.[5]

The United States and British governments had never formally agreed on a set of principles to provide clear guidance on the legality of Jackson's execution of the two British men. As sources of international rules of war, the United States turned to customary practices and jurists' treatises, but neither source provided adequate guidance under these circumstances. Neither the Revolutionary War nor the War of 1812 offered clear standards of customary practices that would have been applicable to prisoners in Florida in 1818. Rather than providing guidance for establishing a principled approach to treatment of prisoners, newspaper articles describing British treatment of prisoners during these two wars had highlighted the worst atrocities—especially the horrendous conditions on British prison ships where thousands of Americans had perished during the Revolution, the killing of American prisoners in Dartmoor prison during the War of 1812, and the British use of Indian allies who had committed brutal acts against captives during both wars.[6]

The Swiss jurist Emer de Vattel made a number of points potentially relevant to Arbuthnot and Ambrister. Private individuals, according to Vattel, could not lawfully make war on their own, without their sovereign's order. Meanwhile, although every nation had the right to defend itself by repelling enemy violence, responding to injuries received, and countering violations of its national rights, it could only undertake such actions as were "necessary" for achieving those lawful goals. Vattel further contended that nations normally had no right to kill prisoners of war or take the life of enemies who had surrendered and laid down arms, although a nation could lawfully execute enemy prisoners who were war criminals, that is, if they had personally violated the laws of war and their crimes warranted the death penalty. But, Vattel argued, a nation could also execute prisoners in retaliation if its enemy had killed prisoners, while in more general terms a nation was not obliged to adhere to the rules of war if the enemy ignored those rules.[7]

Yet it was unclear how rules of war would apply to men like Arbuthnot and Ambrister, nor was it obvious whether the U.S. Constitution and federal statutes were applicable in their cases. The two men were not American citizens or subjects of an enemy country, nor were they acting on American soil, and yet they allegedly had assisted and allied with a group of Florida Indians and fugitive slaves hostile to the United States. So their legal status and rights were ambiguous. Other facts were unclear: Were they making war against the United States, and, if so, was it as agents of Britain or as private individuals? Were they affiliating themselves with the Seminoles and Red Sticks rather than with Britain? If the United States was unrestrained by the laws of war in dealing with those Indians, was the United States also legally unrestricted in its dealings with Arbuthnot and Ambrister? Was it "necessary" to execute the two men? Were they prisoners of war, war criminals, or civilian bystanders? The ambiguity of these issues left room for conflicting interpretations of the legality of the executions, with Jackson's critics as well as his defenders both citing Vattel to support their arguments and referring to past precedent from the Revolutionary War for justification. The two sides reached different conclusions on the main issues in dispute: the applicability and relevance of constraints based on law and precedent, and the effect the executions would have on the United States.

Many commentators, including congressmen and newspaper writers, expressed great concern about the legality of the executions of Arbuthnot and Ambrister. In Congress, the House Committee on Military Affairs proposed a resolution condemning the trials and executions of the two Britons, and at the beginning of the House debate Representative Thomas W. Cobb suggested an additional resolution directing the committee to draft a law prohibiting the execution of army captives "in time of peace, or in time of war with any Indian tribe" without the president's approval. Critics argued that the legal process provided to Arbuthnot and Ambrister did not meet minimal standards of due process and that both the trials and the executions were inconsistent with federal laws, the Constitution, and the laws of war. However, supporters of the executions mounted a vigorous and successful defense, and in the end the House rejected both proposed resolutions.[8]

The widespread publication of the trial records, congressional speeches, military dispatches, diplomatic correspondence, and personal opinions in the press constituted an appeal to popular opinion. Most likely, Jackson held the court-martial proceedings in the expectation that a "court of public opinion" would later deliberate on the case. In fact, Jackson supporter Henry Baldwin articulated that understanding during the congressional debate. Baldwin observed that because the general knew that the executions "would excite much feeling," it was important for him to have an official record of the evidence against Arbuthnot and Ambrister so "that all might judge of their guilt and the propriety of the proceedings." The editor of a prominent newspaper, the *National Register,* agreed on the role of "the newspaper arena" in providing a forum for political and military figures to "appeal to the understandings of the people." The extensive reporting of documents and speeches pertaining to Arbuthnot and Ambrister was "in the nature of an appeal from the constituted authorities, to the undefined sensations of the community," the editor noted. In this case, by "feasting" Jackson in New York, Philadelphia, and Baltimore and toasting him elsewhere throughout the United States after the congressional debate concluded, the people announced that they upheld both Jackson's decisions and Congress's rejection of the censure resolutions. However, the editor expressed some unease about such "complimentary carousings." He was concerned that "[t]he passions of the people" might in some future situation override the more sober decisions of Congress. Scholars John Wertheimer and Elizabeth Dale have pointed out that in the antebellum era, informal courts of public opinion served as a form of "extralegal justice." As will be evident below, the debate about Arbuthnot and Ambrister raised fundamental issues about the uncertain status of formal legal principles when they conflicted with popular opinion in the United States.[9]

Alleged Violations of American Law

In their analysis of the Arbuthnot/Ambrister executions, critics identified five procedural problems under U.S. laws, the Constitution, and American legal principles. First, they claimed that the tribunal that tried Arbuthnot and Ambrister lacked jurisdiction over both the subject matter of the proceedings and the defendants themselves. The jurisdiction of courts-martial, as defined by Congress, did not include war crimes by the enemy. Specifically, as a number of congressmen pointed out, there was nothing in the federal law governing the army that made inciting Indians or aiding and supplying the enemy a crime that could be tried before a court-martial, nor was there any provision allowing noncitizens, who owed no allegiance to the United States, to be charged with conspiring against it outside of U.S. borders, nor did courts-martial have authority to prosecute people categorized as "pirates." In Arbuthnot's and Ambrister's cases, only the charge of spying was potentially within the court-martial's jurisdiction, and, as the court itself conceded, that allegation lacked sufficient grounds for prosecution. Courts-martial, which were intended for U.S. soldiers and officers, were simply not the proper venue for trying enemy combatants or civilians. Because Arbuthnot was a civilian who had committed no military offenses and Ambrister was an enemy combatant who became a prisoner of war upon capture, neither could be subject to a court-martial, critics contended. Moreover, they rejected the claim that the court was just a board of officers who collected evidence and advised Jackson. Because the body that conducted the trials was composed as a court-martial, operated as a court-martial, and was referred to as a court-martial by Jackson, as well as by President James Monroe and Secretary of State John Quincy Adams, critics argued that it was in fact a court-martial. As such, its jurisdiction was limited in accordance with the federal statute. The tribunal had no lawful jurisdiction, so the proceedings were invalid and the executions illegal.[10]

A second legal concern with the Arbuthnot/Ambrister trials was that the court ignored normal rules of evidence, resulting in proceedings that some claimed were devoid of proper legal process. Critics argued that, like civil cases, military proceedings had to adhere to basic principles of due process. Yet the prosecutors used hearsay evidence, while posing leading questions and questions that solicited expressions of opinion rather than facts. Making the process even more suspect was the introduction of hearsay evidence from Indians, who would not have been treated as competent witnesses in most American courts. Furthermore, the court denied Arbuthnot the right to call Ambrister as a witness and inappropriately admitted as evidence certain letters ascribed to Arbuthnot, without proof that he was the author. Additionally, critics alleged, the testimony of William Hambley and Peter Cook, the principal witnesses against the men, was unreliable because of their bias against Arbuthnot. As Representative Joseph Hopkinson of Pennsylvania concluded, "Two lives have been sacrificed, on evidence that would not have been listened to in the most petty court of our country, trying the veriest wretch in our community, on the most petty accusation."[11]

Jackson's detractors also complained that the proceedings failed to satisfy due process requirements because they were governed by the discretion of one man. Contrary to the normal separation of roles in a legal process, Jackson controlled every aspect of the proceedings, including determining the rules, bringing the charges, choosing the judges, appointing the prosecutor, assessing the appropriateness of the sentence, and enforcing the punishment. The *New-England Palladium & Commercial Advertiser* identified the key question: whether the Arbuthnot/Ambrister trials were "such as our republican systems require—whether it is consistent with American principles that one man should possess such power over human life." Crowning his exclusive control of the trial proceedings, Jackson then denied the defendants any right of appeal. Why, critics asked, did he carry out the capital punishment with such "indecent haste"? Would it not have been a good idea to obtain President Monroe's input in such an unusual and sensitive case with its potential international repercussions? Beyond the demands of prudent policy, there was another reason for referring the case to the president: the federal statute governing courts-martial required that sentences be submitted to presidential review before being implemented. Instead, Jackson quickly went ahead with the executions.[12]

Critics next alleged that Jackson violated the U.S. Constitution when he executed Arbuthnot and Ambrister. Even when the laws of war justified taking the life of prisoners in retaliation or as punishment to deter further war crimes by a barbaric enemy, the Constitution authorized Congress, not commanding generals, to provide for such executions. Since Article I, section 8 of the Constitution gave Congress the power to declare war and the power to prescribe punishments for violations of the law of nations, a general could retaliate for an enemy's savage acts or punish a war crime only if Congress authorized such action. By executing Arbuthnot and Ambrister for alleged violations of the law of nations—in the absence of any federal statute permitting such punishment—Jackson had violated the Constitution.[13]

A final concern was that Jackson had overstretched his power and violated basic legal principles when he changed Ambrister's punishment to death. Citing Alexander Macomb's book on martial law, the *Richmond Enquirer* asserted that, by uniform practice, while a general or a president could choose to pardon someone convicted by court-martial, he could not impose a harsher punishment than that determined by the court. The *Boston Intelligencer* expressed a similar view, concluding that when Jackson ordered Ambrister's execution he arbitrarily violated both the laws of nations and U.S. law. The *Massachusetts Spy* was more blunt: altering Ambrister's punishment was the "most arrogant assumption of power which our country has ever witnessed"; it even "amounted to the crime of *murder*." Several members of Congress agreed with the newspapers' position, while others argued that, even if Jackson had the right to execute the men without any trial, he waived that right when he submitted the matter to the military tribunal. He could not later change the sentence that the court imposed on Ambrister. Once Jackson submitted the matter to a court-martial, the executions could no longer be justified as retaliation. The Senate Select Committee's report on the Seminole War accused Jackson of substituting "his own arbitrary will" for the sentence of the court-martial.[14]

Alleged Violations of the Laws of War Regarding Prisoners

Critics also argued that the laws of war did not authorize Jackson to kill prisoners under the existing circumstances. The *Baltimore Telegraph* noted that it had never heard of the doctrine by which Jackson justified his action. "We should like to know where the general finds such a law or such a principle," the newspaper stated. Likewise the *New-York Daily Advertiser* bluntly declared, "We know of no law of war, of nations, or of civilized society, that justifies, or even excuses, the destruction of the life of a prisoner of war," and the *Massachusetts Spy* criticized Jackson for trying to justify the executions "by broaching a *new* principle in the law of nations" by claiming that it was customary practice. In fact, the newspapers pointed out, Jackson misstated the laws of war. Killing prisoners was legally justified only when required for the safety of the army. But the goals of the war against the Seminoles had already been achieved prior to the executions of the two men on April 29, as evidenced by Jackson's own pronouncements in his correspondence of April 20 and 26. Any threat that the two men may have posed to American soldiers or to the United States had been eliminated by their confinement. Their execution was thus unnecessary and unlawful since it neither enhanced the safety of the soldiers nor furthered the goals of the war.[15]

Concern about Rule of Law

These criticisms reflected a deep concern about what was perceived as Jackson's dangerous disrespect for law. Speaker of the House Henry Clay took the lead in a lengthy speech that touched on almost every argument made by Jackson's critics, while expressing particular concern about rule of law. "However guilty these men were," Clay proclaimed, "they should not have been condemned or executed without the authority of the law." He delineated the general principles that "[n]o man could be executed in this free country without two things being shown; 1st. That the law condemns him to death; and, 2dly, That his death is pronounced by that tribunal which is authorized by the law to try him. These principles would reach every man's case, native or foreigner, citizen or alien," were applicable to wartime as well as peacetime, and protected prisoners of war. "The instant quarters are granted to a prisoner," Clay said, "the majesty of the law surrounds and sustains him, and he cannot lawfully be punished with death, without the concurrence of the two circumstances just insisted upon." Allowing a general to have "absolute power of life and death, at his sole discretion," would be "contrary to the genius of all our laws and institutions"; giving one individual the power "to make the rule, to judge, and to execute the rule, or to judge and execute the rule only, was utterly irreconcilable with every principle of free Government, and was the very definition of tyranny itself." Clay added that it was inconsistent with law and ethics to justify Jackson's actions by asserting that he had done the right thing but in the wrong way, as Jackson's supporters contended. "It is not always just," Clay warned, "to do what may be advantageous."[16]

Other congressmen agreed. Representative John Tyler explicitly reminded the House of the importance of the rule of law. "We live in a land where the only rule of our conduct is the law," he proclaimed, and "these proceedings have taken place in the absence of all law." Likewise, Joseph Hopkinson characterized the proceedings as "the most solemn mockery of all the principles of justice; the most daring outrage upon all the guards of liberty and life, that have ever come to my knowledge." Henry R. Storrs of New York maintained that the "proceedings are contrary to all those safeguards which the municipal law has provided for the security of personal liberty," and Virginia representative Charles F. Mercer concluded that the executions were "a stain on the records of the judicial proceedings of this nation." The Senate committee, too, expressed concern about the ways in which the trials and punishments of Arbuthnot and Ambrister failed to follow "the usual and accustomed forms," warning that, in capital cases particularly, a "strict adherence to form" is "the best security against oppression and injustice."[17]

The press likewise expressed concern about Jackson's disrespect for law in executing Arbuthnot and Ambrister. Noting that Jackson had misstated the laws of war and committed "an outrage upon the laws of nations," the *Massachusetts Spy* concluded that the general was "either very ignorant or very regardless of *all* laws." Finding no source for Jackson's asserted justification in the laws of war, the *Baltimore Telegraph* declared sarcastically, "We suppose, however, he is the maker of his own laws." Critics expressed outrage that an American officer could display such disregard for legal process. It was outrageous, one paper said, that "in a country which boasts of being the only free country under heaven—the only country where righteous laws are administered with an impartial hand—the subject of a nation with whom we are at peace—taken in the territory of a nation with whom we are not at war, is dragged before an exasperated tribunal of military chiefs; and, not merely upon the testimony of a rooted foe, but upon what such a foe had heard from other foes, is condemned unheard, and hurried to the gallows without respite." In the *Richmond Enquirer*, pseudonymous essayist "Algernon Sidney" summed up the common view among the critics when he concluded that the executions were "an act of barbarity glossed over with the forms of justice."[18]

From these comments it is evident that, for the critics, "rule of law" required adherence to law as enacted by a valid authority, separation of the powers to make law and adjudicate cases, and observance of fair legal process before punishing an accused person. With regard to Arbuthnot and Ambrister, critics concluded that the United States had violated all three elements of rule of law. They were alarmed that Jackson had substituted his individual will for law as created by the legislature and as explicated by scholars of the law of nations. They were concerned that the court-martial was not a lawful venue for trying the two Britons. And they were disturbed by irregularities evident in the court-martial procedures.

The critics' strident denunciation of the Arbuthnot/Ambrister executions, coupled with their vociferous condemnation of the violation of Spain's sovereign rights, contrasts with their relatively tepid disapproval of the Hillis Hadjo/Homathlemico executions and their apparent indifference to the killing and enslaving of African-descended people. In fact, the critics' view of the concept of "rule of law" was quite limited. They focused on formal procedural criteria and paid little attention to whether the laws were just, or whether they were universally and equally applied.[19] Moreover, it is also notable that although the critics took a stand against utilitarian government action that respected popular opinion more than established legal principles, they did not hesitate to join in the appeal to the "court of public opinion" during the debate about the executions. Nonetheless, critics' advocacy for Arbuthnot and Ambrister's entitlement to protections of international law and procedural rights under American law represented a view of law that diverged sharply from the Jacksonians' perspectives.

U.S. Rationale for the Executions

Naturally, the U.S. government and Andrew Jackson's supporters took a very different view of the executions. They summarily dismissed the due process arguments as irrelevant and inapplicable, while not actually countering those arguments on the merits. The asserted procedural requirements and jurisdictional limitations, they argued, simply did not pertain to Arbuthnot and Ambrister for two reasons. In the first place, the two men did not fall under the protective shield of the U.S. Constitution or federal statutes but instead were covered only by the law of nations. Moreover, under the law of nations Arbuthnot and Ambrister were not entitled to protections as prisoners of war because they had committed crimes in violation of the rules of war.

The first contention, according to Jackson's allies, derived from the fact that Arbuthnot and Ambrister enjoyed no entitlements under the U.S. Constitution or laws because they were noncitizens who were outside of U.S. borders. In Alexander Smyth's words, men who were not American and were not present within U.S. territory "never came under the shade of the umbrella of the Constitution." Moreover, the Constitution distributed authority among the branches of government but nowhere took the power of punishment away from commanding generals. Jackson thus had not violated the Constitution. Pro-Jackson forces further noted that the Arbuthnot/Ambrister trial proceedings were not subject to federal statutory requirements because they were neither courts-martial nor civil court trials. Even though the court that tried the two men may have appeared to have been a court-martial, it was in fact a special court of inquiry charged to investigate, record evidence, and advise the general, but not to reach a verdict and a sentence. Because it was not a statutorily defined court-martial, it thus had no specifically mandated procedures, nor was it required to adhere to strict rules of evidence. The court's jurisdiction, moreover, was not limited to U.S. soldiers and officers, its findings and recommendations were not binding on the commanding general, and there was no obligation to delay sentences of execution pending presidential review. Jackson's advocates claimed that the law of nations, not U.S. legislation, governed a general's authority over prisoners like Arbuthnot and Ambrister.[20]

Jackson's defenders then moved on to the second stage of their argument: that the pertinent component of the law of nations—the laws of war—did not actually provide any procedural guarantees to these two British men. Their illegal actions had removed them from the protections of the laws of war, so they were not entitled to be treated as prisoners of war. Normally, Europeans could rely on the safeguards offered by the law of nations, but, as Jackson himself contended, Arbuthnot and Ambrister were "outlaws." He felt justified in altering Ambrister's punishment because, as he stated in his execution order of April 29, "It is an established principle of the laws of nations that any individual of a nation making war against the citizens of another nation, they being at peace, forfeits his allegiance, and becomes an outlaw and pirate. This is the case of Robert C. Ambrister." Two years later, Jackson's "Memorial" to the Senate labeled both men outlaws and asserted that they were "principals in an unlawful war" that was carried on "in open violation of the laws of war and of nations." The "Memorial" concluded that "[a]s associates of savages, who respected none of the laws of civilized warfare," Arbuthnot and Ambrister "could not claim the benefit or protection of those laws, for they were not parties. They were as much outlaws to all its provisions, as a pirate on the ocean." President Monroe and Secretary of State Adams made a similar argument in their letters and speeches: as allies of Indians, Arbuthnot and Ambrister were not entitled to the usual protections afforded to prisoners of war.[21]

Many newspapers and congressmen agreed that Arbuthnot and Ambrister had placed themselves outside of the shield of law and had become "enemies of the human race, without a country." When foreigners allied themselves with Indians, Jackson's defenders argued, they effectively surrendered their national identity. They "denationalized" or "expatriated" themselves and became "out-laws." Commenting on the executions, the newspapers and congressmen backing Jackson expressed similar sentiments: by allying with "savages" the two men "forfeited the rights of civilized men" and put themselves "beyond the pale of civilized warfare" and "civilized society." Their actions had moved them "out of the protection of the law of civilized warfare," "of the law of nations," even "of all laws and institutions of civilized man." Arbuthnot and Ambrister had become "men whom no laws could restrain, and therefore men whom no law will protect." If captured, therefore, they were not entitled to the rights of prisoners of war, had no right to trial, were subject to the death penalty, and could be executed as soon as they were captured.[22]

Jackson's allies did not venture beyond generalized statements by offering a systematic legal argument for excluding Arbuthnot and Ambrister from the protections of law. Some implied that the men could be executed simply because their allies, the Red Sticks and Seminoles, could also, since the law of nations allowed the United States to treat enemies as those enemies treated Americans. Because Indians put prisoners to death, they claimed (aggregating all "Indians" into a single category), the United States was entitled to put Red Stick prisoners to death in retaliation and their allies warranted the same fate. Curiously, they did not mention the 1813 law that gave the president the power to retaliate against British prisoners of war if their Indian allies perpetrated war crimes against Americans. While the terms of that statute applied only during the War of 1812, it nonetheless could have served as evidence of congressional policies on such matters.[23] Instead of pointing to this kind of precedent, most commentators were content to aver that no law at all protected the two men because they themselves had acted illegally, without being explicit about what made them outlaws.

Alexander Smyth was an exception. During the House debate, the Virginia congressman offered the most detailed explanation of how the basic principles of the rules of war pertained. His analysis focused on the rules' application to Ambrister but stated that the same observations applied in general to Arbuthnot. Referencing treatises written by jurists Emer de Vattel and Georg Friedrich von Martens, Smyth asserted that the laws of war allowed a commanding general to execute prisoners who had violated the usages of war in any of three ways: making war without authority, making unlawful war, or "using means contrary to the laws of war." On the first point, Smyth noted that when an individual waged war against another nation without authority from his own sovereign, and not in the service of another nation, he made war without authority. Ambrister had fought as a rogue individual without authorization from (and contrary to the alliances of) his own government in the service of the Seminoles, a group of "banditti" who were not a nation. On the second criterion, Smyth explained that unlawful war included any war that lacked a just cause or was commenced by individuals who were not a sovereign power. The congressman did not clearly specify why the United States' enemies in the war lacked a just cause, though he implied that Seminoles and Creeks who attacked Americans were engaging in "incursion[s] for havoc and pillage" rather than attempting to remedy any recognizable collective grievance or injury. Smyth did explain that Indians could not constitute a power that could lawfully make war against the United States because they were not a foreign, sovereign nation; rather they were subjects of the United States. Any war waged by Indians was unlawful under the law of nations, and anyone who fought with such Indians committed a war crime. Thus, Ambrister had engaged in an unlawful war because the war had no just cause and was not being waged by a sovereign power. Third, Ambrister used "means contrary to the laws of war," according to Smyth, when he incited savages to commit massacres. The congressman supported his contention by quoting the U.S. commissioners to the Treaty of Ghent, who stated that "the employment of savages, whose known rule of warfare is the indiscriminate torture and butchery of women, children, and prisoners, is, itself, a departure from the principles of humanity observed between all civilized Christian nations, even in war." Instigating such activities violated the rules of war. Having committed three criminal acts—fighting without authority, in an unlawful war, and in an unlawful manner—Ambrister forfeited any entitlement to treatment as a prisoner of war, Smyth concluded. Without specifically addressing Arbuthnot's conduct, Smyth put him in the same legal category as Ambrister. Both men had removed themselves from the protections of the rules of war. They were "outlaws," and therefore they could lawfully be executed.[24]

Law versus National Interest

Jackson's allies derided their opponents' arguments about the trials and executions as narrowly legalistic, and despite their appreciation for Smyth's legal arguments, at certain times during the debate about Arbuthnot and Ambrister they expressed aggressive antilegalist positions. They scorned Jackson's critics for their overreliance on law as the foundation of their arguments, challenged the relevance of law to frontier conflicts involving people who ignored legal restraints themselves, and suggested that only a weak nation would allow itself to be constrained by international legal customs when self-defense was at stake. The lawyers' arguments against Jackson, they said, were deceptive and artificial. Several essays, for example, drew on antilawyer sentiment in disparaging the criticisms of Algernon Sidney. One asserted that in Sidney's essay "[e]very offence is exaggerated with the keen malignity of an experienced lawyer," while another ridiculed him as "wordy, law-quoting, wire-dancing, net-weaving."[25]

Defenders of Jackson's conduct considered procedural nitpicking by lawyers as particularly unsuited to the military context. Military officers needed—and had always asserted—discretion in dealing with prisoners and should not be constrained by legal technicalities, because this would mean going "to war on unequal terms, with our hands tied." Pro-Jackson voices offered examples of officers exercising their discretion in the past, relying especially on analogies between the Seminole War and the American Revolution, and in particular invoking parallels between George Washington and Jackson to show that military power was safe in the latter's hands. A number of congressmen pointed to similarities between Jackson's treatment of Arbuthnot and Ambrister and Washington's handling of John André and Charles Asgill, as well as broader similarities between Jackson's interpretation of the rules of war during hostilities with the Creeks and Seminoles and Washington's approach to dealing with the Iroquois. Jackson, they asserted, was following in Washington's footsteps.[26]

In the weeks leading up to the congressional debate, some newspaper commentators argued that Jackson's actions should be judged by their outcome rather than their adherence to procedural rules. Defenders of the executions maintained that because the end result was correct, the details of the process were less important. A *National Advocate* essay by "Junius Brutus" rejected the notion that jurists' treatises determined the legality of the executions; the general should be judged by common sense and reason rather than abstract principles of legal philosophy. The *Eastern Argus* approved of Jackson's determination that "[t]he forms of law . . . should not stand in the way of public justice and national policy," and the *New York Advocate* thought that Arbuthnot and Ambrister "deserved their fate, whether they were legally executed or not." Likewise, a widely published March 1819 essay, "Strictures on Mr. Lacock's Report on the Seminole War," which responded critically to the Senate committee report, dismissed legalistic criticisms of Jackson. If Arbuthnot and Ambrister were guilty of the crimes, and Jackson had the right to punish them, then "what object have we in cavilling at the mode of their trial?" the author asked, adding that even if there were procedural errors, it did not change the fact that the men were guilty and deserved to be put to death. Strict due process was unnecessary.[27]

During the House debate, congressmen likewise condemned overly legalistic criticisms of Jackson. People should judge the general by the overall justice and practical benefits of his actions rather than on minor legal technicalities, they said. Representative Henry Baldwin (a future Supreme Court justice) expressed this view vociferously, pointing out that sometimes a general was justified in disobeying the law. He referred admiringly to Jackson's conduct during the War of 1812, when the general ensured the safety of New Orleans by proclaiming martial law and refusing to obey habeas corpus writs: "In the hour of danger," Jackson had "dared to violate the laws." Similarly, according to Baldwin, nobody should be second-guessing Jackson's decisions by examining every minute detail of the legal proceedings in the cases of Arbuthnot and Ambrister: "[T]his nation," he asserted, "ought not to be agitated by an inquiry whether their execution was according to the strict and technical forms of law." Richard M. Johnson, a Kentucky representative (and future vice president), responded similarly to the criticism that Jackson had categorized the men as outlaws and pirates: "[W]e are not here," he proclaimed, "to inquire whether General Jackson used technical terms, but whether he did substantially and legally right." He concluded that the two British men were guilty, they deserved the death penalty, and Americans were better off for it. Representative John Holmes summed up the argument: even if the trial by court-martial was illegal, he said, the end result was right.[28]

Critics' Response

Jackson's critics, however, vigorously disputed the arguments in defense of the executions. Some questioned the claim that executing prisoners was warranted as retaliation, pointing out that the Florida Indians had been badly treated and might have had good cause to take up arms against Americans. If their actions were justified, then so were those of Arbuthnot and Ambrister. Because the Seminoles and Creeks had a right to defend themselves, the editors of the *Massachusetts Spy* opined, Arbuthnot and Ambrister were "clearly justified in assisting them to do it." The two British men committed no crimes in befriending the Indians. Rather, they were acting humanely and generously in helping ignorant, weak people to assert their rights under Article 9 of the Treaty of Ghent, rights which the British government had pledged to protect.[29]

Critics of the executions also rejected the idea that Arbuthnot and Ambrister were "outlaws." They contested as a "dangerous doctrine" that was baseless, even preposterous, Jackson's argument that a citizen of a neutral nation who participated in military action against the United States forfeited protections of law. If Jackson's doctrine were true, the *Massachusetts Spy* asked, "how is it, that in every war which has happened for twenty years past, neutral subjects have been suffered with impunity to enlist in the cause of belligerents?" The *Baltimore Telegraph* could find no concept of an "outlaw" in American law. Even England had long ago abandoned the idea that someone who has been declared an outlaw could be entirely unprotected by law and "may be knocked on the head like a wolf by any one that should meet him." Moreover, the House committee report noted, even where law did recognize outlaws, it only applied to the relationship of a person with his own government. Henry Clay and others argued that foreigners who joined forces with an enemy should be treated the same as the enemy's own soldiers. As shown by their customary treatment in previous wars, such men were not outside the laws of war.[30]

Finally, critics pointed out that Arbuthnot was a civilian simply trading normal goods with Indians and acting as a friend to his customers; when he was captured he was unarmed. Meanwhile, Ambrister was just helping the Indians defend themselves. Neither had violated the rules of war by participating in savage acts. Opponents of the executions compared Ambrister's status to that of the Marquis de Lafayette and other foreigners who had fought for the United States during the American Revolution without endorsement by their sovereigns. As the *Dedham Gazette* pointed out, had any foreign supporter of the Revolution "been taken prisoner and ignominiously executed for having intermeddled with us, exciting us to hostilities, and leading us in battle, the whole civilized world would have cried Shame! at the outrage." In fact, Jackson's challengers observed, the American general himself could have been a victim of his own theory. As the *Vermont Intelligencer* pointed out, because Jackson acted without authorization from his government, if the Spanish had taken him captive, he would have been a "freebooter" and, like Arbuthnot and Ambrister, would have had no claim to the privileges of a prisoner of war and could have been executed.[31]

In short, neither Arbuthnot's nor Ambrister's actions took them outside the rule of law, critics argued. Consequently, if the two Britons were combatants at all, they were lawful combatants allied to a nation at war with the United States and thereby entitled to be classified as prisoners of war, with all the protections normally afforded to them. Jackson's opponents condemned the executions as gratuitously cruel, unconscionable, and unlawful.

Debate about the Likely Impact of the Executions

In addition to disputing legal issues, commentators also disagreed about the likely impact of the executions. Jackson's defenders argued that the Britons' fate served as a blunt warning to Europeans not to meddle in U.S.-Indian relations, with Andrew Jackson himself expressing the hope that "the execution of these two unprincipled villains will prove an awful example to the world and convince the Government of Great Britain, as well as her subjects, that certain, though slow retribution awaits those unchristian wretches who, by false promises, delude and excite an Indian tribe to all the horrid deeds of savage war." As Congressman George Poindexter of Mississippi expressed it, "[W]e owe it to the safety and honor of our country to retaliate on the offenders with the utmost rigor and severity, until the subjects of foreign nations shall be taught to dread our vengeance, if they do not respect our rights." An essay in the *Albany Register* declared, "Let it be once understood that every man who is the aider or abettor of Indian warfare is to be punished with death, and we shall have fewer Indian wars." Foreign instigation of Indians was a threat to U.S. sovereignty. Only by acting boldly could the United States deter European incendiaries, protect its borders, and earn respect from abroad, Jackson and his supporters argued. The general's actions boosted the nation's domestic image of military prowess, fortified nationalism and political solidarity, and strengthened the United States' claim to full nationhood, they said.[32] In this view, what James Monroe expressed in the Monroe Doctrine in 1823, Jackson had already conveyed through his actions: Europeans should not intervene in the United States' business in its own neighborhood.

Jackson's advocates also cautioned that condemning the executions as illegal or immoral would reinforce challenges to Indian dispossession and weaken the U.S. bargaining position with Spain, making the acquisition of Florida less likely. More broadly, passage of Representative Cobb's proposed resolutions would halt the spread of civilization and the progress of mankind by stifling and obstructing American expansion at a time when territorial acquisitions were important for furthering the "high destiny of this growing empire." Newspapers articulated the common American view: British agents must not be allowed to "impede our march to glory" nor to "retard the prosperity of the nation" by stirring up Indians and instigating wars. The executions displayed strong national sentiment that neither Indians nor Europeans would be allowed to stand in the way of the inevitable extension of American borders. Moreover, since the executed men were seen as threatening innocent settler families, the executions signaled that protecting those at the vanguard of civilization—the frontier dwellers—was a high national priority. Jackson's champions argued that the magnificent destiny of the United States was at stake, and censuring Jackson for the executions would undermine those important messages.[33]

Although the concept of "manifest destiny" was coined much later, the Seminole War debate evidences the fact that many Americans already believed that the nation was fated to extend all the way to the Pacific. National expansion, power, and prosperity were viewed as more important than adherence to narrow legal procedures. In fact, Jackson's supporters argued, divinely mandated American expansion could not be restrained by narrow principles of domestic or international law. Full U.S. sovereignty included the right to expand. In sum, the executions were seen as not only increasing national security but also bolstering American confidence, reinforcing American authority over Indians and their European allies, and smoothing the nation's path to expansion to the Pacific.

However, critics worried that the events in Florida would damage the United States' reputation for moral rectitude and humane treatment of prisoners. If the United States forfeited its "exalted character," Henry Clay warned, the light of liberty would be dimmer around the world.[34] Others expressed concern about the impact of Jackson's doctrine on U.S. soldiers who had Indian allies by their side, as well as on Americans fighting abroad as private individuals. In late 1818, several newspapers warned that Spain could execute U.S. citizens captured while fighting in South America's rebellions. After King Ferdinand VII ordered the death penalty for any foreigner aiding South American insurgents, the *Kentucky Reporter* observed that the Monroe administration had forfeited the right to challenge future executions of Americans because it could not persuasively "object to an order founded on the very principles on which it has acted, and which it has defended to the Spanish government."[35]

Jackson's critics also argued that the danger went beyond soldiers: the general's failure to follow proper legal process made all Americans vulnerable to arbitrary proceedings. Henry Clay highlighted the threat of military despotism. Excesses that started with unlimited discretion over prisoners might lead to unrestricted power over all citizens, he warned. American newspapers likewise vigorously advised against acquiescing to Jackson's dangerous abuse of power, calling on Congress to protect the nation from tyranny and to demonstrate that "the civil authority is paramount to the military." The *New-York Evening Post* feared that "the military despotism of General Jackson should prove contagious, for, it was not perceived why, if he could thus triumphantly put to death, without the form of trial, prisoners of war, some other military chieftain might not consider himself justified, under particular, and what he might call, urgent circumstances, to make a similar experiment upon our own citizens."[36]

Yet Jackson's supporters dismissed the critics' warnings as insincere, self-serving, partisan rhetoric—mere "political theatre." The *Hampden Patriot* accused Henry Clay—"the great Machiavel of Kentucky"—of defending the "miscreant wretches" Arbuthnot and Ambrister solely to position himself for the 1820 presidential campaign. The article charged that Clay's driving motivation, personal political ambition, was "veiled under the specious garb of 'veneration for the constitution of his country, and anxiety for the unsullied honor of the nation.'"[37]

Jackson himself was blithely dismissive about allegations that he or the army had excessive power. In 1818, he brushed off a state government official's expression of concern about "the liberty of the people prostrated at the feet of military despotism," labeling it mere "cant expressions for political purposes." But his detractors insisted they were motivated by ideology, not politics. The *Connecticut Mirror* countered allegations that Jackson's opponents were just prompted by "party spirit," claiming that such allegations were "disingenuous artifice" and distortions designed to squelch all criticism of Jackson.[38]

Consequences of the Executions

The executions and the debate about them had significant consequences both internationally and domestically. Although many British people were irate about the treatment of their compatriots, government officials wanted cordial relations with the United States and knew it would be prudent to dissociate themselves from Arbuthnot's and Ambrister's behavior. In 1818 the two countries were moving toward resolution of long-standing conflicts, and British officials were unwilling to let events in Florida hamper those discussions. Britain's minister in Washington, Charles Bagot, refrained from any formal objection and told the American secretary of state that Arbuthnot and Ambrister were not government agents. The foreign minister, Robert Stewart (Viscount Castlereagh), also recognized that because the two men had no official status their deaths did not warrant an official protest from Britain. In January 1819, he informed Bagot that the men's unauthorized activities in Florida "deprived them of any claim on their own Gov[ernment] for interfering on their behalf." Prompted by a desire to protect economic ties to the United States, eagerness to foster trade with the Spanish American colonies seeking independence, recognition of the United States' growing power and importance, abandonment of aspirations to hem in the United States geographically, and readiness for peace after years of the Napoleonic Wars, British acquiescence toward the deaths of Arbuthnot and Ambrister marked the end of their military influence with Florida's Indians and blacks and their acceptance of the United States' dominant position in the region.[39]

In the United States, Jackson's critics were unsuccessful in their efforts to obtain congressional censure of his conduct in Florida. After discussing his actions in the Seminole War for three weeks, the House of Representatives voted on February 8, 1819, not to condemn the trials or executions. Two weeks after the House vote—and two days after John Quincy Adams and Luis de Onís signed the treaty in which Spain ceded Florida to the United

States and agreed to a western U.S. boundary that extended American territory to the Pacific Ocean at the 42nd parallel—the Senate committee issued a report critical of the executions, but because many Americans had credited the general with creating an advantageous diplomatic environment, few senators wanted to discuss censuring him while ratification of the Adams-Onís Transcontinental Treaty was pending. The Senate never debated the committee's report.[40]

Jackson's actions in the Seminole War had a significant impact on contemporary domestic politics. Already regarded as a military hero after the Battle of New Orleans, Jackson gained further admiration with the Florida campaigns. The public discussion about Arbuthnot and Ambrister and other issues arising from the war brought heightened attention to the general and provided an occasion for debating core American values. Jackson's popularity soared, eventually propelling him to the White House.

The dispute about Arbuthnot and Ambrister—as prisoners of war, allies of Indians, and European agents hindering U.S. expansion—can also be seen within the context of an emergent challenge to older American ideology, as new attitudes replaced revolutionary-era values, Federalist principles, and Jeffersonian vision. Jackson cared less than Jefferson had about protecting prisoners of war, and, after Jackson's rise in American politics, efforts to develop formal protections for prisoners of war stagnated. U.S. relations with Native peoples also changed: while early presidential administrations had respected tribal sovereignty and favored civilization programs over military expeditions, Jackson pursued more aggressive tactics, and the Jacksonian Democrats continued to undermine tribal sovereignty for decades. Furthermore, Jackson scorned Federalist resistance to expansion and pushed the nation to a new vision of its territorial destiny, while also reinforcing the Jeffersonian idea that North America was the United States' exclusive domain, separate and distinct from Europe's realm. These shifts, of course, correlate with changes in the relative power of the United States, Indian tribes, and European powers in the Americas.[41] The shifts endured long after the Seminole War, as Jackson's position on these issues soon came to dominate in American society.

The Jacksonian position on two other issues—military power and rule of law—reflected a more startling change in national values that did not just respond to altered external conditions. The Seminole War debate revealed a shift in Americans' view of the dangers of a strong army. In the presidential election of 1828, voters swept aside concerns about military despotism and embraced Jackson's boldness as a sign of strong executive leadership. The doctrine of utilitarianism triumphed. The United States endorsed military policies that furthered the nation's security, strength, and prosperity. The goal was the maximization of national interests, rather than achievement of idealistic moral values. In the 1830s and 1840s, Americans enthusiastically pursued expansion as a matter of manifest destiny.

Furthermore, the disagreement about the executions of Arbuthnot and Ambrister revealed a growing divide among Americans about rule of law. On one side of the sharp divide were those who viewed American rule of law and faithfulness to systematic, orderly procedures as paramount national commitments. On the other side were those who valued instinctive justice and popular national goals over legal technicalities and who favored what they considered Jackson's uncorrupted wisdom and common sense over excessive rationalism and intellectualism. Very different mentalities, not just expedient political rhetoric, drove the two sides. On the subject of Arbuthnot and Ambrister, Jackson's critics used legalistic arguments because they were alarmed by his disregard for law, while his defenders took an antilegalist approach because they believed the general's goals were too important to be restrained by rigid observance of law. The first group meticulously itemized each violation of procedural rights, while the second group largely ignored procedure and focused instead on the benefits of the executions. To the first group, which valued rule of law as essential to justice, social stability, and the United States' image abroad, Jackson was simply lawless and his executions of the two British men were deplorable. But the stories of Arbuthnot and Ambrister resonated positively with the second group, men who, like Jackson, favored the "action" end of the law-action spectrum. They praised the general as a man of strong instinctive intelligence who acted decisively to America's advantage rather than allowing himself to be arbitrarily limited by the letter of the law.[42]

Jackson's lasting impact on Americans' attitude toward law was particularly momentous. Historian Christopher Waldrep notes that Andrew Jackson played a significant role in legitimizing "the idea of summary violence administered outside law." He comments that, in executing the two Britons and two Creeks during the Florida campaigns, Jackson acted as a "lyncher." An "energetic enforcer of popular values outside law," Jackson saw himself as accountable not to abstract principles of law but to "popular opinion." To Jacksonians, if the community supported particular acts of violence, then they were democratic and legitimate. In later decades, Americans would use Jackson's previous conduct explicitly as precedent for their own violent acts, as illustrated in an 1859 essay that mentioned the Arbuthnot/Ambrister executions as precedent for justifiable use of "mob law" when necessary to implement the popular will.[43]

This perspective on law became more predominant after the Seminole War, as a strong antilegalist strain emerged in American society. During the

Jacksonian era—the 1830s and 1840s—hostility to lawyers and formal legal process was especially strong, and conflict over the role of law in society became one of the essential elements of the clash between Democrats and Whigs. While Whigs believed in the importance of rule of law to ensure the stability of society and supported the supremacy of abstract legal principles over individual will, Jacksonians saw many statutes as artificial limitations on freedom; they perceived some transgressions as warranted resistance to arbitrary constraints and regarded the legal profession as corrupt and monopolistic. Law reformers of the Jacksonian era demanded that legal issues be resolved not by manipulation of procedural technicalities and complex legal abstractions but by reliance on everyday understandings of right and wrong based on community values and popular will. The widespread rioting and mob violence of the Jacksonian era were an outgrowth of that view of law.[44]

The heated dispute about Arbuthnot and Ambrister had an impact on—and revealed a lot about—domestic politics. Although many historians have emphasized Jacksonianism's roots in class struggle, the Seminole War debate evinces the role of divergent worldviews in determining political affiliation. The case of the two Britons revealed a cultural rift within U.S. society in the 1810s. The executions forced people to articulate underlying values in new ways, raising the profile of ideas that later became central tenets of Jacksonianism, well before the official birth of the Democratic and Whig parties.[45]

In terms of American foreign relations, nationalism, and borders of law, critics and defenders of the treatment of Arbuthnot and Ambrister were both right in anticipating consequences of the Florida campaigns. Both sides saw that the executions would reinforce a more muscular foreign and military policy with regard to Europeans and Indians, though they disputed whether that projected a desirable or an undesirable national image. Moreover, Jackson's supporters correctly predicted that the general's activities in Florida would not only suppress British involvement with Indians along U.S. borders and encourage Spain to cede the Florida territory but also boost American nationalism and pave the way for territorial expansion. As it looked toward Europe, Americans' process of identity formation fixated particularly on Britain. For decades after the United States formally gained independence, Americans remained anxious about a continuing British threat to the young nation's survival. The outcome of the Seminole War helped ease that concern, giving Americans more confidence in the long-term stability and security of the Republic.[46]

The executions of Arbuthnot and Ambrister furthered the U.S. vision of the borders of law in three ways. First, they helped the United States assert itself as an equal of European nations. By executing the two men, the United

States claimed the privileges of full nationhood, including the right to make its own decisions about how to deal with people in its vicinity, whether U.S. citizens, Europeans, Indians, or others. Second, the executions helped the United States define non-European-heritage people and their allies as outside the line of law: Arbuthnot and Ambrister, like Hillis Hadjo, Homathlemico, other Red Sticks, Seminoles, and African-descended people in Florida, were "outlaws" who were unprotected by American and international law. Finally, the executions changed the rules for acting across international borders; the United States asserted jurisdiction to try to execute the two British captives outside of American territory. Underlying the ideas applied to the two British men was a new view of sources of law, applicability of law, and the concept of rule of law, all in the service of American nation-building.

Conclusion

THE EXTENSIVE AND multifaceted justification of U.S. armed hostilities against Spaniards, Creeks and Seminoles, African-descended people, and Britons in Florida in the 1810s forged a stronger, more unified national identity at home and a more assertive role in relations with Europeans. In the course of the war and the ensuing debate, the United States demarcated political, diplomatic, legal, and spatial borders in important and enduring ways.

The Family of Nations

The United States delineated the boundary of the "family of civilized nations," claiming its place in the European legal and diplomatic sphere. Although scholars might disagree on exactly when the United States gained acceptance as a nation equal to European countries, the outcome of the Seminole War evidences that the process was under way by the 1810s: both Spain and Britain acknowledged U.S. sovereignty in new ways. Spain did not declare war in response to aggressive American military action against Indians, blacks, and Spanish officials on Spanish territory, and, in the Adams-Onís Treaty, it acceded completely to U.S. claims to Florida. Britain acknowledged that Alexander Arbuthnot and Robert Ambrister acted without sovereign authority and therefore were subject to U.S. punishment for their activities in Florida. The United Kingdom also did not retaliate against the United States for the executions and proceeded with negotiations on commercial matters, resulting in a treaty that was signed in December 1818. Though Britain continued to see itself as the superior partner for several decades—as indeed it was stronger than other European nations in the mid-nineteenth century—it nonetheless recognized that the law of nations included the United States as a European-heritage state. By the turn of the century, American participation with Europeans in conferences to decide on the rules of international law, such as the Hague conferences of 1899 and 1907, demonstrated the United States' full membership in the same family as Europe.

Racial-Cultural Legal Borders

In the Florida campaigns, the United States also asserted a racially inflected legal border between "civilized" and "savage" peoples. The different legal treatment of Alexander Arbuthnot and Robert Ambrister compared to Hillis Hadjo, Homathlemico, and Garçon provides blunt evidence of the racial-cultural line of law. All five men were captives who were executed during the Seminole War, but their individual racial status determined whether they received any hearing before they were put to death. The United States provided the two Britons with a military trial at St. Marks but did not offer the same to the two Creeks at St. Marks or the African-heritage man at the Prospect Bluff fort.[1] The blatant exclusion of Hillis Hadjo, Homathlemico, and Garçon from legal process helped assert the point that by the early nineteenth century race determined a line of law. Although relative power disparities were a factor, the racial message was clear: nonwhite peoples in and along American territory could be treated as outside the protective umbrella of law.

The United States took the lead in asserting the legal significance of a civilized-savage distinction based on racial classifications because, compared to Europe, it had to deal with more immediate issues of cultural and racial difference. Europeans held slaves abroad, rather than at home, and their domination of indigenous peoples, territory, and resources mostly took place overseas, rather than in the metropolitan center. Consequently, Europeans were able to maintain their self-perception as societies that protected liberty and human rights while they still benefited economically from the exploitation of people and resources in their imperial domains. In contrast, European Americans, who had slavery within their midst and Natives' lands within their borders, were not so geographically removed from the territory they appropriated and the people they exploited. Therefore, earlier than Europeans, Americans needed to be explicit about the exclusive application of law. They had a particular need to develop a special rationale for appropriation and exploitation that would enable them to continue to view themselves as shunning arbitrary and despotic government, adhering to rule of law, and respecting principles of liberty.

The unique scientific and intellectual environment in the United States provided a foundation for a different kind of legal rationale. White Americans' close proximity to nonwhites drove them to develop racial theories ahead of Europeans. The United States' singular racial situation led Americans to play an influential role in developing the concept of racial determinism, the idea that race was biologically rather than environmentally determined. As historian Reginald Horsman observes, because of the presence of different races in the United States, "American writers . . . led Europeans in expounding views of innate racial differences." In the early nineteenth century, as Enlightenment views, which had stressed rationalism and universalism, gave way to Romanticism, which emphasized intuition and particularism, European Americans began openly identifying the nation as a white Republic. They came to see both blacks and Indians as innately inferior, and they drew the border of civic membership in an overtly racial way.[2] Correspondingly, Americans' new rationale for treating blacks and Indians differently from European Americans was based on a doctrine that demarcated a racial line in the application of international law.

Although the practice of Europeans treating non-Europeans differently from Europeans was not new, previous distinctions had been based on religious and behavioral differences rather than on presumed inherent inferiority. Following the American lead, nineteenth-century Europeans came to use race as a determinative factor in their categorization of non-Europeans. In their writings, they still often used cultural language, contending that since backward, barbaric people were incapable of adhering to reciprocal legal principles they could not be bound by law and were unfit for equal legal treatment with advanced, civilized people. In reality, however, European scholars' theories of progress were racially inflected. Crucial to the implementation of their theories was the role of race in determining a society's presumed level of civilization and worthiness for inclusion in the sphere of international law. By the late nineteenth century, although Europeans often justified their refusal to recognize ordinary legal restraints on their conduct toward people in Asia and Africa by claiming that they had failed to meet a standard of civilization, in actuality the perceived inferior peoples were primarily identified by race. Europeans correlated racial attributes with certain ascribed cultural characteristics that, in turn, formed the basis for the presumed civilizational deficiencies. The new racial-cultural line conflicted sharply with the theory of law that formally prevailed at the beginning of the nineteenth century. In principle, that theory presumed that the law of nations was transcultural and universal. The newer view was that international law protected only civilized members of the family of nations and did not constrain such civilized nations in their interactions with polities that were composed of people who, largely because of their racial category, were presumed to be savage or barbaric and to lack sovereignty. By the end of the nineteenth century, Europeans and Americans had formally replaced a universalist, inclusionary legal doctrine with an exclusionary one.[3]

There are various explanations for the emergence of this new view. Some nineteenth-century jurists said an exclusionary notion of law was necessarily concomitant with legal positivism. The rise of positivism undermined the older universalist application of the law of nations. Once natural law was no longer the main foundation of international relations, the argument for universal application lost support. To positivists, the boundaries of law coincided with the extent of shared customs and agreements, which meant limiting the sphere of international law to European and European-descended states. Despite the expansion of global trade relations in the late eighteenth and early nineteenth centuries, one scholar notes, the most "fashionable," well-known nineteenth-century jurists increasingly framed international law narrowly. They relied on intra-European custom and treaties as the primary sources of international law and presumed that expressed intent or consent was the necessary foundation of law. To some jurists, those two premises precluded universal application of legal principles. Increasingly, jurists limited the scope of international law to European-heritage nations.[4]

A related jurisprudential development emerged out of the rise of the nation-state. Medieval legal theory had assumed that natural law applied to all people as individuals. However, the law of nations that accompanied the emergence of the nation-state focused on actions of states and applied only to recognized nations. By the nineteenth century, few European or European American legal thinkers saw the world as a collective community governed by universal principles. Rather, jurists viewed each nation-state as independently self-governing and acting in accordance with its own separate interests. The central focus of international law was the sovereign state. European jurists maintained that the law of nations—including the laws of war—applied only to autonomous nations, not to nonsovereign peoples.[5] Since Europeans saw non-Europeans as less civilized and believed that backward societies could not constitute "nations," some jurists concluded that the sphere of the law of nations had to be exclusive. By the late nineteenth century, mainstream thinkers argued that international law applied only between and among civilized nations. Europeans and European Americans widely presumed that non-European societies were not sovereign and therefore not bound by international law. They further agreed that European societies were not bound by international laws of war when they dealt with non-Europeans.

However, these explanations for the legal border between civilized and savage people do not tell the full story. By arguing that the civilized-savage distinction emerged from other independent doctrinal developments (the rise of positivism and the nation-state), these rationales suggest that an exclusionary view of law was a new vision that emerged incidentally, or even accidentally. In reality, the notion of difference had lurked behind idealistic principles for centuries. Since the civilized-savage dividing line was not new in the late nineteenth century, autonomous developments in legal doctrine at that time do not provide an adequate explanation for the emergence of the line. It is true that European scholars of international law—such as William Edward Hall (treatise first published in 1880), James Lorimer (1883), John Westlake (1894), Thomas Lawrence (1895), and Lassa Oppenheim (1905)—shifted Europe's formal expression of international law principles in the late nineteenth century. European jurists became much more forthright in their assertion of a standard of civilization that determined a group's legal status and rights. To a great extent, however, that shift was instrumental rather than an inadvertent effect of evolving legal doctrine. Europeans needed an approach to law that would be more accommodating of their nineteenth-century imperial activities.

In fact, rather than the emergence of positivism and the nation-state causing racial differences in the application of law, the main thrust of change worked in the opposite way. Perceived racial distinctions reinforced the rise of positivism and underpinned the articulation of narrow definitions of what "nation" and "sovereignty" meant. The circular reasoning that automatically correlated people's racial classification with their presumed degree of sovereignty and nationhood, discussed above, illustrates how supposed racial characteristics impacted ideas about the classification of polities. Racial issues also bolstered a commitment to positive law, especially in the United States. Precisely because European Americans had indigenous and African-descended people both within and alongside their territorial borders, they could not continue the fiction of the universal application of rights under natural law. Instead, they turned to positive law.

Although Americans had relied heavily on universalist natural law ideals during the Revolution, once the nation gained independence its leaders had less incentive to advocate such a view of law in the domestic sphere. They had the opportunity to include in the Constitution the higher principles that were most important to them, and they now had control over lawmaking. It is understandable that the governing elite would not want the American people appealing to extraconstitutional and extralegislative sources of law to trump positive enactments. The Constitution articulated distinctions among European, African, and Native Americans, making such racial lines part of the nation's positive law. The governing elite had no interest in allowing people to use universalist principles to challenge those distinctions.

In the postrevolutionary decades, the elite's self-serving rejection of natural law universalism was particularly evident in the issue of slavery. In the late eighteenth and early nineteenth centuries, Europeans and European Americans increasingly viewed slavery as a creation of positive law—disfavored by natural law but permissible where established and maintained by legislation. Natural law provided a common foundation for American and British abolitionists' challenge to slavery. At the same time, the United States increasingly had to rely on positive law as the only way to legally sustain slavery.[6] For the United States, emphasizing positive rather than natural law helped forestall challenges to the American practice of slavery. Thus, in the domestic sphere, it was in the U.S. interest to deemphasize legal theories that might have universalist application. Moreover, to the extent that relations with Indians and African-descended people could potentially fall within international law, by the 1810s the United States likewise made clear its rejection of a universalist law of nations that was based on natural law.[7] The United States publicly asserted its rejection of universal law in its justifications for the 1816–1818 Florida campaigns, and the principles articulated during the Seminole War debate became a part of Europeans' and Americans' international law doctrine by the late nineteenth century.

Thus, the U.S. defense of its military actions in the 1810s anticipated the solidification of a racially determined civilized-savage border of law. This view of legal doctrine presumed that international law applied only to civilized, sovereign entities. The altered perspective on the applicability of law heightened the global impact of other doctrinal shifts in sources and rationales for law. In determining to what extent it was bound by law in dealing with Indians, blacks, and their British and Spanish allies in the Seminole War, the United States relied heavily on racial-cultural lines between civilized and savage people and between sovereign nation-states and nonsovereign polities. In vociferously articulating that border of law, the United States provided a model rationale for its own later nineteenth-century expansionism as well as for Europe's imperial projects.

Rationales for Extraterritorial Action

Additionally, in the Seminole War the United States asserted its view of law with regard to spatial borders. The extraterritorial nature of the Florida campaigns seemingly conflicted with Europeans' strengthening commitment to territorial sovereignty of nation-states. Yet the United States managed to explain its actions by redefining sovereignty and nationhood. In rationalizing its view of extraterritorial activities, the United States built on its claim to European-style nationhood and its denial of legal protections to "uncivilized" people.

The United States justified its extraterritorial military excursions by claiming its own sovereign rights under the law of nations, including the right of self-preservation. The United States acted out of concern about its own territorial sovereignty—especially fearing intrusion and interference by British, Indian, and black men—and argued that its national security depended on taking control of Florida in order to eliminate threats to its territory and its people. When it executed two Britons and exiled Spanish officers from Florida during the Seminole War, the United States went even further: it insisted that Europeans demonstrate their respect for U.S. sovereignty by recognizing and yielding to the United States as the sole natural dominant power in its regional sphere. In a way that seemed to contradict the formal commitments to both positivism and territorial sovereignty, the United States contended that its popularly supported mission to spread American values, secure control over the nation's "natural" borders, and achieve its providential destiny justified the Florida incursions. These principles provided a foundation for American continentalism as it would be implemented over the course of the nineteenth century. Those principles also anticipated the Monroe Doctrine of 1823. With regard to all territory in the Western Hemisphere, the doctrine asserted a special U.S. position, a position superior to that of Europeans. Thus, at the same time as the United States staked its claim to be part of the European community of civilized nations, it also differentiated between Europe and the Americas. It asserted the natural primacy of the United States, along with its values and political culture, in the Americas. The United States contended that, within its expansive "natural" boundaries, it was entitled to set its own rules for regulating people and controlling territory.

Another kind of line-drawing was just as significant for justifying American extraterritorial action. To rationalize categorizing particular groups and certain territory as outside the bounds of legal constraints, the United States established race-based lines between people who were civilized or savage and between those who were sovereign and nonsovereign. In the Seminole War, the nation relied on the concepts of "pirates" and "outlaws" to sustain those distinctions.

The pirate concept allowed the United States to eliminate territorial and personal boundaries to the government's reach. Using an analogy to pirates on the high seas, it defined Florida as a space where the nation could act extraterritorially. The law of nations recognized that the high seas belonged to no nation yet allowed individual nations to exercise jurisdiction there under certain conditions. Nations shared universal jurisdiction over pirates—people who committed acts of robbery or criminal violence at sea. Territorial boundaries were no barrier to the exercise of authority over people designated as pirates on the ocean.[8] The United States' extension of its sovereignty into Florida by asserting the right to implement the law of nations there parallels Britain's eighteenth-century extension of its jurisdiction over international sea space by asserting the right to punish "pirates" seized anywhere in the oceans.[9] Americans treated Florida as if it were the high seas, that is, a space where no nation exercised exclusive sovereignty and therefore any nation could act to punish lawlessness that threatened national or international interests.

Unlike most European nations, the United States was not bordered on all sides by established nation-states with clear claims to territorial sovereignty. Britain maintained sovereignty in Upper and Lower Canada, but in the South and West the United States abutted lands that, to Americans, seemed to lack a recognizable, assertive sovereign presence. Americans accepted neither local Indian tribes nor remote colonial European nations as truly sovereign authorities in Florida, Texas, and the Louisiana Territory. The United States contended that extraterritorial action in the Seminole War was warranted because Florida was a weakly governed territory and the people there were stateless, like pirates. In the American view, Florida was what pundits today might call a "failed state"—ripe ground for hostile people to set up bases from which to attack the United States. Though the United States had not been militarily strong enough to assert its power over the region immediately after the Revolution, by the mid-1810s the balance of military muscle had shifted, making U.S. military action feasible. The United States used an implicit analogy between Florida and the oceans to justify its extraterritorial action.

The United States further used the pirate concept to identify certain classes of people as subject to unrestrained American military violence. Just as a nation contravened no law when it executed a foreign pirate captured on the ocean, Americans argued, the United States' execution, deportation, and enslavement of "lawless" people in "ungoverned" Florida was entirely consistent with national and international legal mandates. In the American view, neither Indians nor blacks in Florida could claim rights of territorial sovereignty because neither could be a sovereign nation. Moreover, both were presumed uncivilized and lawless. In short, they were like pirates. Anyone allied with them—even a European—was also a pirate. In principles pertaining to pirates as described by leading writers on the law of nations, the United States found a convenient legal rationale for acting extraterritorially. The pirate concept provided a legal premise for acting outside U.S. territorial borders and for committing violence against Spanish, British, Seminole, Creek, and African-descended people there.

The United States also relied on the parallel concept of the "outlaw" to justify its violence against certain categories of people in Florida. By treating blacks, Seminoles, Creeks, and their European allies as outlaws, the United States removed them from the ordinary protections of the law of nations, thus freeing the nation to act against them extraterritorially without having to comply with the laws of war. The United States also denied that its own Constitution and domestic laws could limit its hostilities against Indians and blacks.

Nineteenth-Century Border Law

The United States' aggressive extraterritorial actions in the 1810s provided a model for the future. The doctrines expressed in the Seminole War debate, which later came to dominate legal discourse, provided a foundation for American and European imperialist ventures of the late nineteenth and early twentieth centuries. Although Europeans did not regard the Monroe Doctrine as part of the law of nations and actively acted contrary to the doctrine in several instances in the nineteenth century, they tolerated the United States' claims to hegemony vis-à-vis other polities in the Western Hemisphere. Moreover, they borrowed from some American justifications for territorial expansion to reinforce their own imperial ventures. Most notably, by the late nineteenth century Europeans adopted into their understanding of international law the principle that "civilized" states could acquire sovereignty in "uncivilized," nonsovereign extra-European territory through occupation. Bolstered by legal doctrines that used a standard of civilization to justify extraterritorial expansion and differential legal treatment of racially different, "savage" people, European nations took direct or indirect control of much of Asia, Africa, and the Middle East during the age of imperialism. Having won inclusion in the European legal community, the United States, too, claimed it was entitled to make use of newly formalized legal doctrines as it launched its ventures abroad in such places as the Philippines, Guam, and Puerto Rico. As in the Seminole War, the United States argued that normal principles of international law did not apply universally and that constitutional law did not follow the flag.[10]

Legal doctrines proclaimed in the Seminole War affected not only U.S. and European overseas activities but also the United States' domestic implementation of law. Those doctrines presaged the worldview of the Jacksonian Democrats with regard to blacks and Indians: the Jacksonians were more open about drawing racial lines than their predecessors, the Jeffersonians, had been. In particular, the racial-cultural borderline demarcated in the Seminole War reinforced the notion that law did not protect certain categories of people in the Americas. The boundary of law was marked by ascribed behavior and presumed character, both shaped by racial identity. A vision that left many blacks and Indians categorically outside the law helped reinforce slavery, Indian dispossession, and territorial expansion.[11] Characterizing the victims of the three activities—especially blacks and Indians—as inferior and lawless exempted them from legal protections and justified all three questionable activities yet also allowed white Americans to continue to believe in themselves as law-abiding citizens of a civilized nation.

In the debate about the Seminole War, European Americans made readily apparent the racial line of law, which was to have so many ramifications. The Florida campaigns made it clear that Americans could ignore normal territorial constraints when it came to fugitive slaves. The campaigns further showed that the federal government would act as an agent of the states in defending slave property as defined by slave states. The central government would implement slave states' presumption that blacks were slaves and their notion that fugitive slaves were outside law. Even more fundamentally, the Seminole War made evident that the United States would back up the slave states' assertion that free blacks lacked citizenship. The United States showed that it would not extend equal legal protection to blacks as it did to whites. This racial model continued up through the Civil War. In the antebellum era, the United States continued to act aggressively to support slave states' interests and to extend the fugitive slave provisions of the Constitution and federal laws extraterritorially. In the 1830s and 1840s, Jacksonian Democrats continued the claim that African-descended people were not Americans and could not be part of the American nation—though while on U.S. territory they were obligated to obey American law. In 1857, the Jacksonian-dominated Supreme Court would make this perspective official, ruling in the *Dred Scott* case that blacks could not be citizens and had no rights that whites had to respect. The Privileges and Immunities and Due Process Clauses of the Constitution did not protect the rights of slaves or presumed slaves. African-heritage people were thus declared to be both subject to law and outside protections of law, leaving them without meaningful recourse in the face of violence and enslavement.

Likewise, the Seminole War model with regard to Indians also continued into the antebellum period—and well beyond. The Florida campaigns evidenced the American belief that Indian tribes were not nations holding rights under the law of nations. The expeditions exhibited American disdain for the concept of tribal sovereignty, as well as the American assumption that relations with Indians were a matter of internal, domestic law and politics rather than diplomacy and the law of nations. They further showed that the United States could ignore territorial constraints when it came to relations with Indians: the Republic could extend treaty provisions and national policies extraterritorially. Moreover, even when the United States had obtained treaties through coercion or bribery rather than through tribes' genuine consent, Indians who failed to obey treaty provisions were beyond or outside the law and could be subject to unrestrained American violence. The campaigns of 1816–1818 further demonstrated that the federal government would act as the agent of frontier states that wanted Indians moved out of the way of white settlement. These principles continued in effect throughout the rest of the nineteenth century, as the United States proceeded with its policy of western expansion and Indian removal.

The Seminole War reflected an emerging new view of law. The application of law became more conditional and subjective. Americans came to see some people as outside legal safeguards entirely. With regard to blacks, Creeks, and Seminoles, the United States circumvented international law by denying them the status of civilized nations. Yet, at the same time, the United States denied those groups American citizenship and the protection of U.S. law. Thus, the United States excluded blacks and Indians from the protections of both international and domestic law, using the Seminole War to define itself as a nation and to label Indian tribes and blacks as not Americans and not nations.

The principles of border law that were articulated in the debate on the Seminole War became increasingly dominant in ensuing decades. The nascent ideas of the 1810s regarding legal treatment of both physical boundaries and racial-cultural lines grew to full maturity by the end of the nineteenth century. In the Florida campaigns, the United States was successful in redrawing the line that defined the European family of nations, claiming the young republic's place in the family. At the same time, it asserted its special primacy in its own geographic region. It also articulated a racially determined border between "civilized" and "savage" people and contended that, both internationally and domestically, different laws applied to the former than to the latter. Additionally, the United States asserted a new set of rules for acting across territorial borders, shrewdly employing concepts of piracy, outlawry, racism, sovereignty, continentalism, manifest destiny, and American exceptionalism to justify extraterritorial action. The legal demarcations expressed in the debates had a lasting impact, as they lay the groundwork for the Monroe Doctrine, the *Dred Scott* decision, U.S. westward expansion, and late nineteenth-century interpretations of international law and overseas imperialism.

Appendix

Abbreviations

Notes

Acknowledgments

Index

APPENDIX

Membership in 15th and 17th Congresses and House Debate and Votes on Resolutions concerning the Seminole War

State	Representative in 15th Congress (in February 1819)	Participation in Debate	Resolution: Pensacola	Resolution: Arbuthnot	Resolution: Ambrister	Served in 17th Congress
CT	Sylvester Gilbert		•	•	•	
CT	Ebenezer Huntington		•	•	•	
CT	Jonathan O. Moseley		•	•	•	
CT	Timothy Pitkin		•	•	•	
CT	Samuel B. Sherwood		•	•	•	
CT	Nathaniel Terry		•	•	•	
CT	Thomas S. Williams	•	•	•	•	
DE	Willard Hall		♦	♦	♦	
DE	Louis McLane		♦	♦	♦	x
GA	Joel Abbot		•	♦	♦	x
GA	Thomas W. Cobb	•	•	•	•	
GA	Zadock Cook		•	•	•	
GA	Joel Crawford		•	•	•	
GA	William Terrell		•	•	•	
IL	John McLean		♦	♦	♦	
IN	William Hendricks		♦	—	•	x
KY	Richard C. Anderson, Jr.	♦	♦	♦	♦	
KY	Henry Clay	•	—	—	—	
KY	Joseph Desha	♦	♦	♦	♦	
KY	Richard M. Johnson	♦	♦	♦	♦	
KY	Anthony New		♦	♦	♦	x
KY	Tunstal Quarles		♦	♦	♦	
KY	George Robertson		•	•	•	x
KY	Thomas Speed		•	•	•	
KY	David Trimble		•	•	•	x
KY	David Walker	♦	♦	♦	♦	
LA	Thomas Butler		♦	♦	♦	
MD	Thomas Bayly		•	•	•	x

SYMBOLS

♦ = pro-Jackson position • = anti-Jackson position m = mixed-pro and anti-Jackson position
— = did not vote x = served in 17th Congress

State	Representative in 15th Congress (in February 1819)	Participation in Debate	Resolution: Pensacola	Resolution: Arbuthnot	Resolution: Ambrister	Served in 17th Congress
MD	Thomas Culbreth		•	•	•	
MD	John C. Herbert		•	—	•	
MD	Peter Little		♦	♦	♦	x
MD	George Peter		♦	♦	♦	
MD	Philip Reed	•	•	•	•	x
MD	Samuel Ringgold		♦	♦	♦	
MD	Samuel Smith		♦	♦	♦	x
MD	Philip Stuart		•	•	•	
MA	Benjamin Adams		•	—	•	
MA	Samuel C. Allen		•	•	•	x
MA	Walter Folger, Jr.		♦	♦	♦	
MA	Timothy Fuller	•	•	•	•	x
MA	Joshua Gage		♦	♦	•	
MA	John Holmes	♦	♦	♦	♦	
MA	Enoch Lincoln		•	•	•	
MA	Jonathan Mason		♦	♦	♦	
MA	Elijah H. Mills		•	•	•	
MA	Marcus Morton		♦	♦	♦	
MA	Jeremiah Nelson		•	•	•	x
MA	Benjamin Orr		♦	♦	♦	
MA	Thomas Rice		•	•	•	
MA	Nathaniel Ruggles		•	•	•	
MA	Zabdiel Sampson		♦	♦	♦	
MA	Henry Shaw		♦	♦	♦	
MA	Nathaniel Silsbee		•	♦	♦	
MA	Solomon Strong		•	•	•	
MA	Ezekiel Whitman		•	•	•	x
MA	John Wilson		•	•	•	
MS	George Poindexter	♦	♦	♦	♦	
NH	Josiah Butler		—	—	—	x
NH	Clifton Clagett		♦	♦	♦	
NH	Salma Hale		♦	—	•	
NH	Arthur Livermore		♦	♦	♦	
NH	John F. Parrott		♦	♦	♦	
NH	Nathaniel Upham		♦	♦	—	x
NJ	Ephraim Bateman		♦	♦	♦	x
NJ	Benjamin Bennet		♦	♦	♦	
NJ	Joseph Bloomfield		•	•	•	

SYMBOLS

♦ = pro-Jackson position • = anti-Jackson position m = mixed-pro and anti-Jackson position
— = did not vote x = served in 17th Congress

State	Representative in 15th Congress (in February 1819)	Participation in Debate	Resolution: Pensacola	Resolution: Arbuthnot	Resolution: Ambrister	Served in 17th Congress
NJ	Charles Kinsey		♦	♦	♦	
NJ	John Linn		♦	♦	♦	
NJ	Henry Southard		♦	♦	♦	
NY	Oliver C. Comstock		♦	♦	♦	
NY	Daniel Cruger		♦	♦	♦	
NY	John P. Cushman		•	•	•	
NY	John R. Drake		♦	♦	♦	
NY	Benjamin Ellicott		•	♦	♦	
NY	Josiah Hasbrouck		♦	♦	♦	
NY	John Herkimer		♦	♦	♦	
NY	Thomas H. Hubbard		♦	♦	♦	x
NY	William Irving		•	•	•	
NY	Dorrance Kirtland		♦	♦	♦	
NY	Thomas Lawyer		♦	♦	♦	
NY	David A. Ogden		•	•	♦	
NY	John Palmer		♦	♦	♦	
NY	James Porter		♦	♦	♦	
NY	John Savage		♦	♦	♦	
NY	Philip J. Schuyler		•	•	•	
NY	Tredwell Scudder		♦	♦	♦	
NY	John C. Spencer		•	♦	♦	
NY	Henry R. Storrs	•	•	•	•	
NY	James Tallmadge, Jr.	♦	—	—	—	
NY	John W. Taylor		♦	♦	♦	x
NY	Caleb Tompkins		♦	♦	♦	
NY	George Townsend		—	—	—	
NY	Peter H. Wendover		♦	♦	♦	
NY	Rensselaer Westerlo		•	•	•	
NY	James W. Wilkin		♦	♦	♦	
NY	Isaac Williams, Jr.		♦	♦	♦	
NC	Joseph H. Bryan		♦	♦	♦	
NC	William Davidson		♦	♦	♦	
NC	Weldon N. Edwards		•	•	•	x
NC	Charles Fisher		—	—	—	
NC	Thomas H. Hall		♦	♦	♦	x
NC	James Owen		♦	♦	♦	
NC	Lemuel Sawyer	♦	—	♦	♦	x
NC	Thomas Settle		♦	♦	♦	

SYMBOLS

♦ = pro-Jackson position • = anti-Jackson position m = mixed-pro and anti-Jackson position
— = did not vote x = served in 17th Congress

State	Representative in 15th Congress (in February 1819)	Participation in Debate	Resolution: Pensacola	Resolution: Arbuthnot	Resolution: Ambrister	Served in 17th Congress
NC	Jesse Slocumb		•	•	•	
NC	James S. Smith		•	•	•	
NC	James Stewart		•	•	•	
NC	Felix Walker	♦	♦	♦	♦	x
NC	Lewis Williams		•	•	•	x
OH	Levi Barber		♦	♦	♦	x
OH	Philemon Beecher		•	•	•	
OH	John W. Campbell		♦	♦	♦	x
OH	William Henry Harrison	m	•	♦	•	
OH	Samuel Herrick		♦	♦	♦	
OH	Peter Hitchcock		♦	♦	♦	
PA	William Anderson		—	♦	—	
PA	Henry Baldwin	♦	♦	♦	♦	x
PA	Andrew Boden		♦	♦	♦	
PA	Isaac Darlington		—	—	—	
PA	Joseph Hiester		♦	♦	♦	
PA	Joseph Hopkinson	m	•	♦	♦	
PA	Jacob Hostetter		♦	♦	♦	
PA	William Maclay		•	•	•	
PA	William P. Maclay		•	•	•	
PA	David Marchand		♦	♦	♦	
PA	Robert Moore		•	♦	♦	
PA	Samuel Moore		♦	♦	♦	x
PA	John Murray		♦	♦	•	
PA	Alexander Ogle		♦	—	—	
PA	Thomas Patterson		♦	♦	♦	x
PA	Levi Pawling		•	•	•	
PA	Thomas J. Rogers		♦	♦	♦	x
PA	John Sergeant		♦	♦	♦	
PA	Adam Seybert		♦	♦	♦	
PA	Christian Tarr		♦	♦	♦	
PA	James M. Wallace		♦	♦	♦	
PA	John Whiteside		♦	♦	♦	
PA	William Wilson		•	♦	♦	
RI	John L. Boss, Jr.		—	—	—	
RI	James B. Mason		•	•	•	
SC	Joseph Bellinger		—	—	—	
SC	Elias Earle		—	—	—	

SYMBOLS

♦ = pro-Jackson position • = anti-Jackson position m = mixed-pro and anti-Jackson position
— = did not vote x = served in 17th Congress

State	Representative in 15th Congress (in February 1819)	Participation in Debate	Resolution: Pensacola	Resolution: Arbuthnot	Resolution: Ambrister	Served in 17th Congress
SC	James Ervin	♦	♦	♦	♦	
SC	William Lowndes	m	•	•	♦	x
SC	Henry Middleton		♦	♦	♦	
SC	Stephen D. Miller		—	—	—	
SC	Wilson Nesbitt		♦	—	♦	
SC	Eldred Simkins		•	♦	♦	
SC	Starling Tucker		♦	♦	♦	x
TN	William G. Blount		♦	♦	♦	
TN	Thomas Claiborne		—	—	—	
TN	Samuel Hogg		♦	♦	♦	
TN	Francis Jones	♦	♦	♦	♦	x
TN	George W. L. Marr		♦	♦	♦	
TN	John Rhea	♦	♦	♦	♦	x
VT	Samuel C. Crafts		♦	♦	♦	x
VT	William Hunter		♦	♦	♦	
VT	Orsamus C. Merrill		♦	♦	♦	
VT	Charles Rich		♦	♦	♦	x
VT	Mark Richards		♦	♦	♦	
VA	Archibald Austin		•	•	•	
VA	William Lee Ball		•	•	•	x
VA	Philip P. Barbour	♦	♦	♦	♦	x
VA	Burwell Bassett		♦	♦	♦	x
VA	William A. Burwell		•	♦	♦	
VA	Edward Colston	•	•	•	•	
VA	John Floyd	♦	♦	♦	♦	x
VA	Robert S. Garnett		♦	♦	♦	x
VA	James Johnson	•	•	•	•	
VA	William J. Lewis		•	•	•	
VA	William McCoy		♦	♦	♦	x
VA	Charles F. Mercer	•	•	•	•	x
VA	Hugh Nelson	♦	♦	♦	♦	x
VA	Thomas M. Nelson	•	•	•	•	
VA	Thomas Newton, Jr.		♦	♦	♦	x
VA	John Pegram		•	•	•	
VA	James Pindall		•	•	•	
VA	James Pleasants		•	•	•	
VA	Ballard Smith		♦	♦	♦	
VA	Alexander Smyth	♦	♦	♦	♦	x

SYMBOLS

♦ = pro-Jackson position • = anti-Jackson position m = mixed-pro and anti-Jackson position
— = did not vote x = served in 17th Congress

State	Representative in 15th Congress (in February 1819)	Participation in Debate	Resolution: Pensacola	Resolution: Arbuthnot	Resolution: Ambrister	Served in 17th Congress
VA	George Strother	♦	♦	♦	♦	
VA	Henry St. George Tucker		•	•	•	
VA	John Tyler	•	•	•	•	

Sources: For membership of House of Representatives in 15th Congress (in February 1819): AC, 289–1138; for participation in debate: AC, 527–530, 583–1138; for roll call votes on resolutions: AC, 1135–1138;[1] for membership of House of Representatives in 17th Congress: *Annals of Congress,* House, 17th Cong., 1st sess., 513–1896.

Resolution: Pensacola. That the seizure of the Spanish posts of Pensacola and Barrancas by the U.S. army was unconstitutional. Yea = anti-Jackson position; nay = pro-Jackson position.

Resolution: Arbuthnot. That the House of Representatives does not disapprove of the trial and execution of Alexander Arbuthnot. Yea = pro-Jackson position; nay = anti-Jackson position.

Resolution: Ambrister. That the House of Representatives does not disapprove of the trial and execution of Robert C. Ambrister. Yea = pro-Jackson position; nay = anti-Jackson position.[2]

SYMBOLS

♦ = pro-Jackson position • = anti-Jackson position m = mixed-pro and anti-Jackson position
— = did not vote x = served in 17th Congress

Abbreviations

AC	*Annals of Congress,* House, 15th Cong., 2nd sess.
AC, Appendix	*Annals of Congress,* 15th Cong., 2nd sess., Appendix
ASP-FR	*American State Papers: Foreign Relations*
ASP-MA	*American State Papers: Military Affairs*
Stat.	*Statutes at Large of the United States of America, 1789–1873*

Notes

INTRODUCTION

1. This book uses the terms "blacks," "African-heritage people," "people of African descent," and "African-descended people" interchangeably. The term "African Americans" refers to African-descended people in the United States. Blacks in Florida cannot be referred to collectively as "African Americans" as that term is customarily understood (because not all were from the United States) nor as "free blacks" (because not all were free). How this book refers to people in Florida who had been slaves in the United States and were not enslaved in Florida varies depending on whose perspective is being described. Thus they are sometimes referred to as "refugees" or "free blacks" and sometimes as "fugitive slaves" or "runaway slaves." This book uses the terms "Indians," "American Indians," "Native Americans," "Natives," and "indigenous peoples" to refer collectively to pre-Columbian inhabitants of the Americas and their descendants. When discussing a particular community of Indians, the book employs the most commonly used name for that community, such as "Creeks" and "Seminoles," though those names originated as European Americans' designations for and identification of those groups, as discussed in Chapter 4. The book's description of contemporary statements normally employs the terms as used by the original speakers and writers. Contemporaries writing about the Seminole War often used the terms "Indians" and "Seminoles" in a vague and imprecise manner. American commentators frequently grouped all American Indians together as an indistinguishable mass. This was convenient when a writer wanted to justify American actions as a warranted response to "Indian" behavior but lacked any foundation for allegations against particular Indians. Additionally, the term "Seminoles" sometimes encompassed Red Stick Creeks and at times also included black allies and neighbors. The terms "whites," "European

Americans," "European-heritage people," and European-descended people are used interchangeably. Finally, this book uses both "law of nations" and "international law" to refer to the law governing relations between and among nations. English philosopher and jurist Jeremy Bentham coined the term "international law" in 1789, and subsequently "law of nations" gradually became obsolete. Though this book treats the terms as synonymous, it more often uses "law of nations" when referring to pre-1789 ideas and "international law" to discuss late nineteenth-century doctrines.

2. Although published scholarship provides excellent accounts of the Florida campaigns, including general descriptions of the events and proceedings, scholars have paid little attention to the contemporary public debate and the ideas it revealed about nationhood, law, race, and territoriality. General studies of the Seminole War do not provide substantial analysis of legal issues, and general theoretical works on the history of the law of nations do not address the application of principles to the Seminole War. Moreover, scholars have inadequately examined the application of the laws of war to indigenous and African-descended people in North America. Additionally, few works explore in depth the role of law in early American nation-building in the context of war or foreign policy. A notable exception is Eliga H. Gould, *Among the Powers of the Earth: The American Revolution and the Making of a New World Empire* (Cambridge, MA: Harvard University Press, 2012). Consistently attentive to the role of law in the construction of the nation, Gould analyzes how the United States established its place in the world between the 1750s and the 1820s, when it sought acceptance abroad and dominion at home. His concluding chapter discusses the Seminole War. When *Among the Powers* was published, this book was nearly complete, but it benefited greatly from Gould's insightful earlier essay-length publications, especially "Zones of Law, Zones of Violence: The Legal Geography of the British Atlantic, circa 1772," *William and Mary Quarterly,* 3rd ser., 60 (2003): 471–510; and "The Making of an Atlantic State System: Britain and the United States, 1795–1825," in *Britain and America Go to War: The Impact of War and Warfare in Anglo-America, 1754–1815,* ed. Julie Flavell and Stephen Conway (Gainesville: University Press of Florida, 2004), 241–265.

3. The term "Seminole War" was actually a misnomer. The word "Seminole" was unsuitable and underinclusive because of both the participants' identities and the United States' actual goals. The United States' main enemy combatants in the Florida campaigns included African-descended people as well as Seminoles and Creeks. In fact, as discussed in Chapter 6, there is strong evidence that Florida's blacks were the primary target of the American expeditions. Later, this 1816–1818 war would be known as the First Seminole War, since it would be followed by the Second Seminole War in 1835–1842 and the Third Seminole War in 1855–1858. The term "Seminole War" is also somewhat problematic because, in the course of the debate, some Americans denied that the armed conflicts in Florida constituted "war." Despite these issues, this book will refer to the Florida expeditions as the Seminole War because that is the term most Americans used at the time.

4. Historian Peter Onuf notes that, in the late eighteenth and early nineteenth centuries, "nation" was a "protean concept," and "the terms 'race,' 'nation,'

and 'people' were not yet clearly distinguished." Peter S. Onuf, *Jefferson's Empire: The Language of American Nationhood* (Charlottesville: University Press of Virginia, 2000), 149, 159. For different perspectives on "nations" and "nationalism," see Ernest Gellner, *Nations and Nationalism,* 2nd ed. (Ithaca, NY: Cornell University Press, copyright 2006, printed 2008); Anthony D. Smith, *Nationalism: Theory, Ideology, History,* 2nd ed. (Malden, MA: Polity Press, 2010); and Benedict Anderson, *Imagined Communities: Reflections on the Origin and Spread of Nationalism,* rev. ed. (New York: Verso, 1991).

5. On U.S. eagerness for European countries to accept it as an equal, and on the Constitution as part of an effort to gain European recognition, see Gould, *Among the Powers of the Earth,* chap. 4; and Peter Onuf and Nicholas Onuf, *Federal Union, Modern World: The Law of Nations in an Age of Revolutions, 1776–1814* (Madison, WI: Madison House, 1993). On American concern about foreign reception of the U.S. Constitution, see David M. Golove and Daniel J. Hulsebosch, "A Civilized Nation: The Early American Constitution, The Law of Nations, and the Pursuit of International Recognition," *New York University Law Review* 85, no. 4 (October 2010): 932–1066; and Frederick W. Marks, *Independence on Trial: Foreign Affairs and the Making of the Constitution* (Baton Rouge: Louisiana State University Press, 1973). Mikulas Fabry describes the process by which the United States became a recognized nation in *Recognizing States: International Society and the Establishment of New States since 1776* (New York: Oxford University Press, 2010), 26–36. On criteria for the recognition of states, see also James Crawford, *The Creation of States in International Law,* 2nd ed. (New York: Oxford University Press, 2006).
6. Treaty of Amity, Commerce and Navigation, also known as the Jay Treaty, between the United States and Britain (1794), Stat., 8:116–129; Treaty of Friendship, Limits, and Navigation between Spain and the United States, also known as Pinckney's Treaty or the Treaty of San Lorenzo (1795), Stat., 8:138–153; Treaty between the United States of America and the French Republic, also known as the Louisiana Purchase (1803), ASP-FR, 2:507–508. Eliga Gould concludes that the two treaties signed in the mid-1790s constituted recognition that the United States was "a treaty-worthy sovereign," though it was the Seminole War that "helped place the United States at the head of a new hemispheric community of nations." Gould, *Among the Powers of the Earth,* 140–144, 179–180.
7. On the history of early American foreign policy, see especially William Earl Weeks, *The New Cambridge History of American Foreign Relations,* vol. 1, *Dimensions of the Early American Empire, 1754–1865* (New York: Cambridge University Press, 2013); and William Earl Weeks, *Building the Continental Empire: American Expansion from the Revolution to the Civil War* (Chicago: Ivan R. Dee, 1996).
8. Major General Andrew Jackson to Secretary of War John C. Calhoun, August 10, 1818, ASP-MA, 1:744–745, quotation on 745.
9. Weeks, *History of American Foreign Relations,* 7–12, 34–36, 69–71 (on Benjamin Franklin's and Thomas Jefferson's views on continentalism), chaps. 4 and 5 (on American expansionism from the 1810s to the 1850s). There is an extensive literature on the subject of American exceptionalism and American continentalism in early American history. For a variety of scholarly views, see Seymour Martin Lipset, *American Exceptionalism: A Double-Edged Sword* (New

York: Norton, 1996); Jack P. Greene, *The Intellectual Construction of America: Exceptionalism and Identity from 1492 to 1800* (Chapel Hill: University of North Carolina Press, 1993); Michael Kammen, "The Problem of American Exceptionalism: A Reconsideration," *American Quarterly* 45, no. 1 (March 1993): 1–43; John M. Murrin, "The Jeffersonian Triumph and American Exceptionalism," *Journal of the Early Republic* 20, no. 1 (Spring 2000): 1–25; Julius W. Pratt, "The Ideology of American Expansion," in *Essays in Honor of William E. Dodd by His Former Students at the University of Chicago,* ed. Avery Craven (Chicago: University of Chicago Press, 1935), 335–353; Charles A. Beard, *A Foreign Policy for America* (New York: Alfred A. Knopf, 1940), 12–35; and Charles Vevier, "American Continentalism: An Idea of Expansion, 1845–1910," *American Historical Review* 65, no. 2 (January 1960): 323–335.

10. Thomas Jefferson to Alexander von Humboldt, December 6, 1813, in *The Papers of Thomas Jefferson,* Retirement Series, vol. 7, *28 November 1813 to 30 September 1814,* ed. J. Jefferson Looney (Princeton, NJ: Princeton University Press, 2010), 29–32.

11. Despite jurists' use of universalist language, in fact there always were limitations to the application of natural law. Chapter 4 describes the underlying reality of the Eurocentric and Christian-centric boundaries of natural law in the sixteenth, seventeenth, and eighteenth centuries. Moreover, Europeans' "universal" values often took a judgmental view of cultural diversity and failed to take into account non-European cultures' values. Europeans acted parochially when their theories of universalization of European legal concepts led them to impose their ideals on allegedly inferior people rather than recognizing legal pluralism. However, in some contexts, universalism could be positive. This book focuses on the extent to which the United States regarded itself as universally bound to obey the constraints of the laws of war in armed hostilities against all classes of people. As will be seen, the United States rejected this form of universalism, determining that only certain groups were entitled to the protective provisions of the laws of war.

12. David Armitage points out that the Declaration of Independence drew from positive law as well as natural law. Although the positivist sections of the Declaration focusing on the rights and powers of independent states most directly addressed the document's main purpose, the naturalist portions asserting fundamental individual rights became much more prominent in establishing "the Declaration's place in American national mythology." David Armitage, "The Declaration of Independence and International Law," *William and Mary Quarterly,* 3rd ser., 59 (January 2002): 39–64. For scholarly studies of the role of natural law doctrine in American Revolutionary thought, see Philip Hamburger, "Natural Rights, Natural Law, and the American Constitutions," *Yale Law Journal* 102, no. 4 (January 1993): 907–960; Andrew J. Reck, "Natural Law in American Revolutionary Thought," *Review of Metaphysics* 30, no. 4 (June 1977): 686–714; and Lester H. Cohen, "The American Revolution and Natural Law Theory," *Journal of the History of Ideas* 39, no. 3 (July–September 1978): 491–502.

13. Stephen C. Neff, *War and the Law of Nations: A General History* (New York: Cambridge University Press, 2005).

14. Standard histories of international law posit a distinct change from the seventeenth and eighteenth centuries to the nineteenth century. See, for example,

C. H. Alexandrowicz, "Doctrinal Aspects of the Universality of the Law of Nations," *British Yearbook of International Law* 37 (1961): 506–515. Analyzing the shift in depth but explaining that there were contrary voices in the earlier period is political theory scholar Jennifer Pitts, most recently in "Empire and Legal Universalisms in the Eighteenth Century," *American Historical Review* 117, no. 1 (February 2012): 92–121.

15. On the post–Civil War shift from natural law premodernism to positivistic modern legal thought, see Stephen M. Feldman, *American Legal Thought: Premodernism to Postmodernism* (New York: Oxford University Press, 2000).
16. Other scholars, too, have focused on analyzing the dominant power's legal perspective on a particular subject rather than examining all possible standpoints. For example, Paul G. McHugh's 674-page book, *Aboriginal Societies and the Common Law: A History of Sovereignty, Status, and Self-Determination* (New York: Oxford University Press, 2005), recognizes the importance of aboriginal people's own histories but notes that those histories are not the main concern of his book, which focuses on ways in which British (and British-descended) law shaped relations with indigenous tribes. He comments, "Important as they are, relating those histories is the task of those with access to the indigenous record." Ibid., 62. Likewise, in *The American Indian in Western Legal Thought: The Discourse of Conquest* (New York: Oxford University Press, 1990), Robert A. Williams, Jr., focuses on the status of the American Indian in Western legal thought and does not also examine American Indian views of their own status. Other scholars whose topics might have been conducive to the inclusion of black and Indian voices have noted the difficulty in discerning such voices in the early American Republic. For example, in her book on women's activism in the American debates about Indian removal and slavery, Alisse Portnoy observes that even in the 1830s African Americans lacked the "political presence" and "access to channels of communication" that would have allowed them to engage with whites and participate fully and directly in the debates. Although, as Portnoy makes clear, American Indians had more opportunities to have their views heard in the 1830s, they lacked such outlets two decades earlier. Alisse Portnoy, *Their Right to Speak: Women's Activism in the Indian and Slave Debates* (Cambridge, MA: Harvard University Press, 2005), 136–145.

1. U.S.-SPANISH RELATIONS AND THE FLORIDA CAMPAIGNS

1. Prominent examples of American references to "outlaws" and "banditti" in Florida are Andrew Jackson to Mauricio de Zúñiga, April 23, 1816, included in *Message from the President . . . Transmitting . . . Further Information, in Relation to Our Affairs with Spain,* December 28, 1818 (Washington: E. De Krafft, 1819), 54–55; John Quincy Adams to George W. Erving, November 28, 1818, ASP-FR, 4:539–545; and speeches in Congress by Representatives John Rhea, January 27, 1819, and George Poindexter, February 2, 1819, AC, 869, 956. Spanish accusations appeared in diplomatic letters that were made public in the United States, including Luis de Onís to James Monroe, December 30, 1815, and January 2, 1816, ASP-FR, 4:422–423, 424; and Onís to Adams, July 9, 1817, ASP-FR, 4:441–442. In February 1819, President Monroe provided these three Onís letters, along with other diplomatic correspondence between the United

States and Spain cited in this chapter, to the Senate along with the Adams-Onís treaty. AC, Appendix, 1629–2136. The Onís letters (like other letters written by Spanish officials) were printed in an English translation and thus were readable by members of Congress and other Americans as they discussed the Florida campaigns.

2. "'View of the Southern States': Letters of a Gentleman on a Tour of Business in the Southern States," *Boston Recorder,* July 15, 1817 ("natural and proper"). For a discussion of Jeffersonian Republicans' reasons for coveting Florida, see Frank Lawrence Owsley, Jr., and Gene A. Smith, *Filibusters and Expansionists: Jeffersonian Manifest Destiny, 1800–1821* (Tuscaloosa: University of Alabama Press, 1997), chap. 2. This book uses the singular "Florida" even though sometimes early Americans referred to the territory as the "Floridas," referring to West and East Florida.

3. The following description of the situation in Florida and of American efforts to obtain control of East and West Florida is drawn from scholarly works on the history of the Gulf Coast region: J. C. A. Stagg, *Borderlines in Borderlands: James Madison and the Spanish-American Frontier, 1776–1821* (New Haven, CT: Yale University Press, 2009); James E. Lewis, Jr., *The American Union and the Problem of Neighborhood: The United States and the Collapse of the Spanish Empire, 1783–1829* (Chapel Hill: University of North Carolina Press, 1998); Charles Carroll Griffin, *The United States and the Disruption of the Spanish Empire, 1810–1822* (New York: Octagon Books, 1968); Owsley and Smith, *Filibusters and Expansionists;* Andrew F. McMichael, *Atlantic Loyalties: Americans in Spanish West Florida, 1785–1810* (Athens: University of Georgia Press, 2008); James Gregory Cusick, "The Significance of the War of 1812 in the American South," *Southern Studies: An Interdisciplinary Journal of the South* 20, no. 2 (Fall/Winter 2013): 65–96; James Gregory Cusick, *The Other War of 1812: The Patriot War and the American Invasion of Spanish Florida* (Athens: University of Georgia Press, 2007); James Gregory Cusick, "Some Thoughts on Spanish East and West Florida as Borderlands," *Florida Historical Quarterly* 90, no. 2 (2011): 133–156; J. Leitch Wright, Jr., *Anglo-Spanish Rivalry in North America* (Athens: University of Georgia Press, 1971); Bruce Edward Twyman, *The Black Seminole Legacy and North American Politics, 1693–1845* (Washington, DC: Howard University Press, 1999); and William Earl Weeks, *The New Cambridge History of American Foreign Relations,* vol. 1, *Dimensions of the Early American Empire, 1754–1865* (New York: Cambridge University Press, 2013). On borderlands history more generally, especially the modern shift from rough edges of "borderlands" or "frontiers" to sharpened lines of well-defined "borders," see Jeremy Adelman and Stephen Aron, "From Borderlands to Borders: Empires, Nation-States, and the Peoples In Between in North American History," *American Historical Review* 104, no. 3 (June 1999): 814–841; Michiel Baud and Willem Van Schendel, "Toward a Comparative History of Borderlands," *Journal of World History* 8, no. 2 (1997): 211–242; David J. Weber, "The Spanish Borderlands of North America: A Historiography," *Magazine of History* 14, no. 4 (2000): 5–11; and Andrew R. L. Cayton, "Writing North American History," *Journal of the Early Republic* 22, no. 1 (Spring 2002): 105–111.

4. At the end of the Seven Years' War in 1763, Spain and France both ceded land along the Gulf Coast to Britain, including Florida (from Spain) and Lower

Louisiana east of the Mississippi River (from France). By 1767, Britain had partitioned its Gulf Coast territory at the Apalachicola River into West and East Florida and moved the northern border of West Florida up to the latitude of the mouth of the Yazoo River. The 1783 Treaty of Paris, which returned West and East Florida to Spain, left their boundaries unclear.

5. All of the maps in this book use geographic data from the National Historical Geographic Information System and hydrography data from the National Oceanic and Atmospheric Administration. Minnesota Population Center, National Historical Geographic Information System: Version 2.0 (Minneapolis: University of Minnesota, 2011), http://www.nhgis.org, retrieved October 10, 2013; and National Oceanic and Atmospheric Administration, National Weather Service, National Operational Hydrologic Remote Sensing Center, Lakes and Streams (Chanhassen, MN), http://www.nohrsc.noaa.gov/gisdatasets/, retrieved April 23, 2014.

6. Treaty of Friendship, Limits, and Navigation between Spain and the United States (Pinckney's Treaty or the Treaty of San Lorenzo), October 27, 1795, Stat., 8:138–153.

7. Rafe Blaufarb labels this international rivalry the "Western Question," suggesting that the fall of Spanish America raised issues parallel to those prompted by the decline of the Ottoman Empire (the "Eastern Question"). He also points out that the United States played a role in the South American rebellions, most notably by allowing anti-Spanish privateers to operate out of Baltimore and other American ports. The privateers "forced Spain to fight a costly guerrilla war at sea," and, more generally, the naval insurgency gave the Spanish-American conflict a global dimension. Rafe Blaufarb, "The Western Question: The Geopolitics of Latin American Independence," *American Historical Review* 112, no. 3 (June 2007): 742–763, quotation on 753.

8. James Monroe was secretary of state from April 1811 until March 1817, when he became president. John Quincy Adams succeeded Monroe as secretary of state; he was not able to serve actively in the position until September 1817, when he returned from London after serving as U.S. minister to Britain. Pending Adams's return, Richard Rush was acting secretary of state from March to September 1817. Pedro Cevallos Guerra served as Spanish foreign minister from November 1814 to October 1816, José García de León y Pizarro served October 1816 to September 1818, and Carlos Martínez de Irujo y Tacón served September 1818 to June 1819.

9. Onís to Monroe, December 30, 1815, ASP-FR, 4:422–423.

10. Onís to Adams, December 29, 1817, January 5, 1818, January 24, 1818, March 23, 1818, and October 24, 1818, ASP-FR, 4:452–455, 455–460, 464–467, 480–486, 526–529; "Verus" [Onís], *Observations on the Existing Differences between the Government of Spain and the United States* (Philadelphia: 1817), quotation on 51. See also José García de León y Pizarro to Erving, August 6, 1818, ASP-FR, 4:520.

11. Secretary of state letters addressing the older historical issues are Monroe to Onís, June 10, 1816, ASP-FR, 4:429–431; and Adams to Onís, March 12, 1818, ASP-FR, 4:468–478. Letters stating that it would be useless to discuss those issues include Monroe to Onís, January 25, 1817, ASP-FR, 4:438–439; and Adams to Onís, January 16, 1818, and October 31, 1818, ASP-FR, 4:463–464,

530–531. Adams's unyielding stance in March 1818 earned him domestic support: one newspaper article gleefully contrasted Onís's useless volubility with Adams's firm and succinct letters. "Relations with Spain," *City of Washington Gazette,* March 27, 1818.

12. Pizarro to Erving, July 16, 1817, July 27, 1817, and August 17, 1817, ASP-FR, 4:442–443, 444, 445–449, quotations on 442, 444.
13. Onís to Monroe, December 30, 1815, ASP-FR, 4:422–423, quotations on 423.
14. Monroe to Onís, January 19, 1816, ASP-FR, 4:424–426. Additional American complaints in early 1816 had nothing to do with Florida: Monroe's January 1816 letter especially emphasized that Spain had failed to compensate Americans for ships unlawfully seized and condemned in Spanish ports or for the suspension of Americans' right of deposit—the right to store goods for export—at New Orleans (1798–1801).
15. Monroe first laid out American grievances in Monroe to Onís, January 19, 1816, ASP-FR, 4:424–426. The U.S. envoy to Spain, George W. Erving, also complained of these matters to the Spanish foreign minister, Andrew Jackson protested to the governor of West Florida, and Adams later elaborated on these grievances. Erving to Pedro Cevallos Guerra, August 26, 1816, ASP-FR, 4:433–434; Jackson to Zúñiga, April 23, 1816, included in *Message from the President,* December 28, 1818, 54–55; Adams to Onís, August 24, 1818, ASP-FR, 4:508–509, quotation on 508; Adams to Erving, November 28, 1818, ASP-FR, 4:539–545, quotations on 539; Adams to Onís, November 30, 1818, ASP-FR, 4:545–546. See also Adams to Onís, March 12, 1818, ASP-FR, 4:468–478, at 475–477 (demanding indemnities for French privateers' spoliations against American ships within Spanish jurisdiction) and 478 (noting threat to United States from Amelia Island and Pensacola). Onís's defense of Manrique is in Onís to Adams, March 27, 1818, ASP-FR, 4:486–487, quotation on 486. Article V of Pinckney's Treaty provided that "both Parties oblige themselves expressly to restrain by force all hostilities on the part of the Indian nations living within their boundary: so that Spain will not suffer her Indians to attack the citizens of the United States, nor the Indians inhabiting their territory; nor will the United States permit these last-mentioned Indians to commence hostilities against the subjects of his Catholic Majesty, or his Indians, in any manner whatever." Furthermore, the parties agreed "that in future no treaty of alliance or other whatever (except treaties of peace) shall be made by either party with the Indians living within the boundary of the other." Stat., 8:138–153, quotations on 140, 142.
16. Nathaniel Millett concludes that the population of the Prospect Bluff community reached a peak of between 600 and 750 black inhabitants just prior to the British departure in early 1815 and that its average population between May 1815 and July 1816 was around 300 to 400 people. Nathaniel Millett, *The Maroons of Prospect Bluff and Their Quest for Freedom in the Atlantic World* (Gainesville: University Press of Florida, 2013), 142–145.
17. Jackson to Zúñiga, April 23, 1816; Zúñiga to Jackson, May 26, 1816, included in *Message from the President,* December 28, 1818, 54–55, 55–57, Zúñiga quotation on 57. For later descriptions of the dangers posed by the occupants of the Prospect Bluff fort, see Commodore Daniel T. Patterson to Secretary of the Navy Benjamin W. Crowninshield, August 15, 1816, included in *Letter from*

the Secretary of the Navy Transmitting . . . Documents Relating to the Destruction of the Negro Fort in East Florida, February 1, 1819 (Washington: E. De Krafft, 1819), 13–14; Adams to Erving, November 28, 1818, ASP-FR, 4:539–545; Major General Edmund P. Gaines to Jackson, March 20, 1816, included in *Letter from the Secretary of War . . . Transmitting Information in Relation to the Destruction of the Negro Fort, in East Florida,* February 2, 1819 (Washington: E. De Krafft, 1819), 16–17; and Jackson to Gaines, April 8, 1816, in ibid, 10–11. For other correspondence evidencing the U.S. intention to destroy the fort, see David S. Heidler and Jeanne T. Heidler, *Old Hickory's War: Andrew Jackson and the Quest for Empire,* rev. ed. (Baton Rouge: Louisiana State University Press, 2003), 64–75.

18. For contemporary accounts of the destruction of the Prospect Bluff fort, see Duncan L. Clinch to Robert Butler, August 2, 1816, printed in *National Intelligencer* (Washington, DC), November 15, 1819; Clinch to David Mitchell, August 4, 1816, printed in *City Gazette and Daily Advertiser* (Charleston, SC), August 22, 1816; Patterson to Crowninshield, August 15, 1816, included in *Letter from the Secretary of the Navy Transmitting . . . Documents Relating to the Destruction of the Negro Fort in East Florida,* 13–14; Jairus Loomis to Patterson, August 13, 1816, included in ibid., 15–17; and Marcus C. Buck to his father, August 14, 1816, printed in *Union* (Washington, KY), September 27, 1816. The destruction of the Prospect Bluff fort is discussed in more detail in Chapter 6.

19. Monroe to Congress, included in *Message from the President . . . Communicating Information of the Troops of the United States Having Taken Possession of Amelia Island, in East Florida,* January 13, 1818 (Washington: E. De Krafft, 1818), 3–5, quotations on 4, 3, 4. In addition to this January 1818 report with enclosed documentation, Monroe also provided Congress with additional documents relating to Amelia Island on December 15, 1817, and on March 14, 1818. *Message from the President . . . Communicating Information of the Proceeding of Certain Persons Who Took Possession of Amelia Island and of Galvezton* [*sic*], December 15, 1817 (Washington: E. De Krafft, 1817); and *Message from the President . . . Transmitting the Correspondence between the Department of State, and the Spanish Minister,* March 14, 1818 (Washington: E. De Krafft, 1818).

20. Onís to Adams, January 8, 1818, ASP-FR, 4:463; Adams to Onís, January 16, 1818, ASP-FR, 4:463–464, quotation on 464; U.S. Congress, House committee report on the illicit introduction of slaves from Amelia Island, January 10, 1818, *Annals of Congress,* House, 15th Cong., 1st sess., 646–650. The "No Transfer Resolution," which President James Madison signed on January 17, 1811, was formally titled An Act to Enable the President of the United States to Take Possession of the Country Lying East of the River Perdido, and South of the State of Georgia and the Mississippi Territory, and for Other Purposes. The secret discussions, which took place in both the House and the Senate on January 3–19 and March 3, 1811, are in *Annals of Congress,* House, 11th Cong., 3rd sess., 1117–1148, and *Senate Exec. Journal,* 11th Cong., 3rd sess., 175–186. Secretary of State Adams and President Monroe both explicitly relied on the 1811 act as the administration's source of authority for the occupation of Amelia Island. Adams to John Holmes, chairman of the House Committee on Foreign Relations, January 20, 1819, ASP-FR, 5:12; and *Message from the President . . . Communicating Information of the Troops of the United States Having Taken Possession of Amelia Island, in East Florida,* January 13, 1818.

21. Thomas Jefferson to Alexander von Humboldt, December 6, 1813, in *The Papers of Thomas Jefferson,* Retirement Series, vol. 7, *28 November 1813 to 30 September 1814,* ed. J. Jefferson Looney (Princeton, NJ: Princeton University Press, 2010), 29–32, original emphasis; Alcibiades, *National Register* (Washington, DC), October 26, 1816; Columbus, *Aurora* (Philadelphia, PA), reprinted in *Rhode-Island Republican* (Newport, RI), January 3, 1816; "South America," *National Register,* November 1, 1817; Clay speech in Congress, March 25, 1818, *Annals of Congress,* 15th Cong., 1st sess., Appendix, 1474–1500, quotation on 1482.

    It is interesting to note that when Thomas Jefferson envisioned a line through the mid-Atlantic ocean, he perceived it as distinguishing a peaceful New World from a war-plagued Old World. Likewise, during the Seminole War era other Americans who differentiated between Europe and the Americas perceived the latter as far superior because its governments were (or would be) republics that enhanced liberty rather than monarchies based on oppression and tyranny. This interpretation of Jeffersonian ideas contrasts with an alternative scholarly view that posits that early modern Europeans characterized non-European regions negatively, regarding them as lawless places in contrast to a European zone of law. These concepts of a "line of amity" or of "no peace beyond the line" placed the entire Western Hemisphere, including Europe's own colonies, together on the lawless side of the line. While a fifteenth- to eighteenth-century European view of the Americas as lawless would not necessarily be inconsistent with an early nineteenth-century American view of the Americas as a place of greater freedom, there is reason to question the scholarly characterization of the European view in some regards. While Europeans saw Europe as a region distinct from other regions and sometimes recognized that statutes enacted in the colonies might differ from legislation in effect in the metropolitan center, Europeans did not abandon law outside of Europe. They not only considered themselves as bound by laws and treaties while they were outside of Europe but also made treaties with non-European polities. In that sense, Europeans did not blanketly categorize areas outside Europe as law-free. Thomas Jefferson to John Crawford, January 2, 1812, in *The Papers of Thomas Jefferson,* Retirement Series, vol. 4, *18 June 1811 to 30 April 1812,* ed. J. Jefferson Looney (Princeton, NJ: Princeton University Press, 2007), 394–395. The most prominent example of Europeans recognizing different legislation in their colonial realm than in the metropolitan center is Somerset v. Stewart, 98 E.R. 499 (1772), in which the Court of King's Bench ruled that a slave who was brought to England from the colonies had to be freed. The court did not characterize the colonies as lawless places but rather based its ruling on the fact that although local positive law recognized the institution of slavery in British colonies, there was no such positive law in England. On the concept of the line of amity, see Eliga H. Gould, "Zones of Law, Zones of Violence: The Legal Geography of the British Atlantic, circa 1772," *William and Mary Quarterly,* 3rd ser., 60 (2003): 471–510; and Garrett Mattingly, "No Peace beyond What Line?" *Transactions of the Royal Historical Society* 13 (1963): 145–162.

22. Adams to Onís, March 12, 1818, ASP-FR, 4:468–478, quotation on 478.

23. Onís to Adams, November 16, 1818, ASP-FR, 4:531–533; Adams to Onís, November 30, 1818, ASP-FR, 4: 545–546.
24. Onís to Monroe, February 22, 1816, ASP-FR, 4:426–429; Onís to Adams, July 9, 1817, ASP-FR, 4:441–442; Monroe to Onís, June 10, 1816, ASP-FR, 4:429–431; John Dick, United States attorney for the District of Louisiana, to Monroe, March 1, 1816, ASP-FR, 4:431–432; Adams to Onís, March 12, 1818, ASP-FR, 4:468–478 (on 478); Monroe to Onís, January 19, 1816, ASP-FR, 4:424–426; Jackson to Acting Secretary of War George Graham, December 16, 1817, ASP-MA, 1:689.
25. Onís to Adams, March 27, 1818, ASP-FR, 4:486–487; José Coppinger to Onís, February 10, 1818, ASP-FR, 4:487. Adams appears not to have responded to Onís's March 1818 communication prior to Jackson's invasion. In letters sent in early May and early June, Onís did not comment again on Monroe's speech but instead complained about anti-Spanish adventurers and pirates who were using American ports. Onís to Adams, May 7, 1818, and June 9, 1818, ASP-FR, 4:494, 494–495.
26. Griffin, *United States and the Disruption of the Spanish Empire,* 72, 83, 89, 90, 91, 94. Onís's warning to Adams is in Onís to Adams, March 27, 1818, ASP-FR, 4:486–487.
27. Motion of Senator John Williams of Tennessee, presented January 21, 1818, and agreed to in the Senate, January 22, 1818, *Annals of Congress,* Senate, 15th Cong., 1st sess., 119, 129. In response to the Senate request for information, President Monroe forwarded to the Senate a report prepared by Secretary of War John C. Calhoun. *Message from the President . . . Transmitting a Report from the Secretary of War, in Relation to the Manner the Troops . . . Now Operating against the Seminole Tribe . . . Have Been Subsisted,* January 30, 1818 (Washington: E. De Krafft, 1818). On the bill to increase the pay of soldiers in the Seminole War, see Representative Thomas W. Cobb's motion (April 3, 1818), House resolution referred to committee (April 3), bill proposed by committee (April 4), bill passed in House (April 10), and bill passed in Senate (April 18). *Annals of Congress,* 15th Cong., 1st sess., Appendix, 1672–1673, 1673, 1674, 1715, and *Annals of Congress,* Senate, 15th Cong., 1st sess., 387. For the text of the law, see An Act to Increase the Pay of the Militia While in Actual Service, and for Other Purposes, April 20, 1818, Stat., 3:459. Monroe's special message to Congress prior to Jackson's 1818 invasion was published as *Message from the President . . . Transmitting Information in Relation to the War with the Seminoles,* March 25, 1818 (Washington: E. De Krafft, 1818).
28. The debate on Henry Clay's motion to appropriate money for a minister to Buenos Aires is in *Annals of Congress,* 15th Cong., 1st sess., Appendix, 1464–1655. Clay's and John Forsyth's comments on Florida are in ibid., 1475–1476 (Clay) and 1504 (Forsyth). Others speaking to the issue most directly in the House were Thomas B. Robertson (Louisiana) and George Poindexter (Mississippi) in favor of taking Florida and John Holmes (Massachusetts) against doing so. Ibid., 1537 (Robertson), 1634 (Poindexter), 1581 (Holmes). Clay's proposal failed by a vote of 45 to 115. For newspaper coverage of Forsyth's proposed committee motion, see "Our Affairs with Spain," *Baltimore American,* March 23, 1818, reprinted in *Connecticut Journal* (New Haven, CT),

March 31, 1818; and *National Intelligencer,* April 8, 1818, reprinted in *Mercantile Advertiser* (New York, NY), April 11, 1818. Previously, on February 24, Forsyth had stated in the House that he was "perfectly tired of negotiating on our differences with Spain" and had submitted a resolution requesting the president to present to the House documentation evidencing the status of negotiations with Spain. The House had agreed to the resolution "without opposition." *Annals of Congress,* House, 15th Cong., 1st sess., 1007–1008, quotation on 1008.

29. "The Seminoles," *Boston Patriot and Daily Chronicle,* April 14, 1818; "Relations with Spain," *Niles' Weekly Register* (Baltimore, MD), February 10, 1816; "Spain," *Times* (Hartford, CT), January 27, 1818; "Relations with Spain," *City of Washington Gazette,* March 27, 1818.
30. "Indian War," *Niles' Weekly Register,* February 21, 1818; *Camden (SC) Gazette,* April 11, 1818; *Alexandria (VA) Gazette,* March 23, 1818.
31. Secretary of War John C. Calhoun to Jackson, December 26, 1817, ASP-MA, 1:690.
32. The material in this paragraph and following paragraphs describing the Seminole War is drawn from both primary and secondary sources. Military correspondence provided particularly useful information, and the notes cite specific letters where pertinent. In addition, many newspapers provided accounts of the Seminole War. For a particularly systematic factual account written months after the war, see "A Brief History of the Seminole War, and of the Trial and Execution of Arbuthnot and Ambrister," *Boston Weekly Messenger,* December 31, 1818. That account deems the war to have begun on November 20, 1817, "by an attack upon an Indian village near Fort Scott, by Major Twiggs, under the order of General Gaines," later followed by the attack on Indians near Fowltown.

    Among secondary sources, the most detailed, thorough narrative of the war is Heidler and Heidler, *Old Hickory's War.* Other scholarly publications include John K. Mahon, "The First Seminole War, November 21, 1817–May 24, 1818," *Florida Historical Quarterly* 77 (Summer 1998): 62–67; J. Leitch Wright, Jr., "A Note on the First Seminole War as Seen by the Indians, Negroes, and Their British Advisers," *Journal of Southern History* 34 (November 1968): 565–575; Owsley and Smith, *Filibusters and Expansionists*; Fred Anderson and Andrew R. L. Cayton, *The Dominion of War: Empire and Liberty in North America, 1500–2000* (New York: Viking, 2005), chap. 5; J. Leitch Wright, Jr., *Creeks and Seminoles: The Destruction and Regeneration of the Muscogulge People* (Lincoln: University of Nebraska Press, 1986), chap. 7; Robert V. Remini, *Andrew Jackson and His Indian Wars* (New York: Viking, 2001), chaps. 8–10; Robert V. Remini, *Andrew Jackson,* vol. 1, *The Course of American Empire, 1767–1821* (New York: Harper and Row, 1977; repr. Baltimore: Johns Hopkins University Press, 1998), chap. 23; Frank Lawrence Owsley, Jr., "Prophet of War: Josiah Francis and the Creek War," *American Indian Quarterly* 9 (Summer 1985): 273–293; Frank Lawrence Owsley, Jr., "Ambrister and Arbuthnot: Adventurers or Martyrs for British Honor?" *Journal of the Early Republic* 5 (Fall 1985): 289–308; Daniel Feller, "The Seminole Controversy Revisited: A New Look at Andrew Jackson's 1818 Florida Campaign," *Florida Historical Quarterly* 88, no. 3 (2010): 309–325; William S. Belko, "Epilogue to the War of 1812: The Monroe Administration, American Anglophobia, and the First Seminole

War," in *America's Hundred Years' War: U.S. Expansion to the Gulf Coast and the Fate of the Seminoles, 1763–1858,* ed. William S. Belko (Gainesville: University Press of Florida, 2011), 54–102; John Missall and Mary Lou Missall, *The Seminole Wars: America's Longest Indian Conflict* (Gainesville: University Press of Florida, 2004), chap. 3; and Twyman, *Black Seminole Legacy.* A prominent nineteenth-century account is Joshua R. Giddings, *The Exiles of Florida: Or the crimes Committed by Our Government against the Maroons, Who Fled from South Carolina and Other Slave States, Seeking Protection under Spanish Laws* (Columbus, OH: Follett, Foster, 1858; repr. Baltimore: Black Classic Press, 1997), 46–59.

33. Graham to Gaines, October 30, 1817, and December 2, 1817, ASP-MA, 1:685–686, 687; Calhoun to Gaines, December 9, 1817, and December 16, 1817, ASP-MA, 1:688, 689. Note: although the collection of documents provided to Congress on December 3, 1818, and the Library of Congress's current collection of Letters Sent by the Secretary of War Relating to Indian Affairs show the December 9 letter being signed by Calhoun, the collection of documents provided to Congress on March 25, 1818, and the ASP-MA suggest that Graham signed the letter.

34. Jackson to Graham, December 16, 1817, ASP-MA, 1:689; Jackson to Monroe, January 6, 1818, in *The Papers of Andrew Jackson,* ed. Harold D. Moser et al., 9 vols. (Knoxville: University of Tennessee Press, 1994), 4:166–167; Monroe to Calhoun, January 30, 1818, in *The Papers of John C. Calhoun,* ed. W. Edwin Hemphill, 28 vols. (Columbia: University of South Carolina Press, 1963), 2:104; Calhoun to Jackson, January 29, 1818, and February 6, 1818, ASP-MA, 1:697, 697; Calhoun to Gaines, January 16, 1818, ASP-MA, 1:691–692. Calhoun's authorization to Gaines to enter Florida, and the note informing Jackson of those instructions, are in Calhoun to Gaines, December 26, 1817, ASP-MA, 1:689–690; and Calhoun to Jackson, December 26, 1817, ASP-MA, 1:690. Notably, Monroe omitted Jackson's January 6, 1818, letter (in which the general offered to occupy Florida) from the packet of military correspondence that he provided to Congress in late 1818 and early 1819, and the letter was not otherwise made public at the time.

35. Jackson to Calhoun, March 25, 1818, ASP-MA, 1:698–699; Jackson to José Masot, March 25, 1818, ASP-FR, 4:562.

36. Jackson to Calhoun, April 8, April 9, April 20, April 26, May 5, and June 2, 1818, ASP-MA, 1:699–700, 700, 700–701, 701, 701–702, 708–709, quotation on 700, in April 9 letter. Chapters 4, 6, and 7 provide further details about U.S. military actions against Creeks, Seminoles, blacks, and Britons in Florida.

37. Jackson to Calhoun, April 8, April 9, April 20, April 26, May 5, and June 2, 1818, ASP-MA, 1:699–700, 700, 700–701, 701, 701–702, 708–709, quotations on 702, 701. Two months after the announced end of the war, Jackson instructed Gaines to occupy St. Augustine if there was evidence that the Spanish officers there were supplying and inciting Indians. Such an attack on St. Augustine did not take place because Calhoun countermanded Jackson's order. Jackson to Gaines, August 7, 1818, ASP-MA, 1:744; Calhoun to Gaines, September 1, 1818, ASP-MA, 1:745.

38. "Army News," *Georgia Journal* (Milledgeville, GA), April 14, 1818; "Latest from the Army, via Augusta!" *Reflector* (Milledgeville, GA), April 14, 1818; "Latest from the Army," *Georgia Journal,* April 18, 1818, reprinted in *Charleston*

(SC) City Gazette and Daily Advertiser, April 27, 1818; "Latest News from the Army," *Georgia Journal,* April 21, 1818; "Latest from the Army: Skirmish with the Indians," *Reflector,* April 21, 1818; "Late from the Army," *Georgia Journal,* May 5, 1818. It took just two or three weeks for articles from Georgia newspapers to reach Washington, DC, and the North, where they were widely reprinted. For example, the dramatic April 18 article that gave an account of events through April 9, when American troops left St. Marks and headed toward the maroon towns and Boleck's Town along the Suwannee River, appeared in *City of Washington Gazette,* April 28, 1818; *Washington Whig* (Bridgeton, NJ), May 4, 1818; *New-England Palladium and Commercial Advertiser* (Boston, MA), May 5, 1818; and *Vermont Gazette* (Bennington, VT), May 12, 1818.

39. John Quincy Adams, *Memoirs of John Quincy Adams; Comprising Portions of His Diary from 1795 to 1848,* ed. Charles Francis Adams, 12 vols. (Philadelphia: J. B. Lippincott, 1875, repr. Memphis, TN: General Books, 2009), May 4, 1818, June 18, 1818, and July 8, 1818, 4:54, 65, 67–68.

40. Monroe, second annual message, November 16, 1818, in *The Writings of James Monroe,* ed. Stanislaus Murray Hamilton, 7 vols. (New York: G. P. Putnam's Sons, 1898–1903), 6:75–83; AC, 518, 583 (resolution of House Committee on Military Affairs), 588 (Cobb's resolutions). Cobb's third resolution pertained to treatment of prisoners. Additionally, on the Friday before the House debate was scheduled to commence, Representative John W. Campbell of Ohio submitted another resolution for consideration by the House. The resolution, which the House quickly rejected, proposed that white men who instigated Indians to hostilities or who fought with Indians against the United States be punished as spies. AC, 547 (Campbell's motion, January 15, 1819).

Appointed members of the Select Committee on Military Affairs were Representatives Richard M. Johnson, Philip Reed, Thomas M. Nelson, Ebenezer Huntington, Joshua Gage, James Stewart, and George Peter. The committee's job was to consider portions of President Monroe's annual State of the Union message that related to the war with the Seminole Indians and the proceedings against Arbuthnot and Ambrister. The committee presented its report to the House on January 12, 1819. After a brief discussion, the House agreed to commence full debate on the proposed resolutions the following Monday, giving representatives the opportunity to prepare their remarks. The House intensively debated the Seminole War from January 18 to February 8.

The House and Senate committee reports are in U.S. Congress, House, Committee on Military Affairs, report on the Seminole War, January 12, 1819, in AC, 515–518; and U.S. Congress, Senate, Select Committee, report on the Seminole War, February 24, 1819, *Annals of Congress,* Senate, 15th Cong., 2nd sess., 256–268. The report of the House committee's dissenting minority is in AC, 518–527. The House resolution referring the relevant part of the president's message to a committee and the list of appointed committee members is in AC, 292–293. The House debate on the Seminole War is in AC, 527–530 (January 12, 1819) and 583–1138 (January 18, 1819–February 8, 1819). The votes on resolutions pertaining to the Seminole War are in AC, 548 and 1132–1138.

It should be noted that although the House rejected the proposed censure motions in 1819, two years later it approved a bill that not only decreased the size of the army but also reduced the number of major generals from two to one. The major general who lost his position as a result of the statute was Andrew Jackson. The administration assigned Jackson instead to serve as territorial governor of Florida. An Act to Reduce and Fix the Military Peace Establishment of the United States," March 2, 1821, Stat., 3:615–616.

41. Onís to Adams, June 17, 1818, June 24, 1818, July 8, 1818, and August 5, 1818, ASP-FR, 4:495, 495–496, 496–497, 504–506; Pizarro to Erving, July 26, 1818, August 11, 1818, and August 29, 1818, ASP-FR, 4:518, 522, 522–523. Onís made no mention of Jackson's actions in Florida in his June 9 letter to Adams (ASP-FR, 4:494–495) and first raised the topic in his June 17 letter, after receiving official confirmation about St. Marks from Masot. Onís's July 8 letter was the first to American officials that mentioned Jackson's occupation of Pensacola. Pizarro made no mention of the Florida events in his July 9 or July 18 letters to Erving (ASP-FR, 4:513, 514–516) and first broached the subject of Jackson's entry into Florida and capture of St. Marks with Erving in a July 26 letter. Soon after, Pizarro received Onís's June 20 letter (referenced in Pizarro to Erving, August 11, 1818, ASP-FR, 4:522) informing him about the taking of Pensacola.
42. Onís to Adams, July 8, 1818, and August 5, 1818, ASP-FR, 4:496–497, 504–506, quotations on 496, 504.
43. Onís to Adams, August 5, 1818, ASP-FR, 4:504–506.
44. Pizarro to Erving, July 26, 1818, August 6, 1818, and August 29, 1818, ASP-FR, 4:518, 519, 522–523, quotations on 518, 519, 523. See also Erving to Pizarro, July 28, 1818, ASP-FR, 4:518–519.
45. Adams to Onís, July 23, 1818, August 24, 1818, October 31, 1818, and November 30, 1818, ASP-FR, 4:497–499, 508–509, 530–531, 545–546, quotation on 498.
46. Adams to Erving, November 28, 1818, ASP-FR, 4:539–545. That the administration intended to make public Adams's letters to Onís is evident from Monroe's December 21, 1818, note to Jackson, in which the president states that "[t]his letter will be reported to Congress in a few days, and published of course." Monroe to Jackson, December 21, 1818, in Monroe, *Writings,* 85–87. Historian J. C. A. Stagg comments that Adams's letter was intended to make a case to congressmen and to the European public; its goal was not to persuade Onís. Stagg, *Borderlines in Borderlands,* 201. For a scholarly analysis of the letter, see also William Earl Weeks, "John Quincy Adams's 'Great Gun' and the Rhetoric of American Empire," *Diplomatic History* 14 (1990): 25–42.

    Both Pizarro and Onís had initially continued official negotiations even after learning about Jackson's invasion. Privately, Pizarro apparently wanted to compromise, but the king's council mandated a more aggressive response. William Earl Weeks, *John Quincy Adams and American Global Empire* (Lexington: University Press of Kentucky, 1992), 131. For a description of discussions in the Spanish cabinet and Council of State about Jackson's invasion and the negotiations with the United States, see Griffin, *United States and the Disruption of the Spanish Empire,* 169–177.
47. Monroe to Jackson, July 19, 1818; Monroe to Madison, February 7, 1819; Monroe to Jefferson, July 22, 1818; Monroe to Jackson, December 21, 1818; Monroe to Rush, March 7, 1819; in Monroe, *Writings,* 54–61, 87–89, 62–64, 85–87, 89–92, quotations on 58, 89, 88, 63.

48. Onís to Adams, October 24, 1818, December 12, 1818, and February 1, 1819, ASP-FR, 4:526–530, 612–615, 616–617; Adams to Onís, October 31, 1818, ASP-FR, 4:530–531, quotations on 530 (Adams), 616 (Onís).
49. Letters and written proposals by Adams and Onís dated between October 1818 and February 1819 show the evolution of the negotiations in documents that were made public. See especially Onís to Adams, October 24, 1818, November 16, 1818, December 12, 1818, January 11, 1819, January 16, 1819, February 1, 1819, and February 9, 1819, ASP-FR, 4:526–530, 531–533, 612–615, 615, 615–616, 616–617, 617–619; and Adams to Onís, October 31, 1818, January 29, 1819, February 6, 1819, and February 13, 1819, ASP-FR, 4:530–531, 616, 617, 619–621, quotation on 532 (Onís). Privately, Adams described the negotiations with Onís in Adams, *Memoirs,* July 16, 1818, August 9, 1818, October 25–31, 1818, and January 3–February 25, 1819, 4:70–71, 79, 91–97, 133–177. Examples of previous mention of possible session of Florida include Pizarro to Erving, August 17, 1817, ASP-FR, 4:445–449; and Adams to Onís, January 16, 1818, ASP-FR, 4:463–464. On the history of the treaty negotiations, see Weeks, *John Quincy Adams;* Griffin, *United States and the Disruption of the Spanish Empire,* chaps. 3 and 6; and Stagg, *Borderlines in Borderlands,* chap. 5.

Adams and Onís signed the Treaty of Amity, Settlement, and Limits, between the United States of America and His Catholic Majesty on February 22, 1819, Stat., 8:252–264. While Onís ultimately acceded to a western border that reached the mouth of the Missouri River in the Rocky Mountains, the United States also quietly conceded Texas, which it could have claimed as part of the Louisiana Purchase. Historian William Earl Weeks persuasively argues that, contrary to the common perception, the United States did not have to give up Texas in order to acquire Florida. Instead, he argues, President Monroe was content to yield Texas because he was afraid that adding more slave territory would increase sectional tensions. Weeks, *John Quincy Adams,* 166–168, 123–124, 176; Weeks, *History of American Foreign Relations,* 109–110.

On Jefferson's, Madison's, and Monroe's desire to expand without war, see Owsley and Smith, *Filibusters and Expansionists,* chaps. 1 and 2; and Weeks, *John Quincy Adams,* 26–27, 18.

Robert V. Remini notes that although Adams's diplomacy accomplished the treaty, it would not have been possible without Jackson's military action. He thus credits Jackson with making the continentalist vision possible. Remini, *Course of American Empire,* 388–389. George Herring refers to the United States' "negotiating at gunpoint" and says the country exploited the "Jackson magic" to achieve the treaty. George C. Herring, *From Colony to Superpower: U.S. Foreign Relations since 1776* (New York: Oxford University Press, 2011), 145, 148. Other historians generally agree that the Florida campaigns gave the United States leverage in treaty negotiations. See Walter Nugent, *Habits of Empire: A History of American Expansion* (New York: Vintage Books, 2008), 126; Samuel Flagg Bemis, *John Quincy Adams and the Foundations of American Foreign Policy* (New York: Knopf, 1949), chap. 15; Griffin, *United States and the Disruption of the Spanish Empire,* 176–177, 281; and Bradford Perkins, *The Cambridge History of American Foreign Relations,* vol. 1, *The Creation of a Republic Empire, 1776–1865* (New York: Cambridge University Press, 1993), 154. However, in addition to the American military operation in Florida, there were other factors pressing Spain to agree to a treaty in February 1819, such as Spain's eagerness to establish a border that protected its interests in New Spain and its recognition that after the end of the Napoleonic Wars it could no longer depend on British support. Griffin, *United States and the Disruption of the Spanish Empire,* 92–94; Weeks, *John Quincy Adams,* 53–54, 149–150; Stagg, *Borderlines in Borderlands,* 205.

50. Adams, *Memoirs,* November 16, 1819, 4:275–277. In fact, while Adams was secretary of state the United States acknowledged British sovereignty in Canada in the Convention of 1818. And after the Missouri crisis, Adams would concede that, because of sectional conflict over slavery, territorial expansion could threaten the survival of the Union. In the 1830s and 1840s, he opposed Texas annexation and the Mexican War. Weeks, *John Quincy Adams,* 191–195.

2. RULES OF WAR AND AMERICAN NATION-BUILDING

1. Susan-Mary Grant, *North over South: Northern Nationalism and American Identity in the Antebellum Era* (Lawrence: University Press of Kansas, 2000), 6–10; Peter Parish, "An Exception to Most of the Rules: What Made American Nationalism Different in the Mid-Nineteenth Century?" *Prologue: Quarterly of the National Archives* 27, no. 3 (Fall 1995): 219–229, bibliographic note at 2227–2228; Don H. Doyle and Marco Antonio Pamplona, "Introduction: Americanizing the Conversation on Nationalism," in *Nationalism in the New World,* ed. Don H. Doyle and Marco Antonio Pamplona (Athens: University of Georgia Press, 2006), 1–15; Ernest Gellner, *Nations and Nationalism,* 2nd ed. (Ithaca, NY: Cornell University Press, copyright 2006, printed 2008); Benedict Anderson, *Imagined Communities: Reflections on the Origin and Spread of Nationalism,* rev. ed. (New York: Verso, 1991); Anthony D. Smith, *Nationalism: Theory, Ideology, History,* 2nd ed. (Malden, MA: Polity Press, 2010). Though most political scientists still have not adequately incorporated the United States into broader models of nationalism, one social scientist who discusses early American nationalism in some depth is Liah Greenfeld, *Nationalism: Five Roads to Modernity* (Cambridge, MA: Harvard University Press, 1992), chap. 5. Greenfeld emphasizes ways in which the United States was tied together by a shared set of ideological principles expressed during the American Revolution, constituting a form of civic nationalism.
2. Interesting studies include John M. Murrin, "A Roof without Walls: The Dilemma of American National Identity," in *Beyond Confederation: Origins of the Constitution and American National Identity,* ed. Richard Beeman et al. (Chapel Hill: University of North Carolina Press, 1987), 333–348, at 346–347 (explaining that "the Constitution became a substitute for any deeper kind of national identity" in the early Republic and that, in the "architecture of nationhood," the Constitution provided a roof, but it took decades to build up the national walls); and David Waldstreicher, *In the Midst of Perpetual Fetes: The Making of American Nationalism, 1776–1820* (Chapel Hill: University of North Carolina Press, 1997) (describing early American rituals of nationalism and national political culture).
3. Clinton Rossiter, *The American Quest, 1790–1860: An Emerging Nation in Search of Identity, Unity, and Modernity* (New York: Harcourt Brace Jovanovich, 1971), quotations on 34, 38. Other older historical studies of early development of

the American nation include George Dangerfield, *The Awakening of American Nationalism, 1815–1828* (New York: Harper and Row, 1965); Paul Nagel, *This Sacred Trust: American Nationality, 1798–1898* (New York: Oxford University Press, 1971); Major Wilson, *Space, Time and Freedom: The Quest for Nationality and the Irrepressible Conflict, 1815–1861* (Westport, CT: Greenwood Press, 1974); and Hans Kohn, *American Nationalism: An Interpretive Essay* (New York: Macmillan, 1957).

4. Eliga H. Gould, *Among the Powers of the Earth: The American Revolution and the Making of a New World Empire* (Cambridge, MA: Harvard University Press, 2012). With regard to the Seminole War, Gould remarks that the war "underscored the United States' emergence as a regional power, one that was not only a treaty-worthy nation in its own right but was increasingly able to impose its views on others." Ibid., 179. The 2006 collection of essays edited by Doyle and Pamplona, *Nationalism in the New World,* also takes particularly important strides in rectifying past scholarly neglect of early U.S. nationalism. Especially pertinent to the United States are the essays by Don H. Doyle and Marco Antonio Pamplona, T. H. Breen, Craig Calhoun, Jack P. Greene, Susan-Mary Grant, Barbara Weinstein, and Gary Gerstle. Other recent books that deal with various aspects of American nation-building from a historical more than from a theoretical, social scientific perspective are Kariann Akemi Yokota, *Unbecoming British: How Revolutionary America Became a Postcolonial Nation* (New York: Oxford University Press, 2011); Peter J. Kastor, *Nation's Crucible: The Louisiana Purchase and the Creation of America* (New Haven, CT: Yale University Press, 2004); Peter S. Onuf, *Jefferson's Empire: The Language of American Nationhood* (Charlottesville: University Press of Virginia, 2000); focusing on the Civil War era, Paul Quigley, *Shifting Grounds: Nationalism and the American South, 1848–1865* (New York: Oxford University Press, 2011); Grant, *North over South;* Andre M. Fleche, *The American Civil War in the Age of Nationalist Conflict* (Chapel Hill: University of North Carolina Press, 2012); and, taking a longer historical view, Lloyd Kramer, *Nationalism in Europe and America: Politics, Cultures, and Identities since 1775* (Chapel Hill: University of North Carolina Press, 2011).
5. Although this book focuses on the public debate, it should be noted that many politicians also expressed their views privately. David Heidler and Jeanne Heidler have thoroughly studied the private correspondence of the major figures involved in the Seminole War. The opinions expressed in the letters appear to replicate the arguments made publicly in the newspapers and congressional debate. David S. Heidler and Jeanne T. Heidler, *Old Hickory's War: Andrew Jackson and the Quest for Empire,* rev. ed. (Baton Rouge: Louisiana State University Press, 2003).
6. The newspaper quotation is in *Boston Intelligencer & Evening Gazette,* December 19, 1818. On the relationship between early American newspapers and politics, see Jeffrey L. Pasley, *"The Tyranny of Printers": Newspaper Politics in the Early American Republic* (Charlottesville: University of Virginia Press, 2001); and Carol Sue Humphrey, *The Press of the Young Republic, 1783–1833* (Westport, CT: Praeger, 1996). The comparative statement about coverage of the Seminole War and the Missouri Crisis is from Charles S. Sydnor, *The Development of Southern Sectionalism, 1819–1848* (Baton Rouge: Louisiana State University Press, 1948), 130.

7. One scholarly study, David S. Heidler, "The Politics of National Aggression: Congress and the First Seminole War," *Journal of the Early Republic* 13 (Winter 1993): 501–530, focuses on the congressional debate about the Seminole War, though the article does not concentrate on the substance of representatives' arguments. Instead, it describes the political dynamics of the House debate (the composition of the committees, the voting patterns of men from different geographic regions and party affiliations, and the various political motives driving representatives to support or oppose Jackson). David Heidler and Jeanne Heidler also give a brief overview of the congressional debate in *Old Hickory's War,* chap. 9. Another article, J. M. Opal, "Vengeance and Civility: A New Look at Early American Statecraft," *Journal of the Historical Society* 8, no. 1 (March 2008): 61–83, devotes a few pages to thoughtful, substantive analysis of the Seminole War debate in the course of a study of changing early American views of "vengeance" and "civility." The author argues that, compared to Americans influenced by Enlightenment views, Andrew Jackson represented a more belligerent, vindictive approach to war and statecraft.

   The most thoughtful and thorough book on the history of the law of nations in wartime is Stephen C. Neff, *War and the Law of Nations: A General History* (New York: Cambridge University Press, 2005). Neff does not discuss the actual application of the law of nations in practice, but he provides an excellent history of the theory. Neff's more recent book, *Justice among Nations: A History of International Law* (Cambridge, MA: Harvard University Press, 2014), provides a general history of international law in both wartime and peacetime. The most in-depth study of American international law doctrine in the long nineteenth century, Mark Weston Janis, *The American Tradition of International Law* (New York: Clarendon Press, 2004), also does not focus on the implementation of the law of nations in practice. An important book that focuses primarily on the Civil War era but also includes discussion of the laws of war in the early Republic is John Fabian Witt, *Lincoln's Code: The Laws of War in American History* (New York: Free Press, 2012). A recent essay by Clare Altman provides a thoughtful historiographical overview of scholarship pertaining to the history of the role of law in American empire-building. She concludes that "[l]aw constituted American empire." Clare Altman, "The International Context: An Imperial Perspective on American Legal History," in *A Companion to American Legal History,* ed. Sally E. Hadden and Alfred L. Brophy (Malden, MA: Wiley-Blackwell, 2013), 543–561, quotation on 543.

8. Arguing against passage of Thomas W. Cobb's resolutions and defending Jackson and the administration most vigorously in the House of Representatives were Alexander Smyth (Virginia), Richard M. Johnson (Kentucky), George F. Strother (Virginia), George Poindexter (Mississippi), and James Tallmadge, Jr. (New York). Others speaking in the House on Jackson's behalf were Richard C. Anderson (Kentucky), Henry Baldwin (Pennsylvania), Joseph Desha (Kentucky), James Ervin (South Carolina), John Floyd (Virginia), John Holmes (Massachusetts), Francis Jones (Tennessee), Hugh Nelson (Virginia), John Rhea (Tennessee), Lemuel Sawyer (North Carolina), David Walker (Kentucky), and Felix Walker (North Carolina). Of these congressmen, all were lawyers or had served as judges except the following: Desha, Floyd,

D. Walker, and F. Walker. Though not lawyers or judges, the two Walkers had previous exposure to legal proceedings, since both had been court clerks.

9. Emer de Vattel, *The Law of Nations, or Principles of Natural Law, Applied to the Conduct and Affairs of Nations and Sovereigns* (London: G., G., and J. Robinson, 1797). Vattel (1714–1767) originally published the treatise in 1758 in French as *Le droit des gens; ou, Principes de la loi naturelle appliqués à la conduite et aux affaires des nations et des souverains;* a posthumous French edition of 1773 included Vattel's additional notes. The 1797 English version is a translation of the 1773 edition. In addition to Vattel, the main legal writers cited by commentators in the Seminole War debate were Georg Friedrich von Martens (German, 1756–1821), Hugo Grotius (Dutch, 1583–1645), and Cornelius van Bynkershoek (Dutch, 1673–1743).
10. Arthur Nussbaum, author of a general history of the law of nations, called Vattel "the favorite authority in American theory of international law" in the early Republic. Nussbaum observed that, in part because Vattel was a diplomat who lacked legal training, his work contained unsophisticated, weak legal reasoning but served a practical need for a systematic description of law in the late eighteenth and early nineteenth centuries. Nussbaum found Vattel's treatise to be vague and inconsistent, but he noted that "the ambiguity of Vattel's propositions . . . made it only the easier to refer to his treatise in diplomatic correspondence." Arthur Nussbaum, *A Concise History of the Law of Nations* (New York: Macmillan, 1947), 155–163, quotation on 160.
11. Vattel, *Law of Nations,* xvii ("duty of nations"). For Vattel's additional discussion of treaties and usages, see *Law of Nations,* Preliminaries, sec. 6 (law of nations as the law of nature applied to nations), Prelim., sec. 9 (treaties and customs must conform to natural law), Prelim., sec. 24–26 (customs and usages), book 2, chap. 12, sec. 152–197 [2:12:152–197] (treaties), and 2:15:218–222 (treaty commitments as sacred obligations).
12. Thomas Aquinas (1225–1274) was the most prominent medieval exponent of natural law theory, while John Austin (1790–1859) is best known for developing the principles of positive law in the nineteenth century. Most international law scholars of the late nineteenth and early twentieth centuries expressed a positivist approach, including, for example, Lassa Oppenheim (1858–1919), William Edward Hall (1835–1894), John Westlake (1828–1913), and Thomas Lawrence (1849–1919). Leading scholarly works on the history of international law that have described the medieval natural law tradition and the shift to positive law in the nineteenth century include C. H. Alexandrowicz, "Doctrinal Aspects of the Universality of the Law of Nations," *British Yearbook of International Law* 37 (1961): 506–515; Nussbaum, *Concise History of the Law of Nations;* Neff, *Justice among Nations;* and Antony Anghie, *Imperialism, Sovereignty and the Making of International Law* (New York: Cambridge University Press, 2007).
13. In *Law of Nations,* Vattel discusses just causes of war in chapter 3 (3:3:24–50); lawful conduct against enemies in chapter 8 (3:8:136–159), and lawful conduct against enemies' property in chapter 9 (3:9:160–173). See especially 3:3:26 and 3:3:28 (quotations in the text on the subject of just war), 3:3:43 and 3:8:137 (just means), 3:8:145–147 (killing noncombatants), 3:8:155–157 (using poison), and 3:8:140–141, 149, 152 (executing or enslaving enemy captives). The most

influential just war theorists were Augustine of Hippo, known as Saint Augustine (354–430), and Thomas Aquinas (1225–1274).

14. The issue of universalism was most pertinent in connection with U.S. relations with the Creeks and Seminoles; Chapters 4 and 5 contain an in-depth discussion of how natural law theorists applied their proclaimed universalist ideas to the Native people of the Americas and how Americans reinterpreted those ideas when they defended the Florida campaigns.
15. Vattel, *Law of Nations,* 3:1:1 (defining war as "that state in which we prosecute our right by force"), 3:3:3 (nations' right to employ force), 3:18:339 and 3:18:342–354 (retaliation and reprisals). Vattel's treatment of neutrality and the right of self-defense, discussed in the next few paragraphs of the text, further reinforced the principle that some uses of military force did not automatically constitute war.
16. Ibid., 2:4:49, 2:5:67–68, 3:3:26, and 3:1:3–4 (self-defense), 3:3:26, 3:8:136–137, and 2:9:119 (requirement of necessity).
17. Ibid., 2:4:49–50 (preemptive attacks), 2:18:326–336 (duty to resolve peacefully).
18. Ibid., 2:4:54, 2:7:79–80, 2:7:90–93 (respect for sovereignty and domain).
19. Ibid., 3:6:96–97 (associates), 3:7:103–104 (neutrality), 3:8:133 (allowing retreat for enemy troops), 3:7:111 (trade of neutral nations). In recognizing the concept of neutrality, Vattel took a modern approach that differed significantly from the medieval assumption that there was no room for impartiality because only one side in a war could be viewed as acting justly.
20. Ibid., 3:7:132 (committing hostilities in neutral country), 3:7:120 (asking permission for passage and entering neutral's territory without consent), 3:7:121–123 and 2:9:123 (right to deny entry by foreign troops and exceptions for imminent danger), 3:8:133 (right to enter neutral territory in pursuit of enemy), 3:7:122 (seizure of neutral place).
21. I am indebted to my colleague, Seo Hyun Park, for directing me to political science scholarship on the subject of sovereignty. On the use of "integration" and "insulation" strategies for maximizing state strength vis-à-vis a dominant power, see Seo Hyun Park, "State Sovereignty and Security in Hierarchical East Asia: The Politics of Sovereign-Nationalism in Japan and Korea" (Ph.D. diss., Cornell University, 2009), chap. 1.
22. John Quincy Adams to George W. Erving, November 28, 1818, ASP-FR, 4:539–545, at 541; James Monroe, second annual message, November 16, 1818, in *Writings of James Monroe,* ed. Stanislaus Murray Hamilton, 7 vols. (New York: G. P. Putnam's Sons, 1898–1903), 6:75–83, at 80; memorial of Andrew Jackson to the United States Senate, presented February 23, 1820, ASP-MA, 1:754–760, quotation on 757; AC, 1057–1059 (Baldwin), 972–977 (Poindexter), 682–683 (Smyth).
23. AC, 972–979 (Poindexter), 1059 (Baldwin), 683 (Smyth).
24. Ibid., 977–979 (Poindexter), 1054 (Baldwin), 844–845 (Strother, quotation on 845), 1111 (Floyd).
25. Monroe, second annual message, November 16, 1818, in *Writings,* 6:75–83, at 80; Adams to Erving, November 28, 1818, ASP-FR, 4:539–545, at 541; AC, 975 (Poindexter). Some commentators who questioned the legality of the capture of Spanish posts maintained that restoration of the forts repaired any wrong

that might have been done and allowed the United States to continue negotiations with "clean hands." "The Florida Question—Again," *Richmond (VA) Enquirer,* July 31, 1818.

26. The argument that the United States could attack an enemy within the territory of a neutral nation appeared in numerous places, including "The Florida Question," *Richmond Enquirer,* July 28, 1818; "The Floridas," *National Intelligencer* (Washington, DC), July 27, 1818, reprinted in *National Register* (Washington, DC), August 1, 1818 ("legitimate seat of war"); Adams to Erving, November 28, 1818, ASP-FR, 4:539–545, quotations on 541, 542; Adams to Onís, November 30, 1818, ASP-FR, 4:545–546, quotation on 546; "An Inquiry into the Causes, Conduct and Consequences of the Southern War," *Democratic Press* (Philadelphia, PA), reprinted in *Pittsfield (MA) Sun,* August 5, 1818; AC, 678–679 (Smyth), 962–969 (Poindexter); Judex Judicis, "To Algernon Sidney," *Richmond Enquirer,* January 21, 1819; and Sulpicious, "Capture of Pensacola," *National Advocate* (New York, NY), August 4, 1818. In addition to the editor of the *Richmond Enquirer,* the pseudonymous authors Judex Judicis and Sulpicious also explicitly cited Vattel's rules regarding neutral territory (found in *Law of Nations* at 3:7:133 and 3:7:126) as authority for their positions. The *National Intelligencer* usually expressed the administration's views, and in fact the July 27, 1818, "editorial" cited above apparently was drafted by Attorney General William Wirt and revised and approved by the president's cabinet before submission, though its authorship was not evident in the publication. John Quincy Adams described the evolution of the essay in his diary. John Quincy Adams, *Memoirs of John Quincy Adams; Comprising Portions of His Diary from 1795 to 1848,* ed. Charles Francis Adams, 12 vols. (Philadelphia: J. B. Lippincott, 1875, repr. Memphis, TN: General Books, 2009), July 18, July 21, July 24, July 25, and July 28, 1818, 4:71, 73, 74, 75, 76. Noble E. Cunningham, Jr., *The Presidency of James Monroe* (Lawrence: University Press of Kansas, 1996), 61–63, discusses the essay. See Chapters 4 and 5 for fuller discussion of issues pertaining to the Seminoles and Red Stick Creeks.

27. AC, 839, 842 (Strother, "derelict sovereignty" reference on 842), 603–605 (Holmes, "nominal" jurisdiction on 603); Monroe, second annual message, November 16, 1818, in Monroe, *Writings,* 75–83 ("almost extinct" reference on 77); AC, 1053–1054 (Baldwin), 675–676 (Smyth, quoted phrase on 675), 1109 (Floyd, "impotence"), 519 (House committee minority report), 971 (Poindexter); memorial of Andrew Jackson, ASP-MA, 1:754–760. The Supreme Court case was The Schooner Exchange v. McFaddon, 11 U.S. 116 (1812).

28. AC, 1059 (Baldwin quotation), 842, 844 (Strother); Monroe, second annual message, November 16, 1818, in Monroe, *Writings,* 75–83, at 79–80. Secretary of State Adams called on Spain to punish its Florida officials for their hostile misconduct that created the conditions necessitating American military action. Adams to Onís, November 30, 1818, ASP-FR, 4:545–546, at 545; Adams to Erving, November 28, 1818, ASP-FR, 4:539–545, at 541. Numerous commentators referred to the Spanish royal government's imbecility. Examples are Representatives Strother and Poindexter (AC, 843, 977); *Westchester Herald* (Mount Pleasant, NY), December 1, 1818; *City of Washington Gazette,* July 21, 1818; "General Jackson: Interesting Sketch of General Jackson and His Conduct in the War against the Seminoles," *Franklin Gazette* (Philadelphia,

PA), reprinted in *Spirit of the Times & Carlisle (PA) Gazette,* August 17, 1818; "The Capture of Pensacola," *Kentucky Reporter,* June 24, 1818, reprinted in *American Beacon and Commercial Diary* (Norfolk, VA), July 17, 1818; and "Southern Indians," *Franklin Gazette,* reprinted in *Reflector* (Milledgeville, GA), October 13, 1818.

29. AC, 962–972 (Poindexter); Judex Judicis, "To Algernon Sidney," *Richmond Enquirer,* January 21, 1819; An American Citizen, "Jackson's Justification," *Albany (NY) Argus,* January 5, 1819; Monroe, second annual message, November 16, 1818, in Monroe, *Writings,* 75–83, at 79.

30. Adams to Onís, August 24, 1818, ASP-FR, 4:508–509; Adams to Onís, November 30, 1818, ASP-FR, 4:545–546; Adams to Erving, November 28, 1818, ASP-FR, 4:539–545; Adams to Onís, July 23, 1818, ASP-FR, 4:497–499.

31. AC, 841–845 (Strother, quotation on 841), 606–611 (Holmes), 965–968 (Poindexter), 1054–1055, 1059 (Baldwin), 907 (Anderson), 710 (Jones), 1094 (Desha), 522, 524 (House committee minority report); Monroe, second annual message, November 16, 1818, in Monroe, *Writings,* 75–83, quotation on 80; An American Citizen, "Jackson's Justification," *Albany Argus,* January 5, 1819; "The Surrender of Pensacola," *Genius of Liberty* (Leesburg, VA), August 11, 1818.

32. Treaty of Friendship, Limits, and Navigation between Spain and the United States (Pinckney's Treaty or the Treaty of San Lorenzo), October 27, 1795, Stat., 8:138–153; AC, 677 (Smyth quotation), 868–870 (Rhea, quotation on 869), 522, 524 (House committee minority report); Adams to Onís, August 24, 1818, and October 31, 1818, ASP-FR, 4:508–509, 530–531. Some argued that because the 1795 agreement was effectively a treaty of alliance, as soon as the Seminoles made unprovoked war on the United States and the United States responded, Spain was obligated to take the American side in the conflict. AC, 970–971 (Poindexter).

33. The quotations are from Hampden, "Views of the American Republic—Abroad!" *New-York Columbian,* November 9, 1818. AC, 1094 (Desha); and *National Intelligencer,* September 19, 1818. AC, 839 (Strother); Adams to Erving, November 28, 1818, ASP-FR, 4:539–545, quotation on 541; AC, 671 (R. Johnson). See also AC, 955 (Poindexter), 713–716 (Tallmadge); Junius Brutus, "General Jackson," *National Advocate,* January 16, 1819. One pseudonymous commentator, "Sulpicious," connected the "self-defense" and the "state of war" arguments, asserting that the defensive nature of American acts in Florida meant that there was no state of war at all. He wrote in the *National Advocate:* "[*N*]*o act of war* has been committed by the general, inasmuch as his operations were directly only to the security of our frontier." Sulpicious, "Occupation of Pensacola," *National Advocate,* August 29, 1818.

34. AC, 1056–1057 (Baldwin).

35. The estimate of twenty thousand Americans killed appeared in "An Inquiry into the Causes, Conduct and Consequences of the Southern War," *Democratic Press,* reprinted in *Pittsfield Sun,* August 5, 1818. For the argument that, under the circumstances, the United States was not legally required to respect the southern border, see AC, 519 (House committee minority report, "safeguard"); *Camden (SC) Gazette,* April 11, 1818 ("safe guard"); AC, 709 (Jones, "artificial boundary"), 1053 (Baldwin, "mathematical line"), 602–604 (Holmes, "ideal

line" on 604), 672 (R. Johnson, "ideal line"); Monroe, second annual message, November 16, 1818, in Monroe, *Writings,* 75–83 (quotation on 78); AC, 843 (Strother), 674–676 (Smyth, quotations on 674, 675), 1126–1127 (Ervin, quotation on 1127), 521 (House committee minority report, "dire necessity" quotation), 768 (Barbour), 1093 (Desha); and Themistocles, "To the Honorable Henry Clay, Speaker of the House of Representatives," *National Register,* January 30, 1819.

36. AC, 1125 (Ervin), 840 (Strother), 1056–1057 (Baldwin), 769–770 (Barbour); memorial of Andrew Jackson, ASP-MA, 1:754–760, at 756.

37. AC, 1057 (Baldwin), 842–843 (Strother), 867 (Rhea), 727 (Tallmadge), 905–907 (Anderson, applying principle to St. Marks but not Pensacola), 681–682 (Smyth), 1093–1094 (Desha), 885–886 (Joseph Hopkinson); "The Floridas," *National Intelligencer,* July 27, 1818, reprinted in *National Register,* August 1, 1818; Adams to Erving, November 28, 1818, ASP-FR, 4:539–545 ("indispensably necessary"); Adams to Onís, November 30, 1818, ASP-FR, 4:545–546 ("unforeseen emergencies"). On this topic, Strother, Tallmadge, and Smyth cited Vattel's rules regarding the temporary seizure of a neutral town as authority for their positions, while Desha referred to Vattelian principles without mentioning the jurist by name.

38. Lisa Ford, *Settler Sovereignty: Jurisdiction and Indigenous People in America and Australia, 1788–1836* (Cambridge, MA: Harvard University Press, 2010), 157; Elizabeth Cobbs Hoffman, *American Umpire* (Cambridge, MA: Harvard University Press, 2013), 106.

39. Jay Sexton points out that the United States distinguished its own territorial expansion from European-style colonization on the grounds that acquired territory would be incorporated into the nation on an equal basis with the older territory. Sexton, *The Monroe Doctrine: Empire and Nation in Nineteenth-Century America* (New York: Hill and Wang, 2011).

40. "From Pensacola," *Savannah (GA) Republican,* reprinted in *National Register,* July 11, 1818. AC, 849 (Strother), 937–938 (Poindexter). The Spanish envoy, Luis de Onís, fully recognized the expansionist American mentality. In an 1820 pamphlet that was published in the United States in 1821, he observed: "The Americans, at present, think themselves superiour to all the nations of Europe; and believe that their dominion is destined to extend, now, to the isthmus of Panama, and hereafter, over all the regions of the New World." Luis de Onís, *Memoir upon the Negotiations between Spain and the United States of America* (Madrid: D. M. DeBurgos, 1820; translated by Tobias Watkins, Baltimore: Fielding Lucas, 1821), 23.

41. "Cession of the Floridas," *Niles' Weekly Register* (Baltimore, MD), February 27, 1819; "The Floridas," *Niles' Weekly Register,* March 13, 1819; *National Intelligencer,* February 25, 1819, reprinted in *American* (New York, NY), March 3, 1819; "Florida," *Niles' Weekly Register,* May 1, 1819.

42. Washington, "Spain, Southern America, and the United States," *National Intelligencer,* reprinted in *Northern Whig* (Hudson, NY), November 3, 1818; "America and England," *City of Washington Gazette,* October 14, 1818; *National Intelligencer,* reprinted in *American Beacon and Norfolk & Portsmouth (VA) Daily Advertiser,* October 10, 1818. Commentators who argued that American military actions in Florida were more humane than British conduct overseas

include Libra, "The English & American Character for Humanity, Compared," *Boston Patriot,* May 19, 1819; Libra, "The English & American Character for Humanity, Compared," *Boston Patriot,* June 30, 1819; "Indians," *National Advocate,* July 3, 1818; and Hampden, "Views of the American Republic—Abroad!" *New-York Columbian,* November 9, 1818. These authors contrasted the United States' reasonable defensive actions against Indians and respect for Spanish sovereignty with British "rapacity and brutality" in India.

43. It is interesting that as precedent for entering Spanish Florida, the United States did not point to Britain's assertion during the Napoleonic Wars of the right to visit and search neutral ships. Supporters evidently saw no benefit in making any analogy between Britain's asserted rights with regard to neutral ships and their own asserted rights in neutral Florida, presumably because of the widespread unpopularity of the British position among Americans.

    On the surface, it might appear that the United States' cavalier disregard for Spanish neutrality conflicted with its own previous steadfast support for neutral rights under the law of nations, as critics of the Seminole Wars alleged. However, the United States was not necessarily acting in an inconsistent manner. Historians of the period from 1790 to 1812 do not agree on whether the United States supported neutral rights in that era because the nation was weak and had to placate Britain and France while they were at war, or because such a position served the nation's commercial interests, or because neutral rights and the law of nations were consistent with the nation's republican values, or because such principles were a way to promote international peace and harmony. James Sofka, "American Neutral Rights Reappraised: Identity or Interest in the Foreign Policy of the Early Republic," *Review of International Studies* 26 (2000): 599–622; Stewart Jay, "The Status of the Law of Nations in Early American Law," *Vanderbilt Law Review* 42 (April 1989): 819–849; Douglas J. Sylvester, "International Law as Sword or Shield? Early American Foreign Policy and the Law of Nations," *New York University Journal of International Law and Politics* 32 (Fall 1999): 1–87; Daniel G. Lang, *Foreign Policy in the Early Republic: The Law of Nations and the Balance of Power* (Baton Rouge: Louisiana State University Press, 1985).

44. "America and England," *City of Washington Gazette,* October 14, 1818; Washington, "Spain, Southern America, and the United States," *National Intelligencer,* reprinted in *Northern Whig,* November 3, 1818; AC, 939 (Poindexter).

45. "American President's Speech," *Bell's Messenger* (London), December 28, 1818, reprinted in *Mercantile Advertiser* (New York, NY), March 5, 1819; *London Morning Chronicle,* September 5, 1818, reprinted in *National Intelligencer,* November 28, 1818. In fact, these selective passages were not representative of British newspaper coverage of the Seminole War, which typically focused on sharp criticism of the executions of Alexander Arbuthnot and Robert Ambrister.

46. Pomponius, "Political," *Rhode-Island American, and General Advertiser* (Providence, RI), October 9, 1818; Hampden, "Views of the American Republic—Abroad!" *New-York Columbian,* November 9, 1818.

47. AC, 973–979 (Poindexter), 678, 682 (Smyth), 1059, 1057 (Baldwin), 767–768 (Barbour), 1105–1107 (Floyd), 1091–1092 (Desha), 601–603 (Holmes), 866 (Rhea), 661, 665–666 (R. Johnson); Judex Judicis, "To Algernon Sidney," *Richmond*

Enquirer, January 21, 1819; "An Inquiry into the Causes, Conduct and Consequences of the Southern War," *Democratic Press,* reprinted in *Pittsfield Sun,* August 5, 1818.

48. For arguments based on the 1795 law, see AC, 1128 (Ervin), 601–602 (Holmes), and 767–768 (Barbour). For the argument that the Seminole War was a continuation of an earlier declared war, see AC, 665 (R. Johnson) and 866 (Rhea). For the argument that Congress tacitly approved the invasion, see AC, 1107–1108 (Floyd), 839–840 (Strother), 605 (Holmes), 1121 (Ervin), 677 (Smyth), 709 (Jones), 1058 (Baldwin); and "Political Review," *Niles' Weekly Register,* November 20, 1819. For Monroe's argument that he never authorized Jackson's invasion, see Monroe to Madison, July 20, 1818; Monroe to Richard Rush, March 7, 1819; and Monroe to Jackson, July 19, 1818, in Monroe, *Writings,* 61–62, 89–92, 54–61. Some argued that Monroe's order to return the Spanish posts obviated the constitutional problem. "Political Review," *Niles' Weekly Register,* November 20, 1819.

49. AC, 717–740 (Tallmadge), 682–683 (Smyth), 1128 (Ervin), 843 (Strother); Aristides, "Jackson and the Floridas," letter to the editor, *Nashville (TN) Whig,* reprinted in *Reflector,* October 13, 1818; "The Floridas," *National Intelligencer,* July 27, 1818, reprinted in *National Register,* August 1, 1818. Two years after the invasion, Jackson's "memorial" addressed the issue, ASP-MA, 1:754–760, at 755–756. The quotation about military despotism is from Themistocles, "To the Honorable Henry Clay, Speaker of the House of Representatives," *National Register,* January 30, 1819.

50. "Southern Indians," *Franklin Gazette,* reprinted in *Reflector,* October 13, 1818 (quotation); Judex Judicis, "To Algernon Sidney," *Richmond Enquirer,* January 21, 1819; "An Inquiry into the Causes, Conduct and Consequences of the Southern War," *Democratic Press,* reprinted in *Pittsfield Sun,* August 5, 1818; AC, 767 (Barbour), 1107 (Floyd), 1092–1093 (Desha).

51. The first major American treatise on international law was Henry Wheaton, *Elements of International Law with a Sketch of the History of the Science,* 1st ed. (Philadelphia: Carey, Lea and Blanchard, 1836). Wheaton asserted that positive law, rather than natural law, provided the proper basis for international law.

52. AC, 677 (Smyth); *Annals of Congress,* House, 15th Cong., 1st sess., 1577 (Smyth). Congressman Smyth made the comment about the law of nations in response to Henry Clay's statement that U.S. recognition of the independence of Buenos Aires would give Spain no "just cause" of war. He explained that, under the usage of nations, Spain could interpret an American decision to send an ambassador to Buenos Aires as a reason for war, even if "justice" did not actually provide grounds for war.

    Supporters of the campaigns did not explicitly rely on the Constitution as a source of law, though possibly their arguments could be seen as implicitly using the Constitution's description of the president's powers to argue for expansive executive branch authority in foreign relations, Indian affairs, and military matters. As will be seen in Chapter 3, it was the opponents of the war, rather than supporters, who relied most heavily on constitutional arguments.

53. Gordon S. Wood, *The Radicalism of the American Revolution* (New York: Knopf, 1991) (on American political development from a monarchy to a republic to a

democracy); Alexander Keyssar, *The Right to Vote: The Contested History of Democracy in the United States* (New York: Basic Books, 2000), chap. 2 (on the expansion of the suffrage during the early national period); J. R. Pole, *Political Representation in England and the Origins of the American Republic* (New York: St. Martin's Press, 1966), 308 (on the effect of the War of 1812 on suffrage extension).

54. Stephen M. Feldman, *American Legal Thought: Premodernism to Postmodernism* (New York: Oxford University Press, 2000), chap. 3; Ruth Wedgwood, "The Revolutionary Martyrdom of Jonathan Robbins," *Yale Law Journal* 100, no. 2 (November 1990): 229–368, at 231–233, 363–364. Other scholars have discussed the codification movement that took hold in the decades following the Seminole War. One of the Jacksonians' major contributions to legal reform, the codification movement was intended to ensure that laws were clear, concrete, and founded on popular consent rather than judicial discretion. Morton J. Horwitz, *The Transformation of American Law, 1780–1860* (Cambridge, MA: Harvard University Press, 1977), chap. 1. On the emergence of American democracy and popular sovereignty, see especially Wood, *Radicalism of the American Revolution;* and Sean Wilentz, *The Rise of American Democracy: Jefferson to Lincoln* (New York: Norton, 2005). On the early history of popular constitutionalism in the United States, see Christian Fritz, *American Sovereigns: The People and America's Constitutional Tradition before the Civil War* (New York: Cambridge University Press, 2008); and Larry D. Kramer, *The People Themselves: Popular Constitutionalism and Judicial Review* (New York: Oxford University Press, 2004).

55. Historian Lawrence Frederick Kohl characterizes the Jacksonians' appeal to common sense and the popular will as support for "natural law." Lawrence Frederick Kohl, *The Politics of Individualism: Parties and the American Character in the Jacksonian Era* (New York: Oxford University Press, 1989), chap. 4.

56. For a discussion of the conflicting values of justice and humanitarianism, especially during the U.S. Civil War, see Witt, *Lincoln's Code.*

57. Arthur Nussbaum, a historian of the law of nations, concludes that the Monroe Doctrine did not violate international law, but he also does not view the doctrine as a part of international law. Nussbaum, *Concise History of the Law of Nations,* 183.

58. Alejandro Alvarez, "Latin America and International Law," *American Journal of International Law* 3, no. 2 (April 1909): 269–353; Covenant of the League of Nations, January 10, 1920, available at Yale University's Avalon Project at http://avalon.law.yale.edu/20th_century/leagcov.asp, accessed March 30, 2013; John Westlake, *International Law,* part I, *Peace,* 2nd ed. (Cambridge: Cambridge University Press, 1910), 324 (on the Monroe Doctrine), 101–111 (on title by occupation). For discussion of Latin America's perspectives on international law, see Jorge L. Esquirol, "Latin America," in *The Oxford Handbook of the History of International Law,* ed. Bardo Fassbender and Anne Peters (New York: Oxford University Press, 2012), 553–577. For discussion of the history of regional approaches to international law, see Antony Anghie, "Identifying Regions in the History of International Law," in *Oxford Handbook of the History of International Law,* 1058–1078.

59. Neff, *War and the Law of Nations,* 161–163, 169–172, 197–199. For the argument that realism (rather than idealism) shaped early American diplomacy, see

Norman Graebner, "The Pursuit of Interests and a Balance of Power," in *Major Problems in American Foreign Relations: To 1920,* ed. Dennis Merrill and Thomas G. Paterson, 7th ed. (Boston: Wadsworth, 2009), 12–16.

60. In his study of the political reaction to Jackson's conduct during the War of 1812, Matthew Warshauer explains that Jacksonians not only rejected the revolutionary-era idea that power was an inherent threat to liberty but also argued "that power protected liberty and a military commander, the embodiment of power, was best suited to defend the nation's liberties." Matthew Warshauer, "Andrew Jackson as a 'Military Chieftain,' in the 1824 and 1828 Presidential Elections: The Ramifications of Martial Law on American Republicanism," *Tennessee Historical Quarterly* 57, no. 1 (1998): 4–23, at 19; Matthew Warshauer, *Andrew Jackson and the Politics of Martial Law: Nationalism, Civil Liberties, and Partisanship* (Knoxville: University of Tennessee Press, 2006), chap. 2. On the revolutionary generation's concern about liberty versus power and about standing armies, see Bernard Bailyn, *The Ideological Origins of the American Revolution* (Cambridge, MA: Harvard University Press, 1967, 1992), 55–93 (liberty versus power), and 61–63 and 112–116 (standing armies). Fostering stronger pride and cohesiveness in the early American Republic was particularly important as states expanded the suffrage after the War of 1812. News of Jackson's feats against two European countries, Spain and Britain, was likely to encourage more new voters to join the army or the militias and fight energetically to defend—and extend—the nation's borders. On the connection between expansion of the suffrage and military service, see Keyssar, *Right to Vote,* 37–38.
61. Fiat Justitia, "General Jackson," *National Intelligencer,* reprinted in *Richmond Enquirer,* January 14, 1819.
62. AC, 873 (Hopkinson).

3. CHALLENGES AND CONFLICTS

1. Supporting Thomas W. Cobb's resolutions and criticizing the Florida campaigns most aggressively in the House were Henry Clay (Kentucky), Charles F. Mercer (Virginia), Timothy Fuller (Massachusetts), Edward Colston (Virginia), Henry R. Storrs (New York), Thomas S. Williams (Connecticut), James Johnson (Virginia), John Tyler (Virginia), Thomas M. Nelson (Virginia), and Philip Reed (Maryland). Of these congressmen, all were lawyers or judges except Representative Reed. The most detailed and persistent criticisms in the press were published as five essays in the *Richmond (VA) Enquirer* under the pen name "Algernon Sidney." The Algernon Sidney essays provided thoughtful and sophisticated criticism of the legality of Andrew Jackson's acts. Originally published in December 1818 and January 1819, they appeared widely in the anti-Jackson press throughout the country. Journalists of the time claimed that Algernon Sidney's real identity was Benjamin Watkins Leigh, a Virginia lawyer who was a "consistent democratick republican." *Rhode-Island American, and General Advertiser* (Providence, RI), February 5, 1819; *Boston Commercial Gazette,* February 4, 1819. However, some scholars have speculated that the real author was Virginia lawyer Spencer Roane. See Harry Ammon, *James Monroe: The Quest for National Identity* (New York: McGraw-Hill, 1971), 430.

2. Civis, letter to the editor, *Richmond Enquirer,* July 14, 1818. Other newspapers made similar statements: the *Boston Intelligencer* forthrightly labeled Jackson's invasion "an act of war against Spain," while the *Vermont Intelligencer* asserted, "[W]e conclude that a war exists between the United States and Spain." *Boston Intelligencer & Evening Gazette,* December 19, 1818; "Conquest of Pensacola," *Vermont Intelligencer and Bellows' Falls Advertiser,* July 27, 1818.
3. Algernon Sidney, "To the Hon. John Quincy Adams, Secretary of State," *Richmond Enquirer,* January 12, 1819. During the congressional debate, a number of representatives likewise argued that Jackson's military actions created a state of war with Spain—offensive, not defensive, war. AC, 825–826 (Colston), 747 (Storrs), 1083–1084 (Williams), 589–596 (Cobb), 805 (Mercer), 914 (William Lowndes).
4. AC, 652–653 (Clay), 988 (Fuller).
5. AC, 652–653 (Clay), 989–990 (Fuller), 748–749 (Storrs), 589–596 (Cobb), 626 (J. Johnson); "The Florida Question," *Richmond Enquirer,* July 28, 1818; Algernon Sidney, "To the Hon. John Quincy Adams, Secretary of State," *Richmond Enquirer,* January 12, 1819. The Emer de Vattel quotation appears in connection with his discussion of reprisals in *The Law of Nations, or Principles of Natural Law, Applied to the Conduct and Affairs of Nations and Sovereigns* (London: G., G., and J. Robinson, 1797), 2:18:354. On this subject, Sidney also cited Vattel 2:18:336 and 338, where the jurist reiterated the obligation to pursue peaceful resolution of disputes before taking up arms.
6. Congressman Mercer devoted the most attention to this argument against the claim of military necessity. AC, 802–813.
7. AC, 988–989 (Fuller), 802–805 (Mercer).
8. AC, 992 (Fuller), 589–596 (Cobb), 802–806 (Mercer).
9. AC, 1079–1084 (Williams, specifying number of troops), 926–927 (Tyler, quotation on 926), 649, 652 (Clay), 992–993 (Fuller), 805–808 (Mercer), 747 (Storrs). An editorial in the *Richmond Enquirer* noted that St. Marks "was not in the hands of the Indians, nor was it likely to be so." "A Plain Tale," *Richmond Enquirer,* February 2, 1819.
10. AC, 808–811 (Mercer), 826–827 (Colston), 746 (Storrs); Algernon Sidney, "To the Hon. John Quincy Adams, Secretary of State," *Richmond Enquirer,* January 12, 1819; "A Plain Tale," *Richmond Enquirer,* February 2, 1819.
11. AC, 802–805, 808 (Mercer), 993–994 (Fuller), 622–623 (J. Johnson), 826–827 (Colston), 652 (Clay), 746 (Storrs), 917–919 (Lowndes), 1081–1082 (Williams); "The Florida Question," *Richmond Enquirer,* July 28, 1818; Algernon Sidney, "To the Hon. John Quincy Adams, Secretary of State," *Richmond Enquirer,* January 12, 1819; AC, 807–810 (Mercer).
12. AC, 651–652 (Clay), 996 (Fuller), 747 (Storrs); Algernon Sidney, "To the Hon. John Quincy Adams, Secretary of State," *Richmond Enquirer,* January 12, 1819.
13. AC, 994–995 (Fuller).
14. Algernon Sidney, "To the Hon. John Quincy Adams, Secretary of State," *Richmond Enquirer,* January 12, 1819; AC, 803, 807 (Mercer), 622, 626 (J. Johnson), 585, 595 (Cobb), 1080 (Williams), 1030–1031 (Harrison).
15. AC, 994–995 (Fuller, quoted phrase on 995), 623–626 (J. Johnson); A Calm Observer, "A Few Queries, Addressed to Candid Men," *Richmond Enquirer,* March 9, 1819; *National Messenger* (Georgetown, District of Columbia),

October 30, 1818. Critics also observed that because U.S. actions constituted offensive war, under the law of nations they should have been preceded by a formal declaration of war. The United States issued no such declaration. "Conquest of Pensacola," *Vermont Intelligencer and Bellows' Falls Advertiser,* July 27, 1818.

16. AC, 1083–1084 (Williams), 626 (J. Johnson), 749–751 (Storrs, quotations on 749, 751), 918–919 (Lowndes); Algernon Sidney, "General Jackson," letter to the editor, *Richmond Enquirer,* December 22, 1818.
17. Algernon Sidney, "To the Hon. John Quincy Adams, Secretary of State," *Richmond Enquirer,* January 12, 1819; AC, 649–650 (Clay, quotations on 650), 626 (J. Johnson), 995–996, 1000–1001 (Fuller). Pro-Jackson congressman George F. Strother countered Clay's argument about the British seizure of the Danish fleet. He contended that Jackson was more justified in occupying Pensacola because the city's commander himself had committed acts of war, unlike government officials in Copenhagen, who had maintained their neutrality. AC, 845 (Strother).
18. "The Florida Question," *Richmond Enquirer,* July 28, 1818. During the congressional debate, Representative James Johnson likewise explicitly rejected territorial acquisition as a justification for war. AC, 624.
19. *New-York Evening Post,* December 22, 1818; AC, 995 (Fuller).
20. *National Messenger,* October 30, 1818; "The Florida Question—Again," *Richmond Enquirer,* July 31, 1818; "The Florida Question," *Richmond Enquirer,* July 28, 1818; "Pensacola," *Richmond Enquirer,* June 30, 1818; "A Plain Tale," *Richmond Enquirer,* February 2, 1819.
21. AC, 873 (Joseph Hopkinson), 640 (Clay); "Arbuthnot & Ambrister," *Connecticut Journal,* December 29, 1818; *Northern Whig* (Hudson, NY), January 19, 1819.
22. Congressional critics' explicit references to "just cause" are in AC, 616 (T. Nelson) and 884 (Hopkinson).
23. For the war powers in early American history, see David P. Currie, "Rumors of Wars: Presidential and Congressional War Powers, 1809–1829," *University of Chicago Law Review* 67 no. 1 (2000): 1–40; and Abraham D. Sofaer, *War, Foreign Affairs, and Constitutional Power: The Origins* (Cambridge, MA: Ballinger, 1976), esp. 336–365 on war powers and the Seminole War.
24. A number of members of Congress detailed the constitutional argument. AC, 587–597 (Cobb), 647–648 (Clay), 825–826 (Colston), 914–920 (Lowndes), 926–930 (Tyler), 813–814 (Mercer), 623–625 (J. Johnson), 1083–1084 (Williams), 884 (Hopkinson). Hopkinson explicitly placed the issue in the context of the "just cause" principle, arguing that although the United States had just cause of complaint against Spain, it was up to Congress, not Jackson, to decide whether to proceed to war. Newspaper essayist Algernon Sidney made the same argument. Algernon Sidney, "General Jackson," letter to the editor, *Richmond Enquirer,* December 22, 1818. Numerous newspaper articles likewise made the argument that only Congress could declare war.
25. Inquisitor, "The War Making Power," *Union,* reprinted in *Dedham (MA) Gazette,* September 18, 1818, argued that only Congress had the power to make war against Indians, just as it had exclusive authority over war against "any other sovereign." On the alleged constitutional distinction between Indian

wars occurring within U.S. borders and those taking place in foreign territory, see AC, 825–826 (Colston).

26. Conquest of Pensacola," *Vermont Intelligencer and Bellows' Falls Advertiser,* July 27, 1818; "A Plain Tale," *Richmond Enquirer,* February 2, 1819; A Calm Observer, "A Few Queries, Addressed to Candid Men," *Richmond Enquirer,* March 9, 1819.
27. *New-York Daily Advertiser,* January 10, 1820.
28. For an example of a newspaper comment on this subject, see A Calm Observer, "A Few Queries, Addressed to Candid Men," *Richmond Enquirer,* March 9, 1819. For congressmen's comments, see especially AC, 914 (Lowndes), 930 (Tyler).
29. Algernon Sidney, *Richmond Enquirer,* February 4, 1819; AC, 991–998 (Fuller), 1069–1070 (Reed); Algernon Sidney, "To the Hon. John Quincy Adams, Secretary of State," *Richmond Enquirer,* January 12, 1819; Civis, letter to the editor, *Richmond Enquirer,* July 14, 1818; Monroe to House of Representatives, March 25, 1818, *Annals of Congress,* House, 15th Cong., 1st sess., 1473. The evidence is inconclusive as to whether the Monroe administration actually authorized (or intended for) Jackson to seize Florida. For different interpretations, see David S. Heidler and Jeanne T. Heidler, *Old Hickory's War: Andrew Jackson and the Quest for Empire,* rev. ed. (Baton Rouge: Louisiana State University Press, 2003), 137–141; Robert V. Remini, *Andrew Jackson,* vol. 1, *The Course of American Empire, 1767–1821* (New York: Harper and Row, 1977; repr. Baltimore: Johns Hopkins University Press, 1998), 346–350; Hewitt D. Adams, "Did Jackson Disobey Orders?" *Proceedings of the South Carolina Historical Association* (1968): 44–51; Daniel Feller, "The Seminole Controversy Revisited: A New Look at Andrew Jackson's 1818 Florida Campaign," *Florida Historical Quarterly* 88, no. 3 (2010): 309–325; J. C. A. Stagg, *Borderlines in Borderlands: James Madison and the Spanish-American Frontier, 1776–1821* (New Haven, CT: Yale University Press, 2009), 288–289; and John Missall and Mary Lou Missall, *The Seminole Wars: America's Longest Indian Conflict* (Gainesville: University Press of Florida, 2004), chap. 3.
30. *New-York Daily Advertiser,* January 10, 1820; A. B., "Spanish War," *Georgia Journal,* June 30, 1818; Inquisitor, "The War Making Power," *Union,* reprinted in *Dedham Gazette,* September 18, 1818; AC, 928 (Tyler).
31. Algernon Sidney, *Richmond Enquirer,* February 4, 1819, January 12, 1819, and December 22, 1818.
32. Algernon Sidney, *Richmond Enquirer,* December 22, 1818, and January 12, 1819. Pro-Jackson commentator "Fiat Justitia" defended Jackson against Sidney's allegations regarding the general's past conduct, such as his declaration of martial law in New Orleans. Fiat Justitia, "General Jackson," *National Intelligencer* (Washington, DC), reprinted in *Richmond Enquirer,* January 14, 1819.
33. *Rhode-Island American, and General Advertiser,* March 23, 1819; Aristides, "Communication," *Boston Repertory,* January 19, 1819; "The Florida Question," *Richmond Enquirer,* July 28, 1818; "A Plain Tale," *Richmond Enquirer,* February 2, 1819 ("Watch the military arm"); AC, 653–655 (Clay, quotations on 653, 655); report to constituents by Representative Lewis Williams, *Star & North-Carolina State Gazette* (Raleigh, NC), March 19, 1819; Civis, letter to the editor, *Richmond Enquirer,* July 14, 1818 ("self willed military commander"); "Conquest of

Pensacola," *Vermont Intelligencer and Bellows' Falls Advertiser,* July 27, 1818 ("oriental despotism"); "General Jackson," *Connecticut Journal,* April 6, 1819; A Calm Observer, "A Few Queries, Addressed to Candid Men," *Richmond Enquirer,* March 9, 1819; AC, 928 (Tyler). In fact, some were concerned that Jackson himself might repeat his wrongful conduct, for example, by launching a military campaign in the St. Augustine area without congressional authorization. *Richmond Enquirer,* February 20, 1819.

34. For example, in defiance of the president's and Senate's authority over appointments, Jackson had appointed a revenue collector in Pensacola. As Representative Lewis Williams wrote to his North Carolina constituents, Jackson's conduct in the city was particularly egregious because "it was an exercise by one individual of all the powers of the government." Report to constituents by Representative Lewis Williams, *Star & North-Carolina State Gazette,* March 19, 1819. Algernon Sidney also referred to Jackson's usurping legislative powers in Florida. Algernon Sidney, "To the Hon. John Quincy Adams, Secretary of State," *Richmond Enquirer,* January 12, 1819.
35. A Plain Tale," *Richmond Enquirer,* February 2, 1819; Algernon Sidney, "General Jackson," letter to the editor, *Richmond Enquirer,* December 22, 1818. The "Plain Tale" essay in the *Richmond Enquirer* condemned Jackson for his disrespectful treatment of Georgia governor Rabun, calling it "the most censurable of all his acts" and "a direct insult upon the sovereignty of the states." In his December 22, 1818, essay in the same newspaper, Algernon Sidney explained that, under state constitutions, a governor had authority to appoint the officers of his own state's militia and served as the ex officio commander in chief of the state's military forces. Algernon Sidney said Jackson challenged the validity of one of Governor Rabun's military orders when he wrote: "You, sir, as Governor of a state within my military division, have no right to give a military order while I am in the field." Sidney expressed astonishment that the general would declare "that his command virtually suspends the constitution of Georgia, in respect to the military authority of its executive at least." Permitting Jackson to override a state governor would set a terrible precedent, Sidney warned.
36. The *New-York Daily Advertiser* noted that no law authorized Jackson to raise troops. The paper added that Monroe had directed Jackson to requisition troops from the governors of adjacent states, but instead he just co-opted the Tennessee militia. *New-York Daily Advertiser,* January 10, 1820.
37. "A Plain Tale," *Richmond Enquirer,* February 2, 1819 (quotation); *Richmond Enquirer,* February 20, 1819; A. B., "Spanish War," *Georgia Journal,* June 30, 1818.
38. AC, 654 (Clay).
39. Vattel, *Law of Nations,* 3:7:122 (seizure of neutral place).
40. Ibid., 2:4:49–50 (preemptive attacks), 3:7:121–123 and 2:9:123 (right to deny entry by foreign troops and exceptions for imminent danger), 3:7:133 (right to enter neutral territory in pursuit of enemy), 3:6:96–97 (associates), 3:7:103–104 (neutrality), 3:7:111 (trade of neutral nations).
41. Chris af Jochnick and Roger Normand, "The Legitimation of Violence: A Critical History of the Laws of War," *Harvard International Law Journal* 35 (Winter 1994): 49–95, present particularly strong criticism of early modern

European nations' ventures around the world. For discussion of constitutional issues raised by American territorial expansion, see Gary Lawson and Guy Seidman, *The Constitution of Empire: Territorial Expansion and American Legal History* (New Haven, CT: Yale University Press, 2004). Lauren Benton's comparative study, *A Search for Sovereignty: Law and Geography in European Empires, 1400–1900* (New York: Cambridge University Press, 2010), explains that, despite the theory of territorial sovereignty, early modern nation-states did not actually control defined territories in a clear, consistent, and homogeneous way. Instead, there were numerous territorial irregularities and anomalous legal spaces.

42. William Earl Weeks, *John Quincy Adams and American Global Empire* (Lexington: University Press of Kentucky, 1992), 160; William Earl Weeks, *The New Cambridge History of American Foreign Relations*, vol. 1, *Dimensions of the Early American Empire, 1754–1865* (New York: Cambridge University Press, 2013), 108.

43. The resolutions as originally proposed are in AC, 583 (Committee on Military Affairs resolution regarding Arbuthnot and Ambrister), 588 (resolutions by Thomas W. Cobb regarding seizing Pensacola, executing prisoners, and entering foreign territory), and 547 (John W. Campbell resolution regarding punishing white men who instigated Indian hostilities against the United States). The votes on the resolutions are in AC, 1132–1138 and 548. The appendix contains a chart showing how each member of the House voted on the three resolutions for which there was a roll call vote. There is a disparity between the number reported for the anti-Jackson vote on Arbuthnot (62) and the number of names listed (58), and also a disparity between the number reported for the pro-Jackson vote on Ambrister (107) and the number of names listed (106). The appendix is based on the names actually provided for those votes.

44. When the 15th Congress debated the Seminole War in January–February of 1819, elections for the 16th Congress had already been held (in the fall of 1818). The first opportunity that voters had to select new congressmen after the debate was July–November 1820, when most of the elections for the 17th Congress took place. For the roll call votes, see AC, 1135–1138. The chart in the appendix identifies which members of the 15th Congress also served in the 17th Congress.

45. Commentary alleging personal political motivations included "General Jackson: Extract to the Editor of the Patriot," *Baltimore Patriot & Mercantile Advertiser,* January 29, 1819; Phocion, *Virginia Herald,* reprinted in *Hampden Patriot* (Springfield, MA), February 4, 1819; extract of a letter from Washington, "General Jackson," *Baltimore Patriot & Mercantile Advertiser,* January 21, 1819; and Letter from Wayne, "General Jackson," *Franklin Gazette,* reprinted in *Baltimore Patriot & Mercantile Advertiser,* January 23, 1819. Those denying personal political motivations included "A Plain Tale," *Richmond Enquirer,* February 2, 1819; "Algernon Sidney," *Northern Whig,* January 12, 1819; and "Extract of a Letter to the Editor, Dated Washington, January 18, 1819," *Rhode-Island American, and General Advertiser,* February 2, 1819. The comments on the feasting of Jackson are in "General Jackson, Mr. Lacock, Mr. Clay, and Public Sentiment," *National Register* (Washington, DC), March 20, 1819. By the

1820 election season, editorials, articles, and letters to the editor included few criticisms of individual congressmen for their votes on the Seminole War resolutions.

46. John Quincy Adams, *Memoirs of John Quincy Adams; Comprising Portions of His Diary from 1795 to 1848,* ed. Charles Francis Adams, 12 vols. (Philadelphia: J. B. Lippincott, 1875, repr. Memphis, TN: General Books, 2009), July 20, 1818, and July 25, 1818, 4:113, 120. For an in-depth discussion of political motives and rivalries that drove congressmen to support or oppose Jackson, see David S. Heidler, "The Politics of National Aggression: Congress and the First Seminole War," *Journal of the Early Republic* 13 (Winter 1993): 501–530.
47. McCulloch v. Maryland, 17 U.S. 316 (1819); Dartmouth College v. Woodward, 17 U.S. 518 (1819).
48. Amos S. Hershey, "Incursions into Mexico and the Doctrine of Hot Pursuit," *American Journal of International Law* 13, no. 3 (July 1919): 557–569; Kenneth R. Stevens, *Border Diplomacy: The* Caroline *and McLeod Affairs in Anglo-American-Canadian Relations, 1837–1842* (Tuscaloosa: University of Alabama Press, 1989); Timothy Kearley, "Raising the Caroline," *Wisconsin International Law Journal* 17 (1999): 325–346; Maria Benvenuta Occelli, " 'Sinking' the Caroline: Why the Caroline Doctrine's Restrictions on Self-Defense Should Not Be Regarded as Customary International Law," *San Diego International Law Journal* 4 (2003): 467–490.
49. An Act Vesting in the President of the United States the Power of Retaliation, March 3, 1813, Stat. 2:829–830; *Barbarities of the Enemy, Exposed in a Report of the Committee of the House of Representatives of the United States, Appointed to Inquire into the Spirit and Manner in Which the War Has Been Waged by the Enemy* (Worcester, MA: Isaac Sturtevant, 1814); James Kent, *Commentaries on American Law,* 4 vols. (New York: O. Halsted, 1826), 1:1, 169. Although supporters of the Florida campaigns were eager to show how international law justified their actions with regard to Spain, they were less willing to subject their relations with Indians to European scholars' interpretations of the rules of war. A number of pro-Jackson commentators declared that European treatises simply did not apply to white Americans' conflicts with Indians.
50. Lawyers Chris af Jochnick and Roger Normand express particularly blunt, hard-hitting skepticism about the role of international law in wartime. They deny that laws of war restrain violence. Instead, those laws provide no substantive humanitarian constraints yet serve to legitimate the most barbaric behavior. Jochnick and Normand, "Legitimation of Violence."
51. AC, 1100 (Joseph Desha, "imaginary grounds"); extract of a letter from Washington, "General Jackson," *Baltimore Patriot & Mercantile Advertiser,* January 21, 1819 ("spongy, pompous").
52. AC, 661 (Richard M. Johnson). For similar praise of Jackson as a hero, see AC, 984 (George Poindexter) and 699–703 (Alexander Smyth).

4. CREEKS, SEMINOLES, AND INDIAN WARS

1. J. Leitch Wright, Jr., *Creeks and Seminoles: The Destruction and Regeneration of the Muscogulge People* (Lincoln: University of Nebraska Press, 1986); and Claudio Saunt, *A New Order of Things: Property, Power, and the Transformation of the Creek*

Indians, 1733–1816 (New York: Cambridge University Press, 1999) provide excellent histories of the Creeks and Seminoles. On Creeks and Seminoles in the Seminole War, see also J. Leitch Wright, Jr., "A Note on the First Seminole War as Seen by the Indians, Negroes, and Their British Advisers," *Journal of Southern History* 34 (November 1968): 565–575; Frank Lawrence Owsley, Jr., "Prophet of War: Josiah Francis and the Creek War," *American Indian Quarterly* 9 (Summer 1985): 273–293; David S. Heidler and Jeanne T. Heidler, *Old Hickory's War: Andrew Jackson and the Quest for Empire,* rev. ed. (Baton Rouge: Louisiana State University Press, 2003); John K. Mahon, "The First Seminole War, November 21, 1817–May 24, 1818," *Florida Historical Quarterly* 77 (Summer 1998): 62–67; Robert V. Remini, *Andrew Jackson and His Indian Wars* (New York: Viking, 2001), chaps. 8 and 9; and Robert V. Remini, *Andrew Jackson,* vol. 1, *The Course of American Empire, 1767–1821* (New York: Harper and Row, 1977; repr. Baltimore: Johns Hopkins University Press, 1998), chap. 23.

Most historians still treat U.S. relations with American Indians as an internal, rather than international, matter, and most histories of U.S. foreign policy omit Indians. However, some historians have called for inclusion of U.S.-Indian affairs as part of diplomatic history, and recent surveys of the history of U.S. foreign policy include more discussion of American Indians than was evident in earlier decades. Most notably, while Cambridge University Press's 1993 multivolume history of American foreign relations does not discuss U.S. interactions with Indians (except for a few references to Indian allies of European nations at odds with the United States), its 2013 version includes analysis of U.S. relations with Native American peoples. Compare Bradford Perkins, *The Cambridge History of American Foreign Relations,* vol. 1, *The Creation of a Republic Empire, 1776–1865* (New York: Cambridge University Press, 1993); and William Earl Weeks, *The New Cambridge History of American Foreign Relations,* vol. 1, *Dimensions of the Early American Empire, 1754–1865* (New York: Cambridge University Press, 2013). For an examination of early American diplomacy that includes American Indian nations equally with European powers, see Leonard J. Sadosky, *Revolutionary Negotiations: Indians, Empires, and Diplomats in the Founding of America* (Charlottesville: University of Virginia Press, 2009). Like *Revolutionary Negotiations,* this book studies U.S. relations with non-Europeans alongside an examination of American relations with Europeans.

Scholarly works that examine eighteenth- and nineteenth-century Europe's perspective on the application of the law of nations outside of Europe say little about American Indians. See Antony Anghie, *Imperialism, Sovereignty and the Making of International Law* (New York: Cambridge University Press, 2007), chap. 2; Jennifer Pitts, "Boundaries of Victorian International Law," in *Victorian Visions of Global Order: Empire and International Relations in Nineteenth-Century Political Thought,* ed. Duncan Bell (New York: Cambridge University Press, 2007), 67–88; Jennifer Pitts, "Empire and Legal Universalisms in the Eighteenth Century," *American Historical Review* 117, no. 1 (February 2012): 92–121; Jennifer Pitts, *A Turn to Empire: The Rise of Imperial Liberalism in Britain and France* (Princeton, NJ: Princeton University Press, 2005); Sankar Muthu, *Enlightenment against Empire* (Princeton, NJ: Princeton University Press, 2003); Gerrit W. Gong, *The Standard of "Civilization" in International Society* (New York:

Oxford University Press, 1984); and Martti Koskenniemi, *The Gentle Civilizer of Nations: The Rise and Fall of International Law, 1870–1960* (New York: Cambridge University Press, 2001). In contrast, Robert A. Williams, Jr., and Paul G. McHugh provide thoughtful studies of the application of international legal theory to American Indians. In *The American Indian in Western Legal Thought: The Discourse of Conquest* (New York: Oxford University Press, 1990), Williams presents a comprehensive analysis of how Europeans and European-heritage people used law as an "instrument of empire" in the conquest and colonization of American Indians. He begins with medieval concepts and extends his study through U.S. Supreme Court decisions of the early national period. McHugh's tome, *Aboriginal Societies and the Common Law: A History of Sovereignty, Status, and Self-Determination* (New York: Oxford University Press, 2005), examines aboriginal sovereignty and status under the common law in North America and Australasia from earliest colonization to the present. Also relevant is Lisa Ford's comparative study of Georgia and New South Wales, *Settler Sovereignty: Jurisdiction and Indigenous People in America and Australia, 1788–1836* (Cambridge, MA: Harvard University Press, 2010). Ford explains how the United States displaced indigenous jurisdiction and erased indigenous rights in order to establish its own identity as a modern sovereign nation (and she makes parallel arguments about Australia's relationship with aboriginal people). S. James Anaya, *Indigenous Peoples in International Law* (New York: Oxford University Press, 2000), focuses primarily on present-day issues but provides historical background in chapter 1.

2. Wright, *Creeks and Seminoles,* chap. 1; Saunt, *New Order of Things;* William C. Sturtevant, "Creek into Seminole," in *North American Indians in Historical Perspective,* ed. Eleanor Burch Leacock and Nancy Oestreich Lurie (New York: Random House, 1971), 92–128.
3. Wright, *Creeks and Seminoles,* 133 (quotation), 127 (population estimates), 126 (major Seminole towns).
4. Treaty of Friendship, Limits, and Navigation between Spain and the United States (Pinckney's Treaty or the Treaty of San Lorenzo), October 27, 1795, Stat., 8:138–153.
5. Saunt, *New Order of Things,* 206–207, 241; Sturtevant, "Creek into Seminole"; Wright, *Creeks and Seminoles,* 116–117, 135, 138–142. The United States made treaties with the Creeks at New York (1790), Colerain (1796), Fort Wilkinson (1802), and Washington (1805). The first U.S. treaty with the Seminoles as a separate entity was the Treaty of Moultrie Creek (1823). Stat., 7:35–38, 56–60, 68–70, 96–98, 224–228, quotation on 35.
6. Tecumseh's Speech at Tuckaubatchee, October 1811, as allegedly reported by Samuel Dale. Dale purported to recount the exact language of the speech, but scholars have questioned the authenticity of Dale's report. See, for example, John Sugden, "Early Pan-Indianism: Tecumseh's Tour of the Indian Country, 1811–1812," *American Indian Quarterly* 10, no. 4 (Fall 1986): 273–304, at 288. McIntosh, who was the son of a Coweta Creek woman and a British agent, and a first cousin of Georgia governor George Troup, was the principal leader of the Lower Creeks in the first two decades of the nineteenth century. The information on William McIntosh and Hillis Hadjo is from Wright, *Creeks and Seminoles,* 166–168.

7. Wright, *Creeks and Seminoles,* chap. 6; Saunt, *New Order of Things,* chaps. 11 and 12. Homathlemico's name was spelled in different ways, including "Homathle Mico" and "Hemathlemico."
8. Wright, *Creeks and Seminoles,* chap. 6; Saunt, *New Order of Things;* Gregory Evans Dowd, *A Spirited Resistance: The North American Indian Struggle for Unity, 1745–1815* (Baltimore: Johns Hopkins University Press, 1991); John Sugden, "The Southern Indians in the War of 1812: The Closing Phase," *Florida Historical Quarterly* 60, no. 3 (January 1982): 273–312; Frank Lawrence Owsley, Jr., *Struggle for the Gulf Borderlands: The Creek War and the Battle of New Orleans, 1812–1815* (Gainesville: University Press of Florida, 1981).
9. Sadosky, *Revolutionary Negotiations,* 196–205, quotation on 200. The Jackson quotation is from a letter from Jackson to William Henry Harrison, November 28, 1811, quoted in Bernard Sheehan, *Seeds of Extinction: Jeffersonian Philanthropy and the American Indian* (Chapel Hill: University of North Carolina Press, 1973), 206.
10. Wright, *Creeks and Seminoles,* chap. 6; Saunt, *New Order of Things.*
11. Treaty with the Creeks (Treaty of Fort Jackson), August 14, 1814, Stat., 7:120–122, quotations on 120, 121.
12. Treaty of Peace and Amity between His Britannic Majesty and the United States of America (Treaty of Ghent) December 24, 1814, Stat., 8:218–223, quotation on 222–223. Britain made a parallel commitment with regard to Indian tribes with which it was at war at the time of ratification.
13. Address to the king of England, from the Muscogee Indians, March 10, 1815, ASP-FR, 4:552–553, quotations on 553; Boleck to Coppinger, November 18, 1816, ASP-FR, 4:493. Hillis Hadjo went to London to hand-deliver the 1815 document, in an unsuccessful attempt to solidify an alliance with Britain. The British secretary for war and colonies, the Earl of Bathurst, withheld support for Hillis Hadjo's proposed alliance and treaty.

    In addition to asking British men to write up letters that would be "signed" by Creek or Seminole leaders, the chiefs sometimes asked Britons to include Indian complaints and requests in their own correspondence with American, British, and Spanish officials. Twelve Creek chiefs, including Hillis Hadjo and Homathlemico, even gave British trader Alexander Arbuthnot a power of attorney to authorize him to act on their behalf. Arbuthnot wrote on their behalf to British envoy Charles Bagot, Bahamas governor Charles Cameron, Cuba governor José Cienfuegos, and Indian agent David B. Mitchell. In these letters, and also in letters written on their behalf by Edward Nicolls, Creeks objected to American violence and pledged that Indians would follow a non-aggression policy except when aggression was necessary for self-defense. Power of attorney from the Indian chiefs to Arbuthnot, June 17, 1817, ASP-FR, 4:589; Arbuthnot to Bagot, n.d., ASP-FR, 4:606–607; Arbuthnot to Bagot, n.d., ASP-FR, 4:585; Arbuthnot to Cameron, n.d., ASP-FR, 4:585; Arbuthnot to governor of Havana [Cienfuegos], n.d., ASP-FR, 4:588–589; Arbuthnot to Mitchell, January 19, 1818, ASP-FR, 4:591; Edward Nicolls to Benjamin Hawkins, April 28, 1815, and May 12, 1815, ASP-FR 4:548, 549.
14. On historians' use of documents that ostensibly represent American Indians' perspectives, see Andrew Newman, *On Records: Delaware Indians, Colonists, and the Media of History and Memory* (Lincoln: University of Nebraska Press, 2012);

and Harry Robie, "Red Jacket's Reply: Problems in the Verification of a Native American Speech Text," *New York Folklore* 12 (1986): 99–117.

15. Petition of the chiefs of the Lower Creek Nation to Cameron, n.d., ASP-FR, 4:590.
16. Boleck to Coppinger, May 7, 1816, and November 18, 1816, ASP-FR, 4:492, 493; Cappachimico, McQueen, Charlie Tastonoky, et al., to Charles Bagot, November 8, 1816, Colonial Office 23/66, cited in Wright, *Creeks and Seminoles,*197; General Edmund P. Gaines to the Seminole chiefs, August 1817, ASP-FR, 4:585–586; Chief Kenhagee [Kinache] to General Gaines, n.d., ASP-FR, 4:587; Chiefs Cappachimico [Kinache] and Boleck to Cameron, n.d., ASP-FR, 4:586–587; Accession of Muscogee Indians to the Treaty of Peace of 1814, April 2, 1815, ASP-FR, 4:549. Boleck (sometimes referred to as Bowlegs) was the leading chief along the Suwannee River, having succeeded family members Cowkeeper (Ahaya) and King Payne. Cappichimico, or Kinache (also known as Kenhagee, Heijah, Hachy, and Tom Perryman), was a prominent chieftain in Miccosukee who had fought on the British side in the War of 1812.
17. Monroe to Baker, July 10, 1815, ASP-FR, 4:553–554; Arbuthnot to commanding officer at Fort Gaines, March 3, 1817, ASP-FR, 4:610–611; A. Culloh to Arbuthnot, May 1, 1817, ASP-FR, 4:611.
18. Arbuthnot to a person of rank in England, January 30, 1818, ASP-FR, 4:607–608. For contemporary accounts of events leading up to the war, see "A Brief History of the Seminole War, and of the Trial and Execution of Arbuthnot and Ambrister," *Boston Weekly Messenger,* December 31, 1818; and "A Concise Narrative of the Seminole Campaign, by an Officer Attached to the Expedition," *Spirit of the Times & Carlisle (PA) Gazette,* March 2, 1819.
19. The documentary evidence provided by John Quincy Adams in December 1818 included warnings of such military preparations by Red Sticks and their black allies: George Perryman to Lieutenant Richard M. Sands, February 24, 1817, ASP-FR, 4:596; Sands to Colonial William King, March 15, 1817, ASP-FR, 4:597; Mitchell to Acting Secretary of War George Graham, March 30, 1817, ASP-FR, 4:597; and Culloh to Gaines, [1817], ASP-FR, 4:597. Gaines's correspondence is Gaines to Jackson, November 21, 1817, ASP-FR, 4:597; Gaines to Graham, December 2, 1817, ASP-FR, 4:598; Gaines to Graham, December 4, 1817, ASP-MA, 1:688.
20. Jackson to Graham, December 16, 1817, ASP-MA, 1:689; circular of General Jackson, January 11, 1818, ASP-MA, 1:767.
21. Robert C. Ambrister to Cameron, March 20, 1818, ASP-FR, 4:594. Around the same time, Ambrister also wrote to Nicolls describing the dire situation and requesting assistance. Ambrister to Nicolls, [March 1818?], ASP-FR, 4:594.
22. Wright, *Creeks and Seminoles;* Saunt, *New Order of Things;* Wright, "Note on the First Seminole War"; Owsley, "Prophet of War"; Heidler and Heidler, *Old Hickory's War;* Remini, *Andrew Jackson and His Indian Wars;* Remini, *Course of American Empire.*
23. Jackson to Secretary of War John C. Calhoun, April 8, April 9, April 20, April 26, May 5, and June 2, 1818, ASP-MA, 1:699–700, 700, 700–701, 701, 701–702, 708–709, quotation on 700 (April 9). Mahon, "First Seminole War"; Wright,

"Note on the First Seminole War"; Remini, *Andrew Jackson and His Indian Wars;* Heidler and Heidler, *Old Hickory's War;* Owsley, "Prophet of War."

24. Dowd, *Spirited Resistance,* chap. 9.
25. Wright, *Creeks and Seminoles,* 166–167, 174–177, 198–205, 209–212, 238–242.
26. Treaty with the Florida Tribes of Indians (Treaty of Moultrie Creek), September 18, 1823, Stat., 7:224–228, quotation on 224. In a concurrently signed separate agreement, the United States permitted six leading Seminole signatories of the Treaty of Moultrie Creek to retain their individual lands along the Apalachicola River.
27. Treaty with the Seminole (Treaty of Payne's Landing), May 9, 1832, Stat., 7:368–370.
28. *Seminole Tribune,* http://www.semtribe.com/SeminoleTribune/, accessed March 30, 2013. See also the websites of the Seminole Tribe of Florida, http://www.semtribe.com/, the Miccosukee Tribe of Indians of Florida, http://www.miccosukee.com/, and the Seminole Nation of Oklahoma, http://sno-nsn.gov/ (all accessed March 30, 2013).
29. The House of Representatives debate on the Seminole War is in AC, 527–530 and 583–1138. Most of the House debate about Jackson's actions during the Seminole War focused on his invasion of Florida, seizure of Spanish forts, and execution of British allies of the Seminoles, rather than on Hillis Hadjo and Homathlemico. Tellingly, the resolutions that initiated the debate did not mention the executions of Hillis Hadjo and Homathlemico.
30. An American Citizen, "Jackson's Justification," *Albany (NY) Argus,* January 5, 1819.
31. As previously noted, there is a theoretical difference between the concept that certain natural human rights protect everyone universally (the subject addressed in the text) and the notion of universalization of European understandings of law, though the two ideas are certainly interconnected. In the late nineteenth century, Europeans envisioned an international legal order that was restricted to "civilized" nations, but at the same time they sought to universalize their understanding of law, that is, to spread their legal regimes globally along with their civilization.

    Scholars of the history of international law who discuss evolving ideas of moral universalism, European conceptions of the international community, and the standard of civilization include Stephen C. Neff, *Justice among Nations: A History of International Law* (Cambridge, MA: Harvard University Press, 2014); Gong, *Standard of "Civilization";* Koskenniemi, *Gentle Civilizer of Nations;* Pitts, "Boundaries of Victorian International Law"; Pitts, "Empire and Legal Universalisms" (reference to "distinct legal universe" on 103); and Anghie, *Imperialism, Sovereignty and the Making of International Law.*
32. Pitts, "Empire and Legal Universalisms"; Pitts, "Boundaries of Victorian International Law"; Pitts, *Turn to Empire*; Williams, *American Indian in Western Legal Thought;* Anghie, *Imperialism, Sovereignty and the Making of International Law,* chap. 2.
33. "[B]rotherly correction is as much a part of natural law as brotherly love," Vitoria said, "and since all those peoples are not merely in a state of sin, but presently in a state beyond salvation, it is the business of Christians to correct and direct them." Francisco de Vitoria, "On the American Indians," in *Political*

Writings, ed. Anthony Pagden and Jeremy Lawrance (New York: Cambridge University Press, 1991), 231–292, quotation on 284. For analysis of Vitoria's ideas, see Williams, *American Indian in Western Legal Thought;* Anghie, *Imperialism, Sovereignty and the Making of International Law.* Spain's lack of universalism was also evident within its own borders. By expelling Jews, Muslims, conversos, and moriscos beginning in the late fifteenth century, Spain applied an exclusionary policy to certain classes of its inhabitants in the belief that it would create a more unified nation that could act more forcefully in the world. Like later U.S. policies of Indian removal and "colonization" of African-heritage people, Spain resorted to physical separation and expatriation of its residents based on the presumption that it would build national solidarity. Legally, Spain's action represented a decreased commitment to legal pluralism—a system in which multiple legal authorities coexisted in the same territorial space—and perhaps an early stage of the shift to a state-centered, more uniform legal order. For a global study of that shift in the period from 1400 to 1900, see Lauren Benton, *Law and Colonial Cultures: Legal Regimes in World History, 1400–1900* (New York: Cambridge University Press, 2002).

34. Alberico Gentili, *Three Books on the Law of War,* trans. John C. Rolfe (Oxford: Clarendon Press, 1933), quotations on 125, 122, 122, 41. Gentili wrote his treatise in Latin and first published it in 1598 as *De iure belli libri tres.* For analysis of Gentili's views of American Indians, see Williams, *American Indian in Western Legal Thought,* 194–199.

35. Williams, *American Indian in Western Legal Thought,* 208–221, quotations on 210, 210, 217, 218.

36. John Grenier, *The First Way of War: American War Making on the Frontier, 1607–1814* (New York: Cambridge University Press, 2005).

37. For discussion of how deep cultural differences resulted in frequent execution of captives by both European Americans and "First Nations" peoples in early American wars, see Stephanie Carvin, *Prisoners of America's Wars: From the Early Republic to Guantanamo* (New York: Columbia University Press, 2010), chap. 1. William M. Osborn's book, *The Wild Frontier: Atrocities during the American-Indian War from Jamestown to Wounded Knee* (New York: Random House, 2000), provides a long list of atrocities committed by white settlers and Indians against each other, including numerous murders and frequent killing of prisoners. Among the many other scholarly books on early American white-Indian violence are Matthew C. Ward, *Breaking the Backcountry: The Seven Years' War in Virginia and Pennsylvania, 1754–1765* (Pittsburgh: University of Pittsburgh Press, 2003); Peter Silver, *Our Savage Neighbors: How Indian War Transformed Early America* (New York: Norton, 2008); Wayne E. Lee, *Barbarians and Brothers: Anglo-American Warfare, 1500–1865* (Cary, NC: Oxford University Press, 2011), chaps. 5, 6, and 8; Patrick Griffin, *American Leviathan: Empire, Nation, and Revolutionary Frontier* (New York: Hill and Wang, 2007); Alan Taylor, *The Civil War of 1812: American Citizens, British Subjects, Irish Rebels, and Indian Allies* (New York: Knopf, 2010); Richard Slotkin, *Regeneration through Violence* (Middletown, CT: Wesleyan University Press, 1973); and Richard Drinnon, *Facing West: The Metaphysics of Indian-Hating and Empire-Building* (Minneapolis: University of Minnesota Press, 1980).

38. Emer de Vattel, *The Law of Nations, or Principles of Natural Law, Applied to the Conduct and Affairs of Nations and Sovereigns* (London: G., G., and J. Robinson, 1797), 2:1:7 (imposing dominion), 2:4:59 (imposing religion), 2:7:90 (expelling people from land), 2:7:91 (extending boundaries), 2:7:92 (encroachment on territory), 2:8:97 ("wandering" people).
39. Ibid., 1:18:209, 2:7:97 ("savages").
40. Ibid., 3:8:142 (prisoners), 3:8:145 (noncombatants).
41. Ibid., 1:8:81, 1:18:209, 2:7:97 (importance of cultivation of the earth and right to take Indian land).
42. Ibid., 3:9:167 (enemy property).
43. Ibid., 3:1:1 (quoted definition of "public war"), Preliminaries, sec. 1 (quoted definition of "nations"). See also 3:1:1, 3:1:2, 3:1:4 (definition of "war, " distinction between public war and private war, and rule that only a "sovereign power" has the right to wage war).
44. Williams, *American Indian in Western Legal Thought,* chaps. 6 and 7, analyzes natural law arguments as they specifically pertained to Indians. He discusses the Wharton pamphlet on 298–305, quotation on 299. Williams points out that such American arguments consciously echoed the position taken by British opponents of royal prerogative power in the eighteenth century: Attorney General Charles Pratt (Lord Camden) and Solicitor General Charles Yorke's 1757 opinion supporting the East India Company's right to secure title to territory purchased in India, and the judicial decision in *Campbell v. Hall* (1774) by Chief Justice William Murray (Lord Mansfield). Ibid, 275–280, 298–303.
45. Carvin, *Prisoners of America's Wars,* chap. 1. For a general history of treatment of captives since ancient times, see Alexander Gillespie, *A History of the Laws of War,* vol. 1, *The Customs and Laws of War with regards to Combatants and Captives* (Portland, OR: Hart, 2011), chap. 2.
46. Grenier, *First Way of War,* chaps. 5, 6, and 7. To pressure British officer Henry Hamilton to surrender Fort Sackville, American colonel George Rogers Clark threatened to kill everyone in the fort. To bluntly convey the sincerity of his threat, Clark publicly executed four Indian prisoners near Vincennes. Hamilton was persuaded to give up the fort and was taken into American custody. Interestingly, the Americans subsequently held Hamilton not as a prisoner of war but as a war criminal, owing to his alleged role in instigating Indians to commit brutalities against American settlers. Ibid., 156–157, 16–19.
47. Williams, *American Indian in Western Legal Thought,* chap. 7.
48. Carvin, *Prisoners of America's Wars* (reference to "unrestrained" warfare on 16). An extensive literature describes the American view of a savage-civilization divide, including Roy Harvey Pearce, *Savagism and Civilization: A Study of the Indian and the American Mind* (Berkeley: University of California Press, 1988); and Drinnon, *Facing West.* In the early nineteenth century, the perceived cultural divide (savage versus civilized) took on a racial component as well, as evidenced by the removal of the Cherokees despite their success in the civilization program. See Mary Young, "Racism in Red and Black: Indians and Other Free People of Color in Georgia Law, Politics, and Removal Policy, *Georgia Historical Quarterly* 73 (1989): 492–518; Mary Young, "The Cherokee Nation: Mirror of the Republic," *American Quarterly* 33 (1981): 502–524; Theda

Perdue, *"Mixed Blood" Indians: Racial Construction in the Early South* (Athens: University of Georgia Press, 2003), chap. 3; Daniel K. Richter, "'Believing That Many of the Red People Suffer Much for the Want of Food': Hunting, Agriculture, and a Quaker Construction of Indianness in the Early Republic," in *Race and the Early Republic: Racial Consciousness and Nation-Building in the Early Republic,* ed. Michael A. Morrison and James Brewer Stewart (New York: Rowman and Littlefield, 2002), 27–53; James P. Ronda, "'We Have a Country': Race, Geography, and the Invention of Indian Territory," in *Race and the Early Republic,* 159–175; Reginald Horsman, *Race and Manifest Destiny: The Origins of American Racial Anglo-Saxonism* (Cambridge, MA: Harvard University Press, 1981), chap. 6; Robert F. Berkhofer, Jr., *The White Man's Indian: Images of the American Indian from Columbus to the Present* (New York: Random House, 1978); Robert E. Bieder, *Science Encounters the Indian, 1820–1880: The Early Years of American Ethnology* (Norman: University of Oklahoma Press, 1986), chaps. 1–3; Alden T. Vaughan, "From White Man to Redskin: Changing Anglo-American Perceptions of the American Indian," *American Historical Review* 86 (1982): 917–953; Kathleen Brown, "Native Americans and Early Modern Concepts of Race," in *Empire and Others: British Encounters with Indigenous Peoples, 1600–1850,* ed. Martin Daunton and Rick Halpern (Philadelphia: University of Pennsylvania Press, 1999), 79–100; and Sheehan, *Seeds of Extinction,* chap. 9.

5. CIVILIZATION AND NATIONHOOD

1. AC, 678–679 (Alexander Smyth), 960–961 (George Poindexter).
2. Ibid., 866 (John Rhea), 1128 (James Ervin), 665–666 (Richard M. Johnson), 767–768 (James Barbour), quotations on 866 and 1128.
3. Ibid., 955 (Poindexter), 713–715 (James Tallmadge, Jr.).
4. Ibid., 860, 867 (Rhea quotations), 713–715 (Tallmadge), 1092 (Joseph Desha).
5. Ibid., 633–637 (Henry Clay), 987–988 (Timothy Fuller), quotations on 987, 635.
6. Ibid., 866 (Rhea). For a discussion of how Europeans used cultural differences to justify nineteenth-century colonialism, see Antony Anghie, *Imperialism, Sovereignty and the Making of International Law* (New York: Cambridge University Press, 2007), chap. 2.
7. AC, 638–640 (Clay), 822–823 (Charles F. Mercer).
8. For the 1793 precedent, see AC, 625 (James Johnson).
9. AC, 601–602 (John Holmes), 955–960 (Poindexter), 860–870 (Rhea), 767 (Barbour). Specifically regarding the strength of Indian forces, see ibid., 662 (R. Johnson); regarding the Garretts, see especially ibid., 959–960 (Poindexter); and, regarding St. Marks, ibid., 884–886 (Joseph Hopkinson), 674 (R. Johnson), 681 (Smyth), 865 (Rhea), 905–906 (Richard C. Anderson).
10. *City of Washington Gazette,* July 21, 1818.
11. AC, 802–805 (Mercer), 988–994 (Fuller), 1081–1082 (Thomas S. Williams), 649–650, 652 (Clay), 626 (J. Johnson), 747 (Henry R. Storrs), 927–928 (John Tyler).
12. *Massachusetts Spy, or Worcester Gazette,* December 23, 1818; AC, 989–990 (Fuller), 633–637 (Clay), 786, 804–805 (Mercer), quotation on 990.
13. AC, 1001–1002 (Fuller, quotations on 1001). See also ibid., 654 (Clay).

14. Ibid., 661, 665–666 (R. Johnson, "indiscriminate murder" quotation on 661), 1096 (Desha); John Quincy Adams to George W. Erving, November 28, 1818, ASP-FR, 4:539–545, quotation on 543; "General Jackson's Case," *City of Washington Gazette,* January 20, 1819; "Gen. Jackson," *Albany (NY) Register,* reprinted in *American Mercury* (Hartford, CT), January 5, 1819; "Execution of Prisoners," *Nashville Whig and Tennessee Advertiser,* May 30, 1818, reprinted in *Salem (MA) Gazette,* July 14, 1818; Themistocles, "To the Honorable Henry Clay, Speaker of the House of Representatives," *National Register* (Washington, DC), January 30, 1819; "General Jackson," *Kentucky Reporter* (Lexington, KY), reprinted in *American Watchman* (Wilmington, DE), June 20, 1818; "Arbuthnot and Ambrister," *Eastern Argus* (Portland, ME), December 22, 1818.
15. AC, 898 (Anderson), 613 (Holmes, "indiscriminate massacre" quotation), 1041 (Henry Baldwin); *Narrative of the Tragical Death of Mr. Darius Barber, and His Seven Children Who Were Inhumanly Butchered by the Indians in Camden County, Georgia, January 26, 1818* (Boston: David Hazen, 1818). Some political commentators combined general statements about "Indian" warfare with specific accusations against Florida Indians to make the case that the United States did not have to follow the usual rules of war during the Florida campaigns. AC, 1041 (Baldwin), 120 (Ervin), 851 (Felix Walker); Adams to Erving, November 28, 1818, ASP-FR, 4:539–545, at 543.
16. "Communication," *Boston Patriot and Daily Chronicle,* February 11, 1819; Junius Brutus, "General Jackson," *National Advocate* (New York, NY), January 16, 1819; "Arbuthnot and Ambrister," *Maryland Censor* (Baltimore, MD), reprinted in *National Advocate,* December 19, 1818; AC, 775 (Barbour), 1043 (Baldwin).
17. AC, 989–990, 999–1000 (Fuller, quotation on 999), 802–805, 820–821 (Mercer), 932 (Tyler). Even John Quincy Adams, Jackson's most influential defender, was initially skeptical about the executions of Hillis Hadjo and Homathlemico. Adams's diary entry on May 4, 1818, observed that the two men had been hanged "without due regard to humanity." John Quincy Adams, *Memoirs of John Quincy Adams; Comprising Portions of His Diary from 1795 to 1848,* ed. Charles Francis Adams, 12 vols. (Philadelphia: J. B. Lippincott, 1875, repr. Memphis, TN: General Books, 2009), May 4, 1818, 4:54.
18. AC, 856–869 (Rhea, quotation on 861).
19. Ibid., 1041 (Baldwin), 706 (Francis Jones).
20. Ibid., 704–707 (Jones, quotations on 704, 706), 855–860 (Rhea), 1060, 1053 (Baldwin quotations).
21. Ibid., 726–727 (Tallmadge), 765–766 (Barbour). As will be evident below, openness to tribal sovereignty in Spanish territory did not correlate with support for Florida Indians' rights.
22. Pomponius, "Political," *Rhode-Island American, and General Advertiser* (Providence, RI), October 9, 1818; AC, 678, 685–687 (Smyth), 658–659 (R. Johnson), 841 (George F. Strother), 1106–1107 (John Floyd), 860 (Rhea).
23. AC, 765 (Barbour, "anomalous character of the Indian tribes"), AC, 726 (Tallmadge), 1054 (Baldwin); "The Florida Question," *Richmond (VA) Enquirer,* July 28, 1818 ("peculiar situation of the Indian tribes"); "The Floridas," *National Intelligencer* (Washington, DC), July 27, 1818, reprinted in *National Register,* August 1, 1818 (United States' "peculiar relations with the Indians"); Junius Brutus, "General Jackson," *National Advocate,* January 16, 1819; "Execution of

Prisoners," *Nashville Whig and Tennessee Advertiser,* May 30, 1818, reprinted in *Salem Gazette,* July 14, 1818; Sulpicious, "Occupation of Pensacola," *National Advocate,* August 29, 1818. John Quincy Adams's rejection of Luis de Onís's repeated offer of European mediation prior to Jackson's invasion similarly conveyed the singularity of the American circumstances.

24. AC, 1054 (Baldwin).
25. Ibid., 800–802 (Mercer, quotations on 800, 802), 641, 652–653 (Clay, quotation on 641), 748–749 (Storrs, quotation on 748). Clay made his comments in the context of Arbuthnot's and Ambrister's status, contesting the allegation that the two Britons took themselves outside the laws of war by allying with individuals waging private war. See Chapter 7 for discussion of this issue.
26. On the Acadians, see Eliga H. Gould, *Among the Powers of the Earth: The American Revolution and the Making of a New World Empire* (Cambridge, MA: Harvard University Press, 2012), chap. 1.
27. AC, 765–766 (Barbour), 726–727 (Tallmadge); "The Floridas," *National Intelligencer,* July 27, 1818, reprinted in *National Register,* August 1, 1818 ("legitimate seat of war"); "An Inquiry into the Causes, Conduct and Consequences of the Southern War," *Democratic Press* (Philadelphia, PA), reprinted in *Pittsfield (MA) Sun,* August 5, 1818 ("no territorial bounds"). On the shift from the medieval feudal notion of personal jurisdiction to the more modern concept of territorial jurisdiction in the context of indigenous peoples, see Paul G. McHugh, *Aboriginal Societies and the Common Law: A History of Sovereignty, Status, and Self-Determination* (New York: Oxford University Press, 2005), 68–70 (medieval view), 108–111 (early modern view); and Kal Raustiala, *Does the Constitution Follow the Flag? The Evolution of Territoriality in American Law* (New York: Oxford University Press, 2009).
28. "Arbuthnot and Ambrister," *Eastern Argus,* December 22, 1818. The newspaper described the term "out-laws" in the context of a discussion of the legality of the executions of the two British prisoners, Alexander Arbuthnot and Robert Ambrister.
29. Adams to Erving, November 28, 1818, ASP-FR, 4:539–545, quotations on 542 ("fugitive outlaws from the United States"), 543 ("Indian outlaws"); Adams to Luis de Onís, November 30, 1818, ASP-FR, 4:545–546, quotation on 546 ("fugitive outlaws from the Creek nation"); Jackson to José Masot, May 23, 1818, ASP-MA, 1:712–713, quotation on 712 ("party of outlaws"); Jackson to John C. Calhoun, May 5, 1818, ASP-MA, 1:701–702, quotation on 702 ("outlaws of the old Red Stick party"); AC, 1041 (Baldwin). Note that on the nationhood issue, neither Adams nor Jackson made any explicit connection between the "fugitive outlaw" characterization and the nationhood status of the Red Sticks.
30. *The Statutes at Large, Being a Collection of All the Laws of Virginia from the First Session of the Legislature in the Year 1619,* ed. William Waller Hening, 13 vols. (New York: R. and W. and G. Bartow, 1809–1823), 2:237–238 (1666); *The First Laws of the State of Georgia,* ed. John D. Cushing, 2 vols. (Wilmington, DE: Michael Glazier, 1981), 1:365–370, preamble (1787).
31. AC, 856–869 (Rhea, quotations on 861).
32. Ibid., 1041 (Baldwin), 706–707 (Jones), 678, 685–687 (Smyth).
33. Junius Brutus, "General Jackson," *National Advocate,* January 16, 1819; Adams to Erving, November 28, 1818, ASP-FR, 4:539–545, quoting Vattel on544; AC, 658 (R. Johnson).

34. AC, 898–900 (Anderson), 1096–1097 (Desha), 1041 (Baldwin), 730–731 (Tallmadge), 669 (R. Johnson), 775 (Barbour), 695 (Smyth), quotations on 899, 1096, 1097.
35. Ibid., 704–705 (Jones), 728–729 (Tallmadge), 847 (Strother), 869 (Rhea), 1096–1097 (Desha), 898–900 (Anderson), 669 (R. Johnson), 775 (Barbour); "General Jackson," *Kentucky Reporter,* reprinted in *American Watchman,* June 20, 1818. Not all agreed that Hillis Hadjo had participated in the attack on the Scott party; others blamed him instead for leading the Red Sticks against Americans during the Creek War.
36. AC, 999–1002 (Fuller, "rights of humanity" on 1001 and 1002, "evils of war" on 1002, "useless cruelty" on 999, "Barbarous practices" on 1001, "mercy" on 1000, "extreme rights of war" on 999, "intolerable barbarity" on 999, "without necessity" on 999).
37. Ibid., 932–934 (Tyler, quotation on 933), 754 (Storrs quotation), 820–823 (Mercer, quotations on 822, 823), 639–640 (Clay, quotations on 639, 640).
38. Criticisms of the use of the British flag as a decoy are in AC, 637–638 (Clay), 991 (Fuller), 820 (Mercer). The use of a decoy probably fell within Emer de Vattel's definition of acceptable deceptive practices. Emer de Vattel, *The Law of Nations, or Principles of Natural Law, Applied to the Conduct and Affairs of Nations and Sovereigns* (London: G., G., and J. Robinson, 1797), 3:10:178. Procedural criticisms are in Senate, Select Committee, report on the Seminole War, February 24, 1819, *Annals of Congress,* Senate, 15th Cong., 2nd sess., 256–268, on 261; AC, 821 (Mercer); "Indian War," *National Messenger* (Washington, DC), reprinted in *Salem Gazette,* June 12, 1818. Also noting the absence of a trial: "Short-Metre," *Newburyport (MA) Herald,* January 1, 1819. Additionally, Representative Thomas W. Cobb appeared to include Indians among those who would be protected by his proposed bill prohibiting execution of captives without presidential approval, which was to apply in peacetime or in time of war with Indians. AC, 588 (Cobb). Henry Clay also noted that the executions violated the United States' established past practice—its "long and immemorial usage"—not to kill captives. Ibid., 638–642 (Clay, quotation on 642).
39. AC, 932–933 (John Tyler), 999–1000 (Fuller).
40. Phocion, *Virginia Herald,* reprinted in *Hampden Patriot* (Springfield, MA), February 4, 1819; "Foreign Emissaries," *Aurora* (Philadelphia, PA), reprinted in *Baltimore Patriot & Mercantile Advertiser,* June 11, 1818.
41. Political theory scholar Jennifer Pitts, who has studied the subject in depth, notes that although there was a distinction between "an earlier legal universalism and the later 'European egocentrism,'" the older concept of the law of nations was not as inclusive as some eighteenth-century juridical texts suggest—nor as inclusive as standard historical studies claim. Legal scholars Antony Anghie and Robert A. Williams, Jr., also emphasize early modern European jurists' exceptions to universalism. Jennifer Pitts, "Empire and Legal Universalisms in the Eighteenth Century," *American Historical Review* 117, no. 1 (February 2012): 92–121, quotation on 104; Jennifer Pitts, "Boundaries of Victorian International Law," in *Victorian Visions of Global Order: Empire and International Relations in Nineteenth-Century Political Thought,* ed. Duncan Bell (New York: Cambridge University Press, 2007), 67–88; Jennifer Pitts, *A Turn to Empire: The Rise of Imperial Liberalism in Britain and France* (Princeton, NJ: Princeton University Press, 2005); Robert A. Williams, Jr., *The American Indian in Western*

Legal Thought: The Discourse of Conquest (New York: Oxford University Press, 1990); Anghie, *Imperialism, Sovereignty and the Making of International Law,* chap. 2.

42. AC, 838 (Strother).
43. Henry Wheaton, *Elements of International Law with a Sketch of the History of the Science,* 1st ed. (Philadelphia: Carey, Lea and Blanchard, 1836), chap. 1, quotations on 44, 45.
44. Ibid., 253, 249–250, 209.
45. Ibid., 137, 138–140.
46. Ibid., 82, 88–89.
47. Ibid., 140 ("gradually compelled"), 51 ("sovereign state"), 368–372 (peace treaties); James Kent, *Commentaries on American Law,* 4 vols. (New York: O. Halsted, 1826), 1:45.
48. On late nineteenth-century European imperialism and the rules of war, see especially Anghie, *Imperialism, Sovereignty and the Making of International Law,* chap. 2; and Stephen C. Neff, *War and the Law of Nations: A General History* (New York: Cambridge University Press, 2005), chaps. 6–8. Anghie particularly stresses that interconnected issues of race and culture came to play an important role in European international law doctrine and colonial practices in the late nineteenth century. The outcome of a "racialized" concept of sovereignty, he makes clear, was that non-European states were excluded from the family of nations and had no legal rights over the land they inhabited. Furthermore, there were "virtually no legal restraints" on Europeans in their actions with regard to non-Europeans. In fact, all non-European societies were "outside the sphere of law." Anghie, *Imperialism, Sovereignty and the Making of International Law,* chap. 2, quotations on 99, 103, 62. Paul McHugh, whose work focuses on aboriginal peoples and the law, notes that although the "standard of civilization" came to dominate European legal doctrine regarding indigenous peoples in the second half of the nineteenth century, some jurists, such as Wheaton, proposed the underlying concepts much earlier. McHugh, *Aboriginal Societies and the Common Law,* 201. Legal scholar Lydia Liu observes that Wheaton's approach to international law "cannot but justify the colonial expansion and imperialism of the European powers." Lydia H. Liu, "Henry Wheaton (1785–1848)," in *The Oxford Handbook of the History of International Law,* ed. Bardo Fassbender and Anne Peters (New York: Oxford University Press, 2012), 1132–1136. On late nineteenth-century extraterritorial actions, see Daniel S. Margolies, *Spaces of Law in American Foreign Relations: Extradition and Extraterritoriality in the Borderlands and Beyond, 1877–1898* (Athens: University of Georgia Press, 2011). Margolies explains that in the late nineteenth century powerful nations acted extraterritorially in the land of people who were developmentally, culturally, and religiously different. On the concept of wartime, see Mary L. Dudziak, *War Time: An Idea, Its History, Its Consequences* (New York: Oxford University Press, 2012). Dudziak argues that late nineteenth-century "wars of empire" show how open-ended "wartime" actually has been during much of American and European history. Such wars of empire, which involved perpetual violence, were treated as "matters of imperial governance" that were outside of international law. Ibid, quotation on 31.
49. Eventually, white Americans' racial perspective would lead them to retreat from the earlier conception of the Western Hemisphere as a monolithic unit

that was uniformly distinguishable from the Eastern Hemisphere. As Jacksonians became more prominent in government, their presumption of racial superiority led them to distinguish between Anglo America and Latin America—or, as they usually expressed it, between North and South America. White Americans came to distain nearby Mexico and other Spanish-American countries as "mongrel" nations, and they sought vigorously to avoid that characterization.

50. Rogers M. Smith, *Civic Ideals: Conflicting Visions of Citizenship in U.S. History* (New Haven, CT: Yale University Press, 1997), 54–67, 113–114.
51. These findings complement the work of other scholars who also have identified ways in which violence between whites and Native peoples, as well as European Americans' constituted images of Indians, promoted national identity in the early Republic: Philip J. Deloria's scholarship examines how whites' notions of Indianness played a role in Americans' identity formation, Elise Marienstras discusses the popular representation of Indians and the development of Americans' self-image in the early national era, Susan Scheckel examines how ideas about Indians served a role in creating white Americans' sense of national identity, Carroll Smith-Rosenberg provides an in-depth analysis of how European Americans constituted Indians and African Americans as "Others" in order "to artificially produce a sense of national cohesion for a people with no common heritage," Peter Silver describes how a joint effort to attack and suppress Indians helped heterogeneous European-descended Pennsylvanians develop a more cohesive white American identity in the eighteenth century, and Patrick Griffin describes how American character and ideals developed out of frontier warfare. Philip J. Deloria, *Playing Indian* (New Haven, CT: Yale University Press, 1999); Elise Marienstras, "The Common Man's Indian: The Image of the Indian as a Promoter of National Identity in the Early National Era," in *Native Americans and the Early Republic,* ed. Frederick E. Hoxie et al. (Charlottesville: University Press of Virginia, 1999), 261–296; Susan Scheckel, *The Insistence of the Indian: Race and Nationalism in Nineteenth-Century American Culture* (Princeton, NJ: Princeton University Press, 1998); Carroll Smith-Rosenberg, *This Violent Empire: The Birth of an American National Identity* (Chapel Hill: University of North Carolina Press, 2010), quotation on 21; Peter Silver, *Our Savage Neighbors: How Indian War Transformed Early America* (New York: Norton, 2008); Patrick Griffin, *American Leviathan: Empire, Nation, and Revolutionary Frontier* (New York: Hill and Wang, 2007).
52. Johnson v. McIntosh, 21 U.S. 543 (1823); Cherokee Nation v. Georgia, 30 U.S. 1 (1831). For an analysis of how white Americans of the early Republic "denationalized" Indian polities and saw no place for Native people within the states, see Cynthia Cumfer, "Local Origins of National Indian Policy: Cherokee and Tennessean Ideas about Sovereignty and Nationhood, 1790–1811," *Journal of the Early Republic* 23 (2003): 21–46.
53. On indigenous peoples and territoriality, see McHugh, *Aboriginal Societies and the Common Law,* 294–295 (on the implications of territorial sovereignty) and 149–213 (on sovereignty and indigenous peoples in Anglo-settler communities in the late nineteenth century); and Raustiala, *Does the Constitution Follow the Flag?,* 35–43.

54. For different analyses of Americans' assertion of national distinctiveness, see Eliga H. Gould, "The Making of an Atlantic State System: Britain and the United States, 1795–1825," in *Britain and America Go to War: The Impact of War and Warfare in Anglo-America, 1754–1815,* ed. Julie Flavell and Stephen Conway (Gainesville: University Press of Florida, 2004), 241–265; and Natsu Taylor Saito, *Meeting the Enemy: American Exceptionalism and International Law* (New York: New York University Press, 2010).
55. AC, 1043 (Baldwin).
56. Leonard J. Sadosky, *Revolutionary Negotiations: Indians, Empires, and Diplomats in the Founding of America* (Charlottesville: University of Virginia Press, 2009).
57. For a discussion of how whites in one frontier region used violent private discipline to police Indians, see Brad Asher, *Beyond the Reservation: Indians, Settlers, and the Law in Washington Territory, 1853–1889* (Norman: University of Oklahoma Press, 1999).
58. For a Whig's view of Indian removal, see the analysis of Jeremiah Evarts's "William Penn" essays in Alisse Portnoy, *Their Right to Speak: Women's Activism in the Indian and Slave Debates* (Cambridge, MA: Harvard University Press, 2005), 40–43. The Ord Order of June 1, 1877, which ordered troops into Mexico to capture "lawless" Indians, is described in Margolies, *Spaces of Law,* 9–10.
59. *Legal Borderlands: Law and the Construction of American Borders,* ed. Mary L. Dudziak and Leti Volpp (Baltimore: Johns Hopkins University Press, 2006), originally published as a special issue of *American Quarterly* 57 (September 2005): 593–997. On discussion of ways in which law has been suspended for certain groups ("coolies," immigrants, and African Americans), see the essays in the section titled "Borders of Identity"; for ways in which law has been suspended for certain places (Guano Islands and Guantánamo), see the essays in the section titled "Borders of Territory." On the concept of the "ideological gap," see Dudziak and Volpp, introduction to Dudziak and Volpp, *Legal Borderlands,* 1–18, at 3–4.
60. Linda K. Kerber, "Toward a History of Statelessness," in Dudziak and Volpp, *Legal Borderlands,* 135–157; Linda K. Kerber, "The Stateless as the Citizen's Other: A View from the United States," *American Historical Review* 112, no. 1 (February 2007): 1–34.

6. RACE AND TERRITORIALITY

1. Publications discussing blacks' role in the Florida campaigns include Jane G. Landers, *Atlantic Creoles in the Age of Revolutions* (Cambridge, MA: Harvard University Press, 2010), chap. 5; Jane G. Landers, *Black Society in Spanish Florida* (Urbana: University of Illinois Press, 1999), chap. 10; Gerald Horne, *Negro Comrades of the Crown: African Americans and the British Empire Fight the U.S. before Emancipation* (New York: New York University Press, 2012), chap. 6; Nathaniel Millett, *The Maroons of Prospect Bluff and Their Quest for Freedom in the Atlantic World* (Gainesville: University Press of Florida, 2013); Nathaniel Millett, "Defining Freedom in the Atlantic Borderlands of the Revolutionary Southeast," *Early American Studies* 5, no. 2 (2007): 367–394; Nathaniel Millett, "Britain's 1814 Occupation of Pensacola and America's Response: An Episode

of the War of 1812 in the Southeastern Borderlands," *Florida Historical Quarterly* 84, no. 2 (2005): 229–255; John D. Milligan, "Slave Rebelliousness and the Florida Maroon," *Prologue* 6, no. 1 (1974): 4–18; J. Leitch Wright, Jr., "A Note on the First Seminole War as Seen by the Indians, Negroes, and Their British Advisers," *Journal of Southern History* 34 (November 1968): 565–575; Bruce Edward Twyman, *The Black Seminole Legacy and North American Politics, 1693–1845* (Washington, DC: Howard University Press, 1999); Kenneth Wiggins Porter, "Negroes and the Seminole War, 1817–1818," *Journal of Negro History* 36, no. 3 (1951): 249–280; Claudio Saunt, *A New Order of Things: Property, Power, and the Transformation of the Creek Indians, 1733–1816* (New York: Cambridge University Press, 1999), chap. 12; James W. Covington, "The Negro Fort," *Gulf Coast Historical Review* 5, no. 2 (1990): 78–91; Joseph Becton, "Old Hickory and the Negro Fort," *Pensacola History Illustrated* 2, no. 2 (1986): 25–32; and Rembert W. Patrick, *Aristocrat in Uniform: General Duncan L. Clinch* (Gainesville: University of Florida Press, 1963), chap. 3. For a highly critical account published in 1858, see Joshua R. Giddings, *The Exiles of Florida: Or the Crimes Committed by Our Government against the Maroons, Who Fled from South Carolina and Other Slave States, Seeking Protection under Spanish Laws* (Columbus, OH: Follett, Foster, 1858; repr. Baltimore: Black Classic Press, 1997).

Most textbooks on African American history omit the Seminole War and devote little attention to blacks' military role in the Gulf region. Jan R. Carew, "United We Stand! Joint Struggles of Native Americans and African Americans in the Columbian Era," *Monthly Review* 44, no. 3 (1992): 103–127, observes that scholarly accounts of the war ignore blacks' crucial role because it was intentionally omitted from or misrepresented in contemporary records. Also noting the contemporary erasure of blacks' role are Horne, *Negro Comrades,* 35; Twyman, *Black Seminole Legacy;* Porter, "Negroes and the Seminole War"; and Giddings, *Exiles of Florida.* On southerners' tendency to downplay slave resistance in general, see John Hope Franklin and Loren Schweninger, *Runaway Slaves: Rebels on the Plantation* (New York: Oxford University Press, 1999), chap. 11; and Matthew Mason, *Slavery and Politics in the Early American Republic* (Chapel Hill: University of North Carolina Press, 2006), 125–129. On American slaves and the law, see especially Thomas D. Morris, *Southern Slavery and the Law, 1619–1860* (Chapel Hill: University of North Carolina Press, 1996).

There are no scholarly publications that provide in-depth analysis of the legality of U.S. armed hostilities against African-descended people during the Florida campaigns of 1816–1818. However, a few scholars have included the Seminole War in broader historical studies. Mary Frances Berry includes relevant discussion of issues arising in Florida in the 1810s in her important study of constitutional racism in American history, *Black Resistance/White Law: A History of Constitutional Racism in America* (New York: Penguin Books, 1971, 1994), chap. 4. Don E. Fehrenbacher also examines related issues in *The Slaveholding Republic: An Account of the United States Government's Relations to Slavery* (New York: Oxford University Press, 2001). On the history of race and slavery issues in early American foreign relations, see also David F. Ericson, *Slavery in the American Republic: Developing the Federal Government, 1791–1861* (Lawrence: University Press of Kansas, 2011), chap. 5.

There is little published scholarship analyzing the application of international legal doctrine or sovereignty principles to African-descended people in early nineteenth-century North America. Two notable exceptions are Henry J. Richardson III, *The Origins of African-American Interests in International Law* (Durham, NC: Carolina Academic Press, 2008), which describes the history of African Americans' claims under international law through 1815; and Seymour Drescher and Paul Finkelman, "Slavery," in *The Oxford Handbook of the History of International Law,* ed. Bardo Fassbender and Anne Peters (New York: Oxford University Press, 2012), 890–916, which provides an overview of the history of slavery and international law.

2. Landers, *Black Society in Spanish Florida;* Landers, *Atlantic Creoles;* Christina Snyder, *Slavery in Indian Country: The Changing Face of Captivity in Early America* (Cambridge, MA: Harvard University Press, 2010), chap. 8; John J. TePaske, "The Fugitive Slave: Intercolonial Rivalry and Spanish Slave Policy, 1687–1764," in *Eighteenth-Century Florida and Its Borderlands,* ed. Samuel Proctor (Gainesville: University Presses of Florida, 1975), 1–12; Milligan, "Slave Rebelliousness"; and Patrick Riordan, "Finding Freedom in Florida: Native Peoples, African Americans, and Colonists, 1670–1816," *Florida Historical Quarterly* 75, no. 1 (1996): 24–43. On blacks living among Seminoles, see Saunt, *New Order of Things,* chap. 5; J. Leitch Wright, Jr., *Creeks and Seminoles: The Destruction and Regeneration of the Muscogulge People* (Lincoln: University of Nebraska Press, 1986), chap. 7; Kevin Mulroy, *The Seminole Freedmen: A History* (Norman: University of Oklahoma Press, 2007), chap. 1; Kenneth Wiggins Porter, *The Black Seminoles: History of a Freedom-Seeking People* (Gainesville: University Press of Florida, 1996), 5–7; and Jane L. Landers, "Traditions of African American Freedom and Community in Spanish Colonial Florida," in *The African American Heritage of Florida,* ed. David R. Colburn and Jane L. Landers (Gainesville: University Press of Florida, 1995), 17–41. For different perspectives on blacks' and Indians' overlapping yet distinct experiences in early America, see especially *Confounding the Color Line: The Indian-Black Experience in North America,* ed. James F. Brooks (Lincoln: University of Nebraska Press, 2002); David E. Wilkins, "African Americans and Aboriginal Peoples: Similarities and Differences in Historical Experiences," *Cornell Law Review* 90 (2005): 515–530; Mary Young, "Racism in Red and Black: Indians and Other Free People of Color in Georgia Law, Politics, and Removal Policy, *Georgia Historical Quarterly* 73 (1989): 492–518; and Daniel R. Mandell, "Shifting Boundaries of Race and Ethnicity: Indian-Black Intermarriage in Southern New England, 1760–1880," *Journal of American History* 85 (1998): 466–501.

3. Governor James Glen to the South Carolina Commons House of Assembly, December 11, 1749, describing and quoting from his June–August 1749 letters to the lords commissioners for trade and plantations, printed in *The Colonial Records of South Carolina: The Journal of the Commons House of Assembly, 28 March 1749–19 March 1750,* ed. J. H. Easterby (Columbia: South Carolina Archives Department, 1962), 338–339; Glen to Commons House of Assembly, May 5, 1750, printed in *The Colonial Records of South Carolina: The Journal of the Commons House of Assembly, April 1750–31 August 1751,* ed. R. Nicholas Olsberg (Columbia: University of South Carolina Press, 1974), 92; TePaske, "Fugitive Slave," 10. During the War of Jenkin's Ear, Georgia colonists destroyed Fort Mose but

were unsuccessful in defeating the Spanish in Florida (1740, 1742, 1743); Spanish forces also unsuccessfully invaded Georgia (1742). On Fort Mose (sometimes spelled Mosa or Moosa), see Landers, *Black Society,* chap. 2.

4. Four good examples of revolutionary-era petitions and memorials by African Americans appear on the website of the National Humanities Center: petitions by Prince Hall to the Massachusetts General Court, February 27, 1788; by slaves of New Haven to the Connecticut General Assembly, 1788; by "Free-Men of Colour" to the South Carolina Senate, 1791; and by four free African Americans to Congress, January 23, 1797, available at http://nationalhumanitiescenter.org/pds/maai/community/text4/text4read.htm, accessed March 30, 2013.
5. Henry J. Richardson III, "The 2010–2011 Mitchell Lecture," *Buffalo Human Rights Law Review* 17 (2011): 1–23; Richardson, *Origins of African-American Interests in International Law.*
6. Richard K. Murdoch, "The Seagrove-White Stolen Property Agreement of 1797," *Georgia Historical Quarterly* 42, no. 3 (1958): 258–276.
7. Altogether, it was estimated that by 1814 British officers Edward Nicolls and George Woodbine had trained and armed about one thousand blacks in Florida, including those at Prospect Bluff and also some on Cumberland Island in East Florida and some at Pensacola. After the war, former marine Robert Ambrister carried on the military training effort along the Gulf Coast. Wright, *Creeks and Seminoles,* 165–166, 182, 172. On blacks' military role more generally, see Landers, *Black Society,* chap. 9; Horne, *Negro Comrades,* chaps. 2–5; and Gene Allen Smith, *The Slaves' Gamble: Choosing Sides in the War of 1812* (New York: Palgrave Macmillan, 2013). On fear of black soldiers, see *Annals of Congress,* House, 15th Cong., 1st sess., 1574 (Alexander Smyth); Porter, *Black Seminoles,* 11; and Mulroy, *Seminole Freedmen,* 15–16. Edmund P. Gaines's report on the fort's occupants is in Gaines to Alexander Dallas, May 22, 1815, and deposition of Samuel Jervais, May 9, 1815, enclosed in a letter from Gaines to Dallas, May 14, 1815, ASP-FR, 4:552, 551. Later estimates appear in Secretary of War William H. Crawford to Andrew Jackson, March 15, 1816, and Jackson to Mauricio de Zúñiga, April 23, 1816, included in *Letter from the Secretary of War Transmitting . . . Information in Relation to the Destruction of the Negro Fort, in East Florida,* February 2, 1819 (Washington: E. De Krafft, 1819), 5, 8–9; Lieutenant Colonel Duncan L. Clinch to Adjutant General Robert Butler, August 2, 1816, printed in *National Intelligencer* (Washington, DC), November 15, 1819; and Clinch to Governor David B. Mitchell, August 4, 1816, printed in *City Gazette and Daily Advertiser* (Charleston, SC), August 22, 1816. For a recent in-depth study of the origins of the inhabitants of the fort and the history of the community from 1814 to 1816, see Millett, *Maroons of Prospect Bluff.* Millett estimates that the population of the Prospect Bluff community reached a peak of between 600 and 750 inhabitants just prior to the British departure in early 1815 and that its average population between May 1815 and July 1816 was around 300 to 400 people. Ibid., 142–145.
8. Saunt, *New Order of Things,* 273; *Savannah (GA) Journal,* June 26, 1816, reprinted in *Star and North-Carolina State Gazette* (Raleigh, NC), July 19, 1816.
9. Commodore Daniel T. Patterson to Secretary of the Navy Benjamin W. Crowninshield, August 15, 1816, included in *Letter from the Secretary of the Navy Transmitting . . . Documents relating to the Destruction of the Negro Fort in East Florida,*

February 1, 1819 (Washington: E. De Krafft, 1819), 13–14; John Quincy Adams to George W. Erving, November 28, 1818, ASP-FR, 4:539–545; Gaines to Jackson, March 20, 1816, Jackson to Gaines, April 8, 1816, Jackson to Zúñiga, April 23, 1816, Gaines to Clinch, May 23, 1816, Jackson to Crawford, June 15, 1816, included in *Letter from the Secretary of War Transmitting . . . Information in Relation to the Destruction of the Negro Fort, in East Florida,* February 2, 1819, 16–17, 10–11, 8–9, 23–24, 11–12.

10. For contemporary accounts of the destruction of the fort at Prospect Bluff, see documents included in *Letter from the Secretary of the Navy Transmitting . . . Documents relating to the Destruction of the Negro Fort in East Florida,* February 1, 1819, especially Sailing Master Jairus Loomis to Patterson, August 13, 1816, and Patterson to Crowninshield, August 15, 1816, 15–17, 13–14. See also Clinch to Butler, August 2, 1816, printed in *National Intelligencer,* November 15, 1819; Clinch to Mitchell, August 4, 1816, printed in *City Gazette and Daily Advertiser* (Charleston, SC), August 22, 1816; and Marcus C. Buck to his father, August 14, 1816, printed in *Union* (Washington, KY), September 27, 1816. Loomis reported that 270 people were killed in the fort. Recently, historians have argued that, in fact, most occupants had already left Prospect Bluff before the explosion and that casualties announced by the sailing master and other witnesses were exaggerated. Nathaniel Millett concludes that "[i]n all probability no more than a few dozen maroons died in the American destruction of the fort," while Claudio Saunt similarly estimates that "probably no more than forty [people] lost their lives." Millett, *Maroons of Prospect Bluff,* 144; Saunt, *New Order of Things,* 288. It is also uncertain how many black people were captured from the Prospect Bluff area and then sent to Pensacola or the United States as slaves. Army doctor Marcus Buck estimated "more than one hundred fugitive negroes apprehended," but, in his report to Butler and in a letter to Governor Mitchell, Clinch was vague about how many captives were taken in the expedition. Whatever the number was, Clinch reported that there were some African-descended people from the Prospect Bluff area whom the Americans took back to Camp Crawford (Fort Scott) in Georgia as slaves, allegedly because they belonged to citizens of the state. In his 1856 account, Joshua Giddings referred to the 1816 attack as the "first slave-catching expedition undertaken by the Federal Government." Giddings, *Exiles of Florida,* 39.
11. Patterson to Crowninshield, August 15, 1816, included in *Letter from the Secretary of the Navy Transmitting . . . Documents relating to the Destruction of the Negro Fort in East Florida,* February 1, 1819, 13–14.
12. "Our Southern Border," *Petersburg (VA) Intelligencer,* reprinted in *Camden (SC) Gazette,* September 5, 1816.
13. Richard G. Lowe, "American Seizure of Amelia Island," *Florida Historical Quarterly* 45, no. 1 (July 1966): 18–30, provides a useful overview of the U.S. occupation of the island in 1817. Andrew Jackson described the 1818 expedition in his military reports: Jackson to Secretary of War John C. Calhoun, March 25, April 8, April 9, April 20, April 26, May 5, and June 2, 1818, ASP-MA, 1:698–699, 699–700, 700, 700–701, 701, 701–702, 708–709. On the slave Fernando—renamed Polydore when Jackson took him to Tennessee—see Landers, *Atlantic Creoles,* 184–186, 191–192, 310, 312. It is unclear how many other African-descended inhabitants of Florida were captured and enslaved

as a result of the 1818 campaign. Nathaniel Millett concludes that "the vast majority" of inhabitants of the black towns along the Suwannee River fled south to a settlement known as Angola, not far from Tampa Bay. Millett, *Maroons of Prospect Bluff,* 245.

14. Christopher R. Waldrep, "Jacksonian America," in *Lynching in America: A History in Documents,* ed. Christopher R. Waldrep (New York: New York University Press, 2006), 41–42, quotations on 41.
15. Jackson to Francisco Caso y Luengo, April 6, 1818, AC, Appendix, 2199–2200, quotations on 2199 ("savage foe" and "negro brigands"); Jackson to Calhoun, May 5, 1818, AC, Appendix, 2189–2193, quotation on 2191 ("asylum"); Jackson to Rachel Jackson, April 10, 1818, in *The Papers of Andrew Jackson,* ed. Harold D. Moser et al., 9 vols. (Knoxville: University of Tennessee Press, 1994), 4:191, quotation on 191 ("[b]reak down the hostile savages"); Jackson to José Masot, May 24, 1818, AC, Appendix, 2219–2223; Jackson to Calhoun, June 2, 1818, AC, Appendix, 2207–2210; Gaines to the Seminole chiefs, [August 1817], AC, Appendix, 2037–2038, quotations on 2038; Alexander Arbuthnot to John Arbuthnot, April 2, 1818, AC, Appendix, 2245–2246, quotation on 2246; William McIntosh to Mitchell, April 13, 1818, printed in *Georgia Journal* (Milledgeville, GA), April 28, 1818.
16. On the content of American slave law, see especially Morris, *Southern Slavery and the Law.*
17. AC, 786, 797, 802, 804–805 (Charles F. Mercer, quotations on 802, 804), 988–989 (Timothy Fuller, quotation on 989).
18. Emer de Vattel, *The Law of Nations, or Principles of Natural Law, Applied to the Conduct and Affairs of Nations and Sovereigns* (London: G., G., and J. Robinson, 1797), 2:7:84; Henry Wheaton, *History of the Law of Nations in Europe and America, from the Earliest Times to the Treaty of Washington, 1842* (New York: Gould, Banks, 1845), 739–740. On territorial sovereignty, see Kal Raustiala, *Does the Constitution Follow the Flag? The Evolution of Territoriality in American Law* (New York: Oxford University Press, 2009), chap. 2; and Daniel S. Margolies, *Spaces of Law in American Foreign Relations: Extradition and Extraterritoriality in the Borderlands and Beyond, 1877–1898* (Athens: University of Georgia Press, 2011). On British searches of American ships and impressment of American sailors, see Paul A. Gilje, *Free Trade and Sailors' Rights in the War of 1812* (New York: Cambridge University Press, 2013).
19. For analysis of the interest-convergence theory—that governments only advance blacks' interests when doing so also serves white policy-makers' interests—see Derrick Bell, *Silent Covenants: Brown v. Board of Education and the Unfulfilled Hopes for Racial Reform* (New York: Oxford University Press, 2004).
20. TePaske, "Fugitive Slave," 10, citing Archivo General de Indias, Santo Domingo, Legajo 2584, Carta del governador de la Florida al rey [Letter from the governor of Florida to the king], February 15, 1750.
21. For example, see Henry Baldwin's comments, AC, 1042, 1044.
22. Margolies, *Spaces of Law.* Recently, the issue of extraterritorial abduction and assassination has been the subject of numerous law review articles. One author concludes: "A State that conducts, authorizes, supports, or sponsors extraterritorial abduction violates a well established principle of international law. When one State exercises its police power in the territory of another

State, it exceeds its sphere of jurisdiction permitted under international law, and it violates a fundamental tenet of international law, the respect for the sovereignty and territorial integrity of States." Jianming Shen, "Responsibilities and Jurisdiction Subsequent to Extraterritorial Apprehension," *Denver Journal of International Law and Policy* 23 (Fall 1994): 43–85.

23. The Fugitive Slave Act of 1793 is in Stat., 1:302–305. On fugitive slaves and slave-catchers, see especially Franklin and Schweninger, *Runaway Slaves;* and Sally Haddon, *Slave Patrols: Law and Violence in Virginia and the Carolinas* (Cambridge, MA: Harvard University Press, 2003). On interstate comity, see Paul Finkelman, *An Imperfect Union: Slavery, Federalism, and Comity* (Chapel Hill: University of North Carolina Press, 1981). For an example of a case in which a southern court refused to punish men who had kidnapped an alleged slave from a free state, see *Ohio v. Forbes and Armitage,* which was tried in Franklin Circuit Court of Kentucky, April 10, 1846, cited in Finkelman, *Imperfect Union,* 201n51. In January 1818, just a few months before the spring 1818 invasion of Florida, Congress considered a bill that would have strengthened the 1793 Fugitive Slave Law to make it easier to reclaim fugitive slaves. Among the three members of the subcommittee that drafted the bill was Richard C. Anderson, who defended the Florida campaigns during the congressional debate of January–February 1819. The House and Senate were unable to resolve their differences over the provisions of the bill, so it did not pass. Stanley W. Campbell, *The Slave Catchers: Enforcement of the Fugitive Slave Law, 1850–1860* (Chapel Hill: University of North Carolina Press, 1971), 9.
24. *The Statutes at Large of South Carolina,* ed. Thomas Cooper and David J. McCord, 10 vols. (Columbia, SC: A.S. Johnston, 1836–1873), 7:397–417, sec. 47 (1740); *The Colonial Records of the State of Georgia,* ed. Allen D. Candler, 31 vols. (Atlanta: C. P. Byrd, 1904, 1910, 1911), 18:102–144 (1755). About twenty-five miles south of Amelia Island, the northernmost point of the St. Johns River was south of the Georgia-Florida boundary at the St. Marys River.
25. Attorney General Charles Lee to Secretary of State Timothy Pickering, January 26, 1797, in *Official Opinions of the Attorneys General of the United States,* ed. Benjamin F. Hall (Washington, DC: Robert Farnham, 1852), 1:68. On the U.S.-Canadian border, see *Freedom's Conditions in the U.S.-Canadian Borderlands in the Age of Emancipation,* ed. Tony Freyer and Lyndsay Campbell (Durham, NC: Carolina Academic Press, 2011).
26. AC, 676 (Smyth), 1125 (James Ervin). For scholarly discussion of ways in which military activities to protect slavery furthered the development of the American nation, see Fehrenbacher, *Slaveholding Republic;* and Ericson, *Slavery in the American Republic,* chap 5.
27. See, for example, "Cruel and Unprecedented Murder!" *Richmond (VA) Enquirer,* August 31, 1814.
28. AC, 1039–1040 (Baldwin, "savage negro war" quotation on 1039, "assembled and armed" quotation on 1040), 1109, 1113 (John Floyd, "rebellious slaves," "fiends," "murder, indiscriminately," and "banditti" quotations on 1113), 836 (George F. Strother), 674–675 (Smyth); *Annals of Congress,* House, 15th Cong., 1st sess., 1574 (Smyth quotation).
29. AC, 800–804 (Mercer), 988–989 (Fuller). Jairus Loomis and James Bassett, "Application for Prize Money on the Destruction of a Fort," March 24, 1818,

American State Papers: Naval Affairs, 1:502; H.R. 158, A Bill Authorizing the Payment of a Sum of Money to the Officers and Crews of Gunboats No. 148 and 154, March 24, 1818, passed in the House January 14, 1819 but rejected by the Senate February 8, 1819, *Journal of the House of Representatives* (Washington: E. De Krafft, 1818 [*sic*]), 12:185; *Journal of the Senate* (Washington: E. De Krafft, 1818 [*sic*]), 8:235. Two decades later, in 1839, Congress awarded $5,465 in prize money to the two sailing masters, Loomis and Bassett, or their heirs. An Act for the Relief of Jarius [*sic*] Loomis and Heirs of James Basset [*sic*], Stat., 6:778 (1839).

30. An Act for the Punishment of Certain Crimes against the United States, April 30, 1790, Stat., 1:112; Themistocles, "To the Honorable Henry Clay, Speaker of the House of Representatives," *National Register* (Washington, DC), January 30, 1819; Jackson to Crawford, April 24, 1816, in *Letter from the Secretary of War Transmitting . . . Information in Relation to the Destruction of the Negro Fort, in East Florida,* February 2, 1819. Although explicit reference to fugitive slaves as "land pirates" was not common, it seems that most Americans felt comfortable with the concept. In place of "pirate," however, most people used the word "outlaw," which had an equivalent legal effect. In any case, there does not seem to have been any public challenge to the notion that fugitive slaves could be viewed as "pirates." The term "land pirate" was also used sporadically in the early nineteenth century in reference to people who habitually robbed people on land, alternatively called "highwaymen" or "bandits." At other times the phrase referred to slave stealers, slave traders, land grabbers, or people who stole from shipwrecked boats.

For Vattel on pirates, see *Law of Nations,* 1:6:233. For comprehensive legal analysis of the history of the law of piracy, see Alfred P. Rubin, *The Law of Piracy* (Newport, RI: Naval War College Press, 1988, repr. Honolulu, HI: University Press of the Pacific, 2006). For thoughtful analysis of the concepts of jurisdiction, sovereignty, and piracy in the early modern era, see Lauren Benton, *A Search for Sovereignty: Law and Geography in European Empires, 1400–1900* (New York: Cambridge University Press, 2010), chap. 3. Further discussion of the pirate concept appears in the conclusion of this book.

31. AC, 1040–1041 (Baldwin), quotation on 1040. Baldwin later became a Jackson appointee to the U.S. Supreme Court—and was the only justice to oppose the liberation of the Amistad slaves.
32. Ibid., 1040–1041 (Baldwin), quotation on 1040.
33. On the presumption of slave status based on race, see Morris, *Southern Slavery and the Law,* 21–29; and Landers, *Black Society,* 44.
34. State and federal government failure to provide legal protection to blacks, blatantly evident in the events of 1816–1818, was endemic in early American history. This theme appears prominently in Mary Francis Berry's *Black Resistance/White Law.* Additionally, a wide range of scholars focusing on different time periods or topics has made parallel arguments about the unequal protection of blacks (e.g., Randall Kennedy) and, more broadly, about the racist presumptions and bias of American law (e.g., A. Leon Higginbotham, Jr.). Randall Kennedy, *Race, Crime, and the Law* (New York: Vintage Books, 1997), chap. 2; Leon Higginbotham, Jr., *Shades of Freedom: Racial Politics and Presumptions of the American Legal Process* (New York: Oxford University Press, 1996).

35. William Blackstone, *Commentaries on the Laws of England,* 4 vols. (Oxford, UK: Clarendon Press, 1765–1769), book 4, chap. 24, p. 315. On the history of outlawry in England, see Melissa Sartore, *Outlawry, Governance, and Law in Medieval England* (New York: Peter Lang, 2013).
36. *Statutes at Large of South Carolina,* 7:352–365, preamble (1712), and 7:371–384, preamble (1722). The language is quoted from the 1712 law; there are some slight variations in the 1722 version, most notably that Negroes and slaves were unworthy of being governed by the laws, customs and practices of "England" rather than of "this Province." The South Carolina case is *Ex Parte* Boylston, 33 S.C.L. 20, 2 Strob. 41 (1847), quoted in Andrew W. Fede, "Legitimized Violent Slave Abuse in the American South, 1619–1865: A Case Study of Law and Social Change in Six Southern States," *American Journal of Legal History* 29, no. 2 (1985): 93–150, on 150.
37. Thomas Jefferson, "A Bill concerning Slaves," 1779, available at *Digital History,* ed. Steven Mintz and Sara McNeil, 2013, ID 4108, www.digitalhistory.uh.edu, accessed June 12, 2014.
38. Under South Carolina and Georgia laws, slaves were entitled to a trial when accused of certain criminal acts, and under certain circumstances they were also permitted to bring petitions to court to assert their freedom. So slaves were not entirely outside law. *Statutes at Large of South Carolina,* 7:397–417, secs. 1, 9–19 (1740); *Colonial Records of the State of Georgia,* 18:102–144, secs. 1, 8–19 (1755), 19(1):209–249, secs. 1, 7–19. For Christopher R. Waldrep's analysis of violence against slaves, see *Roots of Disorder: Race and Criminal Justice in the American South, 1817–80* (Urbana: University of Illinois Press, 1998), chap. 2.
39. *The State Records of North Carolina,* vols. 23–25 (Laws, 1669–1790), ed. Walter Clark (Goldsboro, NC: Nash Brothers, 1905–1906), 23:62–66, sec. 9 (1715–1716), 23:191–204, sec. 45, 23:388–390, sec. 9, 23:488–489, sec. 6, 23:975–976, sec. 3; *Statutes at Large of South Carolina,* 7:343–347, secs. 9, 12 (1691); "Governor Archdale's Lawes," Department of Archives and History, Columbia, SC, fols. 60–61, secs. 12, 14, 17 (1696); *Statutes at Large of South Carolina,* 2:280–281, secs. 4–6 (1701), 7:352–365, secs. 2, 14, 15, 19, 24, 30 (1712), 7:371–384, secs. 16, 17, 21, 26, 31 (1722), 3:395–399, sec. 2 (1734), 7:397–417, secs. 5, 17, 25, 27, 47, 49, 56 (1740), 7:420–425, secs. 1, 2, 3 14 (1751); *Colonial Records of the State of Georgia,* 18:102–144 (1755), 18:225–235 (1757), 19(1):209–249, secs. 5, 23, 24, 42 (1770). Virginia set the earliest model for legislation permitting the killing of fugitive slaves. A 1672 law provided that it was lawful to "kill or wound" any runaway slave who resisted apprehension if a warrant had been issued for the slave. Twenty years later, another law provided that any person authorized to apprehend slaves who were "unlawfully absent" from their plantations could "kill and destroy" any of them who "shall resist, runaway, or refuse to deliver and surrender him or themselves" to such person. An Act for the Apprehension and Suppression of Runawayes, Negroes and Slaves, September 1672, and An Act for Suppressing Outlying Slaves, Virginia, April 1691, in *The Statutes at Large: Being a Collection of All the Laws of Virginia, from the First Session of the Legislature, in the Year 1619,* ed. William Waller Hening, 13 vols. (vol. 2, New York: R. and W. and G. Bartow, 1823; vol. 3, Philadelphia: Thomas Desilver, 1823), 2:299–300, 3:86–88.

40. Somerset v. Stewart, 98 E.R. 499 (1772); Eliga H. Gould, *Among the Powers of the Earth: The American Revolution and the Making of a New World Empire* (Cambridge, MA: Harvard University Press, 2012), chap. 3, quotations on 94 and 107. See also Gould, chapters 2 and 5, for a discussion of the colonial law of slavery and of Britain's effort to bring colonial America into Europe's diplomatic republic—especially as that effort was tied to the British abolitionist movement.
41. Fede, "Legitimized Violent Slave Abuse."
42. *Carolina Centinel* (New Bern, NC), September 26, 1818. For other advertisements for outlawed slaves, see "Outlawry," *Cape Fear (NC) Recorder,* April 14, 1821, reprinted in *New-York Evening Post,* May 10, 1821 (slave Cupid, alleged owner Robert W. Brown); *North-Carolina Journal* (Halifax, NC), June 27, 1796 (slave Solomon, owner Sterling Peebles); *Carolina Federal Republican* (New Bern, NC), September 27, 1817 (slaves John and Joe, owner Edmund Hatch, Sr.); and *Carolina Centinel,* March 23, 1822 (slave John Brimmage, owner John R. Good). These early nineteenth-century proclamations closely followed the template of colonial-era outlawry publications. See the advertisement in *North-Carolina Magazine; or, Universal Intelligencer* (New Bern, NC), January 4, 1765 (slaves Peter, Abraham, and Ben, owner Thomas Clifford Howe). Outlawry in North Carolina continued into the 1850s. Fede, "Legitimized Violent Slave Abuse," 113.

    General Jackson was never going to challenge the legitimacy of violent treatment of fugitives. The owner of forty-four slaves in 1820 (and 150 slaves by 1842), the general had once placed an advertisement in the *Tennessee Gazette* offering a fifty-dollar reward for the return of a runaway slave. The advertisement promised that if the slave were found outside of the state, Jackson would also pay "ten dollars extra, for every hundred lashes any person will give him, to the amount of three hundred." Robert V. Remini, *Andrew Jackson,* vol. 1, *The Course of American Empire, 1767–1821* (New York: Harper and Row, 1977; repr. Baltimore: Johns Hopkins University Press, 1998), 133, specifies the number of slaves owned by Jackson. On the advertisement, see Robert P. Hay, " 'And Ten Dollars Extra, for Every Hundred Lashes Any Person Will Give Him, to the Amount of Three Hundred': A Note on Andrew Jackson's Runaway Slave Ad of 1804 and on the Historian's Use of Evidence," *Tennessee Historical Quarterly* 36, no. 4 (1977): 468–478.
43. Themistocles, "To the Honorable Henry Clay, Speaker of the House of Representatives," *National Register,* January 30, 1819.
44. *Statutes at Large of South Carolina,* 7:397–417, sec. 56 (1740); *Journal of the [South Carolina] Commons House of Assembly, 23 April 1750–31 August 1751,* 208, 257; *Columbian Herald* (Charleston, SC), May 28, 1787. For numerous examples of runaways killed, see Herbert Aptheker, "Maroons within the Present Limits of the United States," *Journal of Negro History* 24, no. 2 (1939): 167–184; and Herbert Aptheker, "Additional Data on American Maroons," *Journal of Negro History* 32, no. 4 (1947): 452–460.
45. Jackson to Crawford, June 2, 1816, quoted in David S. Heidler and Jeanne T. Heidler, *Old Hickory's War: Andrew Jackson and the Quest for Empire,* rev. ed. (Baton Rouge: Louisiana State University Press, 2003), 67.

46. *New-York Daily Advertiser,* reprinted in *Otsego (NY) Herald,* March 16, 1818; "Freedom's Battle at Christiana," *Frederick Douglass' Paper* (Rochester, NY), September 25, 1851. Powerful examples of challenges in the 1850s to the fugitive slave law include C. H. Langston, "Should Colored Men Be Subject to the Pains and Penalties of the Fugitive Slave Law?," speech before the U.S. District Court for the Northern District of Ohio, May 12, 1859 (Cleveland: Steam Press of E. Cowles, 1859), printed in *Fugitive Slaves and American Courts,* ed. Paul Finkelman (New York: Garland, 1988), 3–22; and Frederick Douglass's speech against the "Kidnapping Bill" prior to its 1850 passage as the Fugitive Slave Act, printed in *North Star* (Rochester, NY), June 2, 1848. Other abolitionists also criticized the treatment of black slaves or all blacks as "outlaws." See the references to blacks or slaves as "outlaws" in William Jay's written opinion and Horace Mann's speech, quoted, respectively, in "Judge Jay on the Fugitive Law," *North Star,* October 31, 1850; and "Slave Trade and Slavery in the District of Columbia," *National Era* (Washington, DC), April 26, 1849.
47. Robert J. Cottrol, *The Long, Lingering Shadow: Slavery, Race, and Law in the American Hemisphere* (Athens: University of Georgia Press, 2013), chap. 3, quotations on 96, 97, 101, 104. On the Negro Seamen Acts and the legal status of free people of color as they crossed international borders in the early national period, see Michael A. Schoeppner, "Status across Borders: Roger Taney, Black British Subjects, and a Diplomatic Antecedent to the Dred Scott Decision," *Journal of American History* 100, no. 1 (June 2013): 46–67. Schoeppner explains that Attorney General Roger Taney's 1832 opinion about the Negro Seamen Acts—saying they were not unconstitutional or illegal because free blacks could not be part of the British body politic entitled to appeal to treaty rights in U.S. ports—anticipated his later decision as chief justice of the Supreme Court in the *Dred Scott* case (1857). On the concept of "racial nationalism," see William Earl Weeks, *The New Cambridge History of American Foreign Relations,* vol. 1, *Dimensions of the Early American Empire, 1754–1865* (New York: Cambridge University Press, 2013), 123. For an in-depth analysis of ascriptive approaches to American citizenship, see Rogers M. Smith, *Civic Ideals: Conflicting Visions of Citizenship in U.S. History* (New Haven, CT: Yale University Press, 1997). On the role of racialized ideology to build an American national identity during the early national period, see especially the essays in *Race and the Early Republic: Racial Consciousness and Nation-Building in the Early Republic,* ed. Michael A. Morrison and James Brewer Stewart (New York: Rowman and Littlefield, 2002). On connections between race and nationalism in the eighteenth and early nineteenth centuries, see John Wood Sweet, *Bodies Politic: Negotiating Race in the American North, 1730–1830* (Baltimore: Johns Hopkins University Press, 2003). Other examples of historical scholarship dealing with the broad subject of nineteenth-century national expansion, national identity, and racial constructions include Alexander Saxton, *The Rise and Fall of the White Republic: Class Politics and Mass Culture in Nineteenth-Century America* (New York: Verso, 1990); David R. Roediger, *The Wages of Whiteness: Race and the Making of the American Working Class,* rev. ed. (New York: Verso, 1999); and Ronald Takaki, *Iron Cages: Race and Culture in 19th-Century America* (New York: Oxford University Press, 1990). Also of interest is a political science work, Maria Fanis, *Secular Morality and International Security: American and British*

Decisions about War (Ann Arbor: University of Michigan Press, 2011), which analyzes the correlation between the increasing importance of race in American national identity and the United States' decision in the 1840s not to resort to war against Britain (and decision in favor of war against Mexico). On the early history of racial thought in America, see Reginald Horsman, *Race and Manifest Destiny: The Origins of American Racial Anglo-Saxonism* (Cambridge, MA: Harvard University Press, 1981); Winthrop Jordan, *White over Black: American Attitudes toward the Negro, 1550–1812* (Chapel Hill: University of North Carolina Press, 1968); and George M. Frederickson, *The Black Image in the White Mind: The Debate on Afro-American Character and Destiny, 1817–1914* (New York: Harper and Row, 1971). For analysis of how white Americans portrayed the collective status of African-descended people as contrasted with that of American Indians, see Alisse Portnoy, *Their Right to Speak: Women's Activism in the Indian and Slave Debates* (Cambridge, MA: Harvard University Press, 2005), chap. 4.

48. Resolutions of Absalom Jones, Richard Allen, James Forten, and other "People of Colour," January 1817, printed in "Colonization," *American Watchman* (Wilmington, DE), September 20, 1817; letter from Bishop Allen, *Freedom's Journal* (New York, NY), November 2, 1827; "Colonization Society," *Freedom's Journal,* September 7, 1827. John T. McCartney provides a clear description of black nationalist ideas and black integrationist thought in the early Republic in *Black Power Ideologies: An Essay in African-American Political Thought* (Philadelphia: Temple University Press, 1992), chaps. 2 and 3. For different approaches to the early history of black nationalism in early America, see also Patrick Rael, *Black Identity and Black Protest in the Antebellum North* (Chapel Hill: University of North Carolina Press, 2002), chap. 6; and James Sidbury, *Becoming African in America: Race and Nation in the Early Black Atlantic* (New York: Oxford University Press, 2007). Sidbury identifies the period from 1816 to 1826 as "a crucial turning point in the development of a black discourse on African identity in the United States." Ibid, 168.

49. Devon W. Carbado, "Racial Naturalization," in *Legal Borderlands: Law and the Construction of American Borders,* ed. Mary L. Dudziak and Leti Volpp (Baltimore: Johns Hopkins University Press, 2006), 42–66, quotations on 51, 50. The Supreme Court case referred to in the text is Downes v. Bidwell, 182 U.S. 244 (1901).

50. Peter Onuf explains that Jefferson viewed blacks in the United States not only as a permanently distinct nation but also as a captive nation that was necessarily and perpetually in a state of war with the white Republic. Peter S. Onuf, *Jefferson's Empire: The Language of American Nationhood* (Charlottesville: University Press of Virginia, 2000), chap. 5.

51. On the concept of rule of law, see Brian Z. Tamanaha, *On the Rule of Law: History, Politics, Theory* (New York: Cambridge University Press, 2004); Ronald A. Cass, *The Rule of Law in America* (Baltimore: Johns Hopkins University Press, 2001); Paul W. Kahn, *The Reign of Law:* Marbury v. Madison *and the Construction of America* (New Haven, CT: Yale University Press, 1997). The triad of equality, impartiality, and universality is from Kahn, *Reign of Law,* 22. Adherence to a narrow form of rule of law has often been used to make official actions appear to be legitimate when less visible defects in law actually make those actions inequitable and even arbitrary.

52. For analysis of how slavery and the abolitionist movement helped shape evolving understandings of civilization, sovereignty, and international law, see Drescher and Finkelman, "Slavery."

7. MILITARY TRIBUNALS AND RULE OF LAW

1. Two scholarly articles analyze the Arbuthnot/Ambrister trials from a legal perspective: Deborah A. Rosen, "Wartime Prisoners and the Rule of Law: Andrew Jackson's Military Tribunals during the First Seminole War," *Journal of the Early Republic* 28, no. 4 (Winter 2008): 559–595; and Samuel T. Morison, "History and Tradition in American Military Justice," *University of Pennsylvania Journal of International Law* 33 (Fall 2011): 121–171. Legal briefs in recent military tribunal cases that have cited the Arbuthnot/Ambrister trials as precedent include United States v. Ali Hamza Ahmad Suliman al Buhlul, Appellee's Response to Specified Issues, United States Court of Military Commission Review, March 11, 2011, 23–26; and Hamdan v. Rumsfeld, Amicus Curiae Brief of Citizens for the Common Defence, U.S. Supreme Court, February 23, 2006, 8–10.
2. On Alexander Arbuthnot's and Robert Ambrister's backgrounds, trials, and executions, see David S. Heidler and Jeanne T. Heidler, *Old Hickory's War: Andrew Jackson and the Quest for Empire,* rev. ed. (Baton Rouge: Louisiana State University Press, 2003); Frank Lawrence Owsley, Jr., "Ambrister and Arbuthnot: Adventurers or Martyrs for British Honor?" *Journal of the Early Republic* 5 (Fall 1985): 289–308; John K. Mahon, "The First Seminole War, November 21, 1817–May 24, 1818," *Florida Historical Quarterly* 77 (Summer 1998): 62–67; J. Leitch Wright, Jr., "A Note on the First Seminole War as Seen by the Indians, Negroes, and Their British Advisers," *Journal of Southern History* 34 (November 1968): 565–575; Frank Lawrence Owsley, Jr., and Gene A. Smith, *Filibusters and Expansionists: Jeffersonian Manifest Destiny, 1800–1821* (Tuscaloosa: University of Alabama Press, 1997).
3. For a discussion of British policy regarding the United States between the end of the Revolutionary War and the conclusion of the War of 1812, see J. Leitch Wright, Jr., *Britain and the American Frontier, 1783–1815* (Athens: University of Georgia Press, 1975). Britain loomed especially large in the process of American nation-building. Defending against British interference, impressing the British, and establishing an identity that was independent of Britain were all important to Americans in the early national period. See Sam W. Haynes, *Unfinished Revolution: The Early American Republic in a British World* (Charlottesville: University of Virginia Press, 2010); and Kariann Akemi Yokota, *Unbecoming British: How Revolutionary America Became a Postcolonial Nation* (New York: Oxford University Press, 2011). On white Americans' anxiety about British alliance with blacks, see Gerald Horne, *Negro Comrades of the Crown: African Americans and the British Empire Fight the U.S. before Emancipation* (New York: New York University Press, 2012), 5; and Alan Taylor, *The Internal Enemy: Slavery and War in Virginia, 1772–1832* (New York: Norton, 2013), 345, 347.
4. Secretary of State John Quincy Adams to British foreign minister Robert Stewart (Viscount Castlereagh), March 21, 1816, ASP-FR, 4:555.

5. The proceedings of Arbuthnot's and Ambrister's trials are in ASP-MA, 1:721–734. Having examined all the evidence, historian Frank Owsley concludes that the case against Arbuthnot was weak and he should not have been executed. However, he notes, the execution of Ambrister, who had trained and incited Indians and blacks in Florida, might have been justified. Owsley, "Ambrister and Arbuthnot."
6. Past articles or letters published in newspapers describing British treatment of prisoners of war include "Barbarities of the Enemy," *Albany (NY) Argus,* August 17, 1813; "Anglo-Savage Assassination," *Columbian Patriot* (Middlebury, VT), April 12, 1815; General William Henry Harrison to General Vincent, November 3, 1813, printed in *Farmer's Repository* (Charles Town, VA), January 20, 1814; "Old Scraps for News-papers," *True American* (Bedford, PA), September 15, 1813; A Democratic Republican, letter to *The Investigator* (Charleston, SC), November 5, 1812; and "British Humanity," *Statesman* (New York, NY), August 11, 1813.
7. Emer de Vattel, *The Law of Nations, or Principles of Natural Law, Applied to the Conduct and Affairs of Nations and Sovereigns* (London: G., G., and J. Robinson, 1797). On the subjects mentioned in the text, see 3:1:4, 3:15:223 (limitations on private individuals), 2:4:49, 3:1:3, 3:3:26 (national self-defense), 3:3:136–137 (requirement of necessity), 3:8:149, 3:8:140 (prohibition on taking the lives of prisoners of war or other men who have surrendered), 3:8:141, 3:8:149 (punishment of war criminals), 3:8:142 (retaliation), and 3:8:141 (treatment of enemy that did not follow the rules of war).
8. AC, 518, 583 (House committee resolution), 588 (Thomas W. Cobb's resolution), 1132–1136 (vote on those two resolutions). Also rejected by the House was a resolution put forward by a supporter of the U.S. campaigns in Florida. Right before the start of the congressional debate, Representative John W. Campbell proposed a resolution providing that white men who instigated Indians to hostilities or who fought with Indians against the United States be punished as spies. Ibid., 547 (Campbell's motion proposed and rejected).
9. Ibid., 1044–1045 (Henry Baldwin); "General Jackson, Mr. Lacock, Mr. Clay, and Public Sentiment," *National Register* (Washington, DC), March 20, 1819. For drawing my attention to the "court of public opinion," I am indebted to John Wertheimer, who served as commentator for a paper I delivered at an American Society for Legal History conference several years ago. Wertheimer addresses the subject of "the antebellum 'people's court'" at length in chapter 1 of his Ph.D. dissertation, "Free-Speech Fights: The Roots of Modern Free-Expression Litigation in the United States" (Princeton University, 1992), especially on 20–38. I also thank John Wertheimer for referring me to a useful law review publication on the subject, Elizabeth Dale, "A Different Sort of Justice: The Informal Courts of Public Opinion in Antebellum South Carolina," *South Carolina Law Review* 54 (Spring 2003): 627–647, quoted phrase on 630.
10. The Act for Establishing the Rules and Articles for the Government of the Armies of the United States is Stat., 2:359–372 (1806). On the court's lack of jurisdiction, see AC, 516–517 (House committee report), 584 (Cobb), 752 (Henry R. Storrs), 1086 (Thomas S. Williams), 1068–1069 (Philip Reed), 641 (Henry Clay); Algernon Sidney, "General Jackson," letter to the editor,

Richmond (VA) Enquirer, December 22, 1818; "Arbuthnot and Ambrister," *National Intelligencer* (Washington, DC), December 10, 1818, reprinted in *Newport (RI) Mercury,* December 19, 1818. On the categorization of the court as a court-martial, see AC, 815–817 (Charles F. Mercer), 1067 (Reed), 1086 (Williams), 891–892 (Joseph Hopkinson), and 646 (Clay).

11. Minutes of the proceedings of a special court, record of the trials of Alexander Arbuthnot and Robert C. Ambrister, ASP-MA, 1:721–734; AC, 517–518 (House committee report), 817–818 (Mercer), 1067 (Reed), 892 (Hopkinson); "Political," *Union,*" reprinted in *Dedham (MA) Gazette,* December 18, 1818; "Arbuthnot and Ambrister," *Columbian Centinel* (Boston, MA), December 19, 1818; Algernon Sidney, "General Jackson," letter to the editor, *Richmond Enquirer,* December 22, 1818. On the lack of credible evidence, see also the allegations in the June 1818 memorial of Robert Ambrister's father. James Ambrister—who had lived in South Carolina until leaving for the Bahamas with other Tories at the end of American Revolution—referred to the proceedings as a "flagitious mockery of justice" and called for a royal inquiry. James Ambrister to governor of the Bahamas [Charles Cameron], June 29, 1818, printed in "Arbuthnot and Ambrister," *New-England Palladium & Commercial Advertiser* (Boston, MA), September 29, 1818. Most critics of Jackson presumed that a court-martial had to follow the same rules of evidence that governed regular civil courts (House committee report, Cobb, Mercer) or criminal courts (Reed). AC, 517–518 (House committee report), 585 (Cobb), 818 (Mercer), 1067 (Reed).
12. AC, 752 (Storrs), 645 (Clay), 588 (Cobb); *Boston Intelligencer,* December 19, 1818; "Arbuthnot and Ambrister," *New-England Palladium & Commercial Advertiser,* January 29, 1819; "Arbuthnot and Ambrister," *Richmond Enquirer,* December 15, 1818 ("indecent haste"); "Arbuthnot and Ambrister," *National Intelligencer,* December 10, 1818, reprinted in *Newport Mercury,* December 12, 1818; "Arbuthnot and Ambrister," *Columbian Centinel,* December 19, 1818.
13. Congressmen explicitly denying a general's right to execute prisoners included Thomas Williams and James Johnson (AC, 1097, 627–628). Asserting Congress's authority over retaliation: Cobb, Thomas M. Nelson, and Clay (ibid., 587, 618, 644). Claiming the prerequisite of a federal statute punishing a violation of the law of nations: Edward Colston (ibid., 830–831).
14. *Richmond Enquirer,* December 15, 1818; *Boston Intelligencer,* December 19, 1818; "Arbuthnot and Ambrister," *Massachusetts Spy, or Worcester Gazette,* December 16, 1818; "Arbuthnot and Ambrister," *Vermont Intelligencer and Bellows' Falls Advertiser,* December 28, 1818. Arguing in Congress that Jackson had no authority: Mercer and Cobb, AC, 818, 585; arguing that he waived the right: Reed, T. Nelson, and Clay in AC, 1066, 620, 646. The Senate committee's report on the Seminole War is in *Annals of Congress,* Senate, 15th Cong., 2nd sess., 256–268, quotation on 268. Alexander Macomb's treatise was *A Treatise on Martial Law, and Courts-Martial as Practiced in the United States* (Charleston, SC: J. Hoff, 1809; repr. Clark, NJ: Lawbook Exchange, 2007).
15. *Baltimore Telegraph,* reprinted in *Newburyport (MA) Herald,* December 18, 1818; *New-York Daily Advertiser,* May 21, 1818; "Arbuthnot and Ambrister," *Massachusetts Spy, or Worcester Gazette,* December 16, 1818; *Boston Intelligencer,* December 19, 1818; "Arbuthnot and Ambrister," *Richmond Enquirer,* December 15, 1818; Algernon Sidney, "To the Hon. John Quincy Adams, Secretary of

State," *Richmond Enquirer,* January 7, 1819; AC, 830 (Colston), 619 (T. Nelson), 626–627 (J. Johnson), 932 (John Tyler), 893 (Hopkinson), 822 (Mercer).

16. AC, 631–655 (Clay's speech), quotations on 647, 645, 643.
17. Ibid., 934 (Tyler), 892 (Hopkinson), 752 (Storrs), 645 (Clay), 819 (Mercer). The Senate committee did not elaborate on the specific ways in which Jackson had failed to follow the usual forms of justice. Ibid., 268 (Senate committee report quotation).
18. "Arbuthnot and Ambrister," *Massachusetts Spy, or Worcester Gazette,* December 16, 1818; *Baltimore Telegraph,* reprinted in *Newburyport Herald,* December 18, 1818; "Political," *Union,*" reprinted in *Dedham Gazette,* December 18, 1818; Algernon Sidney, "To the Hon. John Quincy Adams, Secretary of State," *Richmond Enquirer,* January 7, 1819.
19. On the concept of rule of law, see Brian Z. Tamanaha, *On the Rule of Law: History, Politics, Theory* (New York: Cambridge University Press, 2004); Ronald A. Cass, *The Rule of Law in America* (Baltimore: Johns Hopkins University Press, 2001); Paul W. Kahn, *The Reign of Law:* Marbury v. Madison *and the Construction of America* (New Haven, CT: Yale University Press, 1997).
20. AC, 845–846 (George F. Strother), 685–696 (Alexander Smyth, quotation on 693), 734–736 (James Tallmadge, Jr.), 904 (Richard C. Anderson), 1047–1051 (Henry Baldwin), 663–664, 669 (Richard M. Johnson), 707 (Francis Jones), 775–779 (James Barbour), 981 (George Poindexter), 1096–1097 (Joseph Desha). A commentator in one newspaper took a different approach to the extraterritoriality issue, based on a fictional crime committed on U.S. soil. The essayist alleged that Arbuthnot and Ambrister had, "within our own dominions," committed an act of treason by instigating a rebellion against the United States. As criminals, the two men were liable for punishment wherever they fled, even if they were on Spanish soil, the writer concluded. Pomponius, "Political," *Rhode-Island American, and General Advertiser* (Providence, RI), October 9, 1818.
21. General orders of Major General Andrew Jackson, April 29, 1818, ASP-MA, 1:734; memorial of Andrew Jackson to the United States Senate, presented February 23, 1820, ASP-MA, 1:754–760, esp. 757; President James Monroe, second annual message to Congress, November 16, 1818, in *The Writings of James Monroe,* ed. Stanislaus Murray Hamilton, 7 vols. (New York: G. P. Putnam's Sons, 1898–1903), 6:75–83, esp. 77; Adams to George W. Erving, November 28, 1818, ASP-FR, 4:539–545. Not surprisingly, the British were unimpressed by Jackson's explanation of legal doctrine. In 1819, a pamphlet written by an English writer dismissed Jackson's "extraordinary" doctrine as expressing an "ignorant interpretation of the term pirate." [J. Freeman Rattenbury], *Narrative of a Voyage to the Spanish Main in the Ship 'Two Friends' . . . with an Appendix Containing a Detail of the Seminole War and the Execution of Arbuthnot and Ambrister* (London: John Miller, 1819), 280.
22. The quotations are from the following: Resolution Approving the Conduct of Major General Andrew Jackson by the House of Representatives and Senate of Mississippi, printed in *Alabama Courier* (Claiborne, AL), March 19, 1819; "Arbuthnot and Ambrister," *Eastern Argus* (Portland, ME), December 22, 1818; *Mississippi State Gazette* (Natchez, MS), June 6, 1818, subsequently reprinted in the *Savannah (GA) Republican,* July 16, 1818 and then in the *Times* (London),

September 3, 1818; AC, 1041 (Baldwin), 846 (Strother), 860, 868 (John Rhea); Junius Brutus, "General Jackson," *National Advocate* (New York, NY), January 16, 1819; and "Foreign Emissaries," *Baltimore Patriot,* June 11, 1818. Accepting that Arbuthnot and Ambrister had no right to treatment as civilized soldiers or prisoners of war under the rules of war, pro-Jackson commentators consigned the two men to various alternative categories—not only "outlaws" but also "pirates," "ruffians," "Indians," "savages," or "wild beasts"—all of which came with undefined, but certainly limited, rights under law. Some argued that they were worse than savages, because they had grown up in a civilized environment. AC, 707 (Jones), 1041 (Baldwin), 846–847 (Strother), 685, 690, 694–695 (Smyth), 613 (John Holmes), 667 (R. Johnson), 732 (Tallmadge); "Jackson's Justification," *Albany Argus,* January 5, 1819; "Indians," *National Advocate,* July 3, 1818; Wyoming, "Arbuthnot and Ambrister," *New-York Columbian,* December 29, 1818; Themistocles, "To the Honorable Henry Clay, Speaker of the House of Representatives," *National Register,* January 30, 1819; "Arbuthnot and Ambrister," *Maryland Censor* (Baltimore, MD), reprinted in *National Advocate,* December 19, 1818. Other state legislatures debating Jackson's conduct in the Seminole War included Pennsylvania, Alabama, and Louisiana. Like Mississippi, the Pennsylvania House of Representatives adopted a resolution approving of Jackson's actions and of Congress's decision not to censure him; the Pennsylvania resolution did not specifically mention the executions. Soon after Alabama was admitted as a state in December of 1819, its legislature endorsed Jackson's conduct in the war. In Louisiana, the state House of Representatives passed a bill for presenting thanks and a sword to Jackson, but the state senate indefinitely postponed any vote on the matter. *Village Record, or Chester and Delaware Federalist* (West Chester, PA), March 31, 1819 (providing text of Pennsylvania resolution dated March 18, 1819); *Camden (SC) Gazette,* January 20, 1820 (reporting Alabama resolution); *Carolina Centinel* (New Bern, NC), February 27, 1819 (providing text of Louisiana bill); *New England Palladium & Commercial Advertiser,* March 19, 1819 (reporting outcome of Louisiana vote on the bill).

23. An Act Vesting in the President of the United States the Power of Retaliation, March 3, 1813, Stat., 2:829–830.
24. AC, 684–689 (Smyth), quotations on 685 ("using means contrary to the laws of war"), 684 ("banditti"), 687 ("incursion[s] for havoc and pillage"), 687 (quotation from treaty commissioners), 684 ("outlaws"). Although noting that both Arbuthnot and Ambrister were punished for their own war crimes, Smyth also described how the principle of retaliation could have justified their executions. Ibid., 689–695 (Smyth).
25. Themistocles, "To the Honorable Henry Clay, Speaker of the House of Representatives," *National Register,* January 30, 1819; "Arbuthnot and Ambrister," *Maryland Censor,* reprinted in *National Advocate,* December 19, 1818; Junius Brutus, "General Jackson," *National Advocate,* January 16, 1819.
26. AC, 1042 (Baldwin), 732 (Tallmadge), 1115 (John Floyd), 1130 (James Ervin), 656–658 (R. Johnson), 688–694, 702–703 (Smyth). Those commentators also made analogies between Jackson's actions and those of George Rogers Clark, Nathanael Greene, and Henry "Light Horse Harry" Lee. However, on the

ground that there was no comparison between the United States and the Seminoles—because the United States was a nation acting lawfully—Jackson's backers denied that there was any analogy between Ambrister and Arbuthnot and foreign fighters in the American Revolution. See, for example, "Communication," *Boston Patriot and Daily Chronicle,* February 11, 1819. For a general discussion of how the U.S. military treated white allies of Indians, see Colin G. Calloway, "Neither White nor Red: White Renegades on the American Indian Frontier," *Western Historical Quarterly* 17 (January 1986): 43–66. Recent studies of the history of U.S. treatment of prisoners of war are Paul J. Springer, *America's Captives: Treatment of POWs from the Revolutionary War to the War on Terror* (Lawrence: University Press of Kansas, 2010); Robert C. Doyle, *The Enemy in Our Hands: America's Treatment of Prisoners of War from the Revolution to the War on Terror* (Lexington: University Press of Kentucky, 2010); and, examining American treatment of wartime captives in the context of the laws of war, Stephanie Carvin, *Prisoners of America's Wars: From the Early Republic to Guantanamo* (New York: Columbia University Press, 2010); the first chapter of each of these books focuses on the American Revolution.

Historian John William Ward provides a good analysis of how Jackson's friends dealt with accusations that he was a dangerous American Napoleon, a man governed by his own will rather than by law. Ward explains that comparing Jackson to Washington was a common way of countering such fears. John William Ward, *Andrew Jackson: Symbol for an Age* (New York: Oxford University Press, 1955), chap. 10. Historian Matthew Warshauer has also found many examples of Jackson and Jacksonians comparing the general to George Washington—as well as examples of Jackson's opponents denying that Jackson was at all like Washington. Matthew Warshauer, "Andrew Jackson as a 'Military Chieftain' in the 1824 and 1828 Presidential Elections: The Ramifications of Martial Law on American Republicanism," *Tennessee Historical Quarterly* 57, no. 1 (1998): 4–23, at 8–10 and 14; Matthew Warshauer, *Andrew Jackson and the Politics of Martial Law: Nationalism, Civil Liberties, and Partisanship* (Knoxville: University of Tennessee Press, 2006), 66.

27. Junius Brutus, "General Jackson," *National Advocate,* January 16, 1819; "Arbuthnot and Ambrister," *Eastern Argus,* December 22, 1818; "General Jackson," *New York Advocate,* reprinted in *Hampden Patriot* (Springfield, MA), December 31, 1818; "Strictures on Mr. Lacock's Report on the Seminole War," March 5, 1819, AC, Appendix, 2350–2361.
28. AC, 1051, 1044–1046 (Baldwin, quotations on 1051, 1044), 664 (R. Johnson quotation), 613 (Holmes).
29. "Arbuthnot and Ambrister," *Massachusetts Spy, or Worcester Gazette,* December 16, 1818.
30. Ibid.; *Baltimore Telegraph,* reprinted in *Newburyport Herald,* December 18, 1818; Algernon Sidney, "To the Hon. John Quincy Adams, Secretary of State," *Richmond Enquirer,* January 7, 1819; "Arbuthnot and Ambrister," *Richmond Enquirer,* December 15, 1818; AC, 517 (House committee report), 267 (Senate committee report), 586 (Cobb), 641–644 (Clay). Clay explained the connection between the status of the Creeks and Seminoles and that of Arbuthnot and Ambrister: since the Florida Indians were "capable of maintaining relations

of peace and war," their hostilities against the United States did not constitute waging private war. Therefore, the two Britons did not take themselves outside the laws of war by allying with them. AC, 641.

31. *Dedham Gazette,* December 18, 1818; "Arbuthnot and Ambrister," *Vermont Intelligencer and Bellows' Falls Advertiser,* December 28, 1818; "Arbuthnot and Ambrister," *Columbian Centinel,* December 19, 1818; *Boston Intelligencer,* December 19, 1818; "Arbuthnot and Ambrister," *Richmond Enquirer,* December 15, 1818; Algernon Sidney, "General Jackson," letter to the editor, *Richmond Enquirer,* December 22, 1818; "Conquest of Pensacola," *Vermont Intelligencer and Bellows' Falls Advertiser,* July 27, 1818; AC, 517 (House committee report), 586 (Cobb), 820, 822 (Mercer), 619 (T. Nelson), 1003 (Timothy Fuller).
32. Jackson to Secretary of War John C. Calhoun, May 5, 1818, ASP-MA, 1:701–702, esp. 702; Jackson to Calhoun, August 10, 1818, ASP-MA, 1:744–745, esp. 745; "Gen. Jackson," *Albany (NY) Register,* reprinted in *American Mercury* (Hartford, CT), January 5, 1819; AC, 1015–1017 (William Henry Harrison), 707 (Jones), 847 (Strother), 614 (Holmes), 699 (Smyth), 1043–1044 (Baldwin), 1115 (Floyd), 1009 (David Walker), 980, 984 (Poindexter), 661 (R. Johnson), 699–703 (Smyth). Ohio representative William Henry Harrison pointed out that the executions would have a salutary effect not only on the southern frontier but also in the Northwest, where there was the threat of a highly dangerous Indian war exacerbated by the potential for the Indians to obtain supplies from British trading posts. AC, 1015–1017 (Harrison).
33. "Jackson's Justification," *Albany Argus,* January 5, 1819; "Foreign Emissaries," *Baltimore Patriot,* June 11, 1818; AC, 849, 838 (Strother).
34. AC, 654 (Clay), 588 (Cobb), 753–754 (Storrs), 797, 819–820 (Mercer), 1001–1002 (Fuller); U.S. Congress, Senate, Select Committee, report on the Seminole War, February 24, 1819, *Annals of Congress,* Senate, 15th Cong., 2nd sess., 256–268, at 267–268; "Arbuthnot and Ambrister," *Columbian Centinel,* December 19, 1818; *Richmond Enquirer,* January 7, 1819, and December 15, 1818.
35. "Arbuthnot and Ambrister," *Columbian Centinel,* December 12, 1818; *City of Washington Gazette,* reprinted in *Hampden Federalist* (Springfield, MA), December 31, 1818; "Outlaws and Pirates," *Kentucky Reporter* (Lexington, KY), May 19, 1819, reprinted in *Poulson's American Daily Advertiser* (Philadelphia, PA), June 4, 1819; "Indian War," *National Messenger* (Washington, DC), reprinted in *Salem (MA) Gazette,* June 12, 1818; *National Intelligencer,* June 19, 1818, reprinted in *New York Evening Post,* June 22, 1818; AC, 1004 (Fuller). Pursuant to the royal decree of January 14, 1819, Spain seized a number of U.S. citizens in South America for having participated in the colonial rebellions but released them by another decree of April 1820. The January 1819 decree is in *British and Foreign State Papers, 1818–1819* (London: James Ridgway, 1835), 1134–1135; documents relating to the Americans subsequently seized in South America are in *British and Foreign State Papers, 1819–1820* (London: James Ridgway, 1834), 1065–1068.
36. AC, 653–655 (Clay), 934 (Tyler), 819 (Mercer); "Arbuthnot and Ambrister," *Massachusetts Spy, or Worcester Gazette,* December 16, 1818; "General Jackson. Direful Effects of Example," *New-York Evening Post,* reprinted in *Rhode-Island American, and General Advertiser,* May 25, 1819; "Arbuthnot and Ambrister," *Connecticut Journal* (New Haven), December 29, 1818; "Arbuthnot and Ambrister," *Columbian Centinel,* December 19, 1818; "Arbuthnot and Ambrister,"

Columbian Centinel, December 12, 1818; Letter from Bostonian, *Boston Daily Advertiser,* January 21, 1819; "Arbuthnot and Ambrister," *New-England Palladium & Commercial Advertiser,* January 29, 1819; "A Warning," *Baltimore Morning Chronicle,* reprinted in *Tennessee Weekly Chronicle* (Clarksville, TN), May 31, 1819; *Connecticut Journal,* April 6, 1819; "Military Despotism," *Rhode-Island American,* reprinted in *Poulson's American Daily Advertiser,* June 8, 1819; "General Jackson," *Poulson's American Daily Advertiser,* September 18, 1920; "Toasts," *Salem Gazette,* July 9, 1919.

37. AC, 980 (Poindexter "political theatre" reference); *Hampden Patriot,* July 8, 1819.
38. "Copy of a Letter from General Jackson to Governor Rabun" [dated August 1, 1818], *Milledgeville (GA) Reflector,* November 10, 1818; *Connecticut Journal,* April 6, 1819; "Democratic Opinions," *Connecticut Mirror* (Hartford, CT), February 1, 1819. The context of the correspondence between Jackson and Rabun was the unauthorized destruction of a Chehaw village on April 23, 1818, by Captain Obed Wright. In the text, the quoted phrase about the liberty of the people is as it was rendered by Jackson rather than as originally stated by Rabun.
39. Bradford Perkins, *Castlereagh and Adams: England and the United States, 1812–1823* (Berkeley: University of California Press, 1964), 289–294, esp. 293; Heidler and Heidler, *Old Hickory's War,* esp. 189–190; William Earl Weeks, *John Quincy Adams and American Global Empire* (Lexington: University Press of Kentucky, 1992), 128–130, 147–150; Robert V. Remini, *Andrew Jackson and His Indian Wars* (New York: Viking, 2001), 166; George Dangerfield, *The Awakening of American Nationalism, 1815–1828* (New York: Harper and Row, 1965), 62–64; Owsley, "Ambrister and Arbuthnot," 306–307. See also Eliga H. Gould, "The Making of an Atlantic State System: Britain and the United States, 1795–1825," in *Britain and America Go to War: The Impact of War and Warfare in Anglo-America, 1754–1815,* ed. Julie Flavell and Stephen Conway (Gainesville: University Press of Florida, 2004), 241–265, at 259–260. The Convention of 1818, agreed upon in December 1818, resolved most of the issues between the United States and Britain that had lingered after the War of 1812.
40. Before the final vote, the House separated the committee's initial resolution disapproving the proceedings in the trial and execution of Arbuthnot and Ambrister into two separate resolutions, one focusing on Arbuthnot and the other on Ambrister. Votes on those resolutions took place in the House of Representatives on February 8, 1819. The proposed resolution to disapprove the trial and execution of Arbuthnot lost by a vote of 108 to 62, while the resolution to condemn the trial and execution of Ambrister lost by a vote of 107 to 63. (The chart in the appendix identifies how each representative voted on the resolutions.) On February 8, the House rejected Representative Cobb's proposed resolution calling for a statute prohibiting the execution of prisoners of war without the approval of the president by a vote of 98 to 57. AC, 1135–1136, 1132.
41. During the American Revolution, Jefferson had spoken up to protect British and German prisoners captured at Saratoga, and after the war he had negotiated a treaty with the king of Prussia guaranteeing humane treatment of prisoners of war. Burrus M. Carnahan, "Reason, Retaliation, and Rhetoric: Jefferson and the Quest for Humanity in War," *Military Law Review* 139 (1993):

83–130; Reginald Horsman, "The Dimensions of an 'Empire for Liberty': Expansion and Republicanism, 1775–1825," *Journal of the Early Republic* 9 (Spring 1989): 1–20.

42. Disagreement over the right of rebellion (such as the Whiskey Rebellion) during the 1790s and disparate contemporary interpretations of the meaning of the election of 1800 exemplified earlier conflicts between law and action. Yet even Thomas Jefferson, who had expressed support for the right of rebellion, regarded Andrew Jackson as "a dangerous man" who was insufficiently restrained by legal principles and process. Historian Sean Wilentz notes that Jefferson considered Jackson "a man of 'terrible' passions, a warrior with little respect for law and constitutions." Sean Wilentz, *The Rise of American Democracy: Jefferson to Lincoln* (New York: Norton, 2005), 248, 851. On the conflicting principles of rule of law and political action based on popular will in the early Republic, see Kahn, *Reign of Law.*

    That Americans of the early Republic were receptive to arguments in favor of popular justice is evidenced by the popularity of James Fenimore Cooper's 1823 novel *The Pioneers.* The final chapters of the novel recount the trial of Natty Bumppo, a "simple, unlettered" frontiersman who allegedly killed a deer illegally, then forcibly resisted the execution of a search warrant in his home and assaulted the man who tried to carry out the search. During the trial, Judge Marmaduke Temple states that he "must be governed by the law," while Bumppo maintains that "there's no guilt in doing what's right." As scholars of law and literature have observed, Cooper highlights the difference between Bumppo, who stands for the principle that conflicts should be governed by common sense and basic moral values, and Temple, who insists that the jury follow the letter of the law. The novel effectively illustrates early Americans' yearning for simple popular justice, those scholars have concluded. James Fenimore Cooper, *The Pioneers; Or, The Sources of the Susquehanna* (New York: Charles Wiley, 1823; repr., New York: Signet, 1964), 329, 346, 354. For an analysis of legal ideas in James Fenimore Cooper's novels, see Robert A. Ferguson, *Law and Letters in American Culture* (Cambridge, MA: Harvard University Press, 1984), 297–304; and David Grimsted, "Rioting in Its Jacksonian Setting," *American Historical Review* 77 (April 1972): 361–397.

43. Waldrep's comments are in *Lynching in America: A History in Documents,* ed. Christopher R. Waldrep (New York: New York University Press, 2006), 41–46; and in Christopher R. Waldrep, "Democracy, and Lynching, in America," in *Signposts: New Directions in Southern Legal History,* ed. Sally E. Hadden and Patricia Hagler Minter (Athens: University of Georgia Press, 2013), 193–217. The 1859 document is James M. Shackleford, "A Little Mob Law in the State of Missouri," *Marshall (MO) Democrat,* July 22, 1859, printed in Waldrep, *Lynching in America,* 78–79. I appreciate Christopher Waldrep's drawing this essay to my attention during a personal conversation at a scholarly conference.

44. For discussion of the Jacksonian and Whig stances on law, see Lawrence Frederick Kohl, *The Politics of Individualism: Parties and the American Character in the Jacksonian Era* (New York: Oxford University Press, 1989), chap. 4. Arthur M. Schlesinger, Jr., argued that Jacksonians were hostile to courts and lawyers because of their democratic and antielitist tendencies. Arthur M.

Schlesinger, Jr., *The Age of Jackson* (New York: Little, Brown, 1945), 322–324. On Jacksonian antilegalism, see especially Grimsted, "Rioting." On the broader early American history of antilegalism, see Richard P. Cole, "Orthodoxy and Heresy: The Nineteenth Century History of the Rule of Law Reconsidered," review of *Heretics in the Temple: Americans Who Reject the Nation's Legal Faith,* by David Ray Papke, *Indiana Law Review* 32 (1999): 1335–1382; Robert W. Gordon, "The American Codification Movement: A Study of Antebellum Legal Reform," *Vanderbilt Law Review* 36 (1983): 431–458; and Richard Ellis, *The Jeffersonian Crisis: Courts and Politics in the Young Republic* (New York: Oxford University Press, 1971). See also Peter Karsten, *Heart versus Head: Judge-Made Law in Nineteenth-Century America* (Chapel Hill: University of North Carolina Press, 1997); Rush Welter, *The Mind of America, 1820–1860* (New York: Columbia University Press, 1975), 82, 421; and Anton-Hermann Chroust, *Rise of the Legal Profession in America* (Norman: University of Oklahoma Press, 1965), 2:57–72. In 1838, Abraham Lincoln famously warned about "the increased disregard for law which pervades the country; the growing disposition to substitute the wild and furious passions, in lieu of the sober judgment of Courts." He cautioned that the "mobocratic spirit" would destroy American government, called for "reason" to take the place of "passion," and appealed for increased "strict obedience" and "reverence for the laws." Abraham Lincoln, "The Perpetuation of Our Institutions," an Address to the Young Men's Lyceum of Springfield, Illinois, January 27, 1838, in *The Portable Abraham Lincoln,* ed. Andrew Delbanco (New York: Penguin, 2009), 17–26.

45. A number of historians of the Jacksonian era have emphasized how men's class status and position on expanded male suffrage influenced their party affiliation. Most notably, see Schlesinger, *Age of Jackson;* Charles Sellers, *The Market Revolution: Jacksonian America, 1815–1846* (New York: Oxford University Press, 1991); Robert V. Remini, "Democracy," in *The Legacy of Andrew Jackson: Essays on Democracy, Indian Removal and Slavery* (Baton Rouge: Louisiana State University Press, 1988); and Wilentz, *Rise of American Democracy.*
46. On American views of Britain during the early period of American identity formation, see Haynes, *Unfinished Revolution;* and Yokota, *Unbecoming British.*

CONCLUSION

1. For the factual circumstances of the executions of the two Britons (Arbuthnot and Ambrister), the two Creeks (Hillis Hadjo and Homathlemico), and the African-heritage man (Garçon), see chapters 7, 4, and 6, respectively.
2. Reginald Horsman, *Race and Manifest Destiny: The Origins of American Racial Anglo-Saxonism* (Cambridge, MA: Harvard University Press, 1981), chaps. 6–9, quotation on 157.
3. On shifting European conceptions of the international community, legal universalism, and the standard of civilization, see especially Jennifer Pitts, "Boundaries of Victorian International Law," in *Victorian Visions of Global Order: Empire and International Relations in Nineteenth-Century Political Thought,* ed. Duncan Bell (New York: Cambridge University Press, 2007), 67–88; Jennifer Pitts, "Empire and Legal Universalisms in the Eighteenth Century," *American*

Historical Review 117, no. 1 (February 2012): 92–121; Antony Anghie, *Imperialism, Sovereignty and the Making of International Law* (New York: Cambridge University Press, 2007); Stephen C. Neff, *Justice among Nations: A History of International Law* (Cambridge, MA: Harvard University Press, 2014); Gerrit W. Gong, *The Standard of "Civilization" in International Society* (New York: Oxford University Press, 1984); and Martti Koskenniemi, *The Gentle Civilizer of Nations: The Rise and Fall of International Law, 1870–1960* (New York: Cambridge University Press, 2001). Of these scholars, Anghie most significantly emphasizes the role of race. Among the publications listed, Pitts, "Boundaries of Victorian International Law," devotes the most attention to the capacity-for-reciprocity argument. In that essay, Pitts also observes that although Victorian-era lawyers tended to agree on the civilized-versus-uncivilized line, some nonjurists pointed out that the juridical theories were hypocritical, ethnocentric, and inconsistent with the actual history of treaty relations with non-European nations.

4. C. H. Alexandrowicz, "Doctrinal Aspects of the Universality of the Law of Nations," *British Yearbook of International Law* 37 (1961): 506–515 ("fashionable" lawyers and authors); Pitts, "Boundaries of Victorian International Law."
5. On the rise of the nation-state and the law of war, see Stephen C. Neff, *War and the Law of Nations: A General History* (New York: Cambridge University Press, 2005), 85–87, 171–172.
6. In *The Antelope,* Chief Justice John Marshall gave higher priority to positive law than natural law as it related to the slave trade. He noted that although slave trading was against natural law, it did not violate the law of nations because it was "authorized and protected by the laws of all commercial nations." *The Antelope,* 23 U.S. 66 (1825). *The Antislavery Argument,* ed. William H. Pease and Jane H. Pease (Indianapolis: Bobbs-Merrill, 1965), 224–256, reprints antislavery speeches and tracts based on natural law and natural rights arguments by Charles Follen (1836), James Forten, Jr. (1836), William Ellery Channing (1842), and Theodore Parker (1854). For an analysis of African Americans' assertion of rights based on natural law in early America, see Henry J. Richardson III, *The Origins of African-American Interests in International Law* (Durham, NC: Carolina Academic Press, 2008). For an in-depth discussion of the use of natural law to support abolitionism, see William M. Wiecek, *The Sources of Antislavery Constitutionalism in America, 1760–1848* (Ithaca, NY: Cornell University Press, 1977).
7. As a relatively weak power in the world immediately after the American Revolution, the United States benefited from a law of nations that presumed the equality of sovereign polities based on natural law principles. Moreover, the Republic found that natural law principles fostered Americans' overseas commerce by supporting U.S. neutrality during the European conflicts of the late eighteenth and early nineteenth centuries. By the mid-1810s, the situation had changed. Dangers to international trade subsided when the Napoleonic Wars ended, and key U.S. military successes bolstered American confidence in the strength of the nation. On the eve of the Seminole War, the United States had less of a stake in a natural-law-based law of nations. Robert Kagan, *Dangerous Nation: America's Foreign Policy from Its Earliest Days to the Dawn of the Twentieth Century* (New York: Vintage, 2007), 61 (arguing that the United States

constantly appealed to international law in the early Republic because it was such a weak nation, rather than because of "any conviction that all international behavior could be regulated by legal mechanisms"); Stewart Jay, "The Status of the Law of Nations in Early American Law," *Vanderbilt Law Review* 42 (April 1989): 819–849 (discussing the role of American weakness in the late eighteenth century); Douglas J. Sylvester, "International Law as Sword or Shield? Early American Foreign Policy and the Law of Nations," *New York University Journal of International Law and Politics* 32 (Fall 1999): 1–87 (disagreeing with Jay's findings and arguing instead that the United States used the law of nations to advance its commercial interests).

8. Alfred P. Rubin, *The Law of Piracy* (Newport, RI: Naval War College Press, 1988, repr. Honolulu, HI: University Press of the Pacific, 2006). Interestingly, an 1820 law labeled transatlantic slave traders "pirates," though in practice African-descended people were much more likely than slave traders to be punished as pirates or outlaws. An Act to Continue in Force "An Act to Protect the Commerce of the United States and Punish the Crime of Piracy," and Also to Make Further Provisions for Punishing the Crime of Piracy, May 15, 1820, Stat., 3:600–601.
9. I am indebted to Lauren Benton for drawing my attention to this analogy several years ago during a conversation at a scholarly conference prior to the publication of her book, *A Search for Sovereignty: Law and Geography in European Empires, 1400–1900* (New York: Cambridge University Press, 2010). See especially chapter 3 of the book, entitled "Sovereignty at Sea: Jurisdiction, Piracy, and the Origins of Ocean Regionalism."
10. Kal Raustiala, *Does the Constitution Follow the Flag? The Evolution of Territoriality in American Law* (New York: Oxford University Press, 2009). On ways in which the United States asserted control extraterritorially, see also Daniel S. Margolies, *Spaces of Law in American Foreign Relations: Extradition and Extraterritoriality in the Borderlands and Beyond, 1877–1898* (Athens: University of Georgia Press, 2011).
11. See Eliga Gould's discussion of the distinctiveness of these three American activities. Eliga H. Gould, "The Making of an Atlantic State System: Britain and the United States, 1795–1825," in *Britain and America Go to War: The Impact of War and Warfare in Anglo-America, 1754–1815,* ed. Julie Flavell and Stephen Conway (Gainesville: University Press of Florida, 2004), 241–265, at 259–260.

APPENDIX

1. In the *Annals of Congress,* there is a disparity between the number reported for the anti-Jackson vote on Arbuthnot (62) and the number of names listed (58) and also a disparity between the number reported for the pro-Jackson vote on Ambrister (107) and the number of names listed (106). This chart is based on the names actually identified for those votes.
2. In the minutes, the motions for roll call votes concerning Arbuthnot and Ambrister were actually presented in a confusing manner. The first motion was presented as follows: "The question was then taken on concurring with the Committee of the Whole in their disagreement to the first branch of the

resolution [proposed by the Committee on Military Affairs], viz: 'That this House disapproves of the trial and execution of Alexander Arbuthnot.'" Subsequently, the second motion was presented as follows: "The question was then taken on concurring with the Committee of the Whole in their disagreement to the first branch of the resolution [proposed by the Committee on Military Affairs], viz: 'That this House disapproves of the trial and execution of Robert C. Ambrister.'"

Acknowledgments

I would like to thank Kathleen McDermott at Harvard University Press for her enthusiastic support of my work. I appreciate the contributions of the entire staff at the press in bringing this book to publication. I am also very grateful for the thoughtful and knowledgeable comments of the anonymous readers; they provided invaluable suggestions for improving the book. Finally, I thank John H. Clark, the Data Visualization and GIS Librarian at Lafayette College, who created the maps that appear in the book.

Portions of Chapter 7, "Military Tribunals and Rule of Law," were first published as "Wartime Prisoners and the Rule of Law: Andrew Jackson's Military Tribunals during the First Seminole War" in *Journal of the Early Republic* 28, no. 4 (Winter 2008): 559–595 and are reprinted here with the permission of the University of Pennsylvania Press. Copyright © 2008 Society for Historians of the Early American Republic.

Index

CPSIA information can be obtained
at www.ICGtesting.com
Printed in the USA
BVHW031152040821
612702BV00018B/109/J

9 780674 967618